GREEK PLAYS

IN MODERN TRANSLATION

EDITED WITH AN INTRODUCTION BY

DUDLEY FITTS

A PERMANENT LIBRARY BOOK

THE DIAL PRESS · NEW YORK · 1947

ACKNOWLEDGMENTS

I am indebted to the following publishers for their permission to reprint certain of these plays: to The Macmillan Company for *King Oedipus* and *Eumenides*; to Harcourt, Brace and Company for *Antigoné*, *Oedipus at Colonus*, and *Alcestis*; to W. W. Norton and Company for *Prometheus Bound*; to the University of Chicago Press for *Hippolytus*; and to New Directions for *Electra*. I am especially grateful to Mr. Richmond Lattimore, of Bryn Mawr College, who at my request translated *The Trojan Women* for this collection; to Mr. Frederic Prokosch, for many helpful suggestions; to my colleagues Dr. Alston Hurd Chase, Mr. Francis McCarthy, and Mr. Norman Etienne Vuilleumier; to Mr. and Mrs. Ralph Osborne; and to Cornelia Fitts, my wife, for her unfailing tact in suppressing the

voces, vagitus et ingens,
infantumque animae flentes in limine meo.

D. F.

TYPOGRAPHY BY EUGENE E. ETTENBERG
PRINTED IN THE UNITED STATES OF AMERICA

ⅎⅎⅎⅎⅎⅎⅎⅎⅎⅎⅎⅎⅎⅎⅎⅎⅎⅎⅎⅎⅎⅎⅎⅎⅎⅎ

CONTENTS

v

DANIELI DEBORÆ
FILIOLIS DILECTISSIMIS
EORVM IN GRATIAM SVO AMORE
FABVLARVM EDITOR
D D D

INTRODUCTION

I

IN THE FOLLOWING PAGES I have collected eleven translations out of a possible twenty known to me which, in varying ways and to different degrees of success, restate Greek tragedy for us in our own terms. The book is designed primarily for the reader with little or no Greek who is nevertheless interested in one of the most significant treasures of our European heritage. It is not intended as an act of scholarship, nor does it pretend to supplant the great translations of the past; it is a supplement rather, an attempt to show that this poetry, however remote from us in time, can yet speak to us with the immediacy and the truth that it had for its original audience.

While these particular plays have not been chosen by caprice, the field of selection was, as I have indicated, narrow. What may be called the Experimental Version is a comparative novelty: although there are many translations in the idiom of the past (to say nothing of the many more in an idiom that never was and never will be), there are few to which we can apply Yeats' dictum* that "a word unfitted for living speech, out of its natural order, or unnecessary to our modern technique, [will] check emotion and tire attention." Nevertheless, the collection, representing as it does about a third of the total number of the tragedies that have come down to us, should give the reader a fairly good idea of the whole. There is one trilogy: for the plays of the Oedipus cycle, although they were not produced as such, do in effect compose one. Since one of my aims was variety, as well of translator as of author, I have substituted Sophocles' *Electra* for the *Choephoroe* in Aeschylus' *Oresteia*; thus the trilogy is, as narrative, preserved. *Prometheus Bound* is the first and only surviving play of another Aeschylean trilogy. The satyr-play with which the trilogies concluded is adumbrated by the *Alcestis* of Euripides—an enigmatic composition which ancient scholarship itself could not classify either as tragedy or as comedy, but which, for lack of an adequate version of the *Cyclops*, may serve here as an example of the lighter treatment of a

* Preface to Sophocles' *King Oedipus* (1928).

serious subject. The remaining three pieces are the *Trojan Women*, the *Medea*, and the *Hippolytus*, also by Euripides, and all of them examples of his rationalistic approach, curiously modern in its mixture of disillusionment and tenderness, to his legendary material. Explanatory notes have been reduced to a minimum and relegated to the Index of Names, but in the Appendix I have reprinted the prefaces and commentaries that accompanied all but three of the plays.

II

Of the many Greek tragic poets whose names are known to us from the commentaries of the grammarians and scholiasts, only three—Aeschylus, Sophocles, and Euripides—survive otherwise than in fragments, and these three are but partially extant: for we know that they wrote nearly three hundred plays, but we possess a mere thirty-two—seven by Aeschylus, seven by Sophocles, and eighteen (counting the *Rhesus*) by Euripides. The proportion is interesting. Aeschylus, the earliest, ruggedest, and most difficult of the three, was a religious and polemical poet interested in explaining and sustaining the social structure of his time. Sophocles was gentler, a mystic, introverted, preoccupied with the theological mystery of man's fate. Euripides, the closest to us in feeling, was a questioner, a religious skeptic, interested rather in character than in institutions and theology; a disbeliever, in conservative eyes, whose summary exposure of the more than human frailties of certain of the gods (Apollo, for instance, in the *Iôn*; Aphroditê in the *Hippolytus*) recalls the Homeric comedy without the Homeric innocence.* It is natural, though perhaps unfortunate, that the survival should be so preponderantly Euripidean. However that may be, if one could imagine that nine-tenths of the greatest period of English literature had vanished except for occasional report, one might guess what the world has lost by the disappearance of all but this small fraction of classic Greek tragedy. Yet in view of what has been saved this is a most profitless crying over spilt milk. For these dramas embody man's noblest expression of his human predicament. Only in Shakespeare shall we find another playwright who can approach them at their highest; but though

---

* There are traces of this quality in Aeschylus, notably in *Prometheus Bound*, where Oceanos is a figure of fun, Hermês a most ungodlike fop, and Zeus himself a blustering papa; but the shattering Aeschylean humor differs *toto caelo* from the insistent psychological probing of Euripides.

the discovery of a lost *Lear* or *Macbeth* might deepen our worship of Shakespeare, I cannot conceive that the digging up in Egypt of the rest of the Promethean trilogy would alter our opinion of Aeschylus, however much more it might tell us about him. His work, as we have it, seems insuperable. ·

One would suppose that a body of literature as impressive as this must have a particular meaning for our own reckless and disheartening times, and indeed it has. Yet these plays, even to the literate general reader, become increasingly unfamiliar. They live in repute, they are accepted as the Classics—and, as "the Classics," they are dismissed. "Macbeth!" snaps Mr. Thurber's all too endemic American Lady. "A book for high-school children!" But they are no longer even that. They have vanished from our curricula nearly as completely as they have lost our concern. They are "there," comfortably in the background along with Berlioz and *Beowulf,* with the unpublished concerti of Vivaldi, the—let everyone make his own list of worthy ghosts, but I should like to suggest the Holy Bible; food for scholars, *esca vermium,* playthings for the eccentric and the escapist; Good Things, too, in their antique way, but not for us in our Atomic Century. The man of letters finds this state of affairs dispiriting, and to the professional classicist it must be something worse than that; but it is an inevitable state of affairs, and one for which neither of these mourners can hold himself quite blameless.

It is easy enough to deplore the technological preoccupation of our age, to accuse the physicists and the economists—to say nothing of the political theorists—of leading our children away from the basic human values represented by the great art of our past. It is as fruitless as it is easy to sigh for a return. A return to what? It seems hardly likely that there will be a revival of interest, on any large scale, in the Greek and Latin languages. Certainly they will not recapture their old authority at the secondary school level, which is where they count. The colleges, by lowering* their entrance requirements, have taken care of that. And even if we could return that way, with the road-signs all pointing *sens unique* against us, should we not find that we had recovered rather the symbols than the thing itself? Compulsory Latin or compulsory Greek, divorced from the general humanistic discipline which as recently as in my father's boyhood was their context, is scarcely more rewarding than compulsory Chapel. Accordingly, if we believe that classical literature has its place

* *Sunt qui altering dicunt legendum.*

in our society; believe, as I most sincerely do, that a certain familiarity with a handful of ancient poets, historians, and philosophers is necessary to salvation; then the only way remaining to us is translation.

III

When I spoke above of the share of blame that teachers of the classics must assume for the disrepute into which their subject has fallen, I was thinking not of their contributions to scholarship, not of the devotion with which they have maintained the struggle in hostile waters, but of the closed-circle remoteness from reality in which so many of them contemplate literature living or dead. No one can study the standard translations of the classics, that aspect of their work which perforce reaches the greatest number of people, without being struck by the killing artificiality that pervades them. It is as though there were fixed conventions for rendering the ancient texts: for serious prose, imitate the Bible and Sir Thomas Browne; for poetry, mix Swinburne with Shelley in lyric passages, assorted Elizabethans in the dramatic. The bookish pastiche that results enforces the unkind assumption that the translator has been guided chiefly by the principle *De mortuis nil nisi mortuum.* At any rate, one must be an imaginative reader indeed who can perceive the living light through the gloom of jargon.

A friend writes me of a performance of *Uncle Vanya* that he attended in a little theatre at some resort. All the actors had been coached to speak their lines with a faint foreign accent, the purpose being, as the director kindly explained, to create the Russian atmosphere necessary to the play. We have all had a comparable experience at the movies, where enemy agents at home converse with one another in broken English. Indeed, we have the august authority of Shakespeare himself: do not the French knights at Agincourt converse in a curious mixture of schoolroom French and excellent English? With these examples in mind, let us investigate a passage of Euripides as he is rendered in the Loeb Library translation— presumably the version to which most people would turn for enlightenment. Here is Medea chatting with King Aegeus of Athens*:

MEDEA   Joy to thee also, wise Pandion's son,
            Aegeus. Whence art thou journeying through this land?
AEGEUS   Leaving the ancient oracle of Phoebus.

* *Med.* 665 sqq.

MEDEA	Why didst thou fare to earth's prophetic navel?
AEGEUS	To ask how seed of children might be mine.
MEDEA	'Fore Heaven!—aye childless is thy life till now?
AEGEUS	Childless I am, by chance of some God's will.
MEDEA	This, with a wife, or knowing not the couch?
AEGEUS	Nay, not unyoked to wedlock's bed am I.
MEDEA	Now what to thee spake Phoebus touching issue?
AEGEUS	Deep words of wisdom not for man to interpret.
MEDEA	Without sin might I know the God's reply?
AEGEUS	O yea—good sooth, it asks a wit most wise.

And so on, for all the world like a pair of clowns escaped from Arden. Now I will not pretend that the Greek of this passage is anything very fine. It is pedestrian enough, saved from utter collapse only by the amusing ripple of the trimeters. Stichomythy, especially in Euripides, lends itself all too easily to this sort of thing. But I must deny that the translator has done anything but make the commonplace absurd. To Greek ears ὀμφαλὸς γῆς presumably was no more strange than *Hub of the Universe* is to ours. The metaphor had died. But it is not dead in English; the anatomical* associations of "navel" are too strong for sober translation, and "centre" or even "heart" would have done better. "Certainly," says Aegeus; "O yea—good sooth," says the translator, as though the king were inexplicably using a Cretan dialect from a half century before his time. True, when he confesses his married state he does express himself in a rather sententious way: "No, I am not unmarried"; but no human being in any age of the world's history has seriously remarked, "Nay, not unyoked to wedlock's bed am I," even if a lady *has* just asked him "This, with a wife, or knowing not the couch?" It is done only in the standard translations.

I have deliberately chosen an unimportant passage in a low key. What happens when this same mortuary method is applied to something more highly charged is more serious. Here is Euripides again, this time at the close of the *Hippolytus*†:

ΘΗΣΕΥΣ

ὦ φίλταθ', ὡς γενναῖος ἐκφαίνει πατρί.

---

* Or pomological, as in a kind of orange; whereat I am disastrously attracted by "seed" in the following verse.

† *Hip.* 1452 sqq.

xii · *INTRODUCTION*

ΙΠΠΟΛΥΤΟΣ
τοιῶνδε παίδων γνησίων εὔχου τυχεῖν.
ΘΗΣΕΥΣ
ὤμοι φρενὸς σῆς εὐσεβοῦς τε κἀγαθῆς.
ΙΠΠΟΛΥΤΟΣ
ὦ χαῖρε καὶ σύ, χαῖρε πολλά μοι, πάτερ.
ΘΗΣΕΥΣ
μή νυν προδῷς με, τέκνον, ἀλλὰ καρτέρει.
ΙΠΠΟΛΥΤΟΣ
κεκαρτέρηται τἄμ'· ὄλωλα γάρ, πάτερ.
κρύψον δέ μου πρόσωπον ὡς τάχος πέπλοις.

Here the stichomythy is anything but perfunctory. Though the language is direct, it is instinct with that ironic pathos which Euripides handles so strikingly—the interplay of γενναῖος and γνησίων; the position of the latter in the slow dying line, as though even in death Hippolytus (with ample provocation, God knows!) could not neglect an opportunity to contrast his own virtue with his father's youthful licentiousness—; and certainly the last verse has the inevitability of true poetry. Here is the Loeb translator:

THES.   Dearest, how noble show'st thou to thy sire!
HIPPOL. Pray to have such sons—sons in wedlock born.
THES.   Woe for thy reverent soul, thy righteous heart!
HIPPOL. Father, farewell thou too—untold farewells!
THES.   Forsake me not, my son!—be strong to bear!
HIPPOL. My strength is overborne—I am gone, my father.
        Cover my face with mantles with all speed.

The only effective touch in this farrago is Theseus' "dearest." All the rest—"how noble show'st thou," "wedlock," "sire," "be strong to bear," "overborne"—is, in both senses of the word, unspeakable. And it is this unspeakableness that is at the root of the matter. The great Victorian translators and their imitators seem never to have reflected that they were concerned with something written for the human voice, for the actual stage. Jebb's prose translations are masterpieces of scholarship; but they can not be read aloud without embarrassment, and it is difficult to imagine an actor projecting their dead phrases in the theatre.* To

* Mr. T. S. Eliot has adequately sung the requiem of Mr. Gilbert Murray as poet-

attempt to recapture the tone of a past age by deliberate archaism of language would seem so immediately absurd as to make comment needless; yet it has been the most common device of all.

IV

It would be pointless to deny that modern English shuns the kind of rhetorical elevation which one finds in these plays and which was once natural enough in English itself. The Tudor translators of Seneca were able to cope with the declamatory eloquence of his poems because their own language was still exuberantly and experimentally alive. They were neither embarrassed by passion nor afraid of excess. Their Seneca was accordingly credible, right for their time and expressed in terms of their time. But we move more circumspectly. If it is not yet time to cry that the glory is departed, it is none the less certain that we are no longer at ease with its once splendid trappings. Yet we long for them; and when the occasion demands something more than the humdrum of our ordinary style, we instinctively turn to them. Unfortunately we can not wear them, and we have no comparable grandeur of our own. This complicates the translator's task, for he is constantly being tempted to indulge in specious beauties—anything rather than the dreary flatness that his language assumes when he compares it with his original.

The ideal translation of a poem should reproduce all the qualities—sonal, intellectual, affective—of the original. Having said this, we must immediately add that it is impossible. "What is well done in one language," wrote Roger Bacon, "can not possibly be reproduced in another with the same authority which it had in the original." This is dogma, and to it every honest translator will subscribe: his reach will for ever exceed his grasp. A lesser ideal, the second best, may be achieved, I think, in either of two ways. It may reproduce as faithfully as possible those elements which can be transferred—the meaning, the image, perhaps by a stroke of luck an occasional cadence—and rest there, preferably accompanied by the original text; or it may move more freely in the direction of re-creation, attempting to communicate to the modern reader whatever the translator conceives to have been the total impact

translator. There is nothing more to be said on that score except to emphasize the almost Sophoclean irony of a situation in which a great Hellenist, actuated solely by the desire to have the plays known and loved, has done as much as any other contemporary to make them unreadable.

of the poem upon its original audience. I am aware that I tread here upon dangerous ground. It is easy for this method to lapse into irresponsible paraphrase, to become an excuse for the translator to write his own poetry and sign it with an illustrious name. This has certainly been done, though not, I think, in this book.* In general, and especially when the language involved has no extensive modern currency, the reader is at the mercy of the translator; indeed he has always been so, even in times more classically minded than our own. But granted that the translator is neither a fool nor a charlatan, this more liberal method of interpretation offers the richer rewards. The dust vanishes, the poem remains: transmuted, of necessity: but a man reading Miss Hamilton's beautiful *Prometheus Bound* or Mr. Lattimore's superb rendering of the *Agamemnon* is reading faithful translation that is also poetry in its own right and in its own way.

V

The plays I shall leave to speak for themselves. They are for the time being: translation for one age is dead or quaint for the age that follows, and there must always be new versions; but they address us now, the best of them, with a healing urgency which we should do well to heed. We are mistaken if we think that these poems, based upon ghastly myths and instinct with a physical violence which is hardly alien to our modern temper, are either childhood exercises or lost dreams. Never more tragically than today has mankind been Oedipus at Thebes, or needed more desperately to ponder the assurance of the dying king that

one word
Makes all those difficulties disappear:
That word is love.

Dudley Fitts

Andover, Massachusetts
September, 1946

* But Yeats' sensitive mishandling of the choruses in *King Oedipus* is clearly suspect; and it is now my opinion—I do not know that my collaborator would agree with me—that Robert Fitzgerald and I permitted ourselves too much latitude in the *Alcestis*, reading into the text a romantic feminism that smacks rather of Ibsen than of Euripides.

Aeschylus

AGAMEMNON

translated by
Richmond Lattimore

ATREUS, King of Argos, quarreled with his younger brother THYESTES and drove him out of the country. When THYESTES returned, a suppliant, the King pretended to forgive him. He held a feast in his honor, but secretly killed the two elder sons of THYESTES, cut them in pieces, and served them to their father, who unwittingly ate of their flesh. When he learned what had happened, THYESTES laid his curse upon the entire house and went once more into exile with his youngest son, AIGISTHOS.

Later, AGAMEMNON and MENELAOS, sons of ATREUS, married KLYTAI-MESTRA and HELEN, daughters of KING TYNDAREUS of Lakedaimon. When HELEN fled with PARIS to Troy, AGAMEMNON assembled all the princes of Greece to force the Trojans to give her back. But at Aulis, where the fleet gathered, contrary winds kept it from putting to sea, until the prophet KALCHAS interpreted a portent to mean that AGAMEMNON must sacrifice his daughter IPHIGENEIA before the winds would change. And this was done.

```
ЛЛЛЛЛЛЛЛЛЛЛЛЛЛЛЛЛЛЛЛЛЛЛ
```

While AGAMEMNON was at Troy, AIGISTHOS returned to Argos and became the Queen's lover. With her help, with a bodyguard of his own spearmen, and with the assistance of many of the people in the city who were angry with AGAMEMNON because of the long war, he won considerable power in Argos. Finally a chain of beacons extending from Mt. Ida to Argolis announced the fall of Troy and the imminent return of AGAMEMNON.

DRAMATIS PERSONÆ:

WATCHMAN   AGAMEMNON
KLYTAIMESTRA   KASSANDRA
HERALD   AIGISTHOS

CHORUS OF ARGIVE ELDERS

AGAMEMNON

SCENE: Argos, before the palace of KING AGAMEMNON. The WATCHMAN,
who speaks the opening lines, is posted on the roof of the palace.
KLYTAIMESTRA's entrances are made from a door in the center of
the stage; all others, from the wings.

[The WATCHMAN, alone.

I ask the gods some respite from the weariness
of this watchtime measured by years I lie awake
elbowed upon the Atreidai's roof dogwise to mark
the great processionals of all the stars of night
burdened with winter and again with heat for men,
dynasties in their shining blazoned on the air,
these stars, upon their wane and when the rest arise.

I wait; to read the meaning in that beacon light,
a blaze of fire to carry out of Troy the rumor
and outcry of its capture; to such end a lady's
male strength of heart in its high confidence ordains.
Now as this bed stricken with night and drenched with dew
I keep, nor ever with kind dreams for company:
since fear in sleep's place stands forever at my head
against strong closure of my eyes, or any rest:
I mince such medicine against sleep failed: I sing,
only to weep again the pity of this house
no longer, as once, administered in the grand way.
Now let there be again redemption from distress,
the flare burning from the blackness in good augury.

[A light shows in the distance.

Oh hail, blaze of the darkness, harbinger of day's

7

Shining, and of processionals and dance and choirs
of multitudes in Argos for this day of grace.
Ahoy!
I cry the news aloud to Agamemnon's queen,
that she may rise up from her bed of state with speed
to raise the rumor of gladness welcoming this beacon,
and singing rise, if truly the citadel of Ilion
has fallen, as the shining of this flare proclaims.
I also, I, will make my choral prelude, since
my lord's dice cast aright are counted as my own,
and mine the tripled sixes of this torchlit throw.

May it only happen. May my king come home, and I
take up within this hand the hand I love. The rest
I leave to silence; for an ox stands huge upon
my tongue. The house itself, could it take voice, might speak
aloud and plain. I speak to those who understand,
but if they fail, I have forgotten everything.

> [*Exit. The* chorus *enters, speaking.*

Ten years since the great contestants
of Priam's right,
Menelaos and Agamemnon, my lord,
twin throned, twin sceptered, in twofold power
of kings from God, the Atreidai,
put forth from this shore
the thousand ships of the Argives,
the strength and the armies.
Their cry of war went shrill from the heart,
as eagles stricken in agony
for young perished, high from the nest
eddy and circle
to bend and sweep of the wings' stroke,
lost far below
the fledgelings, the nest, and the tendance.
Yet someone hears in the air, a god,
Apollo, Pan, or Zeus, the high
thin wail of these sky-guests, and drives

late to its mark
the Fury upon the transgressors.

So drives Zeus the great guest god
the Atreidai against Alexander:
for one woman's promiscuous sake
the struggling masses, legs tired,
knees grinding in dust,
spears broken in the onset.
Danaans and Trojans
they have it alike. It goes as it goes
now. The end will be destiny.
You cannot burn flesh or pour unguents,
not innocent cool tears,
that will soften the gods' stiff anger.

But we; dishonored, old in our bones,
cast off even then from the gathering horde,
stay here, to prop up
on staves the strength of a baby.
Since the young vigor that urges
inward to the heart
is frail as age, no warcraft yet perfect,
while beyond age, leaf
withered, man goes three footed
no stronger than a child is,
a dream that falters in daylight.

> [KLYTAIMESTRA *enters quietly. The* CHORUS
> *continues to speak.*

But you, lady,
daughter of Tyndareus, Klytaimestra, our queen:
What is there to be done? What new thing have you heard?
In persuasion of what
report do you order such sacrifice?
To all the gods of the city,
the high and the deep spirits,
them of the sky and the market places,

the altars blaze with oblations.
The staggered flame goes sky high
one place, then another,
drugged by the simple soft
persuasion of sacred unguents,
the deep stored oil of the kings.
Of these things what can be told
openly, speak.
Be healer to this perplexity
that grows now into darkness of thought,
while again sweet hope shining from the flames
beats back the pitiless pondering
of sorrow that eats my heart.

I have mastery yet to chant the wonder at the wayside
given to kings. Still by God's grace there surges within me
singing magic
grown to my life and power,
how the wild bird portent
hurled forth the Achaians'
twin-stemmed power single hearted,
lords of the youth of Hellas,
with spear and hand of strength
to the land of Teukros.
Kings of birds to the kings of the ships,
one black, one blazed with silver,
clear seen by the royal house
on the right, the spear hand,
they lighted, watched by all
tore a hare, ripe, bursting with young unborn yet,
stayed from her last fleet running.
Sing sorrow, sorrow: but good win out in the end.

Then the grave seer of the host saw through to the hearts
    divided,
knew the fighting sons of Atreus feeding on the hare
with the host, their people.
Seeing beyond, he spoke:

'With time, this foray
shall stalk the castle of Priam.
Before then, under
the walls, Fate shall spoil
in violence the rich herds of the people.
Only let no doom of the gods darken
upon this huge iron forged to curb Troy—
from inward. Artemis the undefiled
is angered with pity
at the flying hounds of her father
eating the unborn young in the hare and the shivering mother.
She is sick at the eagles' feasting.
Sing sorrow, sorrow: but good win out in the end.

Lovely you are and kind
to the tender young of ravening lions.
For sucklings of all the savage
beasts that lurk in the lonely places you have sympathy.
Grant meaning to these appearances
good, yet not without evil.
Healer Apollo, I pray you
let her not with cross winds
bind the ships of the Danaans
to time-long anchorage
forcing a second sacrifice unholy, untasted,
working bitterness in the blood
and faith lost. For the terror returns like sickness to lurk in the
      house;
the secret anger remembers the child that shall be avenged.'
Such, with great good things beside, rang out in the voice of
      Kalchas,
these fatal signs from the birds by the way to the house of the
      princes
wherewith in sympathy
sing sorrow, sorrow: but good win out in the end.

Zeus: whatever he may be, if this name
pleases him in invocation

thus I call upon him.
I have pondered everything
yet I cannot find a way,
only Zeus, to cast this dead weight of ignorance
finally from out my brain.

He who in time long ago was great,
throbbing with gigantic strength,
shall be as if he never were, unspoken.
He who followed him has found
his master, and is gone.
Cry aloud without fear the victory of Zeus,
you will not have failed the truth:

Zeus, who guided men to think,
who has laid it down that wisdom
comes alone through suffering.
Still there drips in sleep against the heart
grief of memory; against
our pleasure we are temperate.
From the gods who sit in grandeur
grace comes somehow violent.

On that day the elder king
of the Achaian ships, no more
strict against the prophet's word,
turned with the crosswinds of fortune,
when no ship sailed, no pail was full,
and the Achaian people sulked
fast against the shore at Aulis
facing Chalkis, where the tides ebb and surge:

and winds blew from the Strymon, bearing
sick idleness, ships tied fast, and hunger,
distraction of the mind, carelessness
for hull and cable,
with time's length bent to double measure
by delay crumbled the flower and pride

of Argos. Then against the bitter wind
the seer's voice clashed out
another medicine
more hateful yet, and spoke of Artemis, so that the kings
dashed their staves to the ground and could not hold their
  tears.

The elder lord spoke aloud before them:
'My fate is angry if I disobey these,
but angry if I slaughter
this child, the beauty of my house,
with maiden blood shed staining
these father's hands beside the altar.
What of these things goes now without disaster?
How shall I fail my ships
and lose my faith of battle?
For them to urge such sacrifice of innocent blood
angrily, for their wrath is great—it is right. May all be well
  yet.'

But when necessity's yoke was put upon him
he changed, and from the heart the breath came bitter
and sacrilegious, utterly infidel
to warp a will now to be stopped at nothing.
The sickening in men's minds, tough,
reckless in fresh cruelty brings daring. He endured then
to sacrifice his daughter
to stay the strength of war waged for a woman,
first offering for the ships' sake.

Her supplications and her cries of father
were nothing, nor the child's lamentation
to kings passioned for battle.
The father prayed, called to his men to lift her
with strength of hand swept in her robes aloft
and prone above the altar, as you might lift
a goat for sacrifice, with guards
against the lips' sweet edge to check
the curse cried on the house of Atreus

by force of bit and speech drowned in strength.
Pouring then to the ground her saffron mantle
she struck the sacrificers with
the eyes' arrows of pity,
lovely as in a painted scene, and striving
to speak—as many times
at the kind festive table of her father
she had sung, and in the clear voice of a stainless maiden
with love had graced the song
of worship when the third cup was poured.

What happened next I saw not, neither speak it.
The crafts of Kalchas fail not of outcome.
Justice so moves that those only learn
who suffer; and the future
you shall know when it has come; before then, forget it.
It is grief too soon given.
All will come clear in the next dawn's sunlight.
Let good fortune follow these things as
she who is here desires,
our Apian land's singlehearted protectress.

[The CHORUS now turns toward KLYTAIMESTRA, and the
leader speaks to her.

I have come in reverence, Klytaimestra, of your power.
For when the man is gone and the throne void, his right
falls to the prince's lady, and honor must be given.
Is it some grace—or otherwise—that you have heard
to make you sacrifice at messages of good hope?
I should be glad to hear, but must not blame your silence.

KLY.   As it was said of old, may the dawn child be born
to be an angel of blessing from the kindly night.
You shall know joy beyond all you ever hoped to hear.
The men of Argos have taken Priam's citadel.

CHORUS   What have you said? Your words escaped my unbelief.

KLY.   The Achaians are in Troy. Is that not clear enough?

CHORUS   This slow delight steals over me to bring forth tears.

KLY.   Yes, for your eyes betray the loyal heart within.

CHORUS   Yet how can I be certain? Is there some evidence?

KLY.   There is, there must be; unless a god has lied to me.

CHORUS   Is it dream visions, easy to believe, you credit?

KLY.   I accept nothing from a brain that is dull with sleep.

CHORUS   The charm, then, of some rumor, that made rich your hope?

KLY.   Am I some young girl, that you find my thoughts so silly?

CHORUS   How long, then, is it since the citadel was stormed?

KLY.   It is the night, the mother of this dawn I hailed.

CHORUS   What kind of messenger could come in speed like this?

KLY.   Hephaistos, who cast forth the shining blaze from Ida.
              And beacon after beacon picking up the flare
              carried it here; Ida to the Hermaian horn
              of Lemnos, where it shone above the isle, and next
              the sheer rock face of Zeus on Athos caught it up;
              and plunging skyward to arch the shoulders of the sea
              the strength of the running flare in exultation,
              pine timbers flaming into gold, like the sunrise,
              brought the bright message to Makistos' sentinel cliffs,
              who, never slow nor in the carelessness of sleep
              caught up, sent on his relay in the courier chain,
              and far across Euripos' streams the beacon flare
              carried to signal watchmen on Messapion.
              These took it again in turn, and heaping high a pile
              of silvery brush flamed it to throw the message on.
              And the flare sickened never, but grown stronger yet
              outleapt the river valley of Asopos like
              the very moon for shining, to Kithairon's scaur
              to waken the next station of the flaming post.
              These watchers, not contemptuous of the far-thrown blaze,
              kindled another beacon vaster than commanded.

The light leaned high above Gorgopis' staring marsh,
and striking Aigyplanktos' mountain top, drove on
yet one more relay, lest the flare die down in speed.
Kindled once more with stintless heaping force, they send
the beard of flame to hugeness, passing far beyond
the promontory that gazes on the Saronic strait
and flaming far, until it plunged at last to strike
the steep rock of Arachnos near at hand, our watchtower.
And thence there fell upon this house of Atreus' sons
the flare whose fathers mount to the Idaian beacon.
These are the changes on my torchlight messengers,
one from another running out the laps assigned.
The first and the last sprinters have the victory.
By such proof and such symbol I announce to you
my lord at Troy has sent his messengers to me.

CHORUS   The gods, lady, shall have my prayers and thanks straightway.
And yet to hear your story till all wonder fades
would be my wish, could you but tell it once again.

KLY.   The Achaians have got Troy, upon this very day.
I think the city echoes with a clash of cries.
Pour vinegar and oil into the selfsame bowl,
you could not say they mix in friendship, but fight on.
Thus variant sound the voices of the conquerors
and conquered, from the opposition of their fates.
Trojans are stooping now to gather in their arms
their dead, husbands and brothers; children lean to clasp
the aged who begot them, crying upon the death
of those most dear, from lips that never will be free.
The Achaians have their midnight work after the fighting
that sets them down to feed on all the city has,
ravenous, headlong, by no rank and file assigned,
but as each man has drawn his shaken lot by chance.
And in the Trojan houses that their spears have taken
they settle now, free of the open sky, the frosts
and dampness of the evening; without sentinels set
they sleep the sleep of happiness the whole night through.

And if they reverence the gods who hold the city
and all the holy temples of the captured land
they, the despoilers, might not be despoiled in turn.
Let not their passion overwhelm them; let no lust
seize on these men to violate what they must not.
The run to safety and home is yet to make; they must turn
the pole, and run the backstretch of the doubled course.
Yet, though the host come home without offence to high
gods, even so the anger of these slaughtered men
may never sleep. Oh, let there be no fresh wrong done!

Such are the thoughts you hear from me, a woman merely.
Yet may the best win through, that none may fail to see.
Of all good things to wish this is my dearest choice.

CHORUS   My lady, no grave man could speak with better grace.
I have listened to the proofs of your tale, and I believe,
and go to make my glad thanksgivings to the gods.
This pleasure is not unworthy of the grief that gave it.

O Zeus our lord and Night beloved,
bestower of power and beauty,
you slung above the bastions of Troy
the binding net, that none, neither great
nor young, might outleap
the gigantic toils
of enslavement and final disaster.
I stare in awe on Zeus of the guests
who wrung from Alexander such payment.
He bent the bow with slow care, that neither
the shaft might hurdle the stars, nor fall
spent to the earth, short driven.

They have the stroke of Zeus to tell of.
This thing is clear and you may trace it.
He acted as he had decreed. A man thought
the gods deigned not to punish mortals
who trampled down the delicacy of things
inviolable. That man was wicked.

The curse on great daring
shines clear; it wrings atonement
from those high hearts that drive to evil,
from houses blossoming to pride
and peril. Let there be
wealth without tears; enough for
the wise man that will ask no further.
There is not any armor
in gold against perdition
for him who spurns the high altar
of Justice down to the darkness.

Persuasion the persistent overwhelms him,
she, strong daughter of designing Ruin.
And every medicine is vain; the sin
smoulders not, but burns to evil beauty.
As cheap bronze tortured
at the touchstone relapses
to blackness and grime, so this man
tested shows vain
as a child that strives to catch the bird flying
and wins shame that shall bring down his city.
No god will hear such a man's entreaty,
but whoso turns to these ways
they strike him down in his wickedness.
This was Paris: he came
to the house of the sons of Atreus,
stole the woman away, and shamed
the guest's right of the board shared.

She left among her people the stir and clamor
of shields and of spearheads,
the ships to sail and the armor.
She took to Ilion her dowry, death.
She stepped forth lightly between the gates
daring beyond all daring. And the prophets
about the great house wept aloud and spoke:
'Alas, alas for the house and for the champions,

alas for the bed signed with their love together.
Here now is silence, scorned, unreproachful.
The agony of his loss is clear before us.
Longing for her who lies beyond the sea
he shall see a phantom queen in his household.
Her images in their beauty
are bitterness to her lord now
where in the emptiness of eyes
all passion has faded.'

Shining in dreams the sorrowful
memories pass; they bring him
vain delight only.
It is vain, to dream and to see splendors,
and the image slipping from the arms' embrace
escapes, not to return again,
on wings drifting down the ways of sleep.
Such have the sorrows been in the house by the hearthside;
such have there been, and yet there are worse than these.
In all Hellas, for those who swarmed to the host
the heartbreaking misery
shows in the house of each.
Many are they who are touched at the heart by these things.
Those they sent forth they knew;
now, in place of the young men
urns and ashes are carried home
to the houses of the fighters.

The god of war, money changer of dead bodies,
held the balance of his spear in the fighting,
and from the corpse-fires at Ilion
sent to their dearest the dust
heavy and bitter with tears shed
packing smooth the urns with
ashes that once were men.
They praise them through their tears, how this man
knew well the craft of battle, how another
went down splendid in the slaughter:

and all for some strange woman.
Thus they mutter in secrecy,
and the slow anger creeps below their grief
at Atreus' sons and their quarrels.
There by the walls of Ilion
the young men in their beauty keep
graves deep in the alien soil
they hated and they conquered.

The citizens speak: their voice is dull with hatred.
The curse of the people must be paid for.
There lurks for me in the hooded night
terror of what may be told me.
The gods fail not to mark
those who have killed many.
The black Furies stalking the man
fortunate beyond all right
wrench back again the set of his life
and drop him to darkness. There among
the ciphers there is no more comfort
in power. And the vaunt of high glory
is bitterness; for God's thunderbolts
crash on the towering mountains.
Let me attain no envied wealth,
let me not plunder cities,
neither be taken in turn, and face
life in the power of another.

[Various members of the CHORUS.

From the beacon's bright message
the fleet rumor runs
through the city. If this be real
who knows? Perhaps the gods have sent some lie to us.

Who of us is so childish or so reft of wit
that by the beacon's messages
his heart flamed must despond again
when the tale changes in the end?

It is like a woman indeed
to take the rapture before the fact has shown for true.

They believe too easily, are too quick to shift
from ground to ground; and swift indeed
the rumor voiced by a woman dies again.

Now we shall understand these torches and their shining,
the beacons, and the interchange of flame and flame.
They may be real; yet bright and dreamwise ecstasy
in light's appearance might have charmed our hearts awry.
I see a herald coming from the beach, his brows
shaded with sprigs of olive; and upon his feet
the dust, dry sister of the mire, makes plain to me
that he will find a voice, not merely kindle flame
from mountain timber, and make signals from the smoke,
but tell us outright, whether to be happy, or—
but I shrink back from naming the alternative.
That which appeared was good; may yet more good be given.

And any man who prays that different things befall
the city, may he reap the crime of his own heart.

[*The* HERALD *enters, and speaks.*

Soil of my fathers, Argive earth I tread upon,
in daylight of the tenth year I have come back to you.
All my hopes broke but one, and this I have at last.
I never could have dared to dream that I might die
in Argos, and be buried in this beloved soil.
Hail to the Argive land and to its sunlight, hail
to its high sovereign, Zeus, and to the Pythian king.
May you no longer shower your arrows on our heads.
Beside Skamandros you were grim; be satisfied
and turn to savior now and healer of our hurts,
my lord Apollo. Gods of the market place assembled,
I greet you all, and my own patron deity
Hermes, beloved herald, in whose right all heralds
are sacred; and you heroes that sent forth the host,

propitiously take back all that the spear has left.
O great hall of the kings and house beloved; seats
of sanctity; divinities that face the sun:
if ever before, look now with kind and glowing eyes
to greet our king in state after so long a time.
He comes, lord Agamemnon, bearing light in gloom
to you, and to all that are assembled here.
Salute him with good favor, as he well deserves,
the man who has wrecked Ilion with the spade of Zeus
vindictive, whereby all their plain has been laid waste.
Gone are their altars, the sacred places of the gods
are gone, and scattered all the seed within the ground.
With such a yoke as this gripped to the neck of Troy
he comes, the king, Atreus' elder son, a man
fortunate to be honored far above all men
alive; not Paris nor the city tied to him
can boast he did more than was done him in return.
Guilty of rape and theft, condemned, he lost the prize
captured, and broke to sheer destruction all the house
of his fathers, with the very ground whereon it stood.
Twice over the sons of Priam have atoned their sins.

CHORUS   Hail and be glad, herald of the Achaian host.

HERALD   I am happy; I no longer ask the gods for death.

CHORUS   Did passion for your country so strip bare your heart?

HERALD   So that the tears broke in my eyes, for happiness.

CHORUS   You were taken with that sickness, then, that brings delight.

HERALD   How? I cannot deal with such words until I understand.

CHORUS   Struck with desire of those who loved as much again.

HERALD   You mean our country longed for us, as we for home?

CHORUS   So that I sighed, out of the darkness of my heart.

HERALD   Whence came this black thought to afflict the mind with fear?

CHORUS   Long since it was my silence kept disaster off.

HERALD   But how? There were some you feared when the kings went
      away?

CHORUS   So much that as you said now, even death were grace.

HERALD   Well: the end has been good. And in the length of time
part of our fortune you could say held favorable,
but part we cursed again. And who, except the gods,
can live time through forever without any pain?
Were I to tell you of the hard work done, the nights
exposed, the huddled quarters, the foul beds—what part
of day's disposal did we not cry out loud?
Ashore, the horror stayed with us and grew. We lay
against the ramparts of our enemies, and from
the sky, and from the ground, the meadow dews came out
to soak our clothes and us, nor ever dry. And if
I were to tell of winter time, when all birds died,
the snows of Ida past endurance she sent down,
or summer heat, when in the lazy noon the sea
fell level and asleep under a windless sky—
but why live such grief over again? That time is gone
for us, and gone for those who died. Never again
need they rise up, nor care again for anything.
Why must a live man count the numbers of the slain,
why grieve at fortune's wrath that fades to break once more?
I call a long farewell to all our unhappiness.
For us, survivors of the Argive armament,
the pleasure wins, pain casts no weight in the opposite scale.
And here, in this sun's shining, we can boast aloud,
whose fame has gone with wings across the land and sea:
'Upon a time the Argive host took Troy, and on
the houses of the gods who live in Hellas nailed
the spoils, to be the glory of days long ago.'
And they who hear such things shall call this city blest
and the leaders of the host; and high the grace of God
shall be exalted, that did this. You have the story.

CHORUS   I must give way; your story shows that I was wrong.

Old men are always young enough to learn, with profit.
But Klytaimestra and her house must hear, above
others, this news that makes luxurious my life.

[KLYTAIMESTRA *comes forward and speaks.*

I raised my cry of joy, and it was long ago
when the first beacon flare of message came by night
to speak of capture and of Ilion's overthrow.
But there was one who laughed at me, who said: 'You trust
in beacons so, and you believe that Troy has fallen?
How like a woman, for the heart to lift so light.'
Men spoke like that; they thought I wandered in my wits,
yet I made sacrifice, and in the womanish strain
voice after voice caught up the cry along the city
to echo in the temples of the gods and bless
and still the fragrant flame that melts the sacrifice.

Why should you tell me then the whole long tale at large
when from my lord himself I shall hear all the story?
But now, how best to speed my preparation to
receive my honored lord come home again—what else
is light more sweet for woman to behold than this,
to spread the gates before her husband home from war
and saved by God's hand?—take this message to the king:
Come, and with speed, back to the city that longs for him,
and may he find a wife within his house as true
as on the day he left her, watchdog of the house
gentle to him alone, fierce to his enemies,
and such a woman in all her ways as this, who has
not broken the seal upon her in the length of days.
With no man else have I known delight, nor any shame
of evil speech, more than I know how to temper bronze.

[KLYTAIMESTRA *goes to the back of the stage.*

HERALD   A vaunt like this, so loaded as it is with truth,
it well becomes a highborn lady to proclaim.

CHORUS   Thus has she spoken to you, and well you understand,
words that impress interpreters whose thought is clear.

But tell me, herald; I would learn of Menelaos,
that power beloved in his own land. Has he survived
also, and come with you back to his home again?

HERALD I know no way to lie and make my tale so fair
that friends could reap joy of it for any length of time.

CHORUS Is there no means to speak us fair, and yet tell the truth?
It will not hide, when truth and good are torn asunder.

HERALD He is gone out of the sight of the Achaian host,
vessel and man alike. I speak no falsehood there.

CHORUS Was it when he had put out from Ilion in your sight,
or did a storm that struck you both whirl him away?

HERALD How like a master bowman you have hit the mark
and in your speech cut a long sorrow to brief stature.

CHORUS But then the rumor in the host that sailed beside,
was it that he had perished, or might yet be living?

HERALD No man knows. There is none could tell us that for sure
except the Sun, from whom this earth has life and increase.

CHORUS How did this storm, by wrath of the divinities,
strike on our multitude at sea? How did it end?

HERALD It is not well to stain the blessing of this day
with speech of evil weight. Such gods are honored apart.
And when the messenger of a shaken host, sad faced,
brings to his city news it prayed never to hear,
this scores one wound upon the body of the people;
and that from many houses many men are slain
by the two-lashed whip dear to the War God's hand, this
turns
disaster double-bladed, bloodily made two.
The messenger so freighted with a charge of tears
should make his song of triumph at the Furies' door.
But, carrying the fair message of our hopes' salvation,
come home to a glad city's hospitality,
how shall I mix my gracious news with foul, and tell

of the storm on the Achaians by God's anger sent?
For they, of old the deepest enemies, sea and fire
made a conspiracy and gave the oath of hand
to blast in ruin our unhappy Argive army.
At night the sea began to rise in waves of death.
Ship against ship the Thracian stormwind shattered us,
and gored and split, our vessels, swept in violence
of storm and whirlwind, beaten by the breaking rain,
drove on in darkness, spun by the wicked shepherd's hand.
But when the sun came up again to light the dawn,
we saw the Aigaian Sea blossoming with dead men,
the men of Achaia, and the wreckage of their ships.
For us, and for our ship, some god, no man, by guile
or by entreaty's force prevailing, laid his hand
upon the helm and brought us through with hull unscarred.
Life-giving fortune deigned to take our ship in charge
that neither riding in deep water she took the surf
nor drove to shoal and break upon some rocky shore.
But then, delivered from death at sea, in the pale day,
incredulous of our own luck, we shepherded
in our sad thoughts the fresh disaster of the fleet
so pitifully torn and shaken by the storm.
Now of these others, if there are any left alive
they speak of us as men who perished, must they not?
Even as we, who fear that they are gone. But may
it all come well in the end. For Menelaos: be sure
if any of them come back that he will be the first.
If he is still where some sun's gleam can track him down,
alive and open-eyed, by blessed hand of God
who willed that not yet should his seed be utterly gone,
there is some hope that he will still come home again.
You have heard all; and be sure, you have heard the truth.

[The HERALD goes out.

CHORUS Who is he that named you so
fatally in every way?
Could it be some mind unseen

in divination of your destiny
shaping to the lips that name
for the bride of spears and blood,
Helen, which is death? Appropriately
death of ships, death of men and cities
from the bower's soft curtained
and secluded luxury she sailed then,
driven on the giant west wind,
and armored men in their thousands came,
huntsmen down the oar blade's fading footprint
to struggle in blood with those
who by the banks of Simoeis
beached their hulls where the leaves break.

And on Ilion in truth
in the likeness of the name
the sure purpose of the Wrath drove
marriage with death: for the guest board
shamed, and Zeus kindly to strangers,
the vengeance wrought on those men
who graced in too loud voice the bride-song
fallen to their lot to sing,
the kinsmen and the brothers.
And changing its song's measure
the ancient city of Priam
chants in high strain of lamentation,
calling Paris him of the fatal marriage;
for it endured its life's end
in desolation and tears
and the piteous blood of its people.

Once a man fostered in his house
a lion cub, from the mother's milk
torn, craving the breast given.
In the first steps of its young life
mild, it played with children
and delighted the old.
Caught in the arm's cradle

they pampered it like a newborn child,
shining eyed and broken to the hand
to stay the stress of its hunger.

But it grew with time, and the lion
in the blood strain came out; it paid
grace to those who had fostered it
in blood and death for the sheep flocks,
a grim feast forbidden.
The house reeked with blood run
nor could its people beat down the bane,
the giant murderer's onslaught.
This thing they raised in their house was blessed
by God to be priest of destruction.

And that which first came to the city of Ilion,
call it a dream of calm
and the wind dying,
the loveliness and luxury of much gold,
the melting shafts of the eyes' glances,
the blossom that breaks the heart with longing.
But she turned in mid-step of her course to make
bitter the consummation,
whirling on Priam's people
to blight with her touch and nearness.
Zeus hospitable sent her,
a vengeance to make brides weep.

It has been made long since and grown old among men,
this saying: human wealth
grown to fulness of stature
breeds again nor dies without issue.
From high good fortune in the blood
blossoms the quenchless agony.
Far from others I hold my own
mind; only the act of evil
breeds others to follow,
young sins in its own likeness.

Houses clear in their right are given
children in all loveliness.

But Pride aging is made
in men's dark actions
ripe with the young pride
late or soon when the dawn of destiny
comes and birth is given
to the spirit none may fight nor beat down,
sinful Daring; and in those halls
the black visaged Disasters stamped
in the likeness of their fathers.

And Righteousness is a shining in
the smoke of mean houses.
Her blessing is on the just man.
From high halls starred with gold by reeking hands
she turns back
with eyes that glance away to the simple in heart,
spurning the strength of gold
stamped false with flattery.
And all things she steers to fulfilment.

> [AGAMEMNON *enters in a* chariot, *with* KASSANDRA
> *beside him. The* CHORUS *speaks to him.*

Behold, my king: sacker of Troy's citadel,
own issue of Atreus.
How shall I hail you? How give honor
not crossing too high nor yet bending short
of this time's graces?
For many among men are they who set high
the show of honor, yet break justice.
If one be unhappy, all else are fain
to grieve with him: yet the teeth of sorrow
come nowise near to the heart's edge.
And in joy likewise they show joy's semblance,
and torture the face to the false smile.
Yet the good shepherd, who knows his flock,

the eyes of men cannot lie to him,
that with water of feigned
love seem to smile from the true heart.
But I: when you marshalled this armament
for Helen's sake, I will not hide it,
in ugly style you were written in my heart
for steering aslant the mind's course
to bring home by blood
sacrifice and dead men that wild spirit.
But now, in love drawn up from the deep heart,
not skimmed at the edge, we hail you.
You have won, your labor is made gladness.
Ask all men: you will learn in time
which of your citizens have been just
in the city's sway, which were reckless.

AGAMEM. To Argos first, and to the gods within the land,
I must give due greeting; they have worked with me to bring
me home; they helped me in the vengeance I have wrought
on Priam's city. Not from the lips of men the gods
heard justice, but in one firm cast they laid their votes
within the urn of blood that Ilion must die
and all her people; while above the opposite vase
the hand hovered and there was hope, but no vote fell.
The stormclouds of their ruin live; the ash that dies
upon them gushes still in smoke their pride of wealth.
For all this we must thank the gods with grace of much
high praise and memory, we who fenced within our toils
of wrath the city; and, because one woman strayed,
the beast of Argos broke them, the fierce young within
the horse, the armored people who marked out their leap
against the setting of the Pleiades. A wild
and bloody lion swarmed above the towers of Troy
to glut its hunger lapping at the blood of kings.

This to the gods, a prelude strung to length of words.
But, for the thought you spoke, I heard and I remember
and stand behind you. For I say that it is true. .

In few men is it part of nature to respect
a friend's prosperity without begrudging him,
as envy's wicked poison settling to the heart
piles up the pain in one sick with unhappiness,
who, staggered under sufferings that are all his own,
winces again to the vision of a neighbor's bliss.
And I can speak, for I have seen, I know it well,
this mirror of companionship, this shadow's ghost,
these men who seemed my friends in all sincerity.
One man of them all, Odysseus, he that sailed unwilling,
once yoked to me carried his harness, nor went slack.
Dead though he be or living, I can say it still.

Now in the business of the city and the gods
we must ordain full conclave of all citizens
and take our counsel. We shall see what element
is strong, and plan that it shall keep its virtue still.
But that which must be healed—we must use medicine,
or burn, or amputate, with kind intention, take
all means at hand that might beat down corruption's pain.

So to the King's house and the home about the hearth
I take my way, with greeting to the gods within
who sent me forth, and who have brought me home once
    more.
My prize was conquest; may it never fail again.

    [KLYTAIMESTRA *comes forward and speaks.*

Grave gentlemen of Argolis assembled here,
I take no shame to speak aloud before you all
the love I bear my husband. In the lapse of time
modesty fades; it is human.
                  What I tell you now
I learned not from another; this is my own sad life
all the long years this man was gone at Ilion.
It is evil and a thing of terror when a wife
sits in the house forlorn with no man by, and hears
rumors that like a fever die to break again,

and men come in with news of fear, and on their heels
another messenger, with worse news to cry aloud
here in this house. Had Agamemnon taken all
the wounds the tale whereof was carried home to me,
he had been cut full of gashes like a fishing net.
If he had died each time that rumor told his death,
he must have been some triple-bodied Geryon
back from the dead with threefold cloak of earth upon
his body, and killed once for every shape assumed.
Because such tales broke out forever on my rest,
many a time they cut me down and freed my throat
from the noose overslung where I had caught it fast.
And therefore is your son, in whom my love and yours
are sealed and pledged, not here to stand with us today,
Orestes. It were right; yet do not be amazed.
Strophios of Phokis, comrade in arms and faithful friend
to you, is keeping him. He spoke to me of peril
on two counts; of your danger under Ilion,
and here, of revolution and the clamorous people
who might cast down the council—since it lies in men's
nature to trample on the fighter already down.
Such my excuse to you, and without subterfuge.

For me: the rippling springs that were my tears have dried
utterly up, nor left one drop within. I keep
the pain upon my eyes where late at night I wept
over the beacons long ago set for your sake,
untended left forever. In the midst of dreams
the whisper that a gnat's thin wings could winnow broke
my sleep apart. I thought I saw you suffer wounds
more than the time that slept with me could ever hold.

Now all my suffering is past, with griefless heart
I hail this man, the watchdog of the fold and hall;
the stay that keeps the ship alive; the post to grip
groundward the towering roof; a father's single child;
land seen by sailors after all their hope was gone;
splendor of daybreak shining from the night of storm;

the running spring a parched wayfarer strays upon.
Oh, it is sweet to escape from all necessity!

Such is my greeting to him, that he well deserves.
Let none bear malice; for the harm that went before
I took, and it was great.
                                        Now, my beloved one,
step from your chariot; yet let not your foot, my lord,
sacker of Ilion, touch the earth. My maidens there!
Why this delay? Your task has been appointed you,
to strew the ground before his feet with tapestries.
Let there spring up into the house he never hoped
to see, where Justice leads him in, a crimson path.

In all things else, my heart's unsleeping care shall act
with the gods' aid to set aright what fate ordained.

     [KLYTAIMESTRA's *handmaidens spread a bright carpet*
       between the chariot and the door. AGAMEMNON
                      speaks.

Daughter of Leda, you who kept my house for me,
there is one way your welcome matched my absence well.
You strained it to great length. Yet properly to praise
me thus belongs by right to other lips, not yours.
And all this—do not try in woman's ways to make
me delicate, nor, as if I were some Asiatic
bow down to earth and with wide mouth cry out to me,
nor cross my path with jealousy by strewing the ground
with robes. Such state becomes the gods, and none beside.
I am a mortal, a man; I cannot trample upon
these tinted splendors without fear thrown in my path.
I tell you, as a man, not god, to reverence me.
Discordant is the murmur at such treading down
of lovely things; while God's most lordly gift to man
is decency of mind. Call that man only blest
who has in sweet tranquillity brought his life to close.
If I could only act as such, my hope is good.

KLY.   Yet tell me this one thing, and do not cross my will.

AGAMEM.   My will is mine. I shall not make it soft for you.

KLY.   It was in fear surely that you vowed this course to God.

AGAMEM.   No man has spoken knowing better what he said.

KLY.   If Priam had won as you have, what would he have done?

AGAMEM.   I well believe he might have walked on tapestries.

KLY.   Be not ashamed before the bitterness of men.

AGAMEM.   The people murmur, and their voice is great in strength.

KLY.   Yet he who goes unenvied shall not be admired.

AGAMEM.   Surely this lust for conflict is not womanlike?

KLY.   Yet for the mighty even to give way is grace.

AGAMEM.   Does such a victory as this mean so much to you?

KLY.   Oh yield! The power is yours. Give way of your free will.

AGAMEM.   Since you must have it—here, let someone with all speed
take off these sandals, slaves for my feet to tread upon.
And as I crush these garments stained from the rich sea
let no god's eyes of hatred strike me from afar.
Great the extravagance, and great the shame I feel
to spoil such treasure and such silver's worth of webs.

So much for all this. Take this stranger girl within
now, and be kind. The conqueror who uses softly
his power, is watched from far in the kind eyes of God,
and this slave's yoke is one no man will wear from choice.
Gift of the host to me, and flower exquisite
from all my many treasures, she attends me here.

Now since my will was bent to listen to you in this
my feet crush purple as I pass within the hall.

KLY.   The sea is there, and who shall drain its yield? It breeds,
precious as silver, ever of itself renewed,
the purple ooze wherein our garments shall be dipped.

And by God's grace this house keeps full sufficiency
of all. Poverty is a thing beyond its thought.
I could have vowed to trample many splendors down
had such decree been ordained from the oracles
those days when all my study was to bring home your life.
For when the root lives yet the leaves will come again
to fence the house with shade against the Dog Star's heat,
and now you have come home to keep your hearth and house
you bring with you the symbol of our winter's warmth;
but when Zeus ripens the green clusters into wine
there shall be coolness in the house upon those days
because the master ranges his own halls once more.

Zeus, Zeus accomplisher, accomplish these my prayers.
Let your mind bring these things to pass. It is your will.

> [AGAMEMNON and KLYTAIMESTRA enter the house.
> KASSANDRA remains in the chariot. The
> CHORUS speaks.

Why must this persistent fear
beat its wings so ceaselessly
and so close against my mantic heart?
Why this strain unwanted, unrepaid, thus prophetic?
Nor can valor of good hope
seated near the chambered depth
of the spirit cast it out
as dreams of dark fancy; and yet time
has buried in the mounding sand
the sea cables since that day
when against Ilion
the army and the ships put to sea.

Yet I have seen with these eyes
Agamemnon home again.
Still the spirit sings, drawing deep
from within this unlyric threnody of the Fury.
Hope is gone utterly,
the sweet strength is far away.

Surely this is not fantasy.
Surely it is real, this whirl of drifts
that spin the stricken heart.
Still I pray; may all this
expectation fade as vanity
into unfulfilment, and not be.

Yet it is true: the high strength of men
knows no content with limitation. Sickness
chambered beside it beats at the wall between.
Man's fate that sets a true
course yet may strike upon
the blind and sudden reefs of disaster.
But if before such time, fear
throw overboard some precious thing
of the cargo, with deliberate cast,
not all the house, laboring
with weight of ruin, shall go down,
nor sink the hull deep within the sea.
And great and affluent the gift of Zeus
in yield of ploughed acres year on year
makes void again sick starvation.

But when the black and mortal blood of man
has fallen to the ground before his feet, who then
can sing spells to call it back again?
Did Zeus not warn us once
when he struck to impotence
that one who could in truth charm back the dead men?
Had the gods not so ordained
that fate should stand against fate
to check any man's excess
my heart now would have outrun speech
to break forth the water of its grief.
But this is so; I murmur deep in darkness
sore at heart; my hope is gone now
ever again to unwind some crucial good
from the flames about my heart.

[KLYTAIMESTRA *comes out from the house again and*
speaks to KASSANDRA.

Kassandra, you may go within the house as well,
since Zeus in no unkindness has ordained that you
must share our lustral water, stand with the great throng
of slaves that flock to the altar of our household god.
Step from this chariot, then, and do not be so proud.
And think—they say that long ago Alkmena's son
was sold in bondage and endured the bread of slaves.
But if constraint of fact forces you to such fate,
be glad indeed for masters ancient in their wealth.
They who have reaped success beyond their dreams of hope
are savage above need and standard toward their slaves.
From us you shall have all you have the right to ask.

CHORUS   What she has spoken is for you, and clear enough.
Fenced in these fatal nets wherein you find yourself
you should obey her if you can; perhaps you can not.

KLY.   Unless she uses speech incomprehensible,
barbarian, wild as the swallow's song, I speak
within her understanding, and she must obey.

CHORUS   Go with her. What she bids is best in circumstance
that rings you now. Obey, and leave this carriage seat.

KLY.   I have no leisure to stand outside the house and waste
time on this woman. At the central altarstone
the flocks are standing, ready for the sacrifice
we make to this glad day we never hoped to see.
You: if you are obeying my commands at all, be quick.
But if in ignorance you fail to comprehend,
speak not, but make with your barbarian hand some sign.

CHORUS   I think this stranger girl needs some interpreter
who understands. She is like some captive animal.

KLY.   No, she is in the passion of her own wild thoughts.
Leaving her captured city she has come to us
untrained to take the curb, and will not understand

until her rage and strength have foamed away in blood.
I shall throw down no more commands for her contempt.

[KLYTAIMESTRA *goes back into the house.*

CHORUS   I, though, shall not be angry, for I pity her.
Come down, poor creature, leave the empty car. Give way
to compulsion and take up the yoke that shall be yours.

[KASSANDRA *descends from the chariot and cries out loud.*

Oh shame upon the earth!
Apollo, Apollo!

CHORUS   You cry on Loxias in agony? He is not
of those immortals the unhappy supplicate.

KASS.   Oh shame upon the earth!
Apollo, Apollo!

CHORUS   Now once again in bitter voice she calls upon
this god, who has not part in any lamentation.

KASS.   Apollo, Apollo!
Lord of the ways, my ruin.
You have undone me once again, and utterly.

CHORUS   I think she will be prophetic of her own disaster.
Even in the slave's heart the gift divine lives on.

KASS.   Apollo, Apollo!
Lord of the ways, my ruin.
Where have you led me now at last? What house is this?

CHORUS   The house of the Atreidai. If you understand
not that, I can tell you; and so much at least is true.

KASS.   No, but a house that God hates, guilty within
of kindred blood shed, torture of its own,
the shambles for men's butchery, the dripping floor.

CHORUS   The stranger is keen scented like some hound upon
the trail of blood that leads her to discovered death.

KASS.   Behold there the witnesses to my faith.

The small children wail for their own death
and the flesh roasted that their father fed upon.

CHORUS   We had been told before of this prophetic fame
of yours; we want no prophets in this place at all.

KASS.   Ah, for shame, what can she purpose now?
What is this new and huge
stroke of atrocity she plans within the house
to beat down the beloved beyond hope of healing?
Rescue is far away.

CHORUS   I can make nothing of these prophecies. The rest
I understood; the city is full of the sound of them.

KASS.   So cruel then, that you can do this thing?
The husband of your own bed
to bathe bright with water—how shall I speak the end?
This thing shall be done with speed. The hand gropes now,
    and the other
hand follows in turn.

CHORUS   No, I am lost. After the darkness of her speech
I go bewildered in a mist of prophecies.

KASS.   No, no, see there! What is that thing that shows?
Is it some net of death?
Or is the trap the woman there, the murderess?
Let now the slakeless fury in the race
rear up to howl aloud over this monstrous death.

CHORUS   Upon what demon in the house do you call, to raise
the cry of triumph? All your speech makes dark my hope.
And to the heart below trickles the pale drop
as in the hour of death
timed to our sunset and the mortal radiance.
Ruin is near, and swift.

KASS.   See there, see there! Keep from his mate the bull.
Caught in the folded web's
entanglement she pinions him and with the black horn

strikes. And he crumples in the watered bath.
Guile, I tell you, and death there in the caldron wrought.

CHORUS   I am not proud in skill to guess at prophecies,
yet even I can see the evil in this thing.
From divination what good ever has come to men?
Art, and multiplication of words
drifting through tangled evil bring
terror to them that hear.

KASS.   Alas, alas for the wretchedness of my ill-starred life.
This pain flooding the song of sorrow is mine alone.
Why have you brought me here in all unhappiness?
Why, why? Except to die with him? What else could be?

CHORUS   You are possessed of God, mazed at heart
to sing your own death
song, the wild lyric as
in clamor for Itys, Itys over and over again
her long life of tears weeping forever grieves
the brown nightingale.

KASS.   Oh for the nightingale's pure song and a fate like hers.
With fashion of beating wings the gods clothed her about
and a sweet life gave her and without lamentation.
But mine is the sheer edge of the tearing iron.

CHORUS   Whence come, beat upon beat, driven of God,
vain passions of tears?
Whence your cries, terrified, clashing in horror,
in wrought melody and the singing speech?
Whence take you the marks to this path of prophecy
and speech of terror?

KASS.   Oh marriage of Paris, death to the men beloved!
Alas, Skamandros, water my fathers drank.
There was a time I too at your springs
drank and grew strong. Ah me,
for now beside the deadly rivers, Kokytos
and Acheron, I must cry out my prophecies.

CHORUS What is this word, too clear, you have uttered now?
A child could understand.
And deep within goes the stroke of the dripping fang
as mortal pain at the trebled song of your agony
shivers the heart to hear.

KASS. O sorrow, sorrow of my city dragged to uttermost death.
O sacrifices my father made at the wall.
Flocks of the pastured sheep slaughtered there.
And no use at all
to save our city from its pain inflicted now.
And I too, with brain ablaze in fever, shall go down.

CHORUS This follows the run of your song.
Is it, in cruel force of weight,
some divinity kneeling upon you brings
the death song of your passionate suffering?
I can not see the end.

KASS. No longer shall my prophecies like some young girl
new-married glance from under veils, but bright and strong
as winds blow into morning and the sun's uprise
shall wax along the swell like some great wave, to burst
at last upon the shining of this agony.
Now I will tell you plainly and from no cryptic speech;
bear me then witness, running at my heels upon
the scent of these old brutal things done long ago.
There is a choir that sings as one, that shall not again
leave this house ever; the song thereof breaks harsh with
    menace.
And drugged to double fury on the wine of men's
blood shed, there lurks forever here a drunken rout
of ingrown vengeful spirits never to be cast forth.
Hanging above the hall they chant their song of hate
and the old sin; and taking up the strain in turn
spit curses on that man who spoiled his brother's bed.
Did I go wide, or hit, like a real archer? Am I
some swindling seer who hawks his lies from door to door?
Upon your oath, bear witness that I know by heart
the legend of ancient wickedness within this house.

CHORUS   And how could an oath, though cast in rigid honesty,
         do any good? And still we stand amazed at you,
         reared in an alien city far beyond the sea,
         how can you strike, as if you had been there, the truth.

KASS.   Apollo was the seer who set me to this work.

CHORUS   Struck with some passion for you, and himself a god?

KASS.   There was a time I blushed to speak about these things.

CHORUS   True; they who prosper take on airs of vanity.

KASS.   Yes, then; he wrestled with me, and he breathed delight.

CHORUS   Did you come to the getting of children then, as people do?

KASS.   I promised that to Loxias, but I broke my word.

CHORUS   Were you already ecstatic in the skills of God?

KASS.   Yes; even then I read my city's destinies.

CHORUS   So Loxias' wrath did you no harm? How could that be?

KASS.   For this my trespass, none believed me ever again.

CHORUS   But we do; all that you foretell seems true to us.

KASS.   But this is evil, see!
         Now once again the pain of grim, true prophecy
         shivers my whirling brain in a storm of things foreseen.
         Look there, see what is hovering above the house,
         so small and young, imaged as in the shadow of dreams,
         like children almost, killed by those most dear to them,
         and their hands filled with their own flesh, as food to eat.
         I see them holding out the inward parts, the vitals,
         oh pitiful, that meat their father tasted of . . .
         I tell you: There is one that plots vengeance for this,
         the strengthless lion rolling in his master's bed,
         who keeps, ah me, the house against his lord's return;
         my lord too, now that I wear the slave's yoke on my neck.
         King of the ships, who tore up Ilion by the roots,
         what does he know of this accursed bitch, who licks

his hand, who fawns on him with lifted ears, who like
a secret death shall strike the coward's stroke, nor fail?
No, this is daring when the female shall strike down
the male. What can I call her and be right? What beast
of loathing? Viper double-fanged, or Skylla witch
holed in the rocks and bane of men that range the sea;
smoldering mother of death to smoke relentless hate
on those most dear. How she stood up and howled aloud
and unashamed, as at the breaking point of battle,
in feigned gladness for his salvation from the sea!
What does it matter now if men believe or no?
What is to come will come. And soon you too will stand
beside, to murmur in pity that my words were true.

CHORUS   Thyestes' feast upon the flesh of his own children
I understand in terror at the thought, and fear
is on me hearing truth and no tale fabricated.
The rest: I heard it, but wander still far from the course.

KASS.   I tell you, you shall look on Agamemnon dead.

CHORUS   Peace, peace, poor woman; put those bitter lips to sleep.

KASS.   Useless; there is no god of healing in this story.

CHORUS   Not if it must be; may it somehow fail to come.

KASS.   Prayers, yes; they do not pray; they plan to strike, and kill.

CHORUS   What man is it who moves this beastly thing to be?

KASS.   What man? You did mistake my divination then.

CHORUS   It may be; I could not follow through the schemer's plan.

KASS.   Yet I know Greek; I think I know it far too well.

CHORUS   And Pythian oracles are Greek, yet hard to read.

KASS.   Oh, flame and pain that sweeps me once again! My lord,
Apollo, King of Light, the pain, aye me, the pain!
This is the woman-lioness, who goes to bed
with the wolf, when her proud lion ranges far away,

and she will cut me down; as a wife mixing drugs
she wills to shred the virtue of my punishment
into her bowl of wrath as she makes sharp the blade
against her man, death that he brought a mistress home.
Why do I wear these mockeries upon my body,
this staff of prophecy, these flowers at my throat?
At least I will spoil you before I die. Out, down,
break, damn you! This for all that you have done to me.
Make someone else, not me, luxurious in disaster . . .
Lo now, this is Apollo who has stripped me here
of my prophetic robes. He watched me all the time
wearing this glory, mocked of all, my dearest ones
who hated me with all their hearts, so vain, so wrong;
called like some gypsy wandering from door to door
beggar, corrupt, half-starved, and I endured it all.
And now the seer has done with me, his prophetess,
and led me into such a place as this, to die.
Lost are my father's altars, but the block is there
to reek with sacrificial blood, my own. We two
must die, yet die not vengeless by the gods. For there
shall come one to avenge us also, born to slay
his mother, and to wreak death for his father's blood.
Outlaw and wanderer, driven far from his own land,
he will come back to cope these stones of inward hate.
For this is a strong oath and sworn by the high gods,
that he shall cast men headlong for his father felled.
Why am I then so pitiful? Why must I weep?
Since once I saw the citadel of Ilion
die as it died, and those who broke the city, doomed
by the gods, fare as they have fared accordingly,
I will go through with it. I too will take my fate.
I call as on the gates of death upon these gates
to pray only for this thing, that the stroke be true,
and that with no convulsion, with a rush of blood
in painless death, I may close up these eyes, and rest.

CHORUS   O woman much enduring and so greatly wise,
you have said much. But if this thing you know be true,

this death that comes upon you, how can you, serene,
walk to the altar like a driven ox of God?

KASS. Friends, there is no escape for any longer time.

CHORUS Yet longest left in time is to be honored still.

KASS. The day is here and now; I can not win by flight.

CHORUS Woman, be sure your heart is brave; you can take much.

KASS. None but the unhappy people ever hear such praise.

CHORUS Yet there is a grace on mortals who so nobly die.

KASS. Alas for you, father, and for your lordly sons.
Ah!

CHORUS What now? What terror whirls you backward from the door?

KASS. Foul, foul!

CHORUS What foulness then, unless some horror in the mind?

KASS. That room within reeks with blood like a slaughter house.

CHORUS What then? Only these victims butchered at the hearth.

KASS. There is a breath about it like an open grave.

CHORUS This is no Syrian pride of frankincense you mean.

KASS. So. I am going in, and mourning as I go
my death and Agamemnon's. Let my life be done.
Ah friends,
truly this is no wild bird fluttering at a bush,
nor vain my speech. Bear witness to me when I die,
when falls for me, a woman slain, another woman,
and when a man dies for this wickedly mated man.
Here in my death I claim this stranger's grace of you.

CHORUS Poor wretch, I pity you the fate you see so clear.

KASS. Yet once more will I speak, and not this time my own
death's threnody. I call upon the Sun in prayer
against that ultimate shining when the avengers strike

these monsters down in blood, that they avenge as well
one simple slave who died, a small thing, lightly killed.

Alas, poor men, their destiny. When all goes well
a shadow will overthrow it. If it be unkind
one stroke of a wet sponge blots all the picture out;
and that is far the most unhappy thing of all.

[KASSANDRA *goes slowly into the house.*

CHORUS   High fortune is a thing slakeless
for mortals. There is no man who shall point
his finger to drive it back from the door
and speak the words: 'Come no longer.'
Now to this man the blessed ones have given
Priam's city to be captured
and return in the gods' honor.
Must he give blood for generations gone,
die for those slain and in death pile up
more death to come for the blood shed,
what mortal else who hears shall claim
he was born clear of the dark angel?

[AGAMEMNON, *inside the house.*

Ah, I am struck a deadly blow and deep within!

CHORUS   Silence: who cried out that he was stabbed to death within
the house?

AGAMEM.   Ah me, again, they struck again. I am wounded twice.

CHORUS   How the king cried out aloud to us! I believe the thing is
done.
Come, let us put our heads together, try to find some safe
way out.

[The *members of the* CHORUS *go about distractedly,*
each one speaking in turn.

Listen, let me tell you what I think is best to do.
Let the herald call all citizens to rally here.

No, better to burst in upon them now, at once,
and take them with the blood still running from their blades.

I am with this man and I cast my vote to him.
Act now. This is the perilous and instant time.

Anyone can see it, by these first steps they have taken,
they purpose to be tyrants here upon our city.

Yes, for we waste time, while they trample to the ground
deliberation's honor, and their hands sleep not.

I can not tell which counsel of yours to call my own.
It is the man of action who can plan as well.

I feel as he does; nor can I see how by words
we shall set the dead man back upon his feet again.

Do you mean, to drag our lives out long, that we must yield
to the house shamed, and leadership of such as these?

No, we can never endure that; better to be killed.
Death is a softer thing by far than tyranny.

Shall we, by no more proof than that he cried in pain,
be sure, as by divination, that our lord is dead?

Yes, we should know what is true before we break our rage.
Here is sheer guessing and far different from sure knowledge.

From all sides the voices multiply to make me choose
this course; to learn first how it stands with Agamemnon.

[The doors of the palace open, disclosing the bodies of
AGAMEMNON and KASSANDRA, with KLYTAIMESTRA
standing over them.

KLY.   Much have I said before to serve necessity,
but I will take no shame now to unsay it all.

How else could I, arming hate against hateful men
disguised in seeming tenderness, fence high the nets
of ruin beyond overleaping? Thus to me
the conflict born of ancient bitterness is not
a thing new thought upon, but pondered deep in time.
I stand now where I struck him down. The thing is done.
Thus have I wrought, and I will not deny it now.
That he might not escape nor beat aside his death,
as fishermen cast their huge circling nets, I spread
deadly abundance of rich robes, and caught him fast.
I struck him twice. In two great cries of agony
he buckled at the knees and fell. When he was down
I struck him the third blow, in thanks and reverence
to Zeus the lord of dead men underneath the ground.
Thus he went down, and the life struggled out of him;
and as he died he spattered me with the dark red
and violent driven rain of bitter savored blood
to make me glad, as gardens stand among the showers
of God in glory at the birthtime of the buds.

These being the facts, elders of Argos assembled here,
be glad, if it be your pleasure; but for me, I glory.
Were it religion to pour wine above the slain,
this man deserved, more than deserved, such sacrament.
He filled our cup with evil things unspeakable
and now himself come home has drunk it to the dregs.

CHORUS   We stand here stunned. How can you speak this way, with
          mouth
          so arrogant, to vaunt above your fallen lord?

KLY.   You try me out as if I were a woman and vain;
          but my heart is not fluttered as I speak before you.
          You know it. You can praise or blame me as you wish;
          it is all one to me. That man is Agamemnon,
          my husband; he is dead; the work of this right hand
          that struck in strength of righteousness. And that is that.

CHORUS   Woman, what evil thing planted upon the earth

or dragged from the running salt sea could you have tasted
    now
to wear such brutality and walk in the people's hate?
You have cast away, you have cut away. You shall go homeless
    now,
crushed with men's bitterness.

KLY.   Now it is I you doom to be cast out from my city
with men's hate heaped and curses roaring in my ears.
Yet look upon this dead man; you would not cross him once
when with no thought more than as if a beast had died,
when his ranged pastures swarmed with the deep fleece of
    flocks,
he slaughtered like a victim his own child, my pain
grown into love, to charm away the winds of Thrace.
Were you not bound to hunt him then clear of this soil
for the guilt stained upon him? Yet you hear what I
have done, and lo, you are a stern judge. But I say to you:
go on and threaten me, but know that I am ready,
if fairly you can beat me down beneath your hand,
for you to rule; but if the god grant otherwise,
you shall be taught—too late, for sure—to keep your place.

CHORUS   Great your design, your speech is a clamor of pride.
Swung to the red act drives the fury within your brain
signed clear in the splash of blood over your eyes.
Yet to come is stroke given for stroke
vengeless, forlorn of friends.

KLY.   Now hear you this, the right behind my sacrament:
By my child's Justice driven to fulfillment, by
her Wrath and Fury, to whom I sacrificed this man,
the hope that walks my chambers is not traced with fear
while yet Aigisthos makes the fire shine on my hearth,
my good friend, now as always, who shall be for us
the shield of our defiance, no weak thing; while he,
this other, is fallen, stained with this woman you behold,
plaything of all the golden girls at Ilion;
and here lies she, the captive of his spear, who saw

wonders, who shared his bed, the wise in revelations
and loving mistress, who yet knew the feel as well
of the men's rowing benches. Their reward is not
unworthy. He lies there; and she who swanlike cried
aloud her lyric mortal lamentation out
is laid against his fond heart, and to me has given
a delicate excitement to my bed's delight.

CHORUS   O that in speed, without pain
and the slow bed of sickness
death could come to us now, death that forever
carries sleep without ending, now that our lord is down,
our shield, kindest of men,
who for a woman's grace suffered so much,
struck down at last by a woman.

Alas, Helen, wild heart,
for the multitudes, for the thousand lives
you killed under Troy's shadow,
you alone, to shine in man's memory
as blood flower never to be washed out. Surely a demon then
of death walked in the house, men's agony.

KLY.   No, be not so heavy, nor yet draw down
in prayer death's ending,
neither turn all wrath against Helen
for men dead, that she alone killed
all those Danaan lives, to work
the grief that is past all healing.

CHORUS   Divinity that kneel on this house and the two
strains of the blood of Tantalos,
in the hands and hearts of women you steer
the strength tearing my heart.
Standing above the corpse, obscene
as some carrion crow she sings
the crippled song and is proud.

KLY.   Thus have you set the speech of your lips
straight, calling by name

the spirit thrice glutted that lives in this race.
From him deep in the nerve is given
the love and the blood drunk, that before
the old wound dries, it bleeds again.

CHORUS   Surely it is a huge
and heavy spirit bending the house you cry,
alas, the bitter glory
of a doom that shall never be done with;
and all through Zeus, Zeus,
first cause, prime mover.
For what thing without Zeus is done among mortals?
What here is without God's blessing?

O king, my king
how shall I weep for you?
What can I say out of my heart of pity?
Caught in this spider's web you lie,
Your life gasped out in indecent death,
struck prone to this shameful bed
by your lady's hand of treachery
and the stroke twin edged of the iron.

KLY.   Can you claim I have done this?
Speak of me never
more as the wife of Agamemnon.
In the shadow of this corpse's queen
the old stark avenger
of Atreus for his revel of hate
struck down this man,
last blood for the slaughtered children.

CHORUS   What man shall testify
your hands are clean of this murder?
How? How? Yet from his father's blood
might swarm some fiend to guide you.
The black ruin that shoulders
through the streaming blood of brothers
strides at last where he shall win requital
for the children who were eaten.

O king, my king
how shall I weep for you?
What can I say out of my heart of pity?
Caught in this spider's web you lie,
your life gasped out in indecent death,
struck prone to this shameful bed
by your lady's hand of treachery
and the stroke twin edged of the iron.

KLY.   No shame, I think, in the death given
this man. And did he not
first of all in this house wreak death
by treachery?
The flower of this man's love and mine,
Iphigeneia of the tears
he dealt with even as he has suffered.
Let his speech in death's house be not loud.
With the sword he struck,
with the sword he paid for his own act.

CHORUS   My thoughts are swept away and I go bewildered.
Where shall I turn the brain's
activity in speed when the house is falling?
There is fear in the beat of the blood rain breaking
wall and tower. The drops come thicker.
Still fate grinds on yet more stones the blade
for more acts of terror.

Earth, my earth, why did you not fold me under
or ever I saw this man lie dead
fenced by the tub in silver?
Who shall bury him? Who shall mourn him?
Shall you dare this who have killed
your lord? Make lamentation,
render the graceless grace to his soul
for huge things done in wickedness?
Who over this great man's grave shall lay
the blessing of tears
worked soberly from a true heart?

KLY.   Not for you to speak of such tendance.
       Through us he fell,
       by us he died; we shall bury.
       There will be no tears in this house for him.
       It must be Iphigeneia
       his child, who else,
       shall greet her father by the whirling stream
       and the ferry of tears
       to close him in her arms and kiss him.

CHORUS Here is anger for anger. Between them
       who shall judge lightly?
       The spoiler is robbed; he killed, he has paid.
       The truth stands ever beside God's throne
       eternal: he who has wrought shall pay; that is law.
       Then who shall tear the curse from their blood?
       The seed is stiffened to ruin.

KLY.   You see truth in the future
       at last. Yet I wish
       to seal my oath with the Spirit
       in the house: I will endure all things as they stand
       now, hard though it be. Hereafter
       let him go forth to make bleed with death
       and guilt the houses of others.
       I will take some small
       measure of our riches, and be content
       that I swept from these halls
       the murder, the sin, and the fury.

          [AIGISTHOS enters, followed at a little distance by his
                      armed bodyguard.

AIGIS. O splendor and exaltation of this day of doom!
       Now I can say once more that the high gods look down
       on mortal crimes to vindicate the right at last,
       now that I see this man—sweet sight—before me here
       sprawled in the tangling nets of fury, to atone
       the calculated evil of his father's hand.

For Atreus, this man's father, King of Argolis—
I tell you the clear story—drove my father forth,
Thyestes, his own brother, who had challenged him
in his king's right—forth from his city and his home.
Yet sad Thyestes came again to supplicate
the hearth, and win some grace, in that he was not slain
nor soiled the doorstone of his fathers with blood spilled.
Not his own blood. But Atreus, this man's godless sire,
angrily hospitable set a feast for him,
in seeming a glad day of fresh meat slain and good
cheer; then served my father his own children's flesh
to feed on. For he carved away the extremities,
hands, feet, and cut the flesh apart, and covered them
served in a dish to my father at his table apart,
who with no thought for the featureless meal before him ate
that ghastly food whose curse works now before your eyes.
But when he knew the terrible thing that he had done,
he spat the dead meat from him with a cry, and reeled
spurning the table back to heel with strength the curse:
'Thus crash in ruin all the seed of Pleisthenes.'
Out of such acts you see this dead man stricken here,
and it was I, in my right, who wrought this murder, I
third born to my unhappy father, and with him
driven, a helpless baby in arms, to banishment.
Yet I grew up, and justice brought me home again,
till from afar I laid my hands upon this man,
since it was I who pieced together the fell plot.
Now I can die in honor again, if die I must,
having seen him caught in the cords of his just punishment.

CHORUS   Aigisthos, this strong vaunting in distress is vile.
You claim that you deliberately killed the king,
you, and you only, wrought the pity of this death.
I tell you then: There shall be no escape, your head
shall face the stones of anger from the people's hands.

AIGIS.   So loud from you, stooped to the meanest rowing bench
with the ship's masters lordly on the deck above?
You are old men; well, you shall learn how hard it is

at your age, to be taught how to behave yourselves.
But there are chains, there is starvation with its pain,
excellent teachers of good manners to old men,
wise surgeons and exemplars. Look! Can you not see it?
Lash not at the goads for fear you hit them, and be hurt.

CHORUS   So then you, like a woman, waited the war out
here in the house, shaming the master's bed with lust,
and planned against the lord of war this treacherous death?

AIGIS.   It is just such words as these will make you cry in pain.
Not yours the lips of Orpheus, no, quite otherwise,
whose voice of rapture dragged all creatures in his train.
You shall be dragged, for baby whimperings sobbed out
in rage. Once broken, you will be easier to deal with.

CHORUS   How shall you be lord of the men of Argos, you
who planned the murder of this man, yet could not dare
to act it out, and cut him down with your own hand?

AIGIS.   No, clearly the deception was the woman's part,
and I was suspect, that had hated him so long.
Still with his money I shall endeavor to control
the citizens. The mutinous man shall feel the yoke
drag at his neck, no cornfed racing colt that runs
free traced; but hunger, grim companion of the dark
dungeon shall see him broken to the hand at last.

CHORUS   But why, why then, you coward, could you not have slain
your man yourself? Why must it be his wife who killed,
to curse the country and the gods within the ground?
Oh, can Orestes live, be somewhere in sunlight still?
Shall fate grown gracious ever bring him back again
in strength of hand to overwhelm these murderers?

AIGIS.   You shall learn then, since you stick to stubbornness of
mouth and hand.
Up now from your cover, my henchmen: here is work for
you to do.

CHORUS   Look, they come! Let every man clap fist upon his hilted
sword.

AIGIS.   I too am sword-handed against you; I am not afraid of death.

CHORUS   Death you said and death it shall be; we take up the word
of fate.

KLY.   No, my dearest, dearest of all men, we have done enough. No
more
violence. Here is a monstrous harvest and a bitter reaping
time.
There is pain enough already. Let us not be bloody now.
Honored gentlemen of Argos, go to your homes now and give
way
to the stress of fate and season. We could not do otherwise
than we did. If this is the end of suffering, we can be content
broken as we are by the brute heel of angry destiny.
Thus a woman speaks among you. Shall men deign to understand?

AIGIS.   Yes, but think of these foolish lips that blossom into leering
gibes,
think of the taunts they spit against me daring destiny and
power,
sober opinion lost in insults hurled against my majesty.

CHORUS   It was never the Argive way to grovel at a vile man's feet.

AIGIS.   I shall not forget this; in the days to come I shall return.

CHORUS   Nevermore, if God's hand guiding brings Orestes home again.

AIGIS.   Exiles feed on empty dreams of hope. I know it. I was one.

CHORUS   Have your way, gorge and grow fat, soil justice, while the
power is yours.

AIGIS.   You shall pay, make no mistake, for this misguided insolence.

CHORUS   Crow and strut, brave cockerel by your hen; you have no
threats to fear.

KLY. These are howls of impotent rage; forget them, dearest; you
   and I
  have the power; we two shall bring good order to our house
   at last.

     [*They enter the house. The doors close. All persons
      leave the stage.*

Sophocles

ELECTRA

translated by
Francis Fergusson

ORESTES, the son of AGAMEMNON and CLYTEMNESTRA, was saved from his father's fate by being sent out of the country to Phocis, where he was befriended by KING STROPHIOS and his son PYLADES. His sister ELECTRA, meanwhile, remained in Argos, enduring the daily insolence of CLYTEM-NESTRA and AEGISTHOS and waiting for the day when the murdered AGAMEMNON should be avenged.

DRAMATIS PERSONÆ:

PAIDAGOGOS

ORESTES

ELECTRA

CHRYSOTHEMIS

CLYTEMNESTRA

AEGISTHOS

CHORUS OF MYCENAEAN WOMEN

ELECTRA

SCENE: *Mycenae, before the palace of* AGAMEMNON.

> [*Dawn.* ORESTES, *the* PAIDAGOGOS, *and* PYLADES *are discovered.*

PAIDAG. Child of that chief who led the army once in Troy,
Son of Agamemnon, here before you lies
For you to see, what you have longed to see.
It is the ancient and beloved Argos
Refuge of Inachos' tormented daughter,
Apollo the Wolfgod's forum. On that side
Hera's familiar altar, and just before you
Golden Mycenae you may see, Orestes,
And that same murderous House of Pelops, whence
Your sister snatched you from your father's killers,
And brought you to me to guard, till you reached the age
When you could avenge that father's murder.

But now, Orestes, and you Pylades,
We must decide at once what's to be done.
The sunlight already bright about us
Has started the early voices of the birds,
And the dark sky of stars has faded.
Before someone emerges from the house,
Come, lay your plans; this is no time to pause,
For you are on the verge of deeds.

OREST. Old friend,
How plainly you show your loyalty to me!
Even in these perils
You urge us on, and lead the way yourself.

I shall explain the plan. Listen acutely
And make corrections if I miss the mark.

When I resorted to the Pythian seer
To learn how I might best avenge my father
Upon his killers, Apollo answered,
With neither shield nor army, secretly
Your own just hand shall deal them their due pay.
With this advice in mind, friend, slip into the house
When you can find an opportunity;
See what goes on, then come report to us.
They won't suspect you; with the changes of time
You'll pass unknown. Tell some such tale as this:
You are a Phocian sent by Phanoteus,
For he you know is their greatest ally.
Tell them on oath that you come to report
Orestes' death in a fatal accident;
Thrown, say, from his speeding chariot
At the Pythian Games: have this your story.
We meanwhile shall adorn my father's tomb
With our shorn hair and our wine-offerings,
As Apollo ordered. We shall return
With that funeral urn we hid in the thicket,
A proof for them of the sweet tale we bring,
That I am already dust and ashes!
What harm is there for me in my rumored death
When I am alive in deed and gaining fame?

But you fathergods, and gods of the country:
O House of my Fathers, on these new paths
Receive me kindly! At the god's urging,
With justice, I come to purify you.
May this land not reject me in dishonor,
But take me in, to make it flourish again.

We have said enough. You go at once, old friend,
And do as I explained. We shall depart,
Obeying Time, which rules all difficult deeds.

[*Wail inside the palace.*

PAIDAG.　I thought I heard a servant cry indoors.

 OREST.   The wretched Electra, can it be?
           Shall we wait to hear what she is wailing?

PAIDAG.   No. Not till we try to do as the god said,
           And pour our lustral offerings to your father.
           We must start with that, for that will give us
           Control and victory in the present action.

                    [*Exeunt* ORESTES, PYLADES *and the* PAIDAGOGOS.
                          Enter ELECTRA *from the palace.*

ELEC.   O day light,
           O air, the sheath of earth,
           How you have shaken with mourning,
           And you have felt
           The breast beaten for grief
           At the hour of night's going.
           Ah, it is with shame I lie
           In that house, mourning all night
           My father's wretched death.
           No far-off wargod killed him,
           My mother with her lover, with
           Cruel Aegisthos, axe to oak,
           Brought down his head.
           In your house no wailing
           But mine, father,
           For such perishing.

           But I will not stop wailing
           While I can see the stars glittering,
           Or this day.
           So a bird cries with her young lost,
           And I scream at my father's doors.
           O dark House, Persephone's,
           O earthy Hermes, and you grave
           Furies, you are aware
           Of murders and adulteries:
           Come! Help! Avenge
           My father's murder!

Send me my brother!
I begin to sink
Under my trouble.

[*Enter the chorus of Mycenaean women. Here begins
the Kommos, or lament sung by actor and chorus.*

CHORUS   Ah Electra, child. Child   [STROPHE 1
Of godless mother. Will you
Still waste for Agamemnon, long since
Guile-snared by that mother, by her delivered
Into the hand of the killer? So may she be
To death delivered. This I dare to pray.

ELEC.   Gentle women,
You come to comfort me.
This I know, but I can never
But I will never
Stop mourning my father dead.
You, in your love,
Abandon me to grief
Only this I crave.

CHORUS   But you shall never bring him back with   [ANTISTROPHE 1
Prayers and weeping from
The common marsh of death: but in that helpless grief
You waste away, your evils are
Unsolved in these tears.
Why then do you feed your misery?

ELEC.   Those heads are weak that cannot hold
The death of parents.
But I have set my heart
With that bewildered bird who tells the god,
Crying *Ityn, Ityn* all night. Ah Niobe,
Unfortunate you are, yet blessed
To weep in stone.

CHORUS   But you are not alone unlucky   [STROPHE 2
Among mortals, child: your kin
Chrysothemis, and

Iphiánassa are so, and that one
Whose youth is hidden, whose sufferings covered, whom
The Mycenean land is to receive,
When the god sends him, as
The King: Orestes.

ELEC.   Him I expect without rest,
Being unwed and childless,
Having my grief, and a fruitlessly evil lot.
Whatever he hears he forgets, or else
Why should he not come as he says?
He longs to, but his longings fall short.

CHORUS   Take heart, child, take heart.   [ANTISTROPHE 2
Still in the sky
Great Zeus sees everything, and rules.
Give over your anger to him,
Neither forgetting, nor hating too much.
Time is an easy god:
Here by the pasture,
Here by the beach of Krisa,
Agamemnon's child will not be iron forever;
No more will the god who rules by Acheron.

ELEC.   But most of life has slipped by,
And will not come to me again.
As one whom no parents bore,
One whom no man cherishes,
As a stranger and a beggar in my father's house,
Meanly clothed:
So I wait here by the empty board.

CHORUS   With a terrible cry,   [STROPHE 3
Agamemnon met
The murdering edge
In his own bed.
Figure of horror, the issue
Of pleasure and slyness, whether
Some god or a mortal the maker.

ELEC.   That was my bitterest day: that night
        The unspeakable supper was like death for me:
        Feast when my father perished at the hands
        That were to take my life away.
        For them O god provide your punishments,
        Never enjoyment of their work's fruits.

CHORUS Stop. Stop speaking so.   [ANTISTROPHE 3
        Can you not think how you distract yourself,
        Make yourself pitifully fail?
        You increase your troubles when you breed
        War in your gloomy soul;
        There's no fighting the strong.

ELEC   I know I am horror-forced,
        And anger will not let me go.
        But I will not hold back
        So long as I live.
        Ah kindly women, from whom shall I hear ever
        The good word in season?
        Leave me, friends,
        Call this trouble issueless.
        So shall I hold my lamentations ceaselessly.

LEADER I speak in kindness, as a faithful mother:
        Do not feed your frenzy.

ELEC.   But where is the end of this evil?
        Where do they dare to forget the dead,
        Among what peoples? There may I be
        Unhonored. Or if I ever wed good fortune,
        Nesting in peace, still may I never fold
        The sharp wings of the wailing due my father.
        If the dead are dust and nothing,
        If they lie disregarded,
        If they are never given
        Their due for murder,
        Then fear and piety are utterly gone
        From among us mortals.

LEADER I came for your sake as well as mine my child.
        If my words are wrong, do as you wish,
        I follow you still.

ELEC.   My friends, I am ashamed, you think I mourn too much.
        But bear with me, since I have no choice;
        What alternative for one who sees the evil?
        And I see it, night and day I see it,
        Not diminishing, growing. My own mother
        Hates me, I live with my father's killers
        And obey them; from them I received the means of life,
        Or perish. And that life: do you suppose
        It is sweet to me to have to see Aegisthos
        In my father's seat, wearing my father's clothes,
        Pouring libations at the hearth
        Where he brought my father down? When I see
        The final insolence accomplished: in my mother's bed
        (If I must call her mother) my father's killer?
        And she is so calloused, so hardened
        With the disease itself, that she fears nothing.
        Now she celebrates her work, remembers
        The day of the month when with guile she killed him,
        To offer the housegods sacrifice and dance.
        But I, watching, keep under cover,
        Bewail the bitter feast-day of my father.
        Yet I cannot wail as I would, for she
        Attacks me: 'Ungodly, ugly girl!
        'Are you the only one whose father died,
        'The only miserable mortal? May you sink to Hell,
        And the gods of Hell not stop your wailing!'
        So she screams till she hears that Orestes is coming.
        Then she will shout in my ear, 'Did you do this?
        'Is this your work, you who stole Orestes from me?
        'But you shall pay for everything!'
        So she screams, and behind her, egging her on,
        Her lover, that illustrious weakling,
        That loud talker, that female fighter!
        But I, waiting for Orestes to bring relief,

I begin to fail. He drains my hope,
My hope of hope, with his delaying.
Here is neither wisdom nor piety, my friends,
But evils, which force me to evil.

LEADER   Tell me, is Aegisthos near? Or has he left the house?

ELEC.   He has left, of course. How should I be out,
If he were near?

LEADER   If he is away, then,
I may speak further with you?

ELEC.   Yes, you may speak.

LEADER   Let me enquire about your brother.
Is he coming? Delaying? I must know.

ELEC.   He says he is coming but does not come.

LEADER   A man with a great work likes to delay.

ELEC.   When I saved him I did not delay.

LEADER   Take courage. He is the man to help those he loves.

ELEC.   I trust him, or I should not still be alive.

LEADER   Hush for now, hush.
Chrysothemis is at the door, your own sister.
She is bringing offerings for the gods of the dead.

[Enter CHRYSOTHEMIS with offerings. She comes from
the palace.

CHRY   Sister, what are you proclaiming out here at the door?
Won't you learn, after all this time
Not to pamper a helpless anger?
And you must know that I too suffer
And that if I had the strength
I too should show them what I think of them.
But in foul weather I lower my sails,
I never threaten when I am helpless.
If you would only do the same! . . . Well,

What I say is immoral, of course,
And you are right. And yet, if I am to breathe freely,
I must listen to what *they* say.

ELEC.   Horrible; the own child of such a father
And you forget him for that mother!
Your moralizing of course is from her,
None of it yours. Well, choose: either be foolish,
Or else be very prudent, and forget
Those who have been dear to you. Consider:
You say you'd show your hatred if you had the strength,
But you give me no help, though I am given
Completely to the cause of vengeance; you dissuade me even.
So we must be cowards too in our misery?
But tell me, what should I gain by silence?
Or I'll tell you. Have I life now? Little;
And yet enough, for I harrow them
To the honor of the dead, if the dead know honor;
While you are a hater in word only,
Living in deed with your father's killers.
I would not yield so—
If they offered me everything that you enjoy,
I would not so yield. For you
Let the tables of life be richly spread,
Let them overflow. For my sole pasturage
I would be unoffending, I do not crave
Your honors—nor would you, if you were wise.
You might have been your father's: be your mother's:
Belong to her who everyone knows is evil,
The betrayer of your dying father and your own kin!

LEADER   By the fear of the gods, no anger!
If you will learn from her, and she from you,
You may still profit from these words.

CHRY.   I am accustomed to what she says, my friends,
And I should never have approached her now,
Had I not heard of a greater misfortune coming
To end her mourning.

ELEC.   What? Tell me of a greater
        And I say no more.

CHRY.   I'll tell you all I heard.
        Unless you stop wailing, they will send you in
        Where you can not see the light of the sun:
        Far away and under a low roof
        You shall sing your sorrows. Think, therefore;
        Do not blame me later, when you suffer,
        But think in time.

ELEC.   And this they really plan?

CHRY.   At once; as soon as Aegisthos returns.

ELEC.   Well then, let him come soon.

CHRY.   What, are you mad?

ELEC.   If that's what he intends, let him come soon!

CHRY.   To bring you suffering? What are you thinking of?

ELEC.   Of escaping you all.

CHRY.   Your life here
        Means nothing to you?

ELEC.   How beautiful it is!

CHRY.   It might have been if you had learned wisdom.

ELEC.   Teach me no treachery to those I love.

CHRY.   I don't. I teach you to yield to the strong.

ELEC.   Go. Fawn. Fawn on the strong. I can not.

CHRY.   Still, it would be well not to fall through *folly*.

ELEC.   I will fall—if I must, to honor my father.

CHRY.   But you know that our father understands.

ELEC.   That's what traitors say.

CHRY.   Then you will not listen
        To what *I* say?

ELEC.	No. I have my wits still.
CHRY.	Then I shall go about my own business.
ELEC.	Where are you going? For whom are those offerings?
CHRY.	My mother sent me with them to our father's grave.
ELEC.	What, to the grave of her mortal enemy?
CHRY.	Of the man she slaughtered, as you like to say.
ELEC.	From whom or what did that inspiration come?
CHRY.	From something she saw in the night, I think.
ELEC.	O fathergods! Come! Help!
CHRY.	Do you take courage From her fear?
ELEC.	If you would tell me what she saw, I should answer that.
CHRY.	I know very little to tell.
ELEC.	But tell me, tell! It is the little things By which we rise or fall.
CHRY.	They say She saw our father with her in the light of day. On the hearth he was, planting his sceptre Which Aegisthos holds now. From that sceptre grew A swelling branch which brought at last The whole land of Mycenae under its shadow. This I heard From one who heard her tell her dream to the sun. It is all I know Except that it was in fear she sent me. Now, by the gods I beg you, listen! Don't fall through folly! It will be the worse for you if you push me away!
ELEC.	Sister, let none of these things touch his tomb. It is against piety, against wisdom,

To offer our father gifts from that woman.
Give them to the wind, or bury them deep in the dust
Where they can never reach our father's bed;
When she is dead, there let her find them.
Only a woman of brass, an iron woman,
Would offer her murder-victim gifts.
Do you suppose the dead man would receive them gladly?
From her who killed him in dishonor and cruelty,
After mutilation washing the blood-stained head
To cleanse herself of murder? No! throw them away,
And cut a lock of hair from your head and one from mine,
And give him also this poor thing, all I have,
This plain and unembroidered belt; then fall on your knees
And pray that a helper may rise for us
Out of the earth, against our enemies: pray
That the young Orestes may come in his strength
To trample them underfoot, so that with fuller hands than
   these
We may make offering. I think, I think
It was he who sent this dream, prophetic of evil.
Therefore help yourself in this, my sister,
And me, and him, the dearest mortal:
Our father lying underground.

LEADER   This girl speaks wisely. You, my friend,
         If you are prudent, will do as she requests.

CHRY.   I will. For it is right to join for action,
         Not wrangle back and forth. But in the name of the gods,
         Let there be silence among you, friends,
         While I make this effort! If my mother hears
         I shall have bitter things to endure.

                                        [*Exit* CHRYSOTHEMIS.

CHORUS   If I am not an utterly false diviner   [STROPHE
         Bereft of mind,
         I am inspired
         By Diké, bringing justice with power.
         She is coming my child, coming in no long time!

My courage
Rises, when
I hear this dream.
Your father, King of the Greeks, did not forget,
Nor did that double-edged bronze-headed axe
That struck him miserably down to shame.

Comes on many feet the many-handed   [ANTISTROPHE
Bronze-shod Fury,
Terrible from ambush.
The godless conjunctions of that mating,
Murder-dabbled, have received no blessing.
Therefore never,
Never in vain
Has this sign come,
To the doers and their helpers! Portents for mortals
Are neither in terrible dreams nor in marvels,
If this night vision is not full of boded good.

Ah Pelops! your ancient   [EPODE
Chariot racing
Has proved unrelenting
To this, our land.
Since Myrtilos was hurled
From his golden car
To an Ocean bed;
Uprooted cruelly, thrown:
Slain with treachery, slain:
Ever,
Ever with us at home
Suffering and shame.

[Enter CLYTEMNESTRA from the palace. She is followed
by a servant girl bearing an offering of fruits.

CLYTEM.   I see you have twisted loose again.
Aegisthos is gone, who always keeps you in
Where you cannot revile your kin publicly.
With him away you do not fear me,

For you have often enough informed the city
That I was a tyrant, lost to all justice,
Outraging you and yours. But it is not I
Who am insolent, I only answer you.
Your father, only he, has been your pretext,
Because I killed him. I killed him: quite clearly
I say this, for I cannot deny it.
But Justice seized him also, not I alone;
And you would have helped too had you been wise.
Because that man whom you still cry for
Was the one Greek who could bear to sacrifice
Your sister. He had not suffered as I had;
He sowed her, and I bore her. So be it.
But tell me why, tell me for whom, he killed her?
For the Argives, you say? But for them
He had no right to offer up my child.
Or was it for his brother Menelaos
My child was slain, and I am not to claim justice?
Did he not himself have two children,
Who rather should have died, since for *their* parents' sake
That voyage was undertaken?
Or had the world of the dead a special craving
To feast, not on their child, but on mine only?
Or did your miserable father lack love
For my child, while tender to Menelaos'?
Choice of an evil and foolish father.
So I believe, and so, though you disagree, I say;
So the dead girl would say, if she were here.
I do not grieve for these things done;
Blame me for them, if you think me wrong
When you can hold your own judgment even.

ELEC.   This time you will not say that it was I
Who started or probed you for these painful things.
But if you allow me I shall speak the truth,
About the dead man and about my sister.

CLYTEM.   I do allow you. If you had always spoken so
I could have listened without pain.

ELEC.   Then I shall speak. You say you killed my father:
          What word more hideous than that avowal,
          Wherever justice lay? But I shall show
          That you killed against justice, in depraved obedience
          To the man with whom you are united now.

          For what offense did Artemis-who-hunts-to-hounds
          Hold all the winds still, there in Aulis?
          I'll tell you: my father once (or so I heard it)
          Playing within the goddess' sacred grove,
          Startled an antlered deer with dappled skin,
          Boasted that he had killed it.
          At that the maiden Artemis grew angry,
          And held the Greeks back, till my father paid,
          With sacrifice of his child, for her stag.
          Such was the sacrifice: there was no other way
          To loose the fleet, either toward home or Troy.
          And so, against his will, constrained, with pain,
          He gave her up: not for his brother's sake.

          But say I'm wrong and you are right,
          Say he offered her up for Menelaos' sake,
          Must you then murder him? And by what law?
          Take care, or in issuing this decree
          You issue yourself remorse and punishment.
          For if a killer merits death
          You must die next, to satisfy that justice.
          Take care, you offer lies for pretexts.

          And now if you will tell me besides
          Why you accept the shameful fruits of your labors;
          Sleep with the very murderer with whom
          You brought my father down; bear children to him,
          Reject your decent children decently born?
          Must I approve? Or will you say
          That all of this is vengeance for your daughter?
          An ugly pretext: because of a daughter
          To join with a mortal enemy in marriage!

But there is no convincing you, you only scream
That I am being insolent to my mother.
Tyrant I call you, no less than mother,
For under you and your lover
I live in misery, while your other child, Orestes,
Barely escaped you, and now wastes in exile.
You say I raised him up to plague you;
I did, I would, I will if I can, be sure of that;
And therefore if you wish you may call me
Foul-mouthed and impious.
For I am close to you, close to your nature.

LEADER   I see she breathes anger, and whether she is just
No more concerns her.

CLYTEM.   Then what attention should she receive,
Attacking her mother, old as she is!
Do you think she would wince from any horror?

ELEC.   I have not lost all sense of shame,
Though you think so. I understand that I
Am lost, that I am beyond the pale.
But it is your heartlessness that forces me;
Crime is quickly learned from crime.

CLYTEM.   A monstrous nursling! She preaches on me
As her text; on what I do, on what I say!

ELEC.   It is you who talk. It is your deeds that talk.
Even in my words it is your deeds that talk!

CLYTEM.   Artemis! Queen! Witness! When Aegisthos comes
She shall diminish this impudence!

ELEC.   Do you see?
Having given me leave to say what I would
She will not listen.

CLYTEM.   And so, though you have had your say,
You will keep me from sacrifice by screaming?

ELEC. Go. I invite you. Sacrifice.
Do not blame my tongue, for I say no more.

[*To servant with offering of fruits.*

CLYTEM. Go, my girl, and take these fruits as offerings
That I may raise a prayer up to the King
And cleanse me of the horrors I contain.

Protecting Phoebos, hear the hid thing I say.
I do not speak among friends,
And it would be wrong to open it to the light
While she is near, or with her murderous voice
She would sow through the city futile words.
Listen so, for so shall I pray.

The spectre that I saw last night, Apollo, King,
In that ambiguous dream:
If it is healthful, then fulfill it; if evil,
Let it turn back against my enemies.
Do not let plotters deprive me of my riches,
But let me live always as I am: in safety:
Having the House of Atreus and the sceptre:
Having the friends that now are near me, having
Those of my children who are not bitter toward me.
Apollo, King: listen graciously;
Grant to all mine all that I beg of you.
Also those other things behind my silence:
I know that you know them, being a god;
Being a child of Zeus you know everything.

[*Enter the* PAIDAGOGOS, *as a traveler.*

PAIDAG. Kind women, may I learn
Whether this is King Aegisthos' house?

LEADER It is; you have guessed rightly.

PAIDAG. And am I right that this is the King's wife?
She seems to be a queen.

LEADER Yes. That is the Queen.

PAIDAG. My greetings, lady. I bring sweet news
         To you and to Aegisthos, from a friend.

CLYTEM. I welcome your words, but must know first who sent you.

PAIDAG. Phanoteus of Phocis, on important matters.

CLYTEM. What are they, stranger? Speak; for I am sure
         That coming from a friend they will be pleasant.

PAIDAG. Orestes is dead, to sum it up briefly.

ELEC.   a-á a-á! This day I die.

CLYTEM. What did you say? What did you say? Don't listen to her!

PAIDAG. Orestes is dead, I tell you again.

ELEC.   a-á a-á! I have ceased to live.

CLYTEM. You: about your business! And you, friend,
         Tell me the truth: how did he die?

PAIDAG. That's what I was sent for, I'll tell you everything.
         First of all, you must know he went
         To the great Greek festival, the Delphic Games.
         And there, to be brief where there is much to tell,
         I never knew such power or such a man.
         Of all the games the judges heralded
         He was acclaimed the victor,
         Orestes, the Illustrious,
         The son of Agamemnon-great-in-Troy.

         Such his beginnings. But when a god lays snares
         No man can get away, though he be strong.

         And so, one day near sundown,
         When the swift chariots gathered for a race,
         He too drove in among the thronging wheels:
         Ten chariots all together, one from Athens.
         At first they all went well, but at the seventh circling
         The Aenian's hard-mouthed foals bolted: swinging round,
         Crashed full into the Barcaean car;

And at that accident one after the other
Collided, smashed up together, heaped
The Krisan plain with wreckage of chariots.
But this the sly Athenian saw, made way
For the turbulent wave of racers down the centre.
Orestes was last, holding his horses in,
Trusting to the finish.
But when he saw that one competitor ahead
He screamed to pierce his horses' ears, gave chase;
And so they sped, the yokes just even,
First one then the other winning by a head.

For the whole course so far unfortunate Orestes
Had driven safely, guided his team aright.
But now he loosed the left-hand rein too far,
Forgetting the goal-post, crashed.
The axle broke and he was thrown
Over the rail and twisted in the reins;
As he struck the ground his team bolted away.
And now the multitude who saw him thrown
Set up a wailing for that youth
Who did such deeds and met such end:
Thrown up, legs first, then dragged along the ground,
Till the other drivers brought his horses to a stop,
And freed the bleeding body which his friends
Could recognize no more.
The Phocians burnt it on a pyre,
And in a little urn their envoys bring
The giant corpse, now paltry dust,
To find a grave here in its native earth.

Such is my tale to you, even in words painful,
But for those who watched, for those who saw
As I saw, with my eyes, the greatest horror.

LEADER   a-á! a-á! It seems our master's tree
         Is withered to the root.

CLYTEM.   O Zeus, these tidings:

Joyful, shall I call them,
Or terrible but advantageous?
It is my misery to save my life
Through the sufferings of my own children.

PAIDAG. Why so disheartened at this news, lady?

CLYTEM. A terrible thing, child-bearing.
Though a mother suffer hate, she cannot hate her child.

PAIDAG. Then it seems we came to you in vain.

CLYTEM. Never in vain: how can you say *in vain*
If you have brought trustworthy evidence
Of his death?—who had his life from mine,
His nourishment from my breasts, then fled?
—Forgot me with this land he left; and ever since
Though never seeing me, has named me
His father's killer who must die in horror?
Neither in the nighttime nor in the daytime
Has sweet sleep covered me, but time in minutes has passed
    me
As one on the verge of death.
And now, on this very day, I lose my fear.
Fear of him, and of her too; for she it was
Living here with me, who was the wider wound,
Draining my life-blood;
And now at last my days are to be free
Both of her and of all her threats!

ELEC. Misery. Now, now may I mourn
Your fate, Orestes, for now is added
Your mother's scorn. Is it not well?

CLYTEM. Not with you; but he is well as he is.

ELEC. Listen, fierce spirit, you the newly dead!

CLYTEM. It listened. And decided well.

ELEC. Exult, for now you have reached your happiness.

CLYTEM. You and Orestes shall not destroy it.

ELEC.   No, it is we who are destroyed, not you.

[*To the* PAIDAGOGOS.

CLYTEM. Your coming would have been a boon indeed
         If you had destroyed this screaming mouth.

PAIDAG. Then I may take my leave, if all is well.

CLYTEM. Not at all, that would be quite unworthy
         Both of me and of my friend who sent you:
         Come in, come in; leave her outside to wail
         Her evils and the evils of her friends.

[CLYTEMNESTRA *and the* PAIDAGOGOS *enter palace.*

ELEC.   Did you think that she was bitterly mourning
         The wretched son who perished so?
         No, she vanished with laughter. Misery.
         Beloved Orestes, your death destroyed me.
         I have lost all heart for my one hope,
         That you would return alive some day
         To avenge my father and me. Where must I go?
         I am alone without you and my father.
         I must go back, I must serve
         My father's murderers, my sorest
         Human affliction. Is it not well with me?
         But never, in such time as may be left me,
         Will I go in to them. Here by the gate
         I will lay my loveless life to dry up.
         If any in the house think me offensive
         Let him put me to death: death would be grace,
         But life is pain, I have no thirst for life.

[STROPHE 1

CHORUS   Where are Zeus' lightnings, where is bright Helios
         If they watch this and hide it away in silence?

ELEC.   e e ai ai

CHORUS   Child, why do you weep?

ELEC.   ai ai

CHORUS	Sh, not that great wail.
ELEC.	You crush me.
CHORUS	How?
ELEC.	On those who are surely going down To the land of death, you place my hope, and so Drain me the more.
CHORUS	I know that King Amphiareus went down [ANTISTROPHE 1 For a woman's golden chain, and now below the ground
ELEC.	ai ai
CHORUS	He rules the dead.
ELEC.	ai ai
CHORUS	Yes, cry, that murderess
ELEC.	Was murdered
CHORUS	Yes.
ELEC.	I know, I know; appeared an avenger For that mourner, but I have none, the one Whisked off, clean gone.
CHORUS	You have really found misery [STROPHE 2
ELEC.	Misery most familiar, Accumulating year by year Stubbornly, on my life.
CHORUS	We have seen its tears
ELEC.	Then do not turn me
CHORUS	Where?
ELEC.	Where no hope is: Of my brother to help me.
CHORUS	His was the fate of all mortals. [ANTISTROPHE 2
ELEC.	To fall among competing hooves?

> To fall, as that wretched one,
> Among the furrowing edges?

CHORUS   Unthinkable that horror.

ELEC.   And he in exile lies

CHORUS   ai ai

ELEC.   Without my burying hands,
Without my tears.

[*Enter* CHRYSOTHEMIS.

CHRY.   My dearest, I am running to you with joy
Because I have good news, and the cessation
Of all your troubles and misfortunes!

ELEC.   And how could you have found me any help
For my misfortunes, when there is none to find?

CHRY.   Orestes is with us, listen to me!
Here in the flesh, just as you see me now!

ELEC.   Poor girl, are you mad? Out of your sorrows
And out of my sorrows, you are making jokes.

CHRY.   No, by our father's hearth, in all soberness,
I do assure you I know that he is here.

ELEC.   Poor girl. And from whom can you have heard
This tale of yours? Who is it you trust so?

CHRY.   Myself I trust, and no one else,
On the clearest evidence of my eyes.

ELEC.   Poor girl. What evidence? What did you see
To make you heat yourself in this crazy fire?

CHRY.   Listen, by the gods, listen! and when you've heard
What I still have to tell, decide if I am mad.

ELEC.   Yes, speak, speak, if it pleases you to speak.

CHRY.   I will, I'll tell you everything I saw.
As I approached our father's sepulchre

I saw that from the top of the barrow
Fresh streams of milk had flowed, and that a wreath
Of many kinds of flowers crowned the tomb.
I marveled as I looked, and I peered about
For fear some one might be approaching me.
But when I saw that everything was quiet
I crept a little closer, and I saw,
Close to the tomb, a lock of new-cut hair.
As I looked, there came to me in my sadness
A familiar image; that sign I saw
Was from my best-beloved Orestes!
I took it in my hands, I did not cry out,
But my eyes, for joy, filled at once with tears.
I knew at once, just as I know now,
That this shining thing could only be from him.
Who else but you or me could have placed it there?
It was not I who did it, that I know;
Nor you: how could you, if you cannot leave the house
Even to offer mourning to the gods?
Our mother certainly would never wish to,
And she could never do it and be unseen:
Orestes it is who made that offering.
Therefore take courage: even for you
The god will not decree the same fate forever.
That fate has been hard so far. But now, at last, the day
Gives promise of good things beginning!

ELEC.   How I pity you for your fondness.

CHRY.   Why? Is this not good news I bring you?

ELEC.   You don't know where you are or what it is you believe.

CHRY.   Am I not to believe what I plainly see?

ELEC.   He is dead, poor girl, and from him will come
          Nothing to save you. Look no more to him.

CHRY.   a-a a-a! From whom did you hear that?

ELEC.   From one who was with him when he was destroyed.

CHRY.   Where is the man? Oh, I am utterly lost.

ELEC.   In the house gratifying our mother.

CHRY.   a-a a-a! And from whom then can have come
        All those death-offerings on my father's grave?

ELEC.   I should think they must have come from one
        Who wished to remember dead Orestes kindly.

CHRY.   Oh, miserable fool. How joyfully
        I ran with those bright tidings, and never knew
        My own delusion! But here I find
        The old evils still, and new ones too.

ELEC.   Yes, that is so. If you take my advice
        You'll lighten the burden of this suffering.

CHRY.   I suppose I am to raise the dead again?

ELEC.   That's not what I said, I'm not so crazed as that.

CHRY.   What do you ask that I am able to do?

ELEC.   To undertake to do what I advise.

CHRY.   If it promises well I shall not hold back.

ELEC.   You know nothing is achieved without toil.

CHRY.   I know. I am with you while my strength lasts.

ELEC.   Then hear what I have decided to do.
        Henceforth, you know, we have with us no friends;
        Death has removed them, and we are left alone.
        As long as I had reports of our brother
        Alive and prospering, I still had hope
        That he would come one day to avenge his father.
        But now that he is gone I turn to you:
        Aegisthos, our father's murderer,
        You, with your sister, unflinchingly must slay.
        So, I hide nothing from you.

        How can you be so cold? What possible hope
        Can you find to stare at? Your lot is wailing

For your father's vanishing wealth, and wailing
While you grow old unmarried and unloved.
You must not hope that you would ever marry,
That man Aegisthos is not so careless
As to permit children of ours to grow
For his own obvious destruction.
But if you follow the advice I give you
You shall show your love for father and brother,
And so step forth as a free woman
Prepared for marriage; all men love the strong.
In the feasts and assemblies of the city
Everyone shall laud us for our male courage,
And that name shall not fail us, living or dead.

My sister, dearest, trust me, join your father,
Side with your brother, put an end to my sorrows
And to your own, in the certainty
That it is shameful for fine beings to live in shame.

LEADER   In these matters forethought is an ally
            Both for the speaker and the listener.

CHRY.   Dear friends, if her forethought hadn't been perverse
            She would have kept the caution she discarded.

What were you thinking of, that you could be ready
For such madness, and ready to ask my help?
Don't you see? You are a woman, not a man;
You are not so strong as those inside the house.
They are growing larger day after day,
We are diminishing, we cannot thrive.
Who would expect to grapple such a man
And then escape unharmed from that folly?
Take care, ugly though our treatment is now
We shall know worse if your words are overheard.
It would solve nothing for us, do us no good,
To win a good report by a shameful death.
Death itself is not hateful, but to need death,
And not be able to get it, is hateful.

I beseech you, before we are quite destroyed,
Before we are rooted out, restrain your anger.
All you have said I shall hold as though unsaid,
Coming to nothing. . . . And you, you be
Reasonable, even now;
Helpless as you are, yield to the strong.

LEADER   Listen, for us mortals there is no scheme
To serve us better than foresight and wisdom.

ELEC.   This of course is the expected answer;
I knew you would reject what I told you.
This work then must be done by me alone.
I shall never refuse it as fruitless.

CHRY.   a-a a-a!
If only you had been of that same mind
When our father died, you could have done all this!

ELEC.   My mind was the same, my spirit weaker then.

CHRY.   Try to keep your spirit always constant.

ELEC.   This advice means that you will not help me.

CHRY.   Your handiwork is likely to end badly.

ELEC.   I envy you your wits, your cowardice I hate.

CHRY.   I shall endure it also when you praise me.

ELEC.   That you will never have to endure from me.

CHRY.   The future shall decide that.

ELEC.   Go: there is no help whatever in you.

CHRY.   There is, but there is no teaching you.

ELEC.   Then go to your mother and tell her everything.

CHRY.   No, I don't hate you as much as that.

ELEC.   But you plainly force me into dishonor.

CHRY.   Dishonor, no; I am careful for you.

ELEC. Am I to accept your sense of what is right?

CHRY. When you are wise you shall guide us both.

ELEC. How hideous to speak so well, and wrongly.

CHRY. You describe your own malady exactly.

ELEC. Why? Don't I seem to you to speak with justice?

CHRY. There may be mischief even in justice.

ELEC. I cannot decide to live by that rule.

CHRY. But if you do what you intend, you'll see I'm right.

ELEC. I will do it, and you shan't divert me.

CHRY. Is this your answer? You won't reconsider?

ELEC. No. Nothing is more hateful than bad advice.

CHRY. It is as though you did not hear what I say.

ELEC. These things have long been clear to me. Nothing has
   changed.

CHRY. Then I shall go. You will never endure
   The things I say, nor I the things you do.

ELEC. Yes, go in there; I shall never follow you,
   Not though you come to begging me on your knees.
   This hunt after vanities is mad.

CHRY. If you think you have all justice with you,
   Continue to think so. When you fall on evil times
   You will accept my words.

       [CHRYSOTHEMIS *slowly enters the palace.*

CHORUS Why, when we see the wise and obedient birds [STROPHE 1
   Heedful of those who dreamed them and brought them to
    birth,
   Can we not do as much?
   Neither the thunder of God
   Nor his laws in the stars
   Shall be hid too long.

O subterranean voice, go, cry cruelly to Atreus' dead sons your
    mirthless news,

[ANTISTROPHE 1

That their house is sick; their children, in the common strife,
Cannot agree, live out of love, two ways of life;
That alone Electra
Betrayed and shaken,
Like bird complaining
Still wails her father.
Death she disregards, she is ready to face it
To snare those furies. What nature so splendid?

None but the lost   [STROPHE 2
Accept imputed shame, or will to live
Without a name, my child.
Therefore you chose the common saeculum of grief,
And through that ugly dearth made your name safe:
Wise, and the best of daughters.

But I would have you live   [ANTISTROPHE 2
Above your enemies' wealth, above their power
Higher than you now are lower.
I see that you labor on a road which is
Not easy, though fertile in the deepest verity,
Which you, in your great piety, bring forth.

[*Enter* ORESTES, *as a weary traveler.* PYLADES *follows
with the urn.*

OREST.   Tell me, ladies, have I been rightly guided,
           And have I nearly finished my journey?

LEADER   What were you seeking? What did you want?

OREST.   I have been seeking a long time for Aegisthos' house.

LEADER   You have come to the right place; your guide was right.

OREST.   Then will one of you tell those inside the house
           That our long-desired company is come?

LEADER   This girl, as the next of kin, must tell them.

[*To* ELECTRA.

OREST. Will you go then, and explain to them that
Certain Phocians, whom Aegisthos expected—

ELEC. a-a a-a! Surely you do not bring
Visible proof of the tale we heard?

OREST. I have not heard your tale. It was old Strophios
Who sent me to bring you news of Orestes.

ELEC. What news, what news, friend? I am seized with dread.

OREST. We offer, as you see, this narrow urn
Containing the small vestiges of his death.

ELEC. a-a a-a! Surely my agony
Lies visible and palpable before me!

OREST. If you are wailing for Orestes' death,
Know that this vessel contains his ashes.

ELEC. Give me the vessel, friend, if it hides him,
Give it to me to hold it in my hands,
For I shall mourn myself and all my race,
Mourning this dust.

[To PYLADES.

OREST. Bring it and give it to her, whoever she is,
For she asks this with no evil intent,
But as a friend or a blood relative.

[PYLADES gives ELECTRA the urn.

ELEC. O ashes of Orestes, best belovèd!
I have you back now, with hope gone;
I did not send you forth so.
Ah, this is nothingness my hands lift up,
And I sent you from your house all shining!
I wish my life might have left me, before
I sent you to a strange land, and with these hands
Saved you from death; you would have died with him
And lain in the one grave with your fathers.
But now, away from home, in another country,
Far from your sister, miserably you died;

And I, with these hands of love, could neither
Wash you nor dress you nor bear the wretched burden
From the hungry fire.
You were tended by the hands of strangers at the end,
And now you come back to me in this little urn.

Ah, the long joyful fruitless care I gave you!
You were never your mother's, always mine,
Of all in the house I alone was your nurse,
I your sister, none had that name but me.
Now with your death this is all wiped out
In a single day, everything snatched away
As though a storm had passed: our father gone,
I dead in you, you vanished into death,
The hateful laughing: remains for my pleasure
That monstrous mother whom you so often told me
That you would punish, when you came.
But the bitter spirit, yours and mine,
Has utterly bereaved us,
Sent me, instead of the belovèd face,
Dust and a vain shadow.

a-a a-a! Pitiful body! a-a a-a!

You came a hard road, my love, it was my death;
A hard road, my love, my brother.
And now you must receive me under your roof,
Nothing to nothing, I with you down there
For the rest of time. Up here it was with us
Share and share alike; and now I crave to die,
And not to be excluded from your grave.
I do not think the dead have grief or mourning.

LEADER Your father was mortal, Electra; think
Orestes mortal. Do not wail too much,
We all must suffer death.

OREST. a-a a-a! What to say? Among the helpless words,
Which to choose? But I can no longer keep from words.

ELEC.   Why do you suffer? Why do you cry out so?

OREST.   Is it you who are Electra?

ELEC.   Yes, it is I.

OREST.   What a piteous change.

ELEC.   Surely it is not I who afflict you so?

OREST.   Oh ruined and dishonored being.

ELEC.   I am as you so cruelly say, my friend.

OREST.   Oh loveless and bitter life!

ELEC.   Why are you so hurt as you see me?

OREST.   How little I knew my own misfortunes.

ELEC.   Did something I said reveal them to you?

OREST.   Seeing you so clearly in your suffering.

ELEC.   Yet what you see is very little.

OREST.   What more painful could there be?

ELEC.   To share one's life with the killers—

OREST.   Of whom? what evil do you mean?

ELEC.   Of my father, and to be forced to serve them—

OREST.   Who forces you to that?

ELEC.   My mother, she is called.

OREST.   How? with violence? does she persecute you?

ELEC.   She persecutes me in every way.

OREST.   And no one is helping you or holding her back?

ELEC.   No. You have given me the dust of my one helper.

OREST.   Poor creature. As I look my pity returns.

ELEC.   You are the only one who has ever pitied me.

OREST.   I am the only one with the same sorrow.

ELEC.	What! you can't be some kinsman of ours?
OREST.	I should answer, if these women were on our side.
ELEC.	They are on our side, take courage and speak.
OREST.	Give back this jar and you shall learn everything.
ELEC.	My friend, do not force me to that.
OREST.	Do as I say and you shall not go wrong.
ELEC.	Don't take away the dearest thing I have.
OREST.	It is impossible.
ELEC.	Ah Orestes, we are forlorn if I may not bury you!
OREST.	Be quiet, you have no right to sorrow.
ELEC.	No right to sorrow for a dead brother?
OREST.	It is wrong to speak of him so.
ELEC.	Am I so dishonored by the dead?
OREST.	No one dishonors you.
ELEC.	Not though I hold here Orestes' body?
OREST.	That is not his body, though meant to be taken for it.
ELEC.	Then where is my wretched brother's grave?
OREST.	There is none, the living have no grave.
ELEC.	What do you say, boy?
OREST.	Nothing that is not true.
ELEC.	He is alive?
OREST.	If I am alive.
ELEC.	Are you he?
OREST.	Look at this ring of my father's and see if I speak the truth.
ELEC.	O sacred day!
OREST.	Sacred day I cry!

ELEC.	O voice, do I hear you?
OREST.	Ask nowhere else.
ELEC.	Do I hold you in my arms?
OREST.	As you shall henceforth.
ELEC.	O dearest friends, women of the city, Look at this Orestes, who through trickery Was dead, and now through trickery is saved!
LEADER	We see him, child, and in this blessèd issue The tears of joy are rising in our eyes.
ELEC.	O son, [STROPHE Son of the most belovèd, You came indeed; You are found, you came, you see what you desired!
OREST.	I am here, but you must be silent.
ELEC.	Why?
OREST.	Be silent so that none within may hear us.
ELEC.	No, by the eternal virgin Artemis, I cannot think them worthy of my fear: That excessive mass of womenfolk Forever inside the house!
OREST.	But think, in women also the wargod Inhabits. You have experience of that.
ELEC.	a-a a-a! Clearly you remind me how insoluble, How unforgettable, is This evil of ours.
OREST.	I know, I know, but now that the chance invites us, We must remember the work we have to do.
ELEC.	O always, [ANTISTROPHE Every moment I have, I would speak out,

And that is just,
For only now am I free to speak.

OREST.   Yes, but you must preserve this freedom.

ELEC.   How?

OREST.   Do not speak too long when we lack the time.

ELEC.   But now that you've come,
Who would give up speech for silence?
Now that beyond thought
I see you, beyond hope?

OREST.   You saw me when the god moved me to come.

ELEC.   Now what you tell me is
More gracious still: if it was indeed a god
Who led you home, divine
I call your coming.

OREST.   I would not restrain your gratitude,
But I am afraid, your too great joy compels me.

ELEC.   After so long, your belovèd coming!   [EPODE
But now that you have really appeared, do not—

OREST.   Do not do what?

ELEC.   Do not despoil me,
Do not deprive me of your face and presence.

OREST.   If anyone tried I should be angry.

ELEC.   You consent?

OREST.   How could I not?

ELEC.   O my friends, hearing the unhoped for voice,
Neither withholding my passionate joys
Nor pouring them forth in cries
Stand I! . . . Now I have you, now you have come,
Shown me the belovèd face
Which even in evils I shall never lose!

OREST.   Say nothing needless: do not tell me
How evil our mother is, nor how
Aegisthos in the house of our fathers
Drains, exhausts and vainly scatters our substance;
The telling of it would destroy our chances.
But show me what is fitting at this moment;
Where and how, hidden or manifest,
We are to end our enemies' laughter.
And do not let our mother recognize
In your shining face, that we are in the house;
Falsely wail as though your fate were upon you.
When we shall have won, then we shall rejoice,
Then we shall laugh freely.

ELEC.   What you wish, my brother, I wish also;
All the pleasure I have I owe to you,
And I should not let you suffer a moment
To gain much for myself; that would never be
The way to serve the beneficent spirit.

You know how we stand, of course; you've heard
That Aegisthos is away from the house,
Our mother within. Do not be afraid
That she will see me smiling with pleasure,
My hatred of her is too old for that;
Besides, since seeing you I have been weeping
For joy. How should I stop, since I have seen you come
Both in death and life? You have worked beyond hope,
So that if my father himself came to me alive
I should think it no marvel, but see and believe;
Therefore lead me as you will.
Alone, I should have done one of two things,
Saved myself in the right way, or found the right death.

OREST.   Be still, I hear someone coming in the house.

[*Enter the* PAIDAGOGOS *from the palace.*

ELEC.   Go in, strangers;

You bring what none in the house will refuse,
Even though receiving it may not be pleasant.

PAIDAG.   You are mad!
Don't you care for life, or were you born witless?
Don't you know that you stand, not on the edge,
But in the midst of the most mortal dangers?
If I had not been waiting all this time
Here, by the door, to watch and to report,
Your plan would have been in the house before you!
This however my caution has prevented.
Now that you've finished all you had to say,
All your insatiable shouting for joy,
Go in. Indecision is fatal;
It is essential to finish up.

OREST.   What reception shall I meet when I go in?

PAIDAG.   A good one. First of all, no one knows you.

OREST.   You must have reported that I was dead.

PAIDAG.   They speak of you as in the world below.

OREST.   Are they glad? Or what do they say?

PAIDAG.   I'll tell you at the proper time; meanwhile
Whatever they do, however bad, is good.

ELEC.   Orestes, tell me, who is this?

OREST.   Don't you understand?

ELEC.   No, and cannot guess.

OREST.   Don't you know the man to whom you gave me once?

ELEC.   What man? What do you mean?

OREST.   The man who through your foresight took me to Phocis.

ELEC.   Is this the one man I could find to trust
When our father was being murdered?

OREST.   Yes. Ask no more.

ELEC.   O sacred light! How did you come, the one rescuer
          Of Agamemnon's house? And was it really you
          Who saved this man and me from many horrors?
          O hands belovèd! O feet come to serve!
          How could you be with me so long and be unknown?
          Destroy me with words, and keep your sweet work hidden?
          Hail, father! Father you are to me! Hail!
          You must know that I have hated and loved you
          Beyond all mankind, in this single day.

PAIDAG.   Enough, I think. The tale of the time between,
          In many revolving nights and days
          Shall make these things all clear to you, Electra.

          Now, you two standing by: now is the time
          To act; now Clytemnestra is alone,
          None of her men are in the house; but think,
          If you delay you will have to fight with them
          And many more much cleverer than they.

OREST.   Pylades, our work permits us no more words;
          Let us go in at once, but first salute the gods
          Who dwell here on the threshold of the house.

               [ORESTES, the PAIDAGOGOS and PYLADES perform a brief
                    ceremony of purification and propitiation.

ELEC.   O Lord Apollo, hear them graciously,
          And hear me too, who came to you so often
          To offer you all I had with these hands.
          For now, Apollo, Light God, Wolf God, with all I have
          I pray beseech and beg you, be propitious
          To us and the things we intend to do;
          Show forth the wages which the gods
          Will pay to men for their ungodliness.

               [The men enter the palace, followed by ELECTRA.

CHORUS   Look, look where the wargod creeps,   [STROPHE
          Blood where he breathes and evil fighting.
          And now within the house pursuing

Crime, go the inescapable hounds;
Now it will not be long
Till my hovering dream come down.

And now led by the dead   [ANTISTROPHE
The stealthy helper enters
His father's wealth, his old abode.
Bloodshed is newly whetted in his hand, and Hermes,
Hiding the snare in darkness,
Leads him to his prize without a pause.

[ELECTRA *enters from the palace.*

ELEC.	Beloved friends, at this very moment The men are at their work. Be silent.	[STROPHE
CHORUS	What work, what are they doing?	
ELEC.	She wreathes the burial urn, the men stand close.	
CHORUS	Why did you come out?	
ELEC.	For fear Aegisthos might come without our knowing. <div align="right">[*Within the house.*</div>	
CLYTEM.	ai ai O loveless rooms alive with death!	
ELEC.	A cry inside. Did you hear it, friends?	
CHORUS	Heard it shivering. It was cruel to hear.	
CLYTEM.	ai ai ai ai Aegisthos, where are you, say?	
ELEC.	Listen, another wail.	
CLYTEM.	Child, child, pity your mother!	
ELEC.	But you did not pity him, nor pity his father.	
CHORUS	O city, O wretched tribe, Your familiar horror is fading.	
CLYTEM.	ai ai I am stricken!	

ELEC.   Strike, if you can, again.

CLYTEM.   ai ai Again! Again!

ELEC.   The same for Aegisthos.

CHORUS   The prayers are answered, the earth-buried live,
           The murderers' blood is seeping down
           To the dead who have been thirsty long;

                    [*The men enter from the palace.*

           The men come forth, the purple hand   [ANTISTROPHE
           Drips with the struggle's sacrifice. I have no blame.

ELEC.   Orestes, how did you fare?

OREST.   Inside there,
           Well, if Apollo guided us well.

ELEC.   Is the woman dead?

OREST.   No longer fear
           That your mother's will could humble you again.

CHORUS   Stop there, Aegisthos is in plain sight.

ELEC.   Why don't you go back!

OREST.   Where do you see him?

ELEC.   Coming from the suburb, full of laughter.

CHORUS   Quick! inside the house! Finish what's well begun!

OREST.   Courage. We shall.

ELEC.   Then go, go!

OREST.   We are gone.

                    [*The men slip back into the palace.*

ELEC.   What's here belongs to me.

CHORUS   Tell this man something pleasing in his ear
           To rush him into the fatal struggle blind.

                    [*Enter* AEGISTHOS.

AEGIS.　Does any of you know where the Phocians are
　　　　Who they say have brought us news
　　　　Of Orestes' death in a chariot-wreck?
　　　　You. I mean you! Yes you, who were before
　　　　So insolent. It is for you, I think,
　　　　Who know the most about it, to inform me.

ELEC.　I know, how could I not? Or else I were
　　　　Careless of the fate of my dearest kin.

AEGIS.　Then where can the strangers be? Come, show me.

ELEC.　Inside; for they have reached their dear hostess.

AEGIS.　Did they really report that he was dead?

ELEC.　Yes, and not only in words, they showed us proof.

AEGIS.　Is it where I can see, to make certain?

ELEC.　Yes, it is there. An unenviable sight.

AEGIS.　What you say pleases me more than usual.

ELEC.　You shall be pleased, if your pleasure is there.

AEGIS.　Silence, I ask, and open out the doors.
　　　　Let all Mycenae and all Argos see,
　　　　So that anyone who still vainly hoped
　　　　For that man's return, may see the corpse
　　　　And take the bit without constraint;
　　　　Learn sense before he meets my punishment.

ELEC.　This is accomplished in me. In this time
　　　　I have learned this wisdom: yield to the strong.

　　　　[*The doors of the palace open, revealing a veiled bier with
　　　　　　the men grouped around it.* AEGISTHOS *approaches.*

AEGIS.　O Zeus, without envy I see this fallen
　　　　Figure: if this is impious I say nothing.

　　　　Take the veil from the face. It is fitting
　　　　For the kindred and also for me to mourn.

OREST.   Lift it yourself. It is for you, not me,
         To see what's lying there and kindly greet it.

AEGIS.   You are right. I will. And you go call me
         Clytemnestra, if she be in the house.

OREST.   She is very close, don't look away.

AEGIS.   a-a a-a What do I see?

OREST.   Why are you afraid? Don't you know the face?

AEGIS.   Into whose terrible snares have I fallen!

OREST.   Haven't you learned that the dead you spoke of are living?

AEGIS.   a-a a-a I see your meaning, you, you
         Are Orestes, you who are speaking to me!

OREST.   You are a seer who has been deceived.

AEGIS.   I am lost! But let me say a word—

ELEC.   Don't let him speak and extend his life with words.
         What good is a little time to a creature
         Who is fatally netted, and must die?
         Kill him as quickly as you can, and give him
         To the diggers of graves, to bury him
         Where we can never see him. That would be
         The only expiation of the old wrongs.

         Go in at once. The struggle is not in words,
         But for your life.

AEGIS.   Why drive me in? If your work is comely,
         Why in the dark? Why not out here?

OREST.   Give me no orders. Go in where you killed my father.
         It is there that you shall die.

AEGIS.   Must this house witness all Pelops' evils,
         Now and to come!

OREST.   Yours it must: that much I can foresee.

AEGIS.   Your foresight did not include your father?

 OREST.   You have much to say, we are slow. Go on.

AEGIS.   You lead.

OREST.   You must go first.

AEGIS.   So I won't escape?

OREST.   No, so you may not die as you please.
          I must make sure that death is bitter for you.
          Justice should always be immediate;
          If the law of death after such deeds
          Were fixed, they would be few.

          [AEGISTHOS, ORESTES, PYLADES, PAIDAGOGOS and ELECTRA
               disappear into the palace. Then the doors open,
                    showing the living and the dead.

LEADER   O Atreus' suffering seed
          To freedom barely emerged
          Through this struggle realized.

Aeschylus

EUMENIDES

translated by
George Thomson

Pursued from country to country by the FURIES after the murder of his mother CLYTEMNESTRA, ORESTES finally took refuge in the temple of his patron, APOLLO, at Delphi. The FURIES followed him remorselessly, entering into the very shrine as he crouched before the navel-stone; but there, before they could harm him, they were overcome by weariness and fell asleep.

DRAMATIS PERSONÆ:

PRIESTESS OF APOLLO   GHOST OF CLYTEMNESTRA

APOLLO   ORESTES

HERMES   ATHENA

CHORUS OF FURIES

CHORUS OF THE ESCORT

EUMENIDES

SCENE: *Before Apollo's temple at Delphi. Later, within the temple.*

[*Enter the* PRIESTESS.

PRIEST.   Chief of the Gods in prayer I venerate,
The first of prophets, Earth; and next to her
Themis, who from her mother, it is said,
Received the seat oracular; and the third,
Another child of Earth, the Titan maid
Phoebe, with free consent here found a home;
And she bestowed it as a birthday gift
On Phoebus, with it lending him her name.
The lakes and rocks of Delos he forsook,
And setting foot on Pallas' harbored shores
Came hither to Parnassus, on his way
Attended with all honor by the Sons
Of Hephaestus, who built a road for him
And tamed the wilderness before his feet.
And when he came, the people worshipped him
Under king Delphus, their lord and governor;
And Zeus, having inspired him with his art,
Set him, the fourth of prophets, on this throne,
Whence he is called Interpreter of Zeus,
Whose son he is, prophetic Loxias.
These Gods then are the preface to my prayers,
And with them I render the homage due
To Pallas of the Precinct, and likewise
The nymphs whose dwelling is the cavernous cliff
Corycian, home of birds and haunt beloved
Of spirits, the region held by Bromius
(This have I not forgotten) when he led
His Bacchants into battle and devised

111

The death of Pentheus like a hunted hare.
So, calling also on Poseidon's power,
Upon the springs of Pleistus, and last of all
On Zeus the Highest, Zeus the Perfecter,
I take my seat on the throne of prophecy.
And may this entry be more blest of them
Than any heretofore! Let Greeks approach
In the accustomed order of the lot;
As the God dictates, so shall I prophesy.

[*She enters the temple, utters a loud cry, and returns.*

Oh horror, horror to utter and behold,
Has driven me back from the house of Loxias;
Strengthless, with dragging step, upon my hands
I run. An aged woman terror-struck
Is nothing, or at most a child again.
I made my way into the laureled shrine
And at the navel stone I saw a man,
Defiled with murder, in suppliant posture, red
Blood dripping from the hands that grasped a sword
Fresh from the scabbard and a topmost branch
Of olive humbly garlanded with wool,
A fleece all silver-white. So much was plain;
But all around, asleep upon the thrones,
Lay a strange company of women—yet
Not women, Gorgons rather; nor again
To Gorgons can I liken them, for those
I saw once in a picture, plundering
The feast of Phineus; but no wings have these,
Yet black and utterly abominable,
Snoring in blasts that none may venture near,
With eyes that run with drops of loathsome rheum,
In raiment clad which it were a sin to bring
Near images of the Gods or roofs of men.
The tribe to which these visitants belong
I never saw, nor know what land could boast
Of such a brood and not repent her pangs.
As for the rest, let him take thought for it
Who owns the house, almighty Loxias,

Prophet and Healer, Interpreter of signs,
Himself of other houses Purifier.

[*The interior of the temple is revealed, as described; with* APOLLO *and* HERMES *standing behind* ORESTES.

APOLLO   I will keep faith, at watch continually,
Close at thy side and vigilant from afar,
And never gentle to thy enemies.
And now thou seest them here in slumber seized,
These ravenous monsters, stretched upon the ground,
Maidens abominable, children gray with years,
With whom no God consorts, nor man nor beast,
Abhorred alike in heaven and on earth,
For evil born, even as the darkness where
They dwell is evil, the abyss of Tartarus.
Yet thou must fly and grow not faint of heart.
They will track down thy steps from shore to shore,
For ever traveling the wide ways of earth
Past island cities, over distant seas,
And nurse thy tribulation patiently
Until thou comest to the citadel
Of Pallas, where in supplication clasp
Her antique image in thine arms; for there,
With judgment of thy suit and gentle charms
Of speech, we shall find out at last a way
From all these evils to deliver thee,
Being moved by me even to kill thy mother.

OREST.   O Lord Apollo, thou knowest what is just,
And since thou knowest, O neglect it not!
Thy strength to do good lacks no warranty.

APOLLO   Remember, let thy heart not yield to fear.
And thou, my brother begotten of one sire,
True to thy name, go with him, guide the feet
Of this my suppliant; for the sanctity
Of outcasts from mankind, who take the road

With guidance fair, is sacred unto Zeus.

[HERMES *and* ORESTES *go. Enter the* GHOST *of*
CLYTEMNESTRA.

GHOST   Oho! asleep! What good are you asleep?
And I, whom you dishonor, am reproached
Among the other dead unceasingly,
Hissed and cast out, homeless, a murderess!
I tell you they malign me shamefully,
While I, so cruelly treated by my own,
Slaughtered myself with matricidal hands,
No deity is indignant for my sake.
O let your conscience look upon these scars!
Remember all those sober blandishments,
Those wineless offerings which you have drunk,
Those sacrificial suppers on the hearth
At many a solemn midnight, which you shared
With none of heaven's deities: and now
All that is rudely trampled in the dust.
And he is gone: light as a fawn he sped
Out of the inmost meshes of your snare
And leapt away, and now he scoffs at you.
O hear as I plead with you for my soul!
O Goddesses of the underworld, awake!
I, Clytemnestra, call you now in dreams!

CHORUS   Mu, mu!

GHOST   Ah, you may mew, but he is fled and gone;
For he has friends far different from mine.

CHORUS   Mu, mu!

GHOST   Still slumbering and still compassionless!
The matricide, Orestes, has escaped!

CHORUS   Oh, oh!

GHOST   Still whining in your drowsiness! Arise!
To do evil is your appointed task.

CHORUS   Oh, oh!

GHOST How sleep and weariness, strong confederates,
Have disenvenomed the fell dragon's rage!

CHORUS Oh, oh! Find the scent, mark him down!

GHOST Though you give tongue like an unerring hound,
You chase the quarry only through your dreams.—
What are you doing? Rise, cast off fatigue!
Let not sleep soothe remembrance of your hurt!—
Let your heart ache with pangs of just reproach,
Which harry a good conscience like a scourge!—
Come, blow about his head your bloody breath,
Consume his flesh with blasts of bellied fire!
On, on, renew the hunt and wear him down!

[Exit.

PARODOS

CHORUS Awake, awake her there as I wake thee!
Still sleeping? Rise, cast slumber underfoot!
Let us see whether our enchantment works.

[STROPHE 1

Alas, alas, for shame! What have we suffered, friends!
Ah, suffered bitterly, and all in vain!
Suffered a fearful hurt, horrible! Oh the pain
Beyond strength to bear!
The game has leapt out of the snare and gone.
In slumber laid low, I let slip the prey.

Aha, son of Zeus, pilferer, pillager! [ANTISTROPHE 1
A youth to trample ancient deities,
Honoring such a suppliant abhorred of God,
An unfilial son!

A God, to steal away the matricide!
O who denies this was unjustly done?

In dream there came to me a dread reproach,   [STROPHE 2
A blow such as might descend from some
Charioteer's stout hand,
Under the ribs, under the flank.
It rankles yet, red and sore,
Chill as frost, like the fell
Assault of public scourger's lash.

This is the doing of the younger Gods,   [ANTISTROPHE 2
Who transgress the powers appointed them.
Dripping with death, red drops
Cover the heel, cover the head.
Behold the Earth's central stone
Black with big stains of blood,
Possessed of vast pollution vile.

A prophet he, his own prophetic cell   [STROPHE 3
He has himself profaned.
His was the act, the asking,
Honoring mortal things, reckless of laws divine
And dealing death to Fates born of old.

He injures me, yet *him* he shall not free,   [ANTISTROPHE 3
Not in the depths of hell,
Ne'er shall he be delivered.
Suppliant unabsolved, soon shall he find his brow
Defiled again with guilt thrice as great.

APOLLO   Out, out, I say, begone! I bid you leave
This mantic cell of your vile presence free;
Or soon a silver scorpion taking wing
From golden bow shall lay on you such smart
That from your swollen bellies you shall retch
The clotted blood from human bodies sucked.
No house is this to be approached by you,

But rather go where heads fall from the block,
Where eyes are gouged, throats slit, and boyhood's bloom
Blasted by gelding knife, where men are stoned,
And limbs lopped, and a piteous whimper heard
From spines impaled in dust. Such festivals
Are your delight and fill heaven with loathing.
So your whole shape and semblance testifies.
A den of lions lapping gore were fit
To entertain you, not this opulent seat
Of prophecy to bear so vile a taint.
Hence, loathsome creatures, hence unshepherded,
A herd for whom there is no love in heaven!

CHORUS   O Lord Apollo, hear us in our turn.
Thou art not an abettor in this work;
Thou art the doer, on thee lies the whole guilt.

APOLLO   How might that be? Prolong thy speech so far.

CHORUS   He slew his mother obedient to thy word.

APOLLO   My word commanded vengeance for his father.

CHORUS   So promising acceptance of fresh blood.

APOLLO   And for it absolution at this house.

CHORUS   Would you insult the band which drove him hither?

APOLLO   My mansion is not fit for such as you.

CHORUS   And yet this is the task appointed us.

APOLLO   What is this power and boasted privilege?

CHORUS   We drive the mother-murderer from home.

APOLLO   What of the woman then who slew her man?

CHORUS   That is not death by kin and common blood.

APOLLO   Dishonored then and set at naught by thee
The marriage-bond which Zeus and Hera seal,
Dishonored too the Cyprian, from whom
Mankind receive their nearest, dearest joys.

What bond is stronger than the bed of man
And wife, which Fate conjoins and Justice guards?
If then on those who slay their dearest thou
Dost not look down in wrath nor punish them,
Then I declare it is unjust in thee
To persecute Orestes—here I see
Anger, there quietness. But in this suit
The goddess Pallas shall regard and judge.

CHORUS   Him will I never leave nor let him go.

APOLLO   Pursue him then, pile up more labor lost.

CHORUS   No words of thine shall circumscribe my powers.

APOLLO   I would disdain such powers as a gift.

CHORUS   Ay, thou art called great at the throne of Zeus.
But I—a mother's blood is calling me
To seek revenge and follow up the hunt.

APOLLO   And I will help and guard my suppliant.
A fearful thing in heaven and on earth
Would be the wrath of such, if I broke faith.

[Interval of one year. Before a shrine of ATHENA in Athens:
enter ORESTES.

OREST.   O Queen Athena, at Loxias' command
I come to thee; receive me mercifully;
An outcast, yet no more with sullied hands,
The edge of my pollution worn away
At distant homes of men, on weary paths
By land and sea alike, obedient
To the prophetic word of Loxias,
Present before thy image, entering
Thy house, O Goddess, here with constant heart
I wait the consummation of my cause.

[Enter the CHORUS.

CHORUS   Aha! here are his traces plain to see.
Step where our dumb informer points the way;

For as the hound pursues the wounded fawn,
So follow I the smell of dripping blood.
With toil and sweat of many a weary day
My bosom pants; all the wide earth I roamed,
And traversing the sea in wingless flight,
Close in his vessel's wake, I follow still.
He must be crouching somewhere here—I feel
My senses wooed with smell of human blood.
—Beware, again beware!
Look on all sides, for fear
He find some escape, foul mother-murderer.
—Ah, here he is, craving help,
As in a close embrace he clasps that divine
Image, awaiting trial for his handiwork.
—It cannot be! The mother's blood he shed
Can ne'er be raised up again.
Low on the ground it lies, scattered away and lost.
—Soon from thy living flesh shalt thou repay
Offerings rich and red; and on an evil draught
From thee my lips shall feed in fat pasturage.
—Alive and wasted, I shall drag thee down
To pay the full price of that terrible act of blood,
—And others shalt thou see in Hell who did
Evil to strangers, Gods,
Or unto those dearest that gave them life,
Each well requited with his just reward.
—For Hades is a stern inquisitor
Of mankind below;
All things are written down in that watchful heart.

OREST. Taught in the school of suffering, I have learnt
The times and seasons when it is right to keep
Silence and when to break it; and in this matter
A wise instructor has charged me to speak.
The blood upon my hands has sunk to sleep,
The matricidal stain is washed away.
Still fresh it was when at the hearth divine
Of Phoebus it was purged by sacrifice.

Too many to recount the men who have
Received since then my presence without hurt;
And now with lips made pure and reverent
I call to my defense this country's Queen,
Athena, who with bloodless victory
Shall win me and my people to her side
In true alliance for all time to come.
So, whether on far shores of Libya,
By Trito's waters, where she came to birth,
Her foot be planted, covered or erect,
Defending those that love her, or her eyes,
Like some brave captain's, watch on Phlegra's heights,
O may she come—far off, she still can hear—
And from these miseries deliver me!

CHORUS   Neither Apollo nor Athena's power
Shall save thee from perdition, when, by all
Abandoned and forsaken, knowing not
Where in the bosom joy resides, shalt thou,
A bloodless shadow, make a feast for fiends.
Hast thou no answer, dost thou spurn me so,
Fattened for me, my consecrated host?
Not slain upon the altar, nay alive
Thou shalt feed me, and now shalt hear a chant
Which binds thee fast unto my purposes.

FIRST STASIMON

O come, let us dance in a ring and declare,
As our purpose is fixed,
To the tune of this terrible music
Those laws whereby
We determine the fortune of mortals.

Just, we avow, are our judgments and righteous.
All those who can show hands cleanly and pure,
Unharmed shall they live for the length of their days,
No anger of ours shall afflict them;
But the man, like him, who hath sinned and conceals
Hands dripping with blood shall be summoned
To attest for the slaughtered the truth of their cause
And to pay for their blood retribution.

[STROPHE 1

Mother Night, thy children cry, hear, black Night,
As we deal to man in dark and day fell judgment!
The son born of Leto hath plundered my powers,
Stealing that trembling hare, held a due sacrifice
Mother's blood to expiate.
> Over the blood now to be shed madness and moil,
> Wither and waste, melody dismal and deathly.
> Hymn of hell to harp untuned,
> Chant to bind the soul in chains,
> Spell to parch the flesh to dust.

[ANTISTROPHE 1

This the Fates who move the whole world through, charged
Unto us to be our task for all time hence,
Watch to keep over all hands that drip red with kindred
Blood, to wait till the Earth open—then down in hell
Freedom hardly shall they find.
> Over the blood now to be shed madness and moil,
> Wither and waste, melody dismal and deathly.
> Hymn of hell to harp untuned,
> Chant to bind the soul in chains,
> Spell to parch the flesh to dust.

[STROPHE 2

Such were the powers decreed as we came into being,
Only to touch not immortals, and none of Olympus
Seeketh a share in our banquets.
Part have we none in the raiment of white, for in such we
  delight not;

Other pleasures are our choice—
    Wreck of the house, when at the hearth
    Blood of its own drippeth in strife.
    Hard on his heels ever we run, and tho' his strength be
      great,
    Lured by fresh blood we waste and wear him out.

[ANTISTROPHE 2

Yet, as we seek to relieve other Gods of this office
And by our own intent endeavor exempt them
So that none call them to question,
Zeus doth debar this brood, bloodstained and abhorrent, from
  converse,
Yea, disdains our company.
    Wreck of the house, when at the hearth
    Blood of its own drippeth in strife.
    Hard on his heels ever we run, and tho' his strength be
      great,
    Lured by fresh blood we waste and wear him out.

[STROPHE 3

Glories of men, how great in the day is their grandeur!
Yet shall they fade in the darkness of hell in dishonor,
Faced with our raiment of sable and dancing
Feet well-tuned to melodies malign.
    Nimbly my feet leap and descend,
    High in the air, down to the earth,
    Heavy the tread of my tiptoe,
    Fugitive steps suddenly tripped up in fatal confusion.

[ANTISTROPHE 3

Caught unawares doth he stumble, his wickedness blinds him,
Such is the cloud of pollution that hovers around him.
Thick on the house is the darkness, a story
Which mankind shall tell with mournful tongue.
    Nimbly my feet leap and descend,
    High in the air, down to the earth,
    Heavy the tread of my tiptoe,
    Fugitive steps suddenly tripped up in fatal confusion.

Our task is such. Armed with quick   [STROPHE 4
Resource and keen memories,
We keep with hard hearts unmoved constant watch on
    human sin.
What all dishonor honor we,
From whence the Gods are barred
By dark corruption foul, region of rugged ways
Both for the quick and dead, for blind and seeing too.

What mortal then boweth not   [ANTISTROPHE 4
In fear and dread, while he hears
The ordinance which Fate made ours, the gift of heaven too,
A perfect power and privilege
Of ancient ages? We
Are not unhonored, tho' deep in the earth the clime
Set for us, sunk in sunless, everlasting gloom.

[Enter ATHENA.

ATHENA   I heard a cry far off, calling to me,
Where by Scamander's waters I received
Possession of the lands which have been given
By the Achaean princes for my own
To have and hold for ever, a chosen gift
To grace the sons of Theseus. Thence I came
In fleet pursuit of never-wearied foot,
With wingless beat of this deep-bosomed aegis—
To such a car my lusty steeds were yoked.
And now, regarding this strange company,
I have no fear, yet wonder fills my eyes.
Who can you be? To all I speak in common,
Both to this stranger seated at my image,
And you, resembling no begotten seed,
Neither like goddesses beheld in heaven
Nor fashioned in the figure of mankind.
But to speak harm of others without cause
Would ill accord with justice and with right.

CHORUS   Daughter of Zeus, in brief thou shalt learn all.

We are the dismal daughters of dark Night,
Called Curses in the palaces of hell.

ATHENA   Your names I know then and your origin.

CHORUS   And now we will acquaint you with our powers.

ATHENA   Teach me those also; I am fain to learn.

CHORUS   We drive the homicide from hearth and home.

ATHENA   And tell me where his persecution ends.

CHORUS   Where to be joyful is a thing unknown.

ATHENA   Is that your hue and cry against this man?

CHORUS   It is; for he thought fit to kill his mother.

ATHENA   He feared, perhaps, some other grave displeasure?

CHORUS   What could have driven him to matricide?

ATHENA   Two parties are there and but half the cause.

CHORUS   Our oath he will not take, nor give his own.

ATHENA   You seek the name of justice, not the act.

CHORUS   How so? Instruct, since thou hast wealth of wit.

ATHENA   Seek not by oaths to make the wrong prevail.

CHORUS   Then try the case and give us a straight judgment.

ATHENA   Will you commit the verdict to my charge?

CHORUS   I will, since thou art worthy, and thy sire.

ATHENA   Stranger, what is thy answer? Let us know
Thy fatherland and family, and what
Misfortune overtook thee, and then meet
The charge they bring against thee. If with trust
In justice thou art stationed at my image,
A holy suppliant, as Ixion was,
Then render on each count a clear reply.

OREST.   O Queen Athena, those last words of thine

Shall be my preface to relieve thy care.
No suppliant I that would be purified.
With hands already spotless I embraced
Thy image and took session at thy shrine;
And I can give thee evidence. The law
Commands the manslayer to hold his peace
Till he has been anointed with the blood
Of new-born beast by purifying hands.
Long since at other houses and on paths
Of land and sea have I been thus absolved.
So, having cast this scruple from thy mind,
I will inform thee of my origin.
I am from Argos, and my father's name—
For asking that I thank thee—Agamemnon,
Marshal of men in ships, with whom of late
The city of Ilium thou hast made to be
No more a city. He died an evil death.
When he returned home, my black-hearted mother
Killed him, entrapped in cunningly contrived
Nets that bore witness to a bath of blood.
Therefore, when I returned from banishment,
I killed my mother—that I do confess—
In retribution for my father's death:
An act not wholly mine, for Loxias
Must answer for it too, who spoke to me
Of bitter anguish to afflict my spirit
If I should fail in vengeance on the guilty.
Whether 'twas just or no, be thou my judge.
I will accept thy ordering of my doom.

ATHENA   Too grave a suit is this for mortal minds
To judge, nor is it right that such as I
Should pass my verdict on a suit of blood
Shed with such bitter wrath attending it;
And all the more since thou hast come to me
A suppliant pure and humbled; and also I
Respect thee, being innocent of wrong
Against my city. But no such gentleness

Has been appointed *these*, and if their plea
Fall short of victory, the poison which
Drips from their angry bosoms to the ground
Will lay this country waste with pestilence.
So stands the matter—let them stay or be
Dismissed, the issue is fraught with injury.
But be it so; since it is come to this,
Judges I will appoint for homicide,
A court set up in perpetuity.
Meanwhile do you call proofs and witnesses
As sworn supports of justice; then, having chosen
The best of all my people, I shall come
To pass true judgment on the present cause.

[*Exit* ATHENA.

SECOND STASIMON

CHORUS   Now shall ancient ordinance   [STROPHE 1
Fall to naught, should the unjust appeal of that accurst
Matricide win the day.
Now shall all men be reconciled by that
Crime to acts of violence;
Many, many a pain awaiteth
Parents in the time to come,
Struck by true-begotten child.

We who watch the works of men   [ANTISTROPHE 1
Shall not send wrath to haunt evildoers, rather lend
Rein to all deeds of blood.
Then shall one, making known his neighbor's plight,
From another seek to learn
End or easement of his trouble—

Wretch, what shifting remedies
Shall he recommend in vain!

Then let none, if e'er he fall   [STROPHE 2
Smitten by disaster, cry
Out in lamentation, 'Oh
Justice, O Furies, hearken to my prayer!'—
Thus shall fathers groan and thus
Stricken mothers weep in vain;
Since the house of Righteousness
Falls in ruins to the ground.

Times there be when fear is well;   [ANTISTROPHE 2
Yea, it must continually
Watch within the soul enthroned.
Needful too straits to teach humility.
Who of those that never nursed
Healthy dread within the heart,
Be they men or peoples, shall
Show to Justice reverence?

Choose a life despot-free,   [STROPHE 3
Yet restrained by rule of law. Thus and thus
God doth administer, yet he appointeth the mean as the
    master in all things.
Hear my word proportionate:
Wickedness breedeth, and pride is the name of her child,
While from the spirit
Of health is born blessedness
Prayed for and prized of all men.

So in brief this I say,   [ANTISTROPHE 3
Bow before the shrine of Right, neither be
Tempted by profit to spurn it with insolent feet; retribution
    shall follow.
Yet abides the end decreed.
See that thy father and mother are rightly esteemed;
Grant to the stranger
Within thy gates all the due
Honors of entertainment.

The man who seeks what is right   [STROPHE 4
Of choice and free will, shall not be unblest;
The seed of just men shall never perish.
Not so the froward and foolish heart that bears
A motley cargo of iniquity.
His outspread sail shall soon be hauled down;
Caught in the growing storm his stout
Mast shall be rent and shattered.

To ears that hear not he cries,   [ANTISTROPHE 4
To angry seas which he cannot master;
His guardian spirit doth laugh to see him,
Who rashly boasted his ship would come to port,
So weak and faint he cannot breast the wave
And sinks unseen with all his riches,
Dashed on the reef of Justice, un-
Looked-on and unlamented.

        [*Enter* ATHENA *with the* JUDGES, *followed by citizens*
                of Athens.

ATHENA   Herald, proclaim, hold back the multitude,
Then let the trump Tyrrhenian, filled with breath
Of human lips, raise its resounding cry!
For while this great tribunal is enrolled,
Silence is meet and study of my laws
For this whole city now and evermore,
And likewise for these litigants, and so
Just judgment shall be given on their cause.

                              [*Enter* APOLLO.

O Lord Apollo, rule where power is thine.
What business is there that concerns thee here?

APOLLO   I come both as a witness, the accused
Being a suppliant at my sanctuary
And purified of bloodshed at my hands,
And also to be tried with him, for I
Must answer for his mother's death. Do thou
Open the case and judge as thou knowest how.

ATHENA The case is open. Yours it is to speak.
The prosecutor shall take precedence
And so instruct us truly what befell.

CHORUS Many in number, we shall be brief in speech.
Give answer to our questions one by one.
First, is it true that thou didst kill thy mother?

OREST. I killed her. That is true, and not denied.

CHORUS So then the first of the three rounds is ours.

OREST. You need not boast that you have thrown me yet.

CHORUS But, having killed her, thou must tell us how.

OREST. I will. With drawn sword leveled at the throat.

CHORUS Who moved, who counselled thee to such an act?

OREST. The oracle of the God who is my witness.

CHORUS The Prophet taught thee to do matricide!

OREST. And I have not repented to this day.

CHORUS Condemned anon, thou shalt tell another tale.

OREST. My father shall defend me from the grave.

CHORUS Ah, having slain thy mother, trust the dead!

OREST. She was polluted with a double crime.

CHORUS How so? Expound thy meaning to the court.

OREST. She slew her husband, and she slew my father.

CHORUS Well, she died guiltless, thou art still alive.

OREST. Why, when she lived, did you not harass her?

CHORUS She was not bound by blood to him she slew.

OREST. And am I then in blood bound to my mother?

CHORUS   How did she nourish thee, abandoned wretch,
                   Within the womb? Dost thou abjure the tie,
                   Nearest and dearest, of a mother's blood?

OREST.   Do *thou* declare thy witness now; pronounce,
                   Apollo, whether I was justified.
                   I killed as I have said; that is confessed;
                   But in thy judgment was it justly done?

APOLLO   Athena's great tribunal, I will say,
                   Justly; and I, as prophet, cannot lie.
                   Never upon my throne of prophecy
                   Have I spoke aught of people, man or woman
                   But what my father Zeus commanded me.
                   How strong that justice is instruct yourselves
                   And do according to my father's will,
                   Whose sovranty no oath shall override.

CHORUS   Zeus, as thou sayest, gave thee this command,
                   To charge Orestes to avenge his father
                   Regardless of dishonoring his mother?

APOLLO   'Tis not the same, to kill a noble man
                   Invested with all majesty from heaven,
                   A woman too to kill him, and not with far
                   Shafts of a valiant Amazon's archery,
                   But in such manner as you shall be told,
                   Thou, Pallas, and this bench of justicers
                   Appointed to give judgment on this cause.
                   When he returned from battle, bringing home
                   A balance for the greater part of good,
                   At first she welcomed him with gentle words,
                   And then, attending while he bathed, at last,
                   His head pavilioned in a trailing robe,
                   She struck him, fettered in those opulent folds.
                   Such was his end—a man, a king whom all
                   The world had honored, a mighty admiral,
                   And such the woman who contrived his death
                   As I have told, seeking to move the hearts
                   Of all who are assembled here to judge.

CHORUS   Then Zeus gives precedence to the father's death
According to thy plea. Yet Zeus it was
Who bound in chains his aged father Kronos.
How shall thy plea be reconciled with that?
Judges, I call upon you to take note.

APOLLO   Abominable monsters loathed of heaven,
Chains may be loosened, there are cures for that
And many a means to bring deliverance;
But once the dust has drunk a dead man's blood,
He shall not rise again—for that no charm
My father has appointed, though all else
He turns and overturns and sets in place
Without the endeavor of a labored breath.

CHORUS   See what this plea for the acquittal means.
He spilt upon the ground his mother's blood,
And shall he still dwell in his father's house?
What altars of the people shall he use,
What holy water grant him fellowship?

APOLLO   That too will I declare, and mark the truth.
The mother is not the parent of the child,
Only the nurse of what she has conceived.
The parent is the father, who commits
His seed to her, a stranger, to be held
With God's help in safekeeping. In proof of this,
Father there might be and no mother: see
A witness here, child of Olympian Zeus,
Begotten not in wedlock neither bred
In darkness of the womb, a goddess whom
No other goddess could have brought to birth.
And therefore, Pallas, since in all things I
Shall strive to make thy land and people great,
I sent this man to be thy suppliant,
A faithful friend to thee eternally,
That thou, Goddess, might find a staunch ally
In him and his hereafter, a covenant
For this thy people to uphold for ever.

ATHENA   Enough has now been spoken. Therefore shall I
Command the judges to record their votes
In righteous judgment according to their minds?

APOLLO   Empty our quiver, every arrow spent.
We wait to hear the issue of the trial.

ATHENA   How shall my ruling be approved by you?

CHORUS   Sirs, you have heard, and vote accordingly
With hearty reverence for your solemn oath.

ATHENA   People of Athens, hear my ordinance
At this first trial for bloodshed. Evermore
This great tribunal shall abide in power
Among the sons of Aegeus; and this hill
Whereon of old the Amazons encamped,
When hate of Theseus rallied them to arms,
And here a city newly fortified
Upraised against his own, and sacrificed
To Ares, whereupon this rock was named
The Areopagus—here Reverence
And inbred Fear enthroned among my people
Shall hold their hands from evil night and day,
Only let them not tamper with their laws;
For, should a stream of mire pollute the pure
Fountain, the lips shall never find it sweet.
I bid my people honor and uphold
The mean between the despot and the slave,
And not to banish terror utterly,
For what man shall be upright without fear?
And if you honor this high ordinance,
Then shall you have for land and commonweal
A stronghold of salvation, such as none
Hath elsewhere in the world, in Scythia
Nor in the isle of Pelops. I establish
This great tribunal to protect my people,
Grave, quick to anger, incorruptible,
And ever vigilant over those that sleep.

Such is my exhortation unto all
My people for all generations. Now
Arise, take each his ballot, and upon
Your solemn oath give judgment. I have spoken.

CHORUS   Remember us, I charge you, visitants
Grave in displeasure, and respect our powers.

APOLLO   I charge you to respect the oracles
Ordained of Zeus and see that they bear fruit.

CHORUS   Bloodshed is not thy office, and henceforth
The shrines which voice thy utterance are unholy.

APOLLO   Then did my Father err when he resolved
To cleanse Ixion, the first murderer?

CHORUS   Prate on; but, if my cause should fail, I shall
Afflict this people with a heavy hand.

APOLLO   Thou art unhonored of all deities
Both young and old, and victory shall be mine.

CHORUS   In the house of Pheres once thou didst the like,
Tempting the Fates to make a man immortal.

APOLLO   Is it not just at all times to befriend
A worshipper, and most in time of need?

CHORUS   Thou didst destroy the ancient dispensations,
Beguiling antique deities with wine.

APOLLO   Thou, failing of the verdict presently,
Shalt spew thy poisons, but they shall do no harm.

CHORUS   Thy youth has trampled on my honored age.
Therefore I wait the verdict, whether or no
Upon this city to let loose my rage.

ATHENA   The final judgment is a task for me;
So for Orestes shall this vote be cast.
No mother gave me birth, and in all things

Save marriage I, my father's child indeed,
With all my heart commend the masculine.
Wherefore I shall not hold of higher worth
A woman who was killed because she killed
Her wedded lord and master of her home.
Upon an equal vote Orestes wins.
Let the appointed judges now proceed
To count the ballots from the emptied urn.

OREST. O bright Apollo, how shall the judgment go?

CHORUS O mother mine, black Night, dost thou behold?

OREST. My hour has come—the halter or the light.

CHORUS And mine—to keep my ancient powers, or perish.

APOLLO Sirs, count the issue of the votes aright;
Divide them as you honor what is just.
If judgment fail, great harm shall come of it;
And oft one vote hath raised a fallen house.

ATHENA He stands acquitted on the charge of blood.
The number of the counted votes is equal.

OREST. O Pallas, O deliverer of my house,
I was an outcast from my country, thou
Hast brought me home again; and men shall say,
Once more he is an Argive and he dwells
In his paternal heritage by the grace
Of Pallas, and of Loxias, and third
Of him who orders all, Deliverer,
Who had regard unto my father's death
And has delivered me. Before I go
I pledge my honor to this land of thine
And to thy people for all plenitude
Of after generations that no prince
Of Argos shall lead forth his serried arms
In war against this city. We ourselves
Out of the grave which then shall cover us
Shall so afflict all those who would transgress

The pledge that I have given, with desperate
Obstructions, wanderings disconsolate
And adverse omens frowning on their march,
That they shall soon repent; but if they keep
Our covenant, continuing to honor
Athena's city with arms confederate,
With blessings rather shall we visit them.
And so farewell. May thou and those who rule
Thy populace stand firm in such a stance
As shall prevail against all enemies,
A strong salvation and victory at arms!

[*Exit.*

KOMMOS

CHORUS   Oho ye younger Gods, since ye have trod under foot
The laws of old and ancient powers purloined,
Then we, dishonored, deadly in displeasure,
Shall spread poison foul
Through the land, with damp contagion
Of rage malignant, bleak and barren, blasting, withering up
the earth,
Mildews on bud and birth abortive. Oh!
Venomous pestilence
Shall sweep this country with infectious death.
To weep?—nay, to work; yea, to work ill, to lay low the
people!
Oh me, many the wrongs of these maids of Night
Mourning their plundered honors!

ATHENA   Let me persuade you from this passionate grief.
You are not vanquished; the issue of the trial

Has been determined by an equal vote.
Nay, Zeus it was who plainly testified,
Himself pronouncing his own evidence,
That for this deed Orestes should not suffer.
And therefore be not angry, let no dread
Displeasures fall upon this country, nor
Corrupt her fruits with drops of rank decay
And keen-edged cankers in the early bud.
Rather accept my honorable word
That ye shall have a cave wherein to dwell
Among this righteous people, and, enthroned
In honor at your altars, shall receive
The adoration of my citizens.

CHORUS   Oho ye younger Gods, since ye have trod under foot
The laws of old and ancient powers purloined,
Then we, dishonored, deadly in displeasure,
Shall spread poison foul
Through the land, with damp contagion
Of rage malignant, bleak and barren, blasting, withering up
    the earth,
Mildews on bud and birth abortive. Oh!
Venomous pestilence
Shall sweep this country with infectious death.
To weep?—nay, to work; yea, to work ill, to lay low the
    people!
Oh me, many the wrongs of these maids of Night
Mourning their plundered honors!

ATHENA   Nay, *not* dishonored; neither let divine
Displeasures plague this mortal populace.
I too confide in Zeus—why speak of that?
And I alone of all divinities
Know of the keys which guard the treasury
Of heaven's thunder. Of that there is no need:
Be moved by my persuasion not to bring
From angry tongues to birth a fruit accursed
Nor sweep this country with calamities.
Calm the black humors of embittered rage,

Reside with me, and share my majesty;
And when from these wide acres you enjoy
Year after year the harvest offerings
That wedlock may be blest with issue, then
You will commend me for my intercession.

CHORUS   Me to be treated so!
Me with the sage wisdom of years to dwell here, oh
Ever debased, oh defiled!
Spirit of spleen and unyielding spite!
Give ear, O Earth!
Ah, the insufferable pangs sink deep.
Hear my passion, hear, black Night!
For the powers once mine, sealed long, long ago,
Have by the younger Gods been snatched all away.

ATHENA   My elder art thou, therefore I indulge
Thy passion; yet, though not so wise as thou,
To me also hath Zeus vouchsafed the gift
Of no mean understanding. I declare,
If you depart from this to other lands,
This country yet shall prove your heart's desire;
For with the tide of years shall flow increase
Of honor to my people; wherefore thou,
Honored among them and enthroned hard by
The temple of Erechtheus, shalt receive
Such homage from the congregated throngs
Of men and women as shall ne'er be yours
Elsewhere in all the world. And so, I pray,
Lay not upon my territories the spur
Of internecine strife to prick the breast
Of manhood flown with passion as with wine;
Implant not in my sons the bravery
Of fighting-cocks, embroiled against their own.
Abroad let battle rage for every heart
Possessed by love of glory—that shall be theirs
In plenty. This then is my offer to you—
To give and take rich benefits and share
My honors in a land beloved of heaven.

CHORUS   Me to be treated so!
         Me with the sage wisdom of years to dwell here, oh
         Ever debased, oh defiled!
         Spirit of spleen and unyielding spite!
         Give ear, O Earth!
         Ah, the insufferable pangs sink deep.
         Hear my passion, hear, black Night!
         For the powers once mine, sealed long, long ago,
         Have by the younger Gods been snatched all away.

ATHENA   I will not weary of my benedictions,
         Lest it be ever said that thou, so old
         A deity, wast driven from the land
         By me and by my mortal citizens,
         Rejected without welcome and despised.
         Nay, if Persuasion's holy majesty,
         The sweet enchantment of these lips divine,
         Is aught to thee, why then, reside with me;
         But if thou wilt not, surely it were wrong
         To lay upon my citizens a load
         Of indignation and pernicious rage,
         Since it is in thy power to own the soil
         Justly attended with the highest honors.

CHORUS   O Queen Athena, what dost thou promise me?

ATHENA   A dwelling free of sorrow. Pray, accept.

CHORUS   Say I accept, what honors shall be mine?

ATHENA   No house shall prosper save by grace from thee.

CHORUS   Wilt thou ensure me this prerogative?

ATHENA   I will, and bless all those who worship thee.

CHORUS   And pledge a warrant for all time to come?

ATHENA   I need not promise what I would not do.

CHORUS   Thy charms are working, and my rage subsides.

ATHENA   Here make thy dwelling where thou shalt win friends.

CHORUS   What song then shall I chant over the land?

ATHENA   A song of faultless victory: from earth and sea,
          From skies above may gentle breezes blow,
          And, breathing sunshine, float from shore to shore;
          That corn and cattle may continually
          Increase and multiply, and that no harm
          Befall the offspring of humanity;
          And prosper too the fruit of righteous hearts;
          For I, as one who tends flowers in a garden,
          Delight in those, the seeds that bring no sorrow.
          Such is thy part; and in the glorious
          Arrays of battle I shall strive until
          This city, over all victorious,
          Enjoy an honored name throughout the world.

THIRD STASIMON

CHORUS   I accept. Here with Pallas I will dwell,   [STROPHE 1
          Honoring the city which
          Zeus Almighty with the aid of Ares
          Holds a fortress for the Gods,
          Jeweled crown of Greece and guardian of her sanctuaries.
          So for her I pray with all
          Graciousness of utterance
          That smiling sun and bounteous earth unite to yield
          Lifelong joys, fortunes fair,
          Light and Darkness reconciled.

ATHENA   As a favor to all of my people have I
          Given homes in the land unto these, whose power
          Is so great and their anger so hard to appease—
          All that concerneth mankind they dispense.

Yet whenever a man falls foul of their wrath,
He knoweth not whence his afflictions approach;
Apprehended to answer the sins of his sires,
He is led unto these to be judged, and the still
Stroke of perdition
In the dust shall stifle his proud boast.

[ANTISTROPHE 1

Ne'er may foul winds be stirred to touch with blight
Budding tree—a grace from me;
Ne'er may parching droughts that blind the newly
Parted blossom trespass here;
Ne'er may blasts of noisome plague advance across the fields;
Rather, Pan in season due
Grant that flocks and herds may yield
A twin increase of yearly wealth, and from the rich
Store which these Gods vouchsafe
May the Earth repay them well.

ATHENA O listen, ye guards of my city, and hear
What blessings they bring you! For great is the power
Of the Furies in heaven and hell, and on earth
Unto some glad music, to others again
They dispense days darkened with weeping.

CHORUS Sudden death cutting short [STROPHE 2
Manhood's prime I bid away;
To all her comely daughters grant
Husband and home, O heavenly wardens of wedlock,
And ye too, dread Fates, born of the same mother's womb,
Spirits of justice divine, dwelling in every household,
Present at every season, weighty in your majesty,
Praised and magnified in every place.

ATHENA Fair blessings are these they bestow on the land,
And my heart is rejoiced.
To the eye of Persuasion I give all praise,
That with favor she looked on the breath of my lips
As I strove to appease these powers that once
Were averted in anger; but Zeus who is Lord

Of the eloquent word hath prevailed, and at last
In contention for blessings we conquer.

CHORUS   Ne'er, I pray, ne'er may that   [ANTISTROPHE 2
                Root of evil, civil strife,
                Rage within her boundaries;
                Ne'er may the earth's dust drink of the blood of her children,
                And wroth thereat thirst greedily after revenge,
                Blood in requital of blood;
                Rather in friendly communion
                Gladness be rendered for gladness,
                All at one in love and hate.
                Therein lies a cure for human ills.

ATHENA   How quick is their sense to discover the paths
                Of a tongue fair-spoken! From these dread shapes
                Great gain do I see for my people: if ye
                Pay homage to these and with favor regard
                Their favor to you, then surely the fame
                Of a city in justice and equity ruled
                Shall be spread as a light unto all men.

      [Enter CHORUS OF THE ESCORT, *carrying crimson robes*
                    and torches.

CHORUS   Joy to you, joy of your justly appointed riches,   [STROPHE 3
                Joy to all the people, blest
                With the Virgin's love, who sits
                Next beside her Father's throne.
                Wisdom ye have learned at last.
                Folded under Pallas' wing,
                Yours at last the grace of Zeus.

ATHENA   Joy to you likewise! Walking before you,
                To the chambers appointed I show you the way,
                Led by the sacred lights of the escort.
                Come with me, come, and let solemn oblations
                Speed you in joy to your homes in the earth,
                Where all that is hurtful imprison, we pray,
                And release what shall guide them to glory.

Lead them, O daughters of Cranaus, lead them,
And let all of you bear
Good will for the good that is given.

[ANTISTROPHE 3

CHORUS   Joy to you, joy—yet again we pronounce our blessing—
Joy to all the citizens,
Mortals, deities alike.
While you hold this land and pay
Homage to our residence,
Ne'er shall you have cause to blame
Change and chance in human life.

ATHENA   I thank you for these words of benison,
And now with flames of torchlit splendor bright
Escort you to your subterranean home,
Attended by the wardens of my shrine,
And justly so; for meet it is that all
The eye of Theseus' people should come forth,
This noble company of maidens fair,
And women wed and venerable in years.
Adorn them well in robes of crimson dye,
And let these blazing torches lead the way,
So that the good will of these residents
Be proved in manly prowess of your sons.

[*The* CHORUS *has put on the crimson robes; and a procession
is drawn up, led by twenty-four young men, who are
followed by the* CHORUS *and their escort, and the
main body of the citizens. The rest is sung as
the procession moves away.*

CHORUS   Pass on your way, O ye powers majestic,   [STROPHE 1
Daughters of darkness, in happy procession.
     Hush, O people, and speak all fair!

Pass to the caverns of earth immemorial   [ANTISTROPHE 1
There to be worshipped in honor and glory.
     Hush, O people, and speak all fair!

Gracious and kindly of heart to our people,   [STROPHE 2
Hither, O holy ones, hither in gladness,
Follow the lamps that illumine the way.
        O sing at the end Alleluia!

Peace to you, peace of a happy communion,   [ANTISTROPHE 2
People of Pallas. Zeus who beholdeth
All with the Fates is at last reconciled.
        O sing at the end Alleluia!

Euripides

THE TROJAN WOMEN

translated by
Richmond Lattimore

FOREWORD

427 B.C. The Lakedaimonian judges . . . caused the [Plataian] prisoners to be led before them one at a time, and asked each man the same question, namely, whether he had done anything during the war to benefit the Lakedaimonians and their allies. Each time they received a negative reply they took the man away and killed him, sparing none. They executed no fewer than two hundred Plataians and twenty-five Athenians who had been besieged with them. They enslaved the women.

Thucydides: III, 68

421 B.C. About the same time that summer the Athenians stormed Skione. They put to death the grown men, and enslaved the women and children.

Thucydides: V, 32

417 B.C. The next winter the Lakedaimonians . . . and their allies . . . took Hysiai, a small place in Argive territory. They killed all free persons whom they caught, and withdrew.

Thucydides: V, 83

416 B.C. [The Melians] were now besieged in force, and after some treasonable activity within the city, they surrendered to the Athenians at the discretion of the latter. The Athenians put to death all the grown men whom they captured, and enslaved the women and children.

Thucydides: V, 116

In [the first year of] the ninety-first Olympiad (415 B.C.) . . . Xenokles and Euripides competed against each other. Xenokles, whoever he may have been, won the first prize with *Oidipous*, *Lykaon*, *Bakchai*, and *Athamas* (a satyr play). Euripides was second with *Alexander*, *Palamedes*, *The Trojan Women*, and *Sisyphos* (a satyr play).

Ælian: Varia Historia II, 8

WHEN Troy fell to the Greeks, the god POSEIDON departed from the city which he had long loved. The men of Troy had been killed; the women, headed by aged HECUBA, PRIAM's queen, assembled before the walls of the burning town to await their departure into slavery.

```
ЛЛЛЛЛЛЛЛЛЛЛЛЛЛЛЛЛЛЛЛЛЛЛЛЛ
```

DRAMATIS PERSONÆ:

POSEIDON	TALTHYBIOS
ATHENE	KASSANDRA
HECUBA	ANDROMACHE
MENELAOS	ASTYANAX

HELEN

CHORUS OF TROJAN WOMEN

THE TROJAN WOMEN

SCENE: *The action takes place shortly after the capture of Troy. All Trojan men have been killed, or have fled; all women and children are captives. The scene is an open space before the city, which is visible in the background, partly demolished, and smoldering. Against the walls are tents, or huts, which temporarily house the captive women. The entrance of the* CHORUS *is made, in two separate groups which subsequently unite, from these buildings, as are those of* KASSANDRA *and* HELEN. *The entrances of* TALTHYBIOS, ANDROMACHE, *and* MENELAOS *are made from the wings. It is imaginable that the gods are made to appear high up, above the level of the other actors, as if near their own temples on the Citadel.*

As the play opens, HECUBA is prostrate on the ground (it is understood that she hears nothing of what the gods say).

[*Enter* POSEIDON.

POSEID.   I am Poseidon. I come from the Aigaian depths
of the sea beneath whose waters Nereid choirs evolve
the intricate bright circle of their dancing feet.
For since that day when Phoibos Apollo and I laid down
on Trojan soil the close of these stone towers, drawn true
and straight, there has always been affection in my heart
unfading, for these Phrygians and for their city;
which smoulders now, fallen before the Argive spears,
ruined, sacked, gutted. Such is Athene's work, and his,
the Parnassian, Epeios of Phokis, architect
and builder of the horse that swarmed with inward steel,
that fatal bulk which passed within the battlements,
whose fame hereafter shall be loud among men unborn,
the Wooden Horse, which hid the secret spears within.

151

Now the gods' groves are desolate, their thrones of power
blood-spattered where beside the lift of the altar steps
of Zeus, Defender Priam was cut down and died.
The ships of the Achaians load with spoils of Troy
now, the piled gold of Phrygia. And the men of Greece
who made this expedition and took the city, stay
only for the favoring stern-wind now to greet their wives
and children after ten years' harvests wasted here.

The will of Argive Hera and Athene won
its way against my will. Between them they broke Troy.
So I must leave my altars and great Ilion,
since once a city sinks into sad desolation
the gods' state sickens also, and their worship fades.
Skamandros' valley echoes to the wail of slaves,
the captive women given to their masters now,
some to Arkadia or the men of Thessaly
assigned, or to the lords of Athens, Theseus' strain;
while all the women of Troy yet unassigned are here
beneath the shelter of these walls, chosen to wait
the will of princes, and among them Tyndareus' child
Helen of Sparta, named—with right—a captive slave.

Nearby, beside the gates, for any to look upon
who has the heart, she lies face upward, Hecuba
weeping for multitudes her multitude of tears.
Polyxena, one daughter, even now was killed
in secrecy and pain beside Achilleus' tomb.
Priam is gone, their children dead; one girl is left,
Kassandra, reeling crazed at King Apollo's stroke,
whom Agamemnon, in despite of the gods' will
and all religion, will lead by force to his secret bed.

O city, long ago a happy place, good-bye;
good-bye, hewn bastions. Pallas, child of Zeus, did this.
But for her hatred, you might stand strong-founded still.

[ATHENE *enters.*

ATHENE   August among the gods, O vast divinity,
closest in kinship to the father of all, may one
who quarreled with you in the past make peace, and speak?

POSEID.   You may, lady Athene; for the strands of kinship
close drawn work no weak magic to enchant the mind.

ATHENE   I thank you for your gentleness, and bring you now
questions whose issue touches you and me, my lord.

POSEID.   Is this the annunciation of some new word spoken
by Zeus, or any other of the divinities?

ATHENE   No; but for Troy's sake, on whose ground we stand, I come
to win the favor of your power, and an ally.

POSEID.   You hated Troy once; did you throw your hate away
and change to pity now its walls are black with fire?

ATHENE   Come back to the question. Will you take counsel with me
and help me gladly in all that I would bring to pass?

POSEID.   I will indeed; but tell me what you wish to do.
Are you here for the Achaians' or the Phrygians' sake?

ATHENE   For the Trojans, whom I hated such a short time since,
to make the Achaians' homecoming a thing of sorrow.

POSEID.   This is a springing change of sympathy. Why must
you hate too hard, and love too hard, your loves and hates?

ATHENE   Did you not know they outraged my temple, and shamed me?

POSEID.   I know that Aias dragged Kassandra there by force.

ATHENE   And the Achaians did nothing. They did not even speak.

POSEID.   Yet Ilion was taken by your strength alone.

ATHENE   True; therefore help me. I would do some evil to them.

POSEID.   I am ready for anything you ask. What will you do?

ATHENE   Make the home voyage a most unhappy coming home.

POSEID.   While they stay here ashore, or out on the deep sea?

ATHENE   When they take ship from Ilion and set sail for home
Zeus will shower down his rainstorms and the weariless beat
of hail, to make black the bright air with roaring winds.
He has promised my hand the gift of the blazing thuderbolt
to dash and overwhelm with fire the Achaian ships.
Yours is your own domain, the Aigaian crossing. Make
the sea thunder to the tripled wave and spinning surf,
cram thick the hollow Euboian fold with floating dead;
that after this Greeks may learn to use with fear
my sacred places, and respect all gods beside.

POSEID.   This shall be done, and joyfully. It needs no long
discourse to tell you. I will shake the Aigaian Sea.
Mykonos' nesses and the swine-back reefs of Delos,
the Kaphereian promontories, Skyros, Lemnos
shall take the washed up bodies of men drowned at sea.
Back to Olympos now, gather the thunderbolts
from your father's hands, then take your watcher's post, to
   wait
the chance, when the Achaian fleet puts out to sea.

That mortal who sacks fallen cities is a fool,
who gives the temples and the tombs, the hallowed places
of the dead to desolation. His own turn must come.

[*The gods leave the stage,* HECUBA *seems to waken, and
gets slowly to her feet as she speaks.*

HECUBA   Rise, stricken head from the dust;
lift up the throat. This is Troy, but Troy
and we, Troy's kings, are perished.
Stoop to the changing fortune.
Steer for the crossing and the death-god,
hold not life's prow on the course against
wave beat and accident.
Ah me,
what need I further for tears' occasion,
state perished, my sons, and my husband?
O massive pride that my fathers heaped

to magnificence, you meant nothing.
Must I be hushed? Were it better thus?
Should I cry a lament?
Unhappy, accursed,
limbs cramped, I lie
backed on earth's stiff bed.
O head, O temples
and sides; sweet, to shift,
let the tired spine rest
weight eased by the sides alternate,
against the strain of the tears' song
where the stricken people find music yet
in the song undanced of their wretchedness.

You ships' prows, that the fugitive
oars swept back to blessed Ilion
over the sea's blue water
by the placid harbors of Hellas
to the flute's grim beat
and the swing of the shrill boat whistles;
you made the crossing, made fast ashore
the Egyptians' skill, the sea cables,
alas, by the coasts of Troy;
it was you, ships, that carried the fatal bride
of Menelaos, Kastor her brother's shame,
the stain on the Eurotas.
Now she has killed
the sire of the fifty sons
Priam; me, unhappy Hecuba,
she drove on this reef of ruin.

Such state I keep
to sit by the tents of Agamemnon.
I am led captive
from my house, an old, unhappy woman,
my head struck pitiful.
Come then, sad wives of the Trojans
whose spears were bronze,

their daughters, brides of disaster,
let us mourn the smoke of Ilion.
And I, as among winged birds
the mother, lead out
the clashing cry, the song; not that song
wherein once long ago
when I held the sceptre of Priam
my feet were queens of the choir and led
the proud dance to the gods of Phrygia.

[*The first* HALF-CHORUS *comes out of the shelter
at the back.*

F.H.C.   Hecuba, what are these cries?
What news now? For through the walls
I heard your pitiful weeping.
And fear shivered in the breasts
of the Trojan women, who within
sob out the day of their slavery.

HECUBA   My children, the ships of the Argives
will move today. The hand is at the oar.

F.H.C.   They will? Why? Ah me. Must I take ship
so soon from the land of my fathers?

HECUBA   I know nothing. I look for disaster.

F.H.C.   Alas.
Poor women of Troy, torn from your homes,
bent to forced hard work.
The Argives push to the run home.

HECUBA   Oh
let her not come forth,
not now, my child
Kassandra, driven delirious
to shame us before the Argives;
not the mad one, to bring fresh pain to my pain.
Ah no.
Troy, ill-starred Troy, this is the end;

your last sad people leave you now
still alive, and broken.

[*The* SECOND HALF-CHORUS *comes out of the shelter
at the back.*

S.H.C.   Ah me. Shivering I left the tents
of Agamemnon to listen.
Tell us, our queen. Did the Argive council
decree our death?
Are the seamen manning the ships now,
oars ready for action?

HECUBA   My child, this was why I came, heart trembling
in the pale light of terror.

S.H.C.   Has a herald come from the Danaans?
Whose wretched slave shall I be ordained?

HECUBA   You are near the lot now.

S.H.C.   Alas.
Who will lead me away? An Argive?
To an island home? To Phthiotis?
Unhappy, surely, and far from Troy.

HECUBA   Ah,
whose wretched slave
shall I be? Where, in my gray age,
a faint drone,
poor image of a corpse,
weak shining among dead men? Shall
I stand and keep guard at their doors,
shall I nurse their children, I who in Troy
held state as a princess?

[*The two half-choruses now unite to form a
single* CHORUS.

CHORUS   Ah me, ah me. So pitiful
your shame and your lamentation.
No longer shall I turn the shifting design

of the shuttle at the looms of Ida.
I shall look no more on the bodies of my sons.
No more. Shall I be a drudge, besides
being forced to the bed of Greek masters?
Night is a queen, but I curse her.
Must I draw the water of Peirene,
a servant at sacred springs?
Might I only be taken to the domain
of Theseus, the bright, the blessed!
Never to the whirl of Eurotas,
detested, who gave us Helen,
not look with slave's eyes on the scourge
of Troy, Menelaos.

I have heard the rumor
of the hallowed ground by Peneios,
bright doorstone of Olympos,
deep burdened in beauty of flower and harvest.
There would I be next after the blessed,
the sacrosanct hold of Theseus.
And they say that the land of Aitna,
the Fire-God's keep against Punic men,
mother of Sicilian mountains, sounds
in the herald's cry for games' garlands;
and the land washed
by the streaming Ionian Sea,
that land watered by the loveliest
of rivers, Krathis, with the red-gold tresses
who draws from the depths of enchanted wells
blessings on a strong people.

See now, from the host of the Danaans
the herald, charged with new tidings, takes
the speed of his way toward us.
What message? What command? Since we count as slaves
even now in the Dorian kingdom.

[TALTHYBIOS *enters, followed by a detail of
armed soldiers.*

TALTHY.   Hecuba, incessantly my ways have led me to Troy
as the messenger of all the Achaian armament.
You know me from the old days, my lady; I am sent,
Talthybios, with new messages for you to hear.

HECUBA   This is it, beloved daughters of Troy; the thing I feared.

TALTHY.   You are all given your masters now. Was this your dread?

HECUBA   Ah, yes. Is it Phthia, then? A city of Thessaly?
Tell me. The land of Kadmos?

TALTHY.   All are allotted separately, each to a man.

HECUBA   Who is given to whom? Oh, is there any hope
left for the women of Troy?

TALTHY.   I understand. Yet ask not for all, but for each apart.

HECUBA   Who was given my child? Tell me, who shall be lord
of my poor abused Kassandra?

TALTHY.   King Agamemnon chose her. She was given to him.

HECUBA   Slave woman to that Lakedaimonian wife?
My unhappy child!

TALTHY.   No. Rather to be joined with him in the dark bed of love.

HECUBA   She, Apollo's virgin, blessed in the privilege
the gold-haired god gave her, a life for ever unwed?

TALTHY.   Love's archery and the prophetic maiden struck him hard.

HECUBA   Dash down, my daughter,
the keys of your consecration,
break the god's garlands to your throat gathered.

TALTHY.   Is it not high favor to be brought to a king's bed?

HECUBA   My poor youngest, why did you take her away from me?

TALTHY.   You spoke now of Polyxena. Is it not so?

HECUBA   To whose arms did the lot force her?

TALTHY.   She is given a guardianship, to keep Achilleus' tomb.

HECUBA   To watch, alas, my child? Over a tomb?
           Tell me, is this their way,
           some law, friend, established among the Greeks?

TALTHY.   Speak of your child in words of blessing. She feels no pain.

HECUBA   What did that mean? Does she live in the sunlight still?

TALTHY.   She lives her destiny, and her cares are over now.

HECUBA   The wife of bronze-embattled Hektor: tell me of her,
           Andromache the forlorn. What shall she suffer now?

TALTHY.   The son of Achilleus chose her. She was given to him.

HECUBA   And I, my aged strength crutched for support on staves,
           whom shall I serve?

TALTHY.   You shall be slave to Odysseus, lord of Ithaka.

HECUBA   Oh no, no!
           Tear the shorn head,
           rip nails through the folded cheeks.
           Must I?
           To be given as slave to serve that vile, that slippery man,
           right's enemy, brute murderous beast,
           that mouth of lies and treachery, that makes void
           faith in things promised
           and that which was beloved turns to hate. Oh, mourn,
           daughters of Ilion, weep as one for me.
           I am gone, doomed, undone,
           O wretched, given
           the worst lot of all.

CHORUS   I know your destiny now, queen Hecuba. But mine?
           What Hellene, what Achaian is my master now?

TALTHY.   Men-at-arms, do your duty. Bring Kassandra forth
           without delay. Our orders are to deliver her
           to the general at once. And afterwards we can bring
           to the rest of the princes their allotted captive women.
           But see! What is that burst of a torch flame inside?
           What can it mean? Are the Trojan women setting fire

to their chambers, at point of being torn from their land
to sail for Argos? Have they set themselves aflame
in longing for death? I know it is the way of freedom
in times like these to stiffen the neck against disaster.
Open, there, open; let not the fate desired by these,
dreaded by the Achaians, hurl their wrath on me.

HECUBA   You are wrong, there is no fire there. It is my Kassandra
whirled out on running feet in the passion of her frenzy.

             [KASSANDRA, *carrying a flaming torch, bursts from*
                         the shelter.

KASS.   Lift up, heave up; carry the flame; I bring fire of worship,
torches to the temple.
Io, Hymen, my lord, Hymenaios.
Blessed the bridegroom.
Blessed am I indeed to lie at a king's side,
blessed the bride of Argos.
Hymen, my lord, Hymenaios.
Yours were the tears, my mother,
yours was the lamentation for my father fallen,
for your city so dear beloved,
but mine this marriage, my marriage,
and I shake out the torch-flare,
brightness, dazzle,
light for you, Hymenaios,
Hecate, light for you,
for the bed of virginity as man's custom ordains.

Let your feet dance, rippling the air; let go the chorus,
as when my father's
fate went in blessedness.
O sacred circle of dance.
Lead now, Phoibos Apollo; I wear your laurel,
I tend your temple,
Hymen O Hymenaios.
Dance, mother, dance too; lead; let your feet
wind in the shifting pattern and follow mine,

keep the sweet step with me,
cry out the name Hymenaios
and the bride's name in the shrill
and the blessed incantation.
O you daughters of Phrygia robed in splendor,
dance for my wedding,
for the lord fate appointed to lie beside me.

CHORUS   Can you not, Queen Hecuba, stop this bacchanal before
her light feet whirl her away into the Argive camp?

HECUBA   Fire God, in mortal marriages you lift up your torch,
but here you throw a melancholy light, not seen
through my hopes that went so high in days gone past. O
  child,
there was a time I dreamed you would not wed like this,
not at the spear's edge, not under force of Argive arms.
Let me take the light; crazed, passionate, you can not carry
it straight enough, poor child. Your fate is intemperate
as you are, always. There is no relief for you.

[*Attendants come from the shelter.* HECUBA *gently takes the
  torch from* KASSANDRA *and gives it to them to carry away.*]

You Trojan women, take the torch inside, and change
to songs of tears this poor girl's marriage melodies.

KASS.   O mother, star my hair with flowers of victory.
I know you would not have it happen thus; and yet
this is a king I marry; then be glad; escort
the bride. Oh, thrust her strongly on. If Loxias
is Loxias still, the Achaians' pride, great Agamemnon
has won a wife more fatal than ever Helen was.
Since I will kill him; and avenge my brothers' blood
and my father's in the desolation of his house.
But I leave this in silence and sing not now the axe
to drop against my throat and other throats than mine,
the agony of the mother murdered, brought to pass
from our marriage rites, and Atreus' house made desolate.
I am ridden by God's curse still, yet I will step so far

out of my frenzy as to make plain this city's fate
as blessed beside the Achaians'. For one woman's sake,
one act of love, these hunted Helen down and threw
thousands of lives away. Their general—clever man—
in the name of a vile woman cut his darling down,
gave up for a brother the sweetness of children in his house,
all to bring back that brother's wife, a woman who went
of her free will, not caught in constraint of violence.
The Achaians came beside Skamandros' banks, and died
day after day, though none sought to wrench their land from
    them
nor their own towering cities. Those the War God caught
never saw their sons again, nor were they laid to rest
decently in winding sheets by their wives' hands, but lie
buried in alien ground; while all went wrong at home
as the widows perished, and barren couples raised and nursed
the children of others, no survivor left to tend
the tombs, and what is left there, with blood sacrificed.
For such success as this congratulate the Greeks.
No, but the shame is better left in silence, for fear
my singing voice become the voice of wretchedness.
The Trojans have that glory which is loveliest:
they died for their own country. So the bodies of all
who took the spears were carried home in loving hands,
brought, in the land of their fathers, to the embrace of earth
and buried becomingly as the rite fell due. The rest,
those Phrygians who escaped death in battle, day by day
came home to happiness the Achaians could not know;
their wives, their children. Then was Hektor's fate so sad?
You think so. Listen to the truth. He is dead and gone
surely, but with reputation, as a valiant man.
How could this be, except for the Achaians' coming?
Had they held back, none might have known how great he
    was.
The bride of Paris was the daughter of Zeus. Had he
not married her, fame in our house would sleep in silence still.
Though surely the wise man will forever shrink from war,
yet if war come, the hero's death will lay a wreath

not lustreless on the city. The coward alone brings shame.
Let no more tears fall, mother, for our land, nor for
this marriage I make; it is by marriage that I bring
to destruction those whom you and I have hated most.

CHORUS   You smile on your disasters. Can it be that you
some day will illuminate the darkness of this song?

TALTHY.   Were it not Apollo who has driven wild your wits
I would make you sorry for sending the princes of our host
on their way home in augury of foul speech like this.
Now pride of majesty and wisdom's outward show
have fallen to stature less than what was nothing worth
since he, almighty prince of the assembled Hellenes,
Atreus' son beloved, has stooped—by his own will—
to find his love in a crazed girl. I, a plain man,
would not marry this woman or keep her as my slave.
You then, with your wits unhinged by idiocy,
your scolding of Argos and your Trojans glorified
I throw to the winds to scatter them. Come now with me
to the ships, a bride—and such a bride—for Agamemnon.

Hecuba, when Laertes' son calls you, be sure
you follow; if what all say who came to Ilion
is true, at the worst you will be a good woman's slave.

KASS.   That servant is a vile thing. Oh, how can heralds keep
their name of honor? Lackeys for despots be they, or
lackeys to the people, all men must despise them still.
You tell me that my mother must be slave in the house
of Odysseus? Where are all Apollo's promises
uttered to me, to my own ears, that Hecuba
should die in Troy? Odysseus I will curse no more,
poor wretch, who little dreams of what he must go through
when he will think Troy's pain and mine were golden grace
beside his own luck. Ten years he spent here, and ten
more years will follow before he at last comes home, forlorn
after the terror of the rock and the thin strait;
Charybdis; and the mountain striding Cyclops, who eats

men's flesh; the Ligurian witch who changes men to swine,
Kirkê; the wreck of all his ships on the salt sea,
the lotus passion, the sacred oxen of the Sun
slaughtered, and dead flesh moaning into speech, to make
Odysseus listening shiver. Cut the story short:
he will go down to the water of death, and return alive
to reach home, and the thousand sorrows waiting there.

Why must I transfix each of Odysseus' labors one by one?
Lead the way, go quick to the house of death where I shall
    take my mate.
Lord of all the sons of Danaos, haughty in your mind of pride,
not by day, but evil in the evil night you shall find your grave
when I lie corpse-cold and naked next my husband's
    sepulchre,
piled in the ditch for animals to rip and feed on, beaten by
streaming storms of winter, I who wore Apollo's sacraments.
Garlands of the god I loved so well, the spirit's dress of pride,
leave me, as I leave those festivals where once I was so gay.
See, I tear your adornments from my skin not yet defiled by
    touch,
throw them to the running winds to scatter, O lord of
    prophecy.
Where is this general's ship, then? Lead me where I must set
    my feet on board.
Wait the wind of favor in the sails; yet when the ship goes out
from this shore, she carries one of the three Furies in my
    shape.
Land of my ancestors, good-bye; O mother, weep no more
    for me.
You beneath the ground, my brothers, Priam, father of us all,
I will be with you soon and come triumphant to the dead
    below,
leaving at my back the wreckage of the house of Atreus.

    [KASSANDRA *is taken away by* TALTHYBIOS *and his soldiers.*
           HECUBA *collapses.*

CHORUS   Handmaids of aged Hecuba, can you not see

how your mistress, powerless to cry out, lies prone? Oh, take
her hand and help her to her feet, you wretched maids.
Will you let an aged helpless woman lie so long?

HECUBA   No. Let me lie where I have fallen. Kind acts, my maids,
must be unkind, unwanted. All that I endure
and have endured and shall, deserves to strike me down.
O gods! What wretched things to call on—gods!—for help
although the decorous action is to invoke their aid
when all our hands lay hold on is unhappiness.
No. It is my pleasure first to tell good fortune's tale,
to cast its count more sadly against disasters now.
I was a princess, who was once a prince's bride,
mother by him of sons preëminent, beyond
the mere numbers of them, lords of the Phrygian domain,
such sons for pride to point to as no woman of Troy,
no Hellene, none in the outlander's wide world might match.
And then I saw them fall before the spears of Greece,
and cut this hair for them, and laid it on their graves.
I mourned their father, Priam. None told me the tale
of his death. I saw it, with these eyes. I stood to watch
his throat cut, next the altar of the protecting god.
I saw my city taken. And the girls I nursed,
choice flowers to wear the pride of any husband's eyes,
matured to be dragged by hands of strangers from my arms.
There is no hope left that they will ever see me more,
no hope that I shall ever look on them again.
There is one more stone to key this arch of wretchedness:
I must be carried away to Hellas now, an old
slave woman, where all those tasks that wrack old age shall be
given me by my masters. I must work the bolt
that bars their doorway, I whose son was Hektor once;
or bake their bread; lay down these withered limbs to sleep
on the bare ground, whose bed was royal once; abuse
this skin once delicate the slattern's way, exposed
through robes whose rags will mock my luxury of long since.
Unhappy, O unhappy. And all this came to pass
and shall be, for the way one woman chose a man.

Kassandra, O daughter, whose excitements were the god's,
you have paid for your consecration now; at what a price!
And you, my poor Polyxena, where are you now?
Not here, nor any boy or girl of mine, who were
so many once, is near me in my unhappiness.
And you would lift me from the ground? What hope? What
    use?
Guide these feet long ago so delicate in Troy,
a slave's feet now, to the straw sacks laid on the ground
and the piled stones; let me lay down my head and die
in an exhaustion of tears. Of all who walk in bliss
call not one happy yet, until the man is dead.

[HECUBA, *after being led to the back of the stage, flings herself*
                    to the ground once more.

CHORUS   Voice of singing, stay
with me now, for Ilion's sake;
take up the burden of tears,
the song of sorrow;
the dirge for Troy's death
must be chanted;
the tale of my captivity
by the wheeled stride of the fourfoot beast of the Argives,
the horse they left in the gates,
thin gold at its brows,
inward, the spears' high thunder.
Our people thronging
the rock of Troy let go the great cry:
'The war is over! Go down,
bring back the idol's enchanted wood
to the Maiden of Ilion, Zeus' daughter.'
Who stayed then? Not one girl, not one
old man, in their houses,
but singing for happiness
let the lurking death in.

And the generation of Troy
swept solid to the gates

to give the goddess
her pleasure: the colt immortal, unbroken,
the nest of Argive spears,
death for the children of Dardanos
sealed in the sleek hill pine chamber.
In the sling of the flax twist shipwise
they berthed the black hull
in the house of Pallas Athene
stone paved, washed now in the blood of our people.
Strong, gay work
deep into black night
to the stroke of the Libyan lute
and all Troy singing, and girls'
light feet pulsing the air
in the kind dance measures;
indoors, lights everywhere,
torchflares on black
to forbid sleep's onset.

I was there also: in the great room
I danced the maiden of the mountains,
Artemis, Zeus' daughter.
When the cry went up, sudden,
bloodshot, up and down the city, to stun
the keep of the citadel. Children
reached shivering hands to clutch
at the mother's dress.
War stalked from his hiding place.
Pallas did this.
Beside their altars the Trojans
died in their blood. Desolate now,
men murdered, our sleeping rooms gave up
their brides' beauty
to breed sons for Greek men,
sorrow for our own country.

[*A wagon comes on the stage. It is heaped with a number of
spoils of war, in the midst of which sits* ANDROMACHE

holding ASTYANAX. *While the chorus continues*
speaking, HECUBA *rises once more.*

Hecuba look, I see her, rapt
to the alien wagon, Andromache,
close to whose beating breast clings
the boy Astyanax, Hektor's sweet child.
O carried away—to what land?—unhappy woman,
on the chariot floor, with the brazen arms
of Hektor, of Troy
captive and heaped beside you
torn now from Troy, for Achilleus' son
to hang in the shrines of Phthia.

ANDRO.   I am in the hands of Greek masters.

HECUBA   Alas

ANDRO.   Must the incantation

HECUBA   Ah me

ANDRO.   of my own grief win tears from you

HECUBA   It must—O Zeus

ANDRO.   my own distress?

HECUBA   O my children

ANDRO.   once. No longer.

HECUBA   Lost, lost, Troy our dominion

ANDRO.   unhappy

HECUBA   and my lordly children.

ANDRO.   Gone, alas

HECUBA   they were mine

ANDRO.   sorrows only.

HECUBA   Sad destiny

ANDRO.   of our city

HECUBA   a wreck, and burning.

ANDRO.   Come back, O my husband.

HECUBA   Poor child, you invoke
a dead man; my son once

ANDRO.   my defender.

HECUBA   And you, whose death shamed the Achaians

ANDRO.   lord of us all once,
O patriarch, Priam,

HECUBA   take me to my death now.

ANDRO.   Longing for death drives deep;

HECUBA   O sorrowful, such is our fortune

ANDRO.   lost our city

HECUBA   and our pain lies deep under pain piled over.

ANDRO.   We are the hated of God, since once your youngest escaping
Death, brought down Troy's towers in the arms of a worthless
     woman,
piling at the feet of Pallas the bleeding bodies of our young
     men
sprawled, kites' food, while Troy takes up the yoke of cap-
     tivity.

HECUBA   O my city, my city forlorn

ANDRO.   abandoned, I weep this

HECUBA   miserable last hour

ANDRO.   of the house where I bore my children.

HECUBA   O my sons, this city and your mother are desolate of you.
Sound of lamentation and sorrow,
tears on tears shed. Home, farewell, since the dead have for-
     gotten
all sorrows, and weep no longer.

CHORUS   They who are sad find somehow sweetness in tears, the song
of lamentation and the melancholy Muse.

ANDRO.   Hecuba, mother of the man whose spear was death
to the Argives, Hektor: do you see what they have done to us?

HECUBA   I see the work of gods who pile tower-high the pride
of those who were nothing, and dash present grandeur down.

ANDRO.   We are carried away, sad spoils, my boy and I; our life
transformed, as the aristocrat becomes the serf.

HECUBA   Such is the terror of necessity. I lost
Kassandra, roughly torn from my arms before you came.

ANDRO.   Another Aias to haunt your daughter? Some such thing
it must be. Yet you have lost still more than you yet know.

HECUBA   There is no numbering my losses. Infinitely
misfortune comes to outrace misfortune known before.

ANDRO.   Polyxena is dead. They cut your daughter's throat
to pleasure dead Achilleus' corpse, above his grave.

HECUBA   O wretched. This was what Talthybios meant, that speech
cryptic, incomprehensible, yet now so clear.

ANDRO.   I saw her die, and left this chariot seat to lay
a robe upon her body and sing the threnody.

HECUBA   Poor child, poor wretched, wretched darling, sacrificed,
but without pity, and in pain, to a dead man.

ANDRO.   She is dead, and this was death indeed; and yet to die
as she did was better than to live as I live now.

HECUBA   Child, no. No life, no light is any kind of death,
since death is nothing, and in life the hopes live still.

ANDRO.   O mother, our mother, hear me while I reason through
this matter fairly—might it even hush your grief?
Death, I am sure, is like never being born, but death
is better thus by far than to live a life of pain,
since the dead with no perception of evil feel no grief,

while he who was happy once, and then unfortunate,
finds his heart driven far from the old lost happiness.
She died; it is as if she never saw the light
of day, for she knows nothing now of what she suffered.
But I, who aimed the arrows of ambition high
at honor, and made them good, see now how far I fall,
I, who in Hektor's house worked out all custom that brings
discretion's name to women. Blame them or blame them not,
there is one act that swings the scandalous speech their way
beyond all else: to leave the house and walk abroad.
I longed to do it, but put the longing aside, and stayed
always within the enclosure of my own house and court.
The witty speech some women cultivate I would
not practice, but kept my honest inward thought, and made
my mind my only and sufficient teacher. I gave
my lord's presence the tribute of hushed lips, and eyes
quietly downcast. I knew when my will must have its way
over his, knew also how to give way to him in turn.
Men learned of this; I was talked of in the Achaian camp,
and reputation has destroyed me now. At the choice
of women, Achilleus' son picked me from the rest, to be
his wife: a lordly house, yet I shall be a slave.
If I dash back the beloved memory of Hektor
and open wide my heart to my new lord, I shall be
a traitor to the dead love, and know it; if I cling
faithful to the past, I win my master's hatred. Yet
they say one night of love suffices to dissolve
a woman's aversion to share the bed of any man.
I hate and loathe that woman who casts away the once
beloved, and takes another in her arms of love.
Even the young mare torn from her running mate and teamed
with another will not easily wear the yoke. And yet
this is a brute and speechless beast of burden, not
like us intelligent, lower far in nature's scale.
Dear Hektor, when I had you I had a husband, great
in understanding, rank, wealth, courage: all my wish.
I was a virgin when you took me from the house
of my father; I gave you all my maiden love, my first.

and now you are dead, and I must cross the sea, to serve,
prisoner of war, the slave's yoke on my neck, in Greece.
No, Hecuba; can you not see my fate is worse
than hers you grieve, Polyxena's? That one thing left
always while life lasts, hope, is not for me. I keep
no secret deception in my heart—sweet though it be
to dream—that I shall ever be happy any more.

CHORUS   You stand where I do in misfortune, and while you mourn
your own life, tell me what I, too, am suffering.

HECUBA   I have never been inside the hull of a ship, but know
what I know only by hearsay and from painted scenes,
yet think that seamen, while the gale blows moderately,
take pains to spare unnecessary work, and send
one man to the steering oar, another aloft, and crews
to pump the bilge from the hold. But when the water is
    troubled
and seas wash over the decks they lose their nerve, and let
her go by the run at the waves' will, leaving all to chance.
So I, in this succession of disasters, swamped,
battered by this storm immortally inspired, have lost
my lips' control and let them go, say anything
they will. Yet still, beloved child, you must forget
what happened with Hektor. Tears will never save you now.
Give your obedience to the new master; let your ways
entice his heart to make him love you. If you do
it will be better for all who are close to you. This boy,
my own son's child, might grow to manhood and bring back—
he alone could do it—something of our city's strength.
On some far day the children of your children might
come home, and build. There still may be another Troy.

But we say this, and others will speak also. See,
here is some runner of the Achaians come again.
Who is he? What news? What counsel have they taken now?

[TALTHYBIOS *enters again with his escort.*

TALTHY.   O wife of Hektor, once the bravest man in Troy,

do not hate me. This is the will of the Danaans and
the kings. I wish I did not have to give this message.

ANDRO. What can this mean, this hint of hateful things to come?

TALTHY. The council has decreed for your son—how can I say this?

ANDRO. That he shall serve some other master than I serve?

TALTHY. No man of Achaia shall ever make this boy his slave.

ANDRO. Must he be left behind in Phrygia, all alone?

TALTHY. Worse; horrible. There is no easy way to tell it.

ANDRO. I thank your courtesy—unless your news be really good.

TALTHY. They will kill your son. It is monstrous. Now you know the
  truth.

ANDRO. Oh, this is worse than anything I heard before.

TALTHY. Odysseus. He urged it before the Greeks, and got his way.

ANDRO. This is too much grief, and more than anyone could bear.

TALTHY. He said a hero's son could not be allowed to live.

ANDRO. Even thus may his own sons some day find no mercy.

TALTHY. He must be hurled from the battlements of Troy.

[*He goes toward* ANDROMACHE, *who clings fast to her child,
as if to resist.*

               No, wait!
Let it happen this way. It will be wiser in the end.
Do not fight it. Take your grief as you were born to take it,
give up the struggle where your strength is feebleness
with no force anywhere to help. Listen to me!
Your city is gone, your husband. You are in our power.
How can one woman hope to struggle against the arms
of Greece? Think, then. Give up the passionate contest.
                 This
will bring no shame. No man can laugh at your submission.
And please—I request you—hurl no curse at the Achaians

for fear the army, savage over some reckless word,
forbid the child his burial and the dirge of honor.
Be brave, be silent; out of such patience you can hope
the child you leave behind will not lie unburied here,
and that to you the Achaians will be less unkind.

ANDRO.   O darling child I loved too well for happiness,
your enemies will kill you and leave your mother forlorn.
Your own father's nobility, where others found
protection, means your murder now. The memory
of his valor comes ill-timed for you. O bridal bed,
O marriage rites that brought me home to Hektor's house
a bride, you were unhappy in the end. I lived
never thinking the baby I had was born for butchery
by Greeks, but for lordship over all Asia's pride of earth.
Poor child, are you crying too? Do you know what they
will do to you? Your fingers clutch my dress. What use,
to nestle like a young bird under the mother's wing?
Hektor can not come back, not burst from underground
to save you, that spear of glory caught in the quick hand,
nor Hektor's fame, nor any strength of Phrygian arms.
Yours the sick leap head downward from the height, the fall
where none have pity, and the spirit smashed out in death.
O last and loveliest embrace of all, O child's
sweet fragrant body. Vanity in the end. I nursed
for nothing the swaddled baby at this mother's breast;
in vain the wrack of the labor pains and the long sickness.
Now once again, and never after this, come close
to your mother, lean against my breast and wind your arms
around my neck, and put your lips against my lips.

       [*She kisses* ASTYANAX *and relinquishes him.*]

Greeks! Your Greek cleverness is simple barbarity.
Why kill this child, who never did you any harm?
O flowering of the house of Tyndareus! Not his,
not God's daughter, never that, but child of many fathers
I say; the daughter of Vindictiveness, of Hate,
of Blood, Death; of all wickedness that swarms on earth.

I cry it aloud: Zeus never was your father, but you
were born a pestilence to all Greeks and the world beside.
Accursed; who from those lovely and accursed eyes
brought down to shame and ruin the bright plains of Troy.
Oh, seize him, take him, dash him to death if it must be done;
feed on his flesh if it is your will. These are the gods
who damn us to this death, and I have no strength to save
my boy from execution. Cover this wretched face
and throw me into the ship and that sweet bridal bed
I walk to now across the death of my own child.

[TALTHYBIOS *gently lifts the child out of the wagon, which
leaves the stage, carrying* ANDROMACHE *away.*

CHORUS   Unhappy Troy! For the sweetness in one woman's arms'
embrace, unspeakable, you lost these thousands slain.

TALTHY.   Come, boy, taken from the embrace beloved
of your mourning mother. Climb the high circle
of the towers your fathers built. There
end life. This was the order.
Take him.

[*He hands* ASTYANAX *to the guards, who lead him out.*

I am not the man
to do this. Some other
without pity, not as I ashamed,
should be herald of messages like this.

[*He goes out.*

HECUBA   O child of my own unhappy child,
shall your life be torn from your mother
and from me? Wicked. Can I help,
dear child, not only suffer? What help?
Tear face, beat bosom. This is all
my power now. O city,
O child, what have we left to suffer?
Are we not hurled
down the whole length of disaster?

CHORUS   Telamon, O king in the land where the bees swarm,
          Salamis the surf-pounded isle where you founded your city
          to front that hallowed coast where Athene broke
          forth the primeval pale branch of olive,
          wreath of the bright air and a glory on Athens the shining:
          O Telamon, you came in your pride of arms
          with Alkmena's archer
          to Ilion, our city, to sack and destroy it
          on that age old venture.

          This was the first flower of Hellenic strength Herakles
              brought in anger
          for the horses promised; and by Simoeis' calm waters
          checked the surf-wandering oars and made fast the ships' stern
              cables.
          From which vessels came out the deadly bow hand,
          death to Laomedon, as the scarlet wind of the flames swept
              over
          masonry straight-hewn by the hands of Apollo.
          This was a desolation of Troy
          twice taken; twice in the welter of blood the walls Dardanian
          went down before the red spear.

          In vain, then, Laomedon's child,
          you walk in delicate pride
          by the golden pitchers
          in loveliest servitude
          to fill Zeus' wine cups;
          while Troy your mother is given to the flame to eat,
          and the lonely beaches
          mourn, as sad birds sing
          for the young lost,
          for the sword hand and the children
          and the aged women.
          Gone now the shining pools where you bathed,
          the fields where you ran
          all desolate. And you
          Ganymede, go in grace by the thrones of God

with your young, calm smile even now
as Priam's kingdom
falls to the Greek spear.

O Love, Love, it was you
in the high halls of Dardanos,
the sky-daughters of melody beside you,
who piled the huge strength of Troy
in towers, the gods' own hands
concerned. I speak no more
against Zeus' name.
But the light men love, who shines
through the pale wings of morning,
balestar on this earth now,
watched the collapse of tall towers:
Dawn. Her lord was of this land;
she bore his children,
Tithonos, caught away by the golden car
and the starry horses,
who made our hopes so high.
For the gods loved Troy once.
Now they have forgotten.

> [MENELAOS *comes on the stage, attended by a detail of*
> *armed soldiers.*

MENEL.   O splendor of sunburst breaking forth this day, whereon
I lay my hands once more on Helen, my wife. And yet
it is not, so much as men think, for the woman's sake
I came to Troy, but against that guest proved treacherous,
who Viking-like carried the woman from my house.
Since the gods have seen to it that he paid the penalty,
fallen before the Hellenic spear, his kingdom wrecked,
I come for her now, the wife once my own, whose name
I can no longer speak with any happiness,
to take her away. In this house of captivity
she is numbered among the other women of Troy, a slave.
And those men whose work with the spear has won her back
gave her to me, to kill, or not to kill, but lead

away to the land of Argos, if such be my pleasure.
And such it is; the death of Helen in Troy I will let
pass, have the oars take her by sea ways back to Greek
soil, and there give her over to execution;
blood penalty for friends who are dead in Ilion here.
Go to the house, my followers, and take her out;
no, drag her out; lay hands upon that hair so stained
with men's destruction. When the winds blow fair astern
we will take ship again and bring her back to Hellas.

HECUBA   O power, who mount the world, wheel where the world rides,
O mystery of man's knowledge, whosoever you be,
Zeus named, nature's necessity or mortal mind,
I call upon you; for you walk the path none hears
yet bring all human action back to right at last.

MENEL.   What can this mean? How strange a way to call on gods.

HECUBA   Kill your wife, Menelaos, and I will bless your name.
But keep your eyes away from her. Desire will win.
She looks enchantment, and where she looks homes are set
    fire;
she captures cities as she captures the eyes of men.
We have had experience, you and I. We know the truth.

[*Men at arms bring* HELEN *roughly out of the shelter.
She makes no resistance.*

HELEN   Menelaos, your first acts are argument of terror
to come. Your lackeys put their hands on me. I am dragged
out of my chambers by brute force. I know you hate
me; I am almost sure. And still there is one question
I would ask you, if I may. What have the Greeks decided
to do with me? Or shall I be allowed to live?

MENEL.   You are not strictly condemned, but all the army gave
you into my hands, to kill you for the wrong you did.

HELEN   Is it permitted that I argue this, and prove
that my death, if I am put to death, will be unjust?

MENEL.   I did not come to talk with you. I came to kill.

HECUBA   No. Menelaos, listen to her. She should not die
unheard. But give me leave to take the opposite case;
the prosecution. There are things that happened in Troy
which you know nothing of, and the long-drawn argument
will mean her death. She never can escape us now.

MENEL.   This is a gift of leisure. If she wishes to speak
she may. But it is for your sake, understand, that I give
this privilege I never would have given to her.

HELEN   Perhaps it will make no difference if I speak well
or badly, and your hate will not let you answer me.
All I can do is to foresee the arguments
you will use in accusation of me, and set against
the force of your charges, charges of my own.

    First, then!
She mothered the beginning of all this wickedness.
For Paris was her child. And next to her the old king,
who would not destroy the infant Alexander, that dream
of the firebrand's agony, has ruined Troy, and me.
This is not all; listen to the rest I have to say.
Alexander was the judge of the goddess trinity.
Pallas Athene would have given him power, to lead
the Phrygian arms on Hellas and make it desolate.
All Asia was Hera's promise, and the uttermost zones
of Europe for his lordship, if her way prevailed.
But Aphrodite, picturing my loveliness,
promised it to him for the word that her beauty surpassed
all others. Think what this means, and all the consequence.
Kypris prevailed, and I was won in marriage: all
for Greek advantage. Asia is not your lord; you serve
no tyrant now, nor take the spear in his defense.
Yet Hellas' fortune was my own misfortune. I,
sold once for my body's beauty stand accused, who should
for what has been done wear garlands on my head.

    I know.

You will say all this is nothing to the immediate charge:
I did run away; I did go secretly from your house.

But when he came to me—call him any name you will:
Paris? or Alexander? or the spirit of blood
to haunt this woman?—he came with a goddess at his side;
no weak one. And you—it was criminal—took ship for Crete
and left me there in Sparta in the house, alone.

You see?

I wonder—and I ask this of myself, not you—
why *did* I do it? What made me run away from home
with the stranger, and betray my country and my hearth?
Challenge the goddess then, show your greater strength than
    Zeus'
who has the other gods in his power, and still is slave
to Aphrodite alone. Shall I not be forgiven?
Still you might have some show of argument against me.
When Paris was gone to the deep places of death, below
ground, and the immortal practice on my love was gone,
I should have come back to the Argive ships, left Troy.
I did try to do it, and I have witnesses,
the tower's gatekeepers and the sentinels on the wall,
who caught me again and again as I let down the rope
from the battlements and tried to slip away to the ground.
For Deiphobos, my second husband: he took me away
by force and kept me his wife against the Phrygians' will.

O my husband, can you kill me now and think you kill
in righteousness? I was the bride of force. Before,
I brought their houses to the sorrow of slavery
instead of conquest. Would you be stronger than the gods?
Try, then. But even such ambition is absurd.

CHORUS   O Queen of Troy, stand by your children and your country!
Break down the beguilement of this woman; since she speaks
well, and has done wickedly. This is dangerous.

HECUBA   First, to defend the honor of the gods, and show
that the woman is a scandalous liar. I will not
believe it! Hera and the virgin Pallas Athene
could never be so silly and empty-headed that

Hera would sell Argos to the barbarians,
or Pallas let Athenians be the slaves of Troy.
They went to Ida in girlish emulation, vain
of their own loveliness? Why? Tell me the reason Hera
should fall so much in love with the idea of beauty.
To win some other lord more powerful than Zeus?
Or has Athene marked some god to be her mate,
she, whose virginity is a privilege won from Zeus,
who abjures marriage? Do not trick out your own sins
by calling the gods stupid. No wise man will believe you.
You claim, and I must smile to hear it, that Aphrodite
came at my son's side to the house of Menelaos;
who could have caught up you and your city of Amyklai
and set you in Ilion, moving not from the quiet of heaven.
Nonsense. My son was handsome beyond all other men.
You looked at him, and sense went Cyprian at the sight,
since Aphrodite is nothing but the human lust,
named rightly, since the word of lust begins the god's name.
You saw him in the barbaric splendor of his robes,
gorgeous with gold. It made your senses itch. You thought,
being queen only in Argos, in little luxury,
that once you got rid of Sparta for the Phrygian city
where gold streamed everywhere, you could let extravagance
run wild. No longer were Menelaos and his house
sufficient to your spoiled luxurious appetites.

So much for that. You say my son took you away
by force. What Spartan heard you cry for help? You did
cry out? Or did you? Kastor, your brother, was there, a young
man, and his twin not yet caught up among the stars.
Then when you had reached Troy, and the Argives at your
    heels
came, and the agony of the murderous spears began,
when the reports came in that Menelaos' side ·
was winning, you would praise him, simply to make my son
unhappy at the strength of his love's challenger,
forgetting your husband when the luck went back to Troy.

You worked hard: not to make yourself a better woman,
but to make sure always to be on the winning side.
You claim you tried to slip away with ropes let down
from the ramparts, and this proves you stayed against your
    will?
Perhaps. But when were you ever caught in the strangling
    noose,
caught sharpening a dagger? Which any noble wife
would do, desperate with longing for her lord's return.
Yet over and over again I gave you good advice:
'Make your escape, my daughter; there are other girls
for my sons to marry. I will help you get away
to the ships of the Achaians. Let the Greeks, and us,
stop fighting.' So I argued, but you were not pleased.
Spoiled in the luxury of Alexander's house
you liked foreigners to kiss the ground before your feet.
All that impressed you.

                And now you dare to come outside,
figure fastidiously arranged, to look upon
the same air as your husband, O abominable
heart, who should walk submissively in rags of robes,
shivering with anxiety, head Scythian-cropped,
your old impudence gone and modesty gained at last
by reason of your sinful life.

                O Menelaos,
mark this, the end of my argument. Be true to your
high reputation and to Hellas. Grace both, and kill
Helen. Thus make it the custom toward all womankind
hereafter, that the price of adultery is death.

CHORUS   Menelaos, keep the ancestral honor of your house.
Punish your wife, and purge away from Greece the stigma
on women. You shall seem great even to your enemies.

MENEL.   All you have said falls into line with my own thought.
This woman left my household for a stranger's bed
of her own free will, and all this talk of Aphrodite
is for pure show. Away, and face the stones of the mob.

Atone for the long labors of the Achaians in
the brief act of dying, and know your penance for my shame.

[HELEN *drops before him and embraces his knees.*

HELEN   No, by your knees! I am not guilty of the mind's
infection, which the gods sent. Do not kill! Have pity!

HECUBA   Be true to the memory of all your friends she murdered.
It is for them and for their children that I plead.

[MENELAOS *pushes* HELEN *away.*

MENEL.   Enough, Hecuba. I am not listening to her now.
I speak to my servants: see that she is taken away
to where the ships are beached. She will make the voyage
       home.

HECUBA   But let her not be put in the same ship with you.

MENEL.   What can you mean? That she is heavier than she was?

HECUBA   A man in love once never is out of love again.

MENEL.   Sometimes; when the beloved's heart turns false to him.
Yet it shall be as you wish. She shall not be allowed
in the same ship I sail in. This was well advised.
And once in Argos she must die the vile death earned
by her vile life, and be an example to all women
to live temperately. This is not the easier way;
and yet her execution will tincture with fear
the lust of women even more depraved than she.

[HELEN *is led out,* MENELAOS *following.*

CHORUS   Thus, O Zeus, you betrayed all
to the Achaians: your temple
in Ilion, your misted altar,
the flame of the clotted sacraments,
the smoke of the skying incense,
Pergamon the hallowed,
the ivied ravines of Ida, washed
by the running snow. The utter

peaks that surprise the sun bolts,
shining and primeval place of divinity.

Gone are your sacrifices, the choirs'
glad voices singing to the gods
night long, deep into darkness;
gone the images, gold on wood
laid, the twelves of the sacred moons,
the magic Phrygian number.
Can it be, can it be, my lord, you have forgotten
from your throne high in heaven's
bright air, my city which is ruined
and the flame storm that broke it?

O my dear, my husband,
O wandering ghost
unwashed, unburied; the sea hull must carry me
in the flash of its wings' speed
to Argos, city of horses, where
the stone walls Cyclopian pasture in sky.
The multitudes of our children stand
clinging to the gates and cry through their tears.
And one girl weeps:
'O mother, the Achaians take me away
lonely from your eyes
to the black ship
where the oars dip surf
toward Salamis the blessed,
or the peak between two seas
where Pelops' hold
keeps the gates at the Isthmos.'

Oh that as Menelaos' ship
makes way through the mid-sea
the bright pronged spear immortal of thunder might smash it
far out in the Aigaian,
as in tears, in bondage to Hellas
I am cut from my country;

as she holds the golden mirror
in her hands, girls' grace,
she, God's daughter.
Let him never come home again, to a room in Lakonia
and the hearth of his fathers;
never more to Pitana's streets
and the bronze gates of the Maiden;
since he forgave his shame
and the vile marriage, the sorrows
of great Hellas and the land
watered by Simoeis.

[TALTHYBIOS *returns. His men carry, laid on the shield of*
HEKTOR, *the body of* ASTYANAX.

But see!
Now evils multiply in our land.
Behold, O pitiful wives
of the Trojans. This is Astyanax,
dead, dashed without pity from the towers, and borne
by the Danaans, who murdered him.

TALTHY.   Hecuba, one last vessel of Achilleus' son
remains, manned at the oar sweeps now, to carry back
to the shores of Phthiotis his last spoils of war.
Neoptolemos himself has put to sea. He heard
news of old Peleus in difficulty and the land
invaded by Akastos, son of Pelias.
Such news put speed above all pleasure of delay.
So he is gone, and took with him Andromache,
whose lamentations for her country and farewells
to Hektor's tomb as she departed brought these tears
crowding into my eyes. And she implored that you
bury this dead child, your own Hektor's son, who died
flung from the battlements of Troy. She asked as well
that the bronze-backed shield, terror of the Achaians once,
when the boy's father slung its defense across his side,
be not taken to the hearth of Peleus, nor the room
where the slain child's Andromache must be a bride

once more, to waken memories by its sight, but given
in place of the cedar coffin and stone-chambered tomb
for the boy's burial. He shall be laid in your arms
to wrap the body about with winding sheets, and flowers,
as well as you can, out of that which is left to you.
Since she is gone. Her master's speed prevented her
from giving the rites of burial to her little child.

The rest of us, once the corpse is laid out, and earth
is piled above it, must raise the mast tree, and go.
Do therefore quickly everything that you must do.
There is one labor I myself have spared you. As
we forded on our way here Skamandros' running water,
I washed the body and made clean the wounds. I go
now, to break ground and dig the grave for him, that my
work be made brief, as yours must be, and our tasks end
together, and the ships be put to sea, for home.

HECUBA   Lay down the circled shield of Hektor on the ground:
a hateful thing to look at; it means no love to me.

　　　　　[TALTHYBIOS *and his escort leave. Two soldiers wait.*

Achaians! All your strength is in your spears, not in
the mind. What were you afraid of, that it made you kill
this child so savagely? That Troy, which fell, might be
raised from the ground once more? Your strength meant
　　nothing, then.
When Hektor's spear was fortunate, and numberless
strong hands were there to help him, we were still destroyed.
Now when the city is fallen and the Phrygians slain,
this baby terrified you? I despise the fear
which is pure terror in a mind unreasoning.

O darling child, how mournful was this death. You might
have fallen fighting for your city, grown to man's
age, and married, and with the king's power like a god's,
and died happy, if there is any happiness here.
But no. You grew to where you could see and learn, my child,

yet your mind was not old enough to win advantage
of fortune. How wickedly, poor boy, your fathers' walls,
Apollo's handiwork, have crushed your pitiful head
tended and trimmed to ringlets by your mother's hand,
and the face she kissed once, where the brightness now is
  blood
shining through the torn bones—too horrible to say more.
O little hands, sweet likenesses of Hektor's once,
now you lie broken at the wrists before my feet;
and mouth beloved whose words were once so confident,
you are dead; and all was false, when you would lean across
my bed, and say: 'Mother, when you die I will cut
my long hair in your memory, and at your grave
bring companies of boys my age, to sing farewell.'
It did not happen; now I, a homeless, childless, old
woman must bury your poor corpse, which is so young.
Alas for all the tendernesses, my nursing care,
and all your slumbers gone. What shall the poet say,
what words will he inscribe upon your monument?
*Here lies a little child the Argives killed, because
they were afraid of him.* That? The epitaph of Greek shame.
You will not win your father's heritage, except
for this, which is your coffin now: the brazen shield.

O shield, who guarded the strong shape of Hektor's arm:
the bravest man of all, who wore you once, is dead.
How sweet the impression of his body on your sling,
and at the true circle of your rim the stain of sweat
where in the grind of his many combats Hektor leaned
his chin against you, and the drops fell from his brow!

Take up your work now; bring from what is left some robes
to wrap the tragic dead. The gods will not allow
us to do it right. But let him have what we can give.

That mortal is a fool who, prospering, thinks his life
has any strong foundation; since our fortune's course

of action is the reeling way a madman takes,
and no one person is ever happy all the time.

[HECUBA's *handmaidens bring out from the shelter a basket of*
robes and ornaments. During the scene which follows,
the body of ASTYANAX *is being made ready for burial.*

CHORUS Here are your women, who bring you from the Trojan spoils
such as is left, to deck the corpse for burial.

HECUBA O child, it is not for victory in riding, won
from boys your age, not archery—in which acts our people
take pride, without driving competition to excess—
that your sire's mother lays upon you now these treasures
from what was yours before; though now the accursed of God,
Helen, has robbed you, she who has destroyed as well
the life in you, and brought to ruin all our house.

CHORUS My heart,
you touched my heart, you who were once
a great lord in my city.

HECUBA These Phrygian robes' magnificence you should have worn
at your marriage to some princess uttermost in pride
in all the East, I lay upon your body now.
And you, once so victorious and mother of
a thousand conquests, Hektor's huge beloved shield:
here is a wreath for you, who die not, yet are dead
with this body; since it is better far to honor you
than the armor of Odysseus the wicked and wise.

CHORUS Ah me.
Earth takes you, child;
our tears of sorrow.
Cry aloud, our mother.

HECUBA   Yes

CHORUS the dirge of the dead

HECUBA   ah me

CHORUS evils never to be forgotten.

HECUBA   I will bind up your wounds with bandages, and be
your healer: a wretched one, in name alone, no use.
Among the dead your father will take care of you.

CHORUS   Rip, tear your faces with hands
that beat like oars.
Alas.

HECUBA   Dear women. . . .

CHORUS   Hecuba, speak to us. We are yours. What did you cry aloud?

HECUBA   The gods meant nothing except to make life hard for me,
and of all cities they chose Troy to hate. In vain
we gave them sacrifices. If the very hand
of God had gripped and crushed this city deep in the ground,
we should have disappeared in darkness, and not given
a theme for music, and the songs of men to come.
You may go now, and hide the dead in his poor tomb;
he has those flowers that are the right of the underworld.
I think it makes small difference to the dead, if they
are buried in the tokens of luxury. All this
is an empty glorification left for those who live.

            [*The soldiers take up and carry away the body
of* ASTYANAX.

CHORUS   Sad mother, whose hopes were so huge
for your life. They are broken now.
Born to high blessedness
and a lordly line
your death was horror.

But see, see
on the high places of Ilion
the torchflares whirling in the hands
of men. For Troy
some ultimate agony.

            [TALTHYBIOS *comes back, with numerous men.*

TALTHY.   I call to the captains who have orders to set fire

to the city of Priam: shield no longer in the hand
the shining flame. Let loose the fire upon it. So
with the citadel of Ilion broken to the ground
we can take leave of Troy, in gladness, and go home.

And I speak to you, in second figure of my orders.
Children of Troy, when the lords of the armament sound
the high echoing crash of the trumpet call, then go
to the ships of the Achaians, to be taken away
from this land. And you, unhappiest and aged woman,
go with them. For Odysseus' men are here, to whom
enslaved the lot exiles you from your native land.

HECUBA   Ah, wretched me. So this is the unhappy end
and goal of all the sorrows I have lived. I go
forth from my country and a city lit with flames.
Come, aged feet; make one last weary struggle, that I
may hail my city in its affliction. O Troy, once
so huge over all Asia in the drawn wind of pride,
your very name of glory shall be stripped away.
They are burning you, and us they drag forth from our land
enslaved. O gods! Do I call upon those gods for help?
I cried to them before now, and they would not hear.
Come then, hurl ourselves into the pyre. How sweet
to die in the flaming ruins of our fathers' house!

TALTHY.   Unhappy creature, ecstatic in your sorrows! Men,
take her, spare not. She is Odysseus' property.
You have orders to deliver her into his hands.

HECUBA   O sorrow.
Kronion, Zeus, lord of Phrygia,
prince of our house, have you seen
the dishonor done to the seed of Dardanos?

CHORUS   He has seen, but the great city
is a city no more, it is gone. There is no Troy.

HECUBA   O sorrow.
Ilion flares.

The chambers of Pergamon take fire,
the citadel and the wall's high places.

CHORUS   Our city fallen to the spear
fades as smoked winged in the sky,
halls hot in the swept fire
and the fierce lances.

HECUBA   O soil where my children grew.

CHORUS   Alas.

HECUBA   O children, hear me; it is your mother who calls.

CHORUS   They are dead you cry to. This is a dirge.

HECUBA   I lean my old body against the earth
and both hands beat the ground.

CHORUS   I kneel to the earth, take up
the cry to my own dead,
poor buried husband.

HECUBA   We are taken, dragged away

CHORUS   a cry of pain, pain

HECUBA   under the slave's roof

CHORUS   away from my country.

HECUBA   Priam, my Priam. Dead
graveless, forlorn,
you know not what they have done to me.

CHORUS   Now dark, holy death
in the brutal butchery closed his eyes.

HECUBA   O gods' house, city beloved

CHORUS   Alas

HECUBA   you are given the red flame and the spear's iron.

CHORUS   You will collapse to the dear ground and be nameless.

HECUBA   Ash as the skyward smoke wing
piled will blot from my sight the house where I lived once.

CHORUS   Lost shall be the name on the land,
all gone, perished. Troy, city of sorrow,
is there no longer.

HECUBA   Did you see, did you hear?

CHORUS   The crash of the citadel.

HECUBA   The earth shook, riven

CHORUS   to engulf the city.

HECUBA   O
shaking, tremulous limbs
this is the way. Forward:
into the slave's life.

CHORUS   Mourn for the ruined city, then go away
to the ships of the Achaians.

             [HECUBA *is led away, and all go out, leaving the*
stage empty.

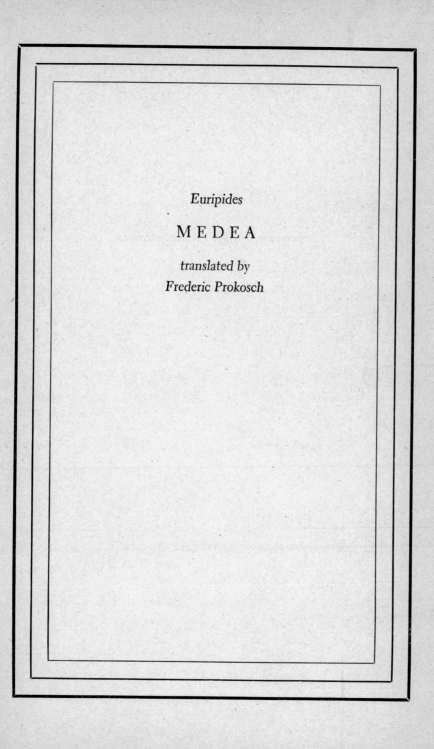

Euripides

M E D E A

translated by
Frederic Prokosch

The princess MEDEA of Colchis fell in love with JASON, who had come to her country in quest of the Golden Fleece, and aided him in his enterprise even to the extent of betraying her father, murdering her brother, and leaving her home for ever in order to live with JASON in Greece. After many vicissitudes they arrived at the court of PELIAS, who had sent JASON on his expedition. Here MEDEA contrived that PELIAS should be barbarously killed by his own daughters. The pair fled the country and took refuge in Corinth, where JASON abandoned MEDEA in order to marry GLAUKE, the daughter of KING KREON.

DRAMATIS PERSONÆ:

MEDEA   ATTENDANT

JASON   NURSE

KREON   AEGEUS

MEDEA'S CHILDREN

A MESSENGER

CHORUS OF CORINTHIAN WOMEN

MEDEA

SCENE: *Corinth, before the house of Medea.*

[The NURSE enters from the house.

NURSE Oh how I wish that famous ship, the Argo, had never made its way through the blue Symplegades to the land of Colchis! How I wish the pine tree had never been felled in the glades of Pelion, and never been hewn into oars for the heroes who went to fetch the Golden Fleece for Pelias! For then my mistress, Medea, would never have sailed to the towers of the land of Iolcos, her heart on fire with love for Jason! Nor would she ever have beguiled the daughters of Pelias into slaying their father, nor have come to live in Corinth with her husband and children. For a long time she found favor with the people here in the land of exile; and she did all things in complete accord with Jason; and indeed it is this— when a woman stands loyally by a man—which brings to men the only sure salvation. But now their love has fallen into decay; and there's hatred everywhere. For Jason has betrayed his children and my mistress; he has taken a royal bride to his bed, the daughter of Kreon, who is the ruler of this land. And poor Medea, scorned and deserted, can do nothing but appeal to the vows they made to one another, and remind him of the eternal pledge they made with their right hands clasped. And she calls upon the gods to witness how Jason is repaying her for her love. She lies half famished; her body is bowed utterly with grief, wasting away the whole day long. So it has been since she learned that he has betrayed her. Never stirring an eye, never lifting her gaze from the ground; and when her friends speak to her in warning she no more listens than a rock listens, or the surging sea wave. Only now and then she turns her snowy neck and quietly laments, and utters her father's name, and the name of her land and home, which she deserted when she followed the man who now brings her such dishonor. Pitiful woman! She has learned at last through all her sufferings how lucky are those who have never lost their native land. She has come to feel a hatred for her children, and no longer wants to see them. Indeed, I fear she may be moving toward some dreadful plan; for her heart is violent. She will never submit to this cruel treatment. I know her well: her anger is great; and I know that any man who makes an enemy of her will have it hard. . . . Look; here come the children; they have been playing. Little they know of their mother's misery; little the hearts of the young can guess of sorrow!

[*The* ATTENDANT *brings in* MEDEA's *children.*

ATTEND. Why are you standing here, in front of the gates? You've been maid for so many years to my mistress; why have you left her alone, then, only to stand outside the gates and lament?

NURSE Listen, old man, who watch over Jason's sons! It's a sad, sad thing for faithful servants like us to see our master's fortunes meet with disaster; it stirs us to the heart. I am so lost in grief, now, that a longing came over me to step outside the gates, and tell the whole wide world and the heavens of my mistress's sorrows!

ATTEND. Poor lady! Hasn't she ceased her weeping yet?

NURSE Ceased? Far from it! This is only the beginning; there is far more to come.

ATTEND. Poor, foolish lady; though I shouldn't call her that; but how little she knows of this latest trouble!

NURSE What do you mean, old man? Come! Don't be afraid to tell me!

ATTEND. Nothing at all; I should never have mentioned it.

NURSE No, no; by your wise old beard I beg you, don't hide anything from your fellow servant! Tell me; and, if you wish, I'll keep it secret.

ATTEND. Well, as I was passing the usual place where the old men sit playing draughts, down by the holy fountain of Pirene, I happened to overhear one of them saying that Kreon, King of the land, intends to send these children, and their mother from Corinth, far away into exile. But whether it was the truth he was speaking, I do not know; I hope and pray it wasn't the truth.

NURSE And will Jason allow this thing to happen to his sons, even though he is on bad terms with their mother?

ATTEND. Old ties give way to new ones; and his love for this family of ours is dying away.

NURSE Oh, it looks dark indeed for us; new sorrows are being added to old ones, even before the old ones have faded!

ATTEND. Be still, be still; don't whisper a word of it. This isn't the proper time to tell our mistress.

NURSE O little children, do you hear how your father feels toward you? May evil befall him! But no; he is still my master. Yet how cruelly he has betrayed his dear ones!

ATTEND. And which of us has not done the same? Haven't you learned long ago, my dear, how each man loves himself far more than his neighbor? Some, perhaps, from honest motives; some for private gain. So you see how Jason deserts his children for the pleasure of his new bride.

NURSE Go back into the house, children; all will be well. Try to keep them out of the way, old man; keep them far from their mother as long as she feels this desperate anger. I have already seen the fire in her eyes as she watched them, almost as though she were wishing them harm. I am sure her anger won't end till she has found a victim. Let's hope the victim will be an enemy, and not a friend!

[*Within the house.*

MEDEA Lost, oh lost! I am lost
In my sufferings. I wish, oh I wish
That I could die. . . .

NURSE   My dear children, what did I tell you?
        Your mother's mind is filled with the wildest
        Fancies; her heart is wild with anger!
        Run quickly back into the house.
        Keep out of her sight. Do not
        Go near her. Beware of the wildness
        And bitterness of her heart!
        Go, quickly, quickly!
        I can feel that her fury will rise
        And redouble! I can hear
        In that cry the rising thunderstorm,
        I can feel the approach of thunder and lightning!
        Oh what will she do, in the pride
        And torment of her soul? What
        Evil thing will she do?

        [*The* ATTENDANT *takes the children into the house.*

                                                    [*Within.*

MEDEA   Oh, I have suffered
        And suffered enough for all these tears!
        I call destruction upon you, all, all of you,
        Sons of a doomed mother, and the father too!
        May ruin fall on the entire house!

NURSE   I am full of pity,
        Full of deep pity for you! Yet why
        Do the children share their father's crime?
        Why should you hate them? O my poor children,
        I fear some outrage will befall you!
        Yes, strange and terrible is the temper of princes.
        There is none they need to obey;
        There is none that can check them:
        There is nothing to control
        The madness of their mood.
        How much better off are the rest of us
        Who've been taught to live equally
        With our neighbors! All I wish
        Is to grow old quietly, not in pride,
        But only in humble security.

It's the moderate thing that always sounds
Best to our ears; and indeed it is
The moderate thing that is best in practice.
For power grows beyond control;
Power brings comfort to no man.
And I say, the greater the power, the greater
The ruin when it finally falls.

[Enter the CHORUS of Corinthian women. The following
lines are chanted.

CHORUS   I heard the voice,
I heard the loud lament
Of the pitiful lady from Colchis:
Oh tell me, mother, is she still
Unquiet? As I stood
By the house with the double gates
I heard the sound of weeping from within.
I grieve for the sorrow of this family
Which I have come to love.

NURSE   There is no family left; it has gone,
It has gone forever. The master now
Has a royal bride in the bed beside him,
And our mistress is withering away
In her chamber, and finds no solace
Or warmth in words
That friends can utter.

[Within.

MEDEA   Oh how I wish that a stroke of lightning
Would fall from heaven and shatter my head!
Why should I live any longer?
Death would bring release; in death
I could leave behind me the horror of living.

CHORUS   Did you hear, almighty Zeus?
O earth, O heaven, did you hear
The cry of woe this woman has uttered?
Oh why, poor lady, should you long
For that unutterable haven of rest?

Death only can bring it; and death comes only too soon!
No, no, there is no need to pray for death.
And if your man is drawn
To a new love, remember,
Such things occur often; do not feel hurt.
For God will be your ultimate friend and judge
In this as in all matters.
So do not mourn too much,
Do not waste away in sorrow
For the loss of the one you loved!

[Within.

MEDEA   Great Themis, O lady Artemis, look down
On all I am suffering; and suffering in spite
Of all the vows my husband made me.
I pray that I may some day see
Him and his bride brought down to ruin
And their palace ruined for all the wrong
They dared to do me without cause.
O my own father, my own country,
Shameful it was of me to leave you,
And to have killed my brother before I left you!

NURSE   Do you hear what she says? Do you hear
How loudly she cries to Themis, the goddess of promises,
And to Zeus, whom men think of as the Emperor of Vows?
One thing I know. It is no small thing
That draws such anger from our mistress!

CHORUS   Let her come forth and see us,
Let her listen to our words of warning,
Let her lay aside the rage and violence of her heart;
Never shall I refuse to help my friends,
Never shall they turn to me in vain.
Go, go, and bring her from the house
That we may see her; speak kindly to her!
Hurry, before she does some violent thing.
I feel her passion rising to a new pitch.

NURSE   Yes; I shall go; but I deeply doubt
Whether I can persuade my mistress.

Still, I shall gladly go and try;
Though she glares upon her servants, those
That approach and dare to speak to her,
With the fiery look of a lioness with cubs!
You would be right, I think,
If you called both ignorant
And trivial those poets of old who wrote
Their songs for festivities and banquets,
Graceful and pleasant sounds for men
Who lived in gaiety and leisure.
For none of them learned a way
For the song or the musicians
To still man's suffering. And suffering it is
From which all killing springs, and all calamity
Which falls on the homes of men.
Yet it would be a blessing, surely,
If songs could heal the wounds which sorrow
Inflicts on men! What good is music
And singing at an idle banquet? It seems to me
That men who are sitting at the banquet table
Have pleasure enough already . . .

[*The* NURSE *goes into the house.*

CHORUS   I heard a cry that was heavy and sick with sorrow.
Loud in her bitterness she cries
On the man who betrayed her marriage bed!
Full of her wrongs she cries
To the gods, to Themis, to the bride of Zeus,
To the Keeper of Vows, who brought her away
To the shores of Greece which face the shores of Asia,
Through the straits at night to the gateway opening
On the unlimited salty sea.

[*Toward the end of this song,* MEDEA *enters from the house.*

MEDEA   Ladies of Corinth, I have come forth from my house, lest you should feel bitterness toward me; for I know that men often acquire a bad name for their pride—not only the pride they show in public, but also the pride of retirement; those who live in solitude, as I do, are frequently thought to be proud. For there is no justice in the view one man takes of another, often hating him before he has suffered wrong, hating him even before he has seen his true character. Therefore a foreigner above all should fit into the ways of a city. Not even a native citizen, I think, should risk offending his neighbors by rudeness or pride.

But this new thing has fallen upon me so unexpectedly, my strength is broken. O my friends, my life is shattered; my heart no longer longs for the blessings of life, but only for death! There was one man through whom I came to see the world's whole beauty: and that was my husband; and he has turned out utterly evil. O women, of all creatures that live and reflect, certainly it is we who are the most luckless. First of all, we pay a great price to purchase a husband; and thus submit our bodies to a perpetual tyrant. And everything depends on whether our choice is good or bad—for divorce is not an honorable thing, and we may not refuse to be married. And then a wife is plunged into a way of life and behavior entirely new to her, and must learn what she never learned at home—she must learn by a kind of subtle intuition how to manage the man who lies beside her. And if we have the luck to handle all these things with tact and success, and if the husband is willing to live at our side without resentment, then life can become happy indeed. But if not, I'd rather be dead. A man who is disgusted with what he finds at home, goes forth to put an end to his boredom, and turns to a friend or companion of his own age; while we at home continue to think of him, and of him only.

And yet people say that we live in security at home, while the men go forth to war. How wrong they are! Listen: I'd rather be sent three times over to the battlefront than give birth to a single child.

Still, my friends, I realize that all this applies not to you but to me; you after all have a city of your own, and a family home, and a certain pleasure in life, and the company of your friends. But I am utterly lonely, an exile, cast off by my own husband—nothing but a captive brought here from a foreign land—without a mother or brother, without a single kinsman who can give me refuge in this sea of disaster. Therefore, my ladies, I ask only one thing of you: promise me silence. If I can find some way, some cunning scheme of revenge against my husband for all that he has done to me, and against the man who gave away his daughter, and against the daughter who is now my husband's wife: then please be silent. For though a woman is timid in everything else, and weak, and terrified at the sight of a sword: still, when things go wrong in this thing of love, no heart is so fearless as a woman's; no heart is so filled with the thought of blood.

CHORAG. Yes; I promise this. You will be right, Medea, in avenging yourself on your husband. It does not surprise me to see you lost in despair . . . But look! I see Kreon, our king, approaching: he will have some news to tell us.

[*Enter* KREON, *with his following.*

KREON Listen to me, Medea! You, with your angry looks and all that bitterness against your husband: I order you to leave my kingdom! I order you to go with both your children into exile, and immediately. This is my decree. And I will not return to my house until I have hurled you beyond the borders of my kingdom.

MEDEA Oh, now I am lost indeed! This is the end of all things for me! Now my enemies are bearing down on me in all their force; and I have no refuge left in this hour of ruin. And yet, let me ask you this one thing, Kreon: why is it, Kreon, you are sending me away?

KREON I am afraid of you. I need no longer pretend otherwise. I am afraid you will do my daughter some mortal harm. And I have many reasons for being afraid of this. You are a cunning woman, Medea, expert in all kinds of magic, so I hear. And you are enraged by the loss of your husband's love. I have also heard them say that you are planning some kind of mischief against Jason and the bride, and the bride's father, myself, as well. It is against these things I take precautions. I tell you, Medea, I'd rather incur your hatred now than be soft-hearted and later learn to regret it.

MEDEA   This is not the first time, Kreon! Many times before has this strange reputation done me harm. A sensible man should never nowadays bring up his children to be too clever or exceptional. For one thing, these talents never bring them profit; for another, they end by bringing envy and hatred from others. If you present new ideas to a group of fools, they'll think you ignorant as well as idle. And if your fame should come to exceed the established reputations, they'll hate you for it. This has been my own experience. Some think me clever, and resent it; some think me not so very clever after all, and disapprove. And you, Kreon, are somehow afraid that I may do something to harm you. But you need not worry. It isn't for someone like me to quarrel with kings. After all, why should I? You haven't harmed me. You've allowed your daughter to marry as you saw fit. I hate my husband, certainly; but as for you, I feel you have acted reasonably enough. I don't grudge you for your good fortune. I wish you luck with your daughter's marriage, Kreon, but beg you only, let me live on in this land. I have been wronged, but I shall remain quiet, and submit to those above me.

KREON   Your words are gentle enough, Medea. Yet in my heart I can't help dreading that you are planning some evil; and I trust you now even less than before. It is easier to deal with a quick-tempered man or woman than with one who is subtle and soft-spoken. No. You must go at once. Make no more speeches. It is settled. You are my enemy, and there is nothing you can do to prolong your stay in my country.

MEDEA   I implore you! By your knees, by your newly wed daughter!

KREON   You are wasting your words. You will never persuade me.

MEDEA   Then you'll drive me out without listening to my prayers?

KREON	I shall; for I love my own family more than you.
MEDEA	O my country! How my heart goes back to you now!
KREON	I, too, love my country above all things, except my children.
MEDEA	How cruelly passionate love can deal with men!
KREON	And yet, it all depends on the luck men have.
MEDEA	O Zeus, never forget the man who caused this!
KREON	Go now; go. Spare me this useless trouble.
MEDEA	No trouble, no pain, nothing has been spared me!
KREON	Soon one of my men shall lead you away by force.
MEDEA	Not that, Kreon, not that! I beg you, Kreon.
KREON	It seems you insist on creating a disturbance.
MEDEA	I will go. I will go. That is not what I intended.
KREON	Why all this commotion, then? What is it you want?
MEDEA	Let me stay here just a single day longer, Kreon. Let me stay and think over where I shall go in exile, and how I shall find a living for my children, for whom their father has completely failed to provide. Take pity on them, Kreon! You too have children of your own; you too must have a soft place in your heart for them. What happens to me now no longer matters; I only grieve for the suffering that will come to my children.
KREON	I am not a cruel man, Medea. I have often made blunders, out of sheer compassion. Even now I feel I am making a mistake. All the same, have it your way. But let me warn you! If tomorrow at sunrise still finds you and your children within the frontiers of my land, you shall die for it. That is my verdict; it is final. So stay this one day longer, if you must. One day is not enough to bring disaster.

[*Exit* KREON *with his following.*]

CHORAG.	Pitiful woman! Oh we pity The sorrows you suffer!

Where will you turn now? Who can help you?
What home remains, what land
Is left to save you from destruction?
O Medea, you have been hurled by heaven
Into an ocean of despair.

MEDEA   Everything has gone wrong. None can deny it. But not quite everything is lost; don't give up hope, my friends! There still are troubles in store for the young bride, and for the bridegroom too. Do you think I would have fawned on that old man without some plan and purpose? Certainly not. I would never have touched him with my hands. But now, although he could have crushed all my plans by instant exile, he has made a fatal error; he has given me one day's reprieve. One day in which I can bring death to the three creatures that I loathe: the father, the bride, my husband. There are many manners of death which I might use; I don't quite know yet which to try. Shall I set fire to the bridal mansion? Or shall I sharpen a sword and steal into the chamber to the wedding bed and plunge it into their hearts? One thing stands in my way. If I am caught making my way into the bridal room on such an errand, I shall surely be put to death, and my foes will end by triumphing over me. Better to take the shortest way, the way I am best trained in: better to bring them down with poison. That I will do, then. And after that? Suppose them dead. What city will take me in then? What friend will offer me shelter in his land, and safety, and a home? None. Then best to wait a little longer; perhaps some sure defense will appear, and I can set about this murder in stealth and stillness. And if no help should come from fate, and even if death is certain, still I can take at last the sword in my own hand and go forth boldly to the crime, and kill. Yes, by that dark Queen whom I revere above all others, and whom I now invoke to help me, by Hecate who dwells in my most secret chamber: I swear no man shall injure me and not regret it. I will turn their marriage into sorrow and anguish! Go now, go forward to this dangerous deed! The time has come for courage. Remember the suffering they caused you! Never

shall you be mocked because of this wedding of Jason's, you
who are sprung from a noble father and whose grandfather
was the Sun-God himself! You have the skill; what is more,
you are a woman: and it's always a woman who is incapable
of a noble deed, yet expert in every kind of mischief!

CHORUS   [STROPHE 1

The sacred rivers are flowing back to their sources!
The order of the world is being reversed!
Now it is men who have grown deceitful,
Men who have broken their sacred vows.
The name of woman shall rise to favor
Again; and women once again
Shall rise and regain their honor: never
Again shall ill be said of women!

Those poets of old shall cease at last   [ANTISTROPHE 1
To sing of our faithlessness. Never
On us did Phoebus, the god of music,
Lavish the talents of the lyre,
Else I should long ago have sung
A song of rebuttal to the race
Of men: for the years have many things
To tell of them as well as of us!

You sailed away from your father's dwelling   [STROPHE 2
With your heart on fire, Medea! And you passed
Between the rocky gates of the seas;
And now you sleep on a foreign shore,
In a lonely bed: now you are driven
Forth, and far away from the land
Once more you go in exile and dishonor!

Gone is the dignity of vows,   [ANTISTROPHE 2
Gone from great Hellas the sense of honor.
It has flown and vanished in the skies.
And now no father's dwelling house
Stands as a refuge from this storm!

Now another princess lies
In the bed which once was yours, and rules your home!

[As the CHORUS approaches the end of the song,
JASON enters.

JASON This is not the first time I have noticed how difficult it is to deal with a violent temper. Ah, Medea, if you had patiently accepted the will of our ruler, you might have stayed on quietly in this land and this house. But now your pointless complaints are driving you into exile. Not that I minded them myself; I didn't mind it at all when you called Jason an evil man. But, considering your references to the King himself, you may count yourself lucky that your punishment is exile. Personally, I have always done my best to calm the King's anger, and would have liked to see you stay on here. But you refused to give up this sort of folly, and kept on slandering him; with the result that you are facing banishment. Nevertheless, in spite of your behavior, I feel inclined to do you a favor; I have come to make some sort of provision for you and the children, my dear, so that you won't be penniless when you are in exile; for I know that exile will not be easy. And even though you hate me, Medea, my thoughts of you will continue to be friendly as always.

MEDEA You filthy coward! That is the only name I can find for you, you and your utter lack of manliness! And now you, who are the worst of my enemies, now you too have chosen to come to me! No; it isn't courage which brings you, nor recklessness in facing the friends you have injured; it is worse than that, it is the worst of all human vices: shamelessness. Still, you did well to come to me, for now I can ease my heart by reviling you: and perhaps you too will suffer as you listen.

Let me begin, then, at the very beginning. I saved your life; every Greek who sailed with you on the Argo knows I saved you, when you were sent to tame the fire-breathing bulls and to yoke them, and to sow the deadly fields. Yes, and I killed the many-folded serpent who lay guarding the Golden

Fleece, forever wakeful, coil upon coil. And I raised a beacon of light to bring you to safety. Freely I deserted my own father and my own home; and followed you to Iolcos, to the hills of Pelion; and all this time my love was stronger than my reason. And I brought death to Pelias by his own daughters' hands; I utterly destroyed the household. All of these things I did for you, traitor! And you forsook me, and took another wife, even though I had borne your children. Had you been childless, one might have pardoned your wish for a second wedding. But now all my faith in your vows has vanished. I do not know whether you imagine that the gods by whom you swore have disappeared, or that new rules are now in vogue in such matters; for you must be aware that you have broken your vows to me. Oh this poor right hand, which you so often pressed! These knees, which you so often used to embrace! And all in vain, for it was an evil man that touched me! How wildly all my hopes have fallen through! . . .

Come, Jason, I shall speak to you quite frankly, as though we still were friends. Can I possibly expect any kindness from someone like you? Still, let us assume that I can: it will only make you appear still more ignoble. Very well. Where shall I go? Home to my father? Home to him and the land I betrayed when I followed you? Or back to the pitiful daughters of Pelias? What a fine welcome they would give me, who arranged the death of their own father! So this is how it now stands with me. I am loathed by my friends at home; and for your sake I made enemies of others whom I need never have harmed. And now, to reward me for all this, look, look, how doubly happy you've made me among the women of Hellas! Look what a fine, trustworthy husband I have had in you! And now I am to be cast forth into exile, in utter misery, alone with my children and without a single friend! Oh, this will be a shameful shadow upon you, as you lie in your wedding bed! That your own children, and their mother, who saved your life, should go wandering around the world like beggars! . . . O Zeus, why have you given us a way to tell true gold from the counterfeit, but no way, no emblem branded on a man's body whereby we can tell the true man from the false?

CHORAG.   Dreadful is the anger, and past all healing, when lovers in fury turn against each other!

JASON   The time has come, it seems, when I must speak, and speak well, and like a good helmsman reef up my sail and weather the tempest of your tongue . . . And since you dwell so heavily on all the favors you did me, Medea, I am certain that I owe the safety of my voyage to Aphrodite alone among gods and men. Not that I doubt your skill; but all the same, I prefer not to dwell on this notion that love, with all its irresistible power, compelled you to save my life. I don't think we need go into details. I admit that you meant well, and did your best. But when it comes to this matter of my safety, let me point out that you got rather more than you gave. First of all, instead of living in a barbaric land, you've come to Greece and enjoyed contact with a country where justice and law prevail, and not brute force; and what is more, the Greeks thought rather highly of you. You even acquired a certain fame here. Whereas, if you had stayed on in that outer fringe of the world, your name would now be quite unknown. Frankly, I'd rather have real fame and distinction than mighty stores of gold in my halls or the talent to sing more sweetly than Orpheus. That is my answer to your version of all my labors; remember, it was you who brought up this matter.

As for your bitter attack on my marriage with the princess, I think I can prove first of all that it was a shrewd move; secondly, a thoroughly sober one; and finally, that I did it in your interest and that of your children . . . Wait! Please remain calm . . . Since I had come from Iolcos involved in every kind of trouble, and an exile, what could be luckier for me than marriage with the King's own daughter? It was not—since it is this that seems to rankle in you—it was not that I grew weary of going to bed with you, and began to look around for a new wife. Nor was it that I was anxious to have more children. The two we have are quite enough; I don't complain. No, it was this, first of all: that we might live in comfort, and not in poverty. Believe me, I have learned how a man's friends desert him the moment he is penniless . . . And then I wanted to bring up my sons in a manner worthy of my position; I even hoped that by having more sons, who would live as brothers to yours, we might draw the entire family into harmony, and all be happy. You yourself need no more children; but I would do well to help the sons I have through the sons I hope to have. Do you disagree with all this? You would agree if it weren't for this matter of love which rankles in you. But you women have developed such curious notions: you think that all is well as long as your life at night runs smoothly. But if something happens which upsets your way of love, then all that you once found lovely and desirable you now find hateful. Believe me, it would have been better far if men could have thought up some other way of producing children, and done away with women; then no evil would ever have come to men.

CHORAG. O Jason, you have given this speech of yours a convincing enough air; and yet I somehow feel, though perhaps I shouldn't say so, that you have acted wickedly in betraying your wife.

MEDEA I suppose I am different in many ways from most people, for I feel that the worst punishment should fall on the man who speaks brilliantly for an evil cause, the man who knows he can make an evil thing sound plausible and who dares to do so. And still, such a man isn't really so very wise after all. Listen, Jason. You need not bring forth these clever phrases and specious arguments; for a single word from me will destroy you. Consider: had you not been a coward, Jason, you would have spoken frankly to me first, and not concealed your wedding plans from the one who loved you.

JASON And you, no doubt, would have done all you could to help me, if I had spoken of this matter: you, who even now cannot control the rage in your heart.

MEDEA   It wasn't this that restrained you. No. It was that you thought it might not be altogether proper, as you grew older, to have a foreign wife.

JASON   You may be quite sure of one thing, Medea. It was not because of any woman that I made this royal marriage. It was as I said before: because I wanted security for you, and also to be the father of royal children bound by blood to our two children: a thing which would have brought welfare to all of us.

MEDEA   I don't want the kind of welfare that is brought by suffering. I don't want the kind of safety which ends in sorrow.

JASON   Reflect on that opinion, Medea; it will make you wiser. Don't search for sorrow in prosperity. Don't keep looking for pain in a piece of good luck.

MEDEA   Go on; mock me. You at least have a home to turn to. But I am going into exile, and alone.

JASON   It was you who made this choice; there is no one else to blame.

MEDEA   How so? By marrying and deserting you?

JASON   You called down an evil curse on the royal house.

MEDEA   I have brought a curse to your own house too, I think.

JASON   Well, I don't propose to go into this any further. But if you'd like to take along some of my money into exile, for your own need and that of the children, please say so. I am prepared to be generous on this point, and even to give you letters to friends of mine abroad who will treat you well. It would be madness for you to refuse this offer. It will be to your own gain, Medea, if you give up your anger.

MEDEA   I will never accept favors from friends of yours; and I'll accept nothing from you, so please don't offer it. Gifts from a coward bring luck to no one.

JASON   Very well then. I call upon the gods to witness that I have tried in every way to help you and the children. It is you who refuse my offers. It is you who are stubbornly rejecting your friends. And for this, Medea, you will surely suffer.

MEDEA   Please go! I can see you are longing to be with your new sweetheart. Aren't you lingering too long outside her bedroom? Go, and taste the joys of your wedding. Go, and God help you; you may end by regretting this kind of wedding!

[JASON goes out.

CHORUS   When love has passed its limits   [STROPHE 1
It brings no longer good:
It brings no peace or comfort to any soul.
Yet while she still moves mildly there is no fire
So sweet as that which is lit by the goddess of love.
Oh never, upon me, Cypris,
Send forth from your golden bow
The unerring arrow poisoned with desire!

Let my heart be temperate: for that   [ANTISTROPHE 1
Is the wisest gift of the gods.
Let not that terrible goddess drive
Me to jealousy or rage! Oh let me never
Be one of those who incessantly are driven
To some new, forbidden longing!
Let her guide us gently toward the man we choose;
Let her bless our beds with repose.

O my country, my own home   [STROPHE 2
Let me never leave my city,
Let me never lose my way
In that dark and pitiless life
Where each new day brings sorrow!
O, let me first succumb
To death, yes, let me die
Before I suffer the hopeless
Grief of the loss of a home!

I have seen it with my own eyes,   [ANTISTROPHE 2
I have heard my own heart tell me:
There is no city, no,

No friend who will give you pity
In the hour of your deepest woe.
O, let him perish in darkness
Who is faithless to his friends
And lets his heart stay frozen!
Let no such man be my friend!

[MEDEA *has been sitting in despair on the stairway during
this song.* AEGEUS *enters.*

AEGEUS   Joy to you, Medea! This is the best kind of greeting between old friends!

MEDEA   And joy to you, Aegeus, son of Pandion, King of Athens! How does it happen that you have set foot in this country?

AEGEUS   I have come from the ancient oracles of Phoebus.

MEDEA   And why did you visit that great centre of prophecy?

AEGEUS   I went to ask how I might bring fertility to my seed.

MEDEA   Tell me, has your life been childless hitherto?

AEGEUS   Some divine visitation, I think, has made me childless.

MEDEA   Have you a wife, or not?

AEGEUS   I have, Medea.

MEDEA   And what did Phoebus tell you about begetting children?

AEGEUS   Words far too subtle for any man to understand.

MEDEA   Is it proper for you to tell me what he said?

AEGEUS   Certainly; what I need is cleverness like yours.

MEDEA   Then what were the God's words? Tell me, if I may hear them.

AEGEUS   That I shouldn't loosen the hanging neck of the wine skin . . .

MEDEA   Till when? What must you do first? Where must you go?

AEGEUS   Till I have returned again to my native home.

MEDEA	Then why have you come sailing to this land?
AEGEUS	There is a man called Pittheus, who is King of Troezen.
MEDEA	A son of Pelops, so they say, and a man of piety.
AEGEUS	I want to discuss this oracle of the God with him.
MEDEA	He is a man full of skill and experience in these matters.
AEGEUS	As well as the dearest of my old spear-bearing friends.
MEDEA	Good luck to you then! And success to your wishes!
AEGEUS	But why do you look so pale and woebegone?
MEDEA	O Aegeus, my husband has turned out to be the vilest of men!
AEGEUS	What do you mean? Tell me what has made you so unhappy.
MEDEA	Jason is wronging me, and utterly without provocation.
AEGEUS	What has he done? Tell me more clearly, Medea.
MEDEA	He has taken another wife to take my place.
AEGEUS	Does he really dare to do such a cruel thing!
MEDEA	He does indeed! He loved me once, but no longer.
AEGEUS	Has he fallen in love? Has he wearied of your bed?
MEDEA	Ah, he's a great lover! But never true to his love. . . .
AEGEUS	Let him go, then, if he is really as bad as you say.
MEDEA	He's in love with the idea of marrying royalty.
AEGEUS	And who is the father of this princess? Please go on.
MEDEA	Her father is Kreon, King of Corinth.
AEGEUS	Indeed, Medea, I understand your grief.
MEDEA	I am lost. And there is more: I am being banished!
AEGEUS	Banished? By whom? This is something new you tell me.
MEDEA	Kreon is driving me from Corinth into banishment.
AEGEUS	Does Jason consent? This is a contemptible thing.

MEDEA   Not in so many words, but he has not really opposed it. O Aegeus, I beg you, I implore you, by your beard and by your knees, I beseech you, have pity on me! Have pity on a friend who is in trouble! Don't let me wander about in exile! Let me come to your land of Athens, let me find refuge in your halls! And there, with heaven's consent, you may find your love grow fertile and be blessed with children, and your life at last end happily. You don't know, Aegeus, how good your luck has been, for I shall end your sterility; I shall bring power to your seed; for I know of drugs that can do this.

AEGEUS   There are many reasons, my dear lady, why I should like to do this for you: first, for the sake of the children you promise me (for in that matter, frankly, I'm at my wits' end). But let me state my position. If you arrive in Athens, I shall stand by you as I am bound to do. But I must warn you first, my friend: I won't agree to take you with me. If you arrive at my halls of your own accord, you shall live there in safety; I shan't surrender you to anyone. But you yourself must manage your escape from this land, for I have no wish to incur ill will among my friends here.

MEDEA   Very well. So be it. Make me a formal pledge on this, and I shall be satisfied.

AEGEUS   Do you distrust me? What is it that troubles you?

MEDEA   I trust you, yes. But the house of Pelias, and Kreon as well, both detest me. If you are bound to me by an oath, then, when they come to drag me away from your country, I know you will remain true to your vow and stand by me. Whereas, if it's only a promise, you might not be in a position to resist their demands; for I am weak, and they have both money and a royal house to help them.

AEGEUS   You show considerable foresight in these matters, I must say. Still, if you insist, I shan't refuse you. From my own point of view, too, it might be just as well to have an excuse like this oath to present to your enemies . . . Now name your gods.

MEDEA   Swear by the plain of Earth, and by my father's father Helios, the Sun God, and in one sweeping phrase by the whole host of the gods. . . .

AEGEUS Swear to do what, or not to do what? Tell me.

MEDEA Swear that you will never cast me from your land, nor ever, as long as you live, allow an enemy of mine to carry me away.

AEGEUS I swear by the Earth, and by the holy light of Helios, the Sun God, and by the entire host of the gods, that I will abide by the terms you have just made.

MEDEA Very well. And if you should fail, what curse are you willing to incur?

AEGEUS Whatever happens to such as disregard the gods.

MEDEA Go in peace, Aegeus. All is well, now; I shall arrive in your city as soon as I possibly can—after I have done what I must do, and accomplished what I desire.

[AEGEUS *goes out.*

CHORAG. May Hermes, the God of Travelers,
Go with you on your way, Aegeus,
And bring you safely home!
And may you find the thing you have been seeking
For so long; you seem to be a generous man.

MEDEA O Zeus, and Justice who are the child of Zeus, and light of the Sun God! Now, my friends, has come the hour of my triumph! Now I have started on the road; now I know that I shall bring revenge on the ones I hate. For at the very moment that my doom looked darkest of all, this man Aegeus appeared, like a harbor for all my hopes; and to him I can fasten the cable of my ship when I come to the town and fortress of Pallas Athene. And now let me tell you all of my plans. Listen; they will not be idle words, or pleasant. I shall send a servant to Jason and ask for an interview. And when he comes, I shall be soft and conciliatory; I shall tell him that I've thought better of it; that I agree; that even the treacherous marriage with the princess, which he is celebrating, strikes me as sensible, and all for the best. However, I shall beg him to let the children stay on here: not that I'd dream of leaving my babies to be insulted in a land that loathes me; but purely as a stratagem; and I shall kill the king's own daughter. For I shall send them with gifts in their little hands, to be offered to the bride to preserve them from banishment: a finely woven dress and a golden diadem. And if she takes these things and wears them on her body, she, and whoever touches her, will die in anguish; for I shall rub these things with deadly poison. That will be that; but it is the next thing I must do which sets me weeping. For I will kill my own children! My own dear children, whom none shall take from me. And when I have brought ruin on the house of Jason, I shall flee from the land and flee from the murder of my children; for it will be a terrible deed to do! It isn't easy, my friends, to bear the insults of one's enemies. And so it shall be. For what have I left in life? I have no land, no home, no harbor to protect me. What a fool I was to leave my father's house, to put my faith in the words of a Greek! And for this he will pay the penalty, so help me God. Never again will he see his sons alive; never will he have a son by this new bride. For she is doomed to die, and die hideously from the power of my poison. Let no man think I am a feeble, frail-hearted woman who sits with folded hands: no, let them know me for the opposite of that—one who knows how to hurt her enemies and help her friends. It is lives like this that are longest remembered!

CHORAG. Since you have told us all your plans, let me say this to you: do not do this thing!

MEDEA There is nothing else I can do. It is forgivable that you should say this: but remember, you have not suffered as I have!

CHORAG. Woman, can you really bring yourself to destroy your own flesh and blood?

MEDEA I can; for in that way I can hurt my husband most cruelly.

CHORAG. And yourself as well! You will be the most miserable of women.

MEDEA   Then I will; no matter. No word of warning now can stop me!

         [*The* NURSE *enters;* MEDEA *turns to her.*

MEDEA   Go and tell Jason to come to me. And remember, I send you
         on a mission of great secrecy. Say nothing of the plans I have
         prepared; don't say a word, if you are loyal to your mistress
         and loyal to the race of woman!

CHORUS   Oh listen! We know of a land   [STROPHE 1
         Where dwell the sons of Erechtheus,
         Fed on the food of wisdom, and blessed with the blood of
            gods,
         Raised on a soil still holy and still unconquered; and there
         Moving amid that glittering air where the legends
         Say that lovely Harmonia, the golden-haired,
         Brought forth the Sacred Nine, the Pierian Muses!

         And where they say that Cypris,   [ANTISTROPHE 1
         The divine one, sailed to draw the
         Water out of the wandering stream of Cephisus, and the
            gentle
         Winds passed over the land: and over her glittering
         Head the long, sweet-scented rose wreaths
         Were wound by the Loves, who sit by Wisdom's side
         And in all virtuous deeds are the friends of mortals.

         Then how can this city, O how   [STROPHE 2
         Can these sacred streams which welcome
         Only the ones they love,
         O tell, how can they welcome
         You who are evil? You
         Who are killing your sons? O think
         Of the sons you plan to slay,
         Of the blood you plan to shed!
         We beg, we implore you, Medea:
         Do not murder your sons!

         Oh where can your hand or your heart,   [ANTISTROPHE 2
         Medea, find the hardness

To do this frightful thing
Against your sons? O how
Can you look on them and yet
Not weep, Medea? How
Can you still resolve to slay them?
Ah, when they fall at your feet
For mercy, you will not be able
To dip your hand in their blood!

[JASON *enters.*

JASON   I have come at your bidding, Medea. For although you are full of hatred for me, this small favor I will grant you; I will listen to you, my lady, and hear what new favor you are asking.

MEDEA   Jason, I beg your forgiveness for what I have said! Surely you can afford to forgive my bad temper: after all, there has been much love between us! I have reasoned with myself and reproached myself. 'Poor fool,' I said, 'Why am I so distraught? Why am I so bitter against all good advice, why am I so angry at the rulers of this country, and my husband as well, who does the best he can for me in marrying a royal princess, and in having royal children, who will be brothers to my own? Why not stop complaining? What is wrong with me, when the gods are being so generous? Don't I have my children to consider? Don't I realize that we are exiles after all, and in need of friends?' . . . And when I had thought all this over, Jason, I saw how foolish I'd been, and how silly my anger. So now I agree with you. I think you are well advised in taking this new wife; and I was mad. I should have helped you in your plans, I should have helped arrange the wedding. I should have stood by the wedding bed and been happy to wait on your bride. But we women are—well, I shan't say entirely worthless; but we are what we are. And you men shouldn't stoop to our level: you shouldn't reply to our folly with folly. I give in. I admit I was wrong. I have thought better of it all. . . .

[*She turns toward the house.*

Come, come, my children, come out from the house, come and greet your father, and then say good-bye to him. Give up your anger, as your mother does; be friends with him again, be reconciled!

[*The* ATTENDANT *enters with the children.*

We have made peace now; our bitterness is gone. Take his right hand . . . O God: I can't help thinking of the things that lie dark and hidden in the future! . . . My children, hold out your arms—the way one holds them in farewell after a long, long life . . . I am close to tears, my children! I am full of fear! I have ended my quarrel with your father at last, and look! My eyes are full of tears.

CHORAG. And our eyes too are filling with tears. O, do not let disasters worse than the present descend on you!

JASON I approve of your conduct, Medea; not that I blame you for anything in the past. It is natural for a woman to be furious with her husband when he begins to have other affairs. But now your heart has grown more sensible, and your mind is changed for the better; you are behaving like a woman of sense. And of you, my sons, your father will take good care, and make full provision, with the help of God. And I trust that in due time you with your brothers will be among the leading men in Corinth. All you need to do is grow up, my sons; and as for your future, you may leave it safely in the hands of your father, and of those among the gods who love him. I want to see you when you've grown to be men, tall and strong, towering over my enemies! . . . Medea, why are your eyes wet with tears? Why are your cheeks so pale? Why are you turning away? Don't these happy words of mine make you happy?

MEDEA It is nothing. I was only thinking about these children.

JASON Take heart, then. I shall look after them well.

MEDEA I will, Jason. It is not that I don't trust you. Women are weak; and tears come easily to them.

JASON   But why should you feel disturbed about the children?

MEDEA   I gave birth to them, Jason. And when you prayed that they might live long, my heart filled with sorrow to think that all these things must happen . . . Well now: I have told you some of the things I called you here to tell you; now let me tell you the rest. Since the ruler of this land has resolved to banish me, and since I am considered an enemy, I know it will be best for me not to stand in your way, or in the way of the King, by living here. I am going forth from this land into exile. But these children—O let them feel that you are protecting them, and beg of Kreon not to banish them!

JASON   I doubt whether I can persuade him; still, I will try.

MEDEA   Or at least ask your wife to beg her father to do this, and give the children reprieve from exile.

JASON   I will try; and with her I think I shall succeed.

MEDEA   She's a woman, after all; and like all other women. And I will help you in this matter; I will send the children to her with gifts far more exquisite, I am sure, than any now to be found among men—a finely woven dress and a diadem of chased gold. There; let one of the servants go and bring me these lovely ornaments.

> [One of the ATTENDANTS goes into the house.

And she'll be happy not in one way, but a thousand! With so splendid a man as you to share her bed, and with this marvelous gown as well, which once the Sun God Helios himself, my father's father, gave his descendants.

> [The ATTENDANT returns with the poisoned dress and diadem.

There, my children, take these wedding presents in your hands and take them as an offering to the royal princess, the lucky bride; give them to her; they are not gifts to be scorned.

JASON   But why do you give them away so rashly, Medea? Do you think the royal palace is lacking in dresses, or in gold? Keep them. Don't give them away. If my wife really loves me, I am sure she values me more highly than gold.

MEDEA No; don't say that, Jason. For I have heard it said that gifts can persuade even the gods; and men are governed more by gold than by words! Luck has fallen on your bride, and the gods have blessed her fortune. She is young: she's a princess. Yet I'd give not only gold but my life to save my children from exile. Enter that rich palace together, children, and pray to your father's new bride; pray to my mistress, and beg her to save you from banishment. Present this garment to her; and above all let her take the gift from you with her own hands. Go; don't linger. And may you succeed, and bring back to your mother the good news for which she longs!

[Exit JASON, *the* ATTENDANT, *and the children bearing the poisoned gifts.*]

CHORUS No hope now remains for the children's lives!   [STROPHE 1
No, none. Even now they are moving toward death;
The luckless bride will accept the gown that will kill her,
And take the golden crown, and hold it
In her hand, and over her golden head will
Lift the garment of Hell!

[ANTISTROPHE 1
The grace and glitter of gold will enchant her:
She will put on the golden robe and wear
The golden crown: and deck herself as the bride
Of Death. And thus, pitiful girl,
Will fall in the trap; will fall and perish.
She will never escape!

You likewise, O miserable groom,   [STROPHE 2
Who planned a royal wedding ceremony,
Do not see the doom you are bringing
Upon your sons; and the terrible death

Now lying in wait for your bride. Pity
Upon you! O, how you are fallen!

And I weep for you too, Medea,   [ANTISTROPHE 2
O mother who are killing your sons,
Killing in revenge for the loss
Of your love: you whom your lover Jason
Now has deserted and betrayed
To love and marry another mistress!

[*Enter* ATTENDANT *with the children.*

ATTEND. My lady, your children are reprieved from exile. The royal bride was delighted to receive your gifts with her own hands. And there is peace between her and your children . . . Medea! Why are you so distraught at this lucky moment? Why are you turning your head away? Are you not happy to hear this news, my lady?

MEDEA Oh, I am lost!

ATTEND. That cry does not suit the news I have brought you, surely!

MEDEA I am lost! I am lost!

ATTEND. Have I told you of some disaster, without knowing it? Was I wrong in thinking that my news was good?

MEDEA You have said what you have said: I do not wish to blame you.

ATTEND. Then why are you so disturbed? Why are you weeping?

MEDEA Oh, my old friend, I can't help weeping. It was I, it was I and the gods, who planned these things so badly.

ATTEND. Take heart, Medea. Your sons will bring you back to your home some day.

MEDEA And I'll bring others back to their homes, long before that happens!

ATTEND. And often before this, mothers have been parted from their sons. Bear your troubles, Medea, as all mortals must bear them.

MEDEA   I will, I will. Go back into the house; and plan your daily work for the children.

[*The* ATTENDANT *goes into the house, and* MEDEA *turns to her children.*

MEDEA   O my children, my children, you will still have a city, you will still have a home where you can dwell forever, far away from me, far forever from your mother! But I am doomed to go in exile to another land, before I can see you grow up and be happy, before I can take pride in you, before I can wait on your brides and make your marriage beds, or hold the torch at your wedding ceremony! What a victim I am of my own self-will! It was all in vain, my children, that I reared you! It was all in vain that I grew weary and worn, and suffered the anguish and pangs of childbirth! Oh pity me! Once I had great hopes for you; I had hopes that you'd look after me in my old age, and that you'd lovingly deck my body with your own hands when I died, as all men hope and desire. But now my lovely dreams are over. I shall love you both. I shall spend my life in grief and solitude. And never again will you see your mother with your own dear eyes; now you will pass into another kind of life. Ah, my dear children, why do you look at me like this? Why are you smiling your sweet little smiles at me? O children, what can I do? My heart gives way when I see the joy shining in my children's eyes. O women, I cannot do it! . . . Farewell to all my plans! I will take my babies away with me from this land. Why should I hurt their father by hurting them? Why should I hurt myself doubly? No: I cannot do it. I shall say good-bye to my plans . . . And yet—O, what is wrong with me? Am I willing to see my enemies go unpunished? Am I willing to be insulted and laughed at? I shall follow this thing to the end. How weak I am! How weak to let my heart be touched by these soft sentiments! Go back into the house, my children . . . And if anyone prefers not to witness my sacrifice, let him do as he wishes! My poor heart—do not do this thing! My poor heart, have pity on them, let them go, the little children! They'll bring cheer to you, if you let them live with you in exile! . . . No, by all the avenging Furies, this shall not be! Never shall I surrender my children to the insolence and mockery of my enemies! It is settled. I have made my decision. And since they must die, it is their mother who must kill them. Now there is no escape for the young bride! Already the crown is on her head; already the dress is hanging from her body; the royal bride, the princess is dying! This I know. And now—since I am about to follow a dreadful path, and am sending them on a path still more terrible—I will simply say this: I want to speak to my children.

[*She calls and the children come back; she takes them in her arms.*

Come, come, give me your hands, my babies, let your mother kiss you both. O dear little hands, dear little lips: how I have loved them! How fresh and young your eyes look! How straight you stand! I wish you joy with all my heart; but not here; not in this land. All that you had here your father has stolen from you. . . . How good it is to hold you, to feel your soft young cheeks, the warm young sweetness of your breath. . . . Go now; leave me. I cannot look at you any longer . . . I am overcome. . . .

[*The children go into the house again.*

Now at last I understand the full evil of what I have planned. At last I see how my passion is stronger than my reason: passion, which brings the worst of woes to mortal man.

[*She goes out at the right, toward the palace.*

CHORAG. Many a time before
I have gone through subtler reasoning,
Many times I have faced graver questioning
Than any woman should ever have to face:
But we women have a goddess to help us, too,
And lead us into wisdom.
Not all of us; perhaps not many;
But some women there are who are capable of wisdom.
And I say this: that those who have never

Known the fullness of life and never had children,
Are happier far than those who are parents.
For the childless, who never discover whether
Their children grow up to be a cause for joy or for pain,
Are spared many troubles:
While those who know in their houses
The sweet presence of children—
We have seen how their lives are wasted by worry.
First they fret about how they shall raise them
Properly; and then how to leave them enough
Money to live on; and then they continue
To worry about whether all this labor
Has gone into children that will turn out well
Or turn out ill: and the question remains unanswered.
And let me tell of one more trouble,
The last of all, and common to all mortals:
For suppose you have found enough
For them to live on, and suppose
You have seen them grow up and turn out well;
Still, if fate so decrees it, Death
Will come and tear away your children!
What use is it, then, that the gods
For the sake of children
Should pile on us mortals,
After all other griefs,
This grief for lost children? This grief
Greater by far than any?

[MEDEA *comes out of the house.*

MEDEA   I have been waiting in suspense, ladies; I have waited long to
learn how things will happen . . . Look! I see one of Jason's
servants coming toward us; he is panting; and the bearer of
news, I think; of bad news . . .

[A MESSENGER *rushes in.*

MESS.   Fly, Medea, fly! You have done a terrible thing, a thing
breaking all human laws: fly, and take with you a ship for
the seas, or a chariot for the plains!

MEDEA   Why? What reason have you for asking me to fly?

MESS.   She lies dead! The royal princess, and her father Kreon too! They have died: they have been slain by your poisons!

MEDEA   You bring me blessèd news! Now and from now on I count you among my friends, my benefactors!

MESS.   What! Are you insane? Are you mad, Medea? You have done an outrage to the royal house: does it make you happy to hear it? Can you hear of this dreadful thing without horror?

MEDEA   I too have words to say in reply to yours. Do not be impatient, my friend. Tell me: how did they die? You will make me doubly happy if you say they died in anguish!

MESS.   When those two children, your own babies, Medea, came with their father and entered the palace of the bride, it gave joy to all of us, the servants who have suffered with you; for instantly all through the house we whispered that you had made up your quarrel with your husband. One of us kissed your children's hands, and another their golden hair, and I myself was so overjoyed that I followed them in person to the women's chambers. And there stood our mistress, whom we now serve instead of you; and she kept her eyes fixed longingly on Jason. When she caught sight of your children, she covered up her eyes, and her face grew pale, and she turned away, filled with petulance at their coming. But your husband tried to soothe the bride's ill humor, and said: 'Do not look so unkindly at your friends! Do not feel angry: turn your head to me once more, and think of your husband's friends as your own friends! Accept these gifts, and do this for my sake: beg of your father not to let these children be exiled!' And then, when she saw the dress, she grew mild and yielded, and gave in to her husband. And before the father and the children had gone far from her rooms, she took the gorgeous robe and put it on; and she put the golden crown on her curly head, and arranged her hair in the shining mirror, smiling as she saw herself reflected. And then she rose from her chair and walked across the room, stepping softly and delicately on

her small white feet, filled with delight at the gift, and
glancing again and again at the delicate turn of her ankles.
And after that it was a thing of horror we saw. For suddenly
her face changed its color, and she staggered back, and began
to tremble as she ran, and reached a chair just as she was
about to fall to the ground. An old woman servant, thinking
no doubt that this was some kind of seizure, a fit sent by Pan,
or some other god, cried out a prayer: and then, as she
prayed, she saw the flakes of foam flow from her mouth, and
her eyeballs rolling, and the blood fade from her face. And
then it was a different prayer she uttered, a terrible scream,
and one of the women ran to the house of the King, and
another to the newly wedded groom to tell him what had
happened to the bride; and the whole house echoed as they
ran to and fro.

Let me tell you, time enough for a man to walk two hundred
yards passed before the poor lady awoke from her trance, with
a dreadful scream, and opened her eyes again. A twofold
torment was creeping over her. The golden diadem on her
head was sending forth a violent stream of flame, and the
finely woven dress which your children gave her was beginning to eat into the poor girl's snowy soft flesh. And she
leapt from her chair, all on fire, and started to run, shaking
her head to and fro, trying to shake off the diadem; but the
gold still clung firmly, and as she shook her hair the fire
blazed forth with double fury. And then she sank to the
ground, helpless, overcome; and past all recognition except
to the eye of a father—for her eyes had lost their normal
expression, and the familiar look had fled from her face, and
from the top of her head a mingled stream of blood and fire
was pouring. And it was like the drops falling from the bark
of a pine tree when the flesh dropped away from her bones,
torn loose by the secret fangs of the poison. And terror kept
all of us from touching the corpse; for we were warned by
what had happened.

But then her poor father, who knew nothing of her death,

came suddenly into the house and stumbled over her body, and cried out as he folded his arms about her, and kissed her, and said: 'O my child, my poor child, which of the gods has so cruelly killed you? Who has robbed me of you, who am old and close to the grave? O my child, let me die with you!' And he grew silent and tried to rise to his feet again, but found himself fastened to the finely spun dress, like vine clinging to a laurel bough, and there was a fearful struggle. And still he tried to lift his knees, and she writhed and clung to him; and as he tugged, he tore the withered flesh from his bones. And at last he could no longer master the pain, and surrendered, and gave up the ghost. So there they are lying together: and it is a sight to send us weeping. . . .

As for you, Medea, I will say nothing of your own problems: you yourself must discover an escape from punishment. I think, and I have always thought, the life of men is a shadow; and I say without fear that those who are wisest among all men, and probe most deeply into the cause of things—they are the ones who suffer most deeply! For, believe me, no man among mortals is happy; if wealth comes to a man, he may be luckier than the rest; but happy—never.

[*Exit* MESSENGER.

CHORAG.   It seems that heaven has sent, today, a heavy load of evils upon Jason; and he deserves them. Alas, poor girl, poor daughter of Kreon! I pity you and your anguish; and now you are gone, all because of your wedding with Jason: gone away to the halls of Hades!

MEDEA   Women, the deed shall be done! Swiftly I will go and kill my children, and then leave the land: and not delay nor let them be killed by a crueler hand. For die they must in any case: and if they must be slain, it is I, their mother who gave them life, who must slay them! O my heart, my heart, arm yourself in steel! Do not shrink back from this hideous thing which has to be done! Come, my hand, and seize the sword, take it and step forward to the place where my life's true sorrow begins! Do not be a coward . . . do not think of the

children, and how dear they are to you who are their mother!
For one brief day, Medea, forget your children; and then
forever after you may mourn; for though you will kill them,
they were dear to you, very dear . . . I am a miserable woman!

[*With a cry* MEDEA *rushes into the house.*

CHORUS   O Earth, and the all-brightening   [STROPHE
Beam of the Sun, look, look
Upon this lost one, shine upon
This pitiful woman before she raises
Her hand in murder against her sons!
For lo! these are the offspring
Of thine own golden seed, and I fear
That divine blood may now be shed by men!
O Light flung forth by Zeus,
O heavenly Light,
Hold back her hand,
Restrain her, and drive out
This dark demoniac fury from the house!

Was it all in vain, Medea,   [ANTISTROPHE
What you suffered in bearing your sons?
Was it utterly in vain
You bore the babes you loved, after you left
Behind you that dark passage through the straits
And past the perilous rocks, the blue Symplegades?
Wretched woman, how has it happened
That your soul is torn by anger
And darkened by the shadow of death?
Heavy will be the price
To pay for kindred blood staining the earth!
Heavy the woe sent down by heaven
On the house of the killer for such a crime!

[*A cry is heard from the children within.*

CHORAG.   Listen! Do you hear? Do you hear the children crying?
Hate-hardened heart! O woman born for evil!

[*Crying within.*

1ST SON   What can I do? How can I run from mother's hands?

[*Crying within.*

2ND SON   I don't know! We are lost, we are lost, brother!

CHORAG.   Shall I enter the house? Oh surely
           I must help! I must save these children from murder!

[*Within.*

1ST SON   Help, in the name of heaven! We need your help!

[*Within.*

2ND SON   Now, now it's coming closer! The sword is falling!

CHORAG.   Oh, you must be made of stone or steel,
           To kill the fruit of your womb
           With your own hands, unhappy woman!
           I have heard of only one,
           Of all the women who ever lived, who laid
           Her hand upon her children: it was Ino,
           Who was driven insane by the Gods
           When the wife of Zeus sent her wandering from her home.
           And wild with grief at killing her children,
           She flung herself from the sea-battered cliff
           And plunged into the sea, and in the sea
           Rejoined her two dead children.
           Can anything so dreadful ever happen again?
           Woe flows forth from the bed of a woman
           Whom fate has touched with trouble!
           Great is the grief that they have brought on men!

[*Enter* JASON *with his attendants.*

JASON   Ladies, you have been sitting near this house! Tell me! Is
           Medea, is the woman who did this frightful thing, still in the
           house? Or has she fled already? O believe me, she'll have to
           hide deep under the earth, or fly on wings through the sky,
           if she hopes to escape the vengeance of the royal house! Does
           she dream, after killing the rulers of the land, that she herself
           can escape from these halls unpunished? But I am thinking

of her far less than of her children; for she herself will duly suffer at the hands of those she wronged. Ladies, I have come to save the lives of my boys, lest the royal house should harm them in revenge for this vile thing done by their mother.

CHORAG. O Jason, you do not yet know the full depth of your misery, or you would not have spoken those words!

JASON What do you mean? Is she planning to kill me also?

CHORAG. Your boys are dead; dead at their mother's hand.

JASON What have you said, woman? You are destroying me!

CHORAG. You may be sure of this: your children are dead.

JASON Oh where did she kill them? Was it here, or in the house?

CHORAG. Open the doors, and you will see their murdered bodies!

JASON Open the doors! Unlock the bolts! Undo the fastenings! And let me see this twofold horror! Let me see my murdered boys! Let me look on her whom I shall kill in vengeance!

[His attendants rush to the door. MEDEA appears above the house in a chariot drawn by dragons. The dead children are at her side.

MEDEA Why do you batter at the doors? Why do you shake these bolts, in quest of the dead and their murderess? You may cease your trouble, Jason; and if there is anything you want to say, then say it! Never again shall you lay your hand on me; so swift is the chariot which my father's father gave me, the Sun God Helios, to save me from my foes!

JASON Horrible woman! Now you are utterly loathed by the gods, and by me, and by all mankind. You had the heart to stab your children; you, their own mother, and to leave me child-less; you have done these fearful things, and still you dare to gaze as ever at the sun and the earth! O I wish you were dead! Now at last I see clearly what I did not see on the day I brought you, loaded with doom, from your barbarous home to live in Hellas—a traitress to your father and your native land. On me too the gods have hurled the curse which has haunted you. For you killed your own brother at his fireside, and then came aboard our beautiful ship the Argo. And that was how it started. And then you married me, and slept with me, and out of your passion bore me children; and now, out of your passion, you have killed them. There is no woman in all of Greece who would dare to do this. And yet I passed them over, and chose you instead; and chose to marry my own doom! I married not a woman, but a monster, wilder of heart than Scylla in the Tyrrhenian Sea! But even if I hurled a thousand insults at you, Medea, I know I could not wound you: your heart is so hard, so utterly hard. Go, you wicked sorceress; I see the stains of your children's blood upon you! Go; all that is left to me now is to mourn. I shall never lie beside my newly wedded love; I shall never have my sons, whom I bred and brought up, alive beside me to say a last farewell! I have lost them forever, and my life is ended.

MEDEA   O Jason, to these words of yours I could make a long reply; but Zeus, the father, himself well knows all that I did for you, and what you did to me. Destiny has refused to let you scorn my love, and lead a life of pleasure, and mock at me; nor were the royal princess and the matchmaker Kreon destined to drive me into exile, and then go untormented! Call me a monster if you wish; call me the Scylla in the Tyrrhenian Sea. For now I have torn your heart: and this indeed was destined, Jason!

JASON   You too must feel the pain; you will share my grief, Medea.

MEDEA   Yes; but the pain is milder, since you cannot mock me!

JASON   O my sons, it was an unspeakable mother who bore you!

MEDEA   O my sons, it was really your father who destroyed you!

JASON   But I tell you: it was not my hand that slew them!

MEDEA   No; but your insolence, and your new wedding slew them!

JASON   And you thought this wedding cause enough to kill them?

MEDEA   And you think the anguish of love is trifling for a woman?

JASON   Yes, if her heart is sound: but yours makes all things evil.

MEDEA   Your sons are dead, Jason! Does it hurt you when I say this?

JASON   They will live on, Medea, by bringing suffering on you.

MEDEA   The gods are well aware who caused all this suffering.

JASON   Yes, the gods are well aware. They know your brutal heart.

MEDEA   You too are brutal. And I am sick of your bitter words!

JASON   And I am sick of yours. Oh Medea, it will be easy to leave you.

MEDEA   Easy! Yes! And for me too! What, then, do you want?

JASON   Give me those bodies to bury, and to mourn.

MEDEA   Never! I will bury them myself. I will bring them myself to Hera's temple, which hangs over the Cape, where none of their enemies can insult them, and where none can defile their graves! And in this land of Corinth I shall ordain a holy feast and sacrifice, forever after, to atone for this guilt of killing. And I shall go myself to Athens, to live in the house of Aegeus, the son of Pandion. And I predict that you, as you deserve, will die without honor; and your head crushed by a beam of the shattered Argo; and then you will know the bitter end of all my love for you!

JASON   May the avenging fury of our sons destroy you! May Justice destroy you, and repay blood with blood!

MEDEA   What god, what heavenly power would listen to you? To a breaker of oaths? To a betrayer of love?

JASON   Oh, you are vile! You sorceress! Murderess!

MEDEA   Go to your house. Go, and bury your bride.

JASON   Yes, I shall go; and mourn for my murdered sons.

MEDEA   Wait; do not weep yet, Jason! Wait till age has sharpened your grief!

JASON	Oh my sons, whom I loved! My sons!
MEDEA	It was I, not you, who truly loved them.
JASON	You say you loved them; yet you killed them.
MEDEA	Yes. I killed them to make you suffer.
JASON	Medea, I only long to kiss them one last time.
MEDEA	Now, now, you long to kiss them! Now you long to say farewell: but before, you cast them from you!
JASON	Medea, I beg you, let me touch the little bodies of my boys!
MEDEA	No. Never. You speak in vain.
JASON	O Zeus, high in your heaven, have you heard these words? Have you heard this unutterable cruelty? Have you heard this woman, this monster, this murderess? And now I shall do the only thing I still can do! Yes! I shall cry, I shall cry aloud to heaven, and call on the gods to witness how you killed my sons, and refused to let me kiss them farewell, or touch them, or give them burial! Oh, I'd rather never have seen them live, than have seen them slaughtered so!

[*The chariot carries* MEDEA *away.*

CHORAG.	Many, many are the things That Zeus determines, high on the Olympian throne; Many the things beyond men's understanding That the gods achieve, and bring to pass. Many the things we think will happen, Yet never happen. And many the things we thought could never be, Yet the gods contrive. Such things have happened on this day, And in this place!

Euripides

HIPPOLYTUS

translated by
David Grene

As a young man, theseus, King of Athens, had a son, hippolytus, by queen hippolyta of the Amazons. Later he married phaedra, daughter of king minos of Crete. The youth hippolytus offended aphrodite, Goddess of Love, by his neglect of her in the service of artemis; accordingly she brought it about that phaedra should fall irremediably in love with her own stepson.

DRAMATIS PERSONÆ:

APHRODITE	HIPPOLYTUS
ARTEMIS	THESEUS
PHAEDRA	MESSENGER
NURSE	SERVANT

CHORUS OF HUNTSMEN

CHORUS OF TROEZENIAN LADIES

HIPPOLYTUS

SCENE: *Troezen, before the palace of Theseus.*

PROLOGUE

APHRO.   I am called the Goddess Cypris:
I am mighty among men and they honor me by many names.
All those that live and see the light of sun
from Atlas' Pillars to the tide of Pontus
are mine to rule.
Such as worship my power in all humility,
I exalt in honor.
But those whose pride is stiff-necked against me
I lay by the heels.
There is joy in the heart of a god also
when honored by men.

Now I will quickly tell you the truth of this story.

Hippolytus, son of Theseus by the Amazon,
pupil of holy Pittheus,
alone among the folk of this land of Troezen has blasphemed
    me
counting me vilest of the gods in Heaven.
He will none of the bed of love nor marriage,
but honors Artemis, Zeus' daughter,
counting her greatest of the gods in Heaven
he is with her continually, this Maiden Goddess, in the
    greenwood.

245

They hunt with hounds and clear the land of wild things,
mortal with immortal in companionship.
I do not grudge him such privileges: why should I?
But for his sins against me
I shall punish Hippolytus this day.
I have no need to toil to win my end:
much of the task has been already done.

Once he came from Pittheus' house to the country of Pandion
that he might see and be initiate in the holy mysteries.
Phaedra saw him
and her heart was filled with the longings of love.
This was my work.
So before ever she came to Troezen
close by the rock of Pallas in view of this land,
she dedicated a temple to Cypris.
For her love, too, dwelt in a foreign land.
Ages to come will call this temple after him,

[She points to where the temple stood above the Dionysiac
    Theater where our performance was taking place.

the temple of the Goddess established here.
When Theseus left the land of Cecrops,
flying from the guilty stain of the murder of the Pallantids,
condemning himself to a year's exile
he sailed with his wife to this land.
Phaedra groans in bitterness of heart
and the goads of love prick her cruelly,
and she is like to die.
But she breathes not a word of her secret and none of the
    servants
know of the sickness that afflicts her.
But her love shall not remain thus aimless and unknown.
I will reveal the matter to Theseus and all shall come out.
Father shall slay son with curses,—
this son that is hateful to me.
For once the lord Poseidon, Ruler of the Sea,
granted this favor to Theseus
that three of his prayers to the god should find answer.

Renowned shall Phaedra be in her death, but none the less
die she must.
Her suffering does not weigh in the scale so much
that I should let my enemies go untouched
escaping payment of that retribution
that honor demands that I have.
Look, here is the son of Theseus, Hippolytus!
He has just left his hunting.
I must go away.
See the great crowd that throngs upon his heels
and shouts the praise of Artemis in hymns!
He does not know
that the doors of death are open for him,
that he is looking on his last sun.

SCENE I

[Enter HIPPOLYTUS, attended by friends and servants
carrying nets, hunting spears, etc.

HIPPOL.   Follow me singing
the praises of Artemis,
Heavenly One, child of Zeus,
Artemis!
We are the wards of your care.

[The CHORUS of HUNTSMEN chant.

Hail, holy and gracious!
Hail daughter of Zeus!
Hail maiden daughter of Zeus and Leto!
Dweller in the spacious sky!
Maid of the Mighty Father!
Maid of the golden glistening house!

Hail!
Maiden Goddess most beautiful of all the heavenly host that
    lives in Olympus!

[HIPPOLYTUS *advances to the altar on the right of the stage,*
    the altar of ARTEMIS, *and lays a garland on it, praying.*

My Goddess Mistress, I bring you ready woven
this garland. It was I that plucked and wove it,
plucked it for you in your inviolate meadow.
No shepherd dares to feed his flock within it:
no reaper plies a busy scythe within it:
only the bees in springtime haunt the inviolate meadow.
Its gardener is the spirit reverence who
refreshes it with water from the river.
Not those who by instruction have profited
to learn, but in whose very soul the seed
of chastity towards all things alike
nature has deeply rooted, they alone
may gather flowers there! the wicked may not.

Loved mistress, here I offer you this coronal;
it is a true worshipper's hand that gives it you
to crown the golden glory of your hair.
With no man else I share this privilege
that I am ever with you and to your words
can answer words. True, I may only hear:
I may not see God face to face.
I pray that with such sweet companionship
my chariot wheels may graze the ultimate mark
set at the finish of life's stadium
even as I began the race.

SERV.   King,—for I will not call you 'Master,' that belongs
    to the gods only— will you take good advice?

HIPPOL.   Certainly I will take good advice. I am not a fool.

SERV.   In men's communities one rule holds good,
    do you know it, King?

HIPPOL.   Not I. What is this rule?

SERV.   Men hate the haughty of heart who will not be
the friend of every man.

HIPPOL.   And rightly too:
For haughty heart breeds arrogant demeanor.

SERV.   And affability wins favor, then?

HIPPOL.   Abundant favor. Aye, and profit, too,
at little cost of trouble.

SERV.   Do you think
that it's the same among the gods in Heaven?

HIPPOL.   If we in our world and the gods in theirs
know the same usages,—Yes.

SERV.   Then, King, how comes it
that for a holy goddess you have not even
a word of salutation?

HIPPOL.   Which goddess?
Be careful, or you will find that tongue of yours
may make a serious mistake.

SERV.   This goddess here
who stands before your gates, the goddess Cypris.

HIPPOL.   I worship her,—but from a long way off,
for I am chaste.

SERV.   Yet she's a holy goddess,
and fair is her renown throughout the world.

HIPPOL.   Men make their choice: one man honors one god,
and one another.

SERV.   Well, good fortune guard you!
if you have the mind you should have.

HIPPOL.   God of nocturnal prowess is not my god.

SERV.   Honor the gods, son; gods are jealous of honor.

HIPPOL.   Go, men, into the house and look to supper.
A plentiful table is an excellent thing
after the hunt. And you (*singling out two*) rub down my
        horses.

When I have eaten I shall exercise them.
For your Cypris here,—a long good-bye to her!

[*The old man is left standing alone on the stage.*
He prays before the statue of Aphrodite.

O Cypris Mistress, we must not imitate
the young men when they have such thoughts as these.
As fits a slave to speak, here at your image
I bow and worship. You should grant forgiveness
when one that has a young tempestuous heart
speaks foolish words. Seem not to hear them.
You should be wiser than mortals, being gods.

[*Enter* CHORUS OF TROEZENIAN LADIES, *servants in*
PHAEDRA'S *house.*

CHORUS   There is a rock streaming with water,   [STROPHE
whose source, men say, is Ocean,
and it pours from the heart of its stone a spring
where pitchers may dip and be filled.
My friend was there and in the river water
she dipped and washed the royal purple robes,
and spread them on the rock's warm back
where the sunbeams played.
It was from her I heard at first
of the news of my mistress' sorrow.

She lies on her bed within the house,   [ANTISTROPHE
within the house, and fever wracks her
and she hides her golden head in fine spun robes.
This is the third day
she has eaten no bread
and her body is pure and fasting.
For she would willingly bring her life to anchor
at the end of its voyage
the gloomy harbour of death.

Is it Pan's frenzy that possesses you   [STROPHE
or is Hecate's madness upon you, maid?
Can it be the holy Corybantes,

or the mighty Mother who rules the mountains?
Are you wasted in suffering thus,
for a sin against Dictynna Queen of hunters?
Are you perhaps unhallowed having offered
no sacrifice to her from taken victims?
For she goes through the waters of the Lake,
can travel on dry land beyond the sea,
the eddying salt sea.

Can it be that some other woman's love,   [ANTISTROPHE
a secret love that hides itself from you,
has beguiled your husband
the son of Erechtheus
our sovran lord, that prince of noble birth?
Or has some sailor from the shores of Crete
put in at this harbour hospitable to sailors,
bearing a message for our queen,
and so because he told her some calamity
her spirit is bound in chains of grief
and she lies on her bed in sorrow?

Unhappy is the compound of woman's nature;   [EPODE
the torturing misery of helplessness,
the helplessness of childbirth and its madness
are linked to it for ever.
My body too has felt this thrill of pain,
and I called on Artemis, Queen of the Bow;
she has my reverence always
as she goes in the company of the gods.

SCENE II

[Enter the NURSE, supporting PHAEDRA. Servants follow
carrying a couch and pillows.

NURSE   A weary thing is sickness and its pains!

What must I do now?
Here is light and air, the brightness of the sky.
I have brought out the couch on which you tossed
in fever,—here clear of the house.
Your every word has been to bring you out,
but when you're here, you hurry in again.
You find no constant pleasure anywhere
for when your joy is upon you, suddenly
you're foiled and cheated.
There's no content for you in what you have
for you're forever finding something dearer,
some other thing—because you have it not.
It's better to be sick than nurse the sick.

Sickness is single trouble for the sufferer:
but nursing means vexation of the mind,
and hard work for the hands beside.

The life of man entire is misery:
he finds no resting place, no haven from calamity.
But something other dearer still than life
the darkness hides and mist encompasses;
we are proved luckless lovers of this thing
that glitters in the underworld: no man
can tell us of the stuff of it expounding
what is, and what is not: we know nothing of it.
Unpiloted we're helplessly adrift
upon a sea of legends, lies and fantasy.

                                        [*To the servants.*

PHAED.   Lift me up! Lift my head up! All the muscles
           are slack and useless. Here, you, take my hands.
           They're beautiful, my hands and arms!
           Take away this hat! It is too heavy to wear.
           Take it away! Let my hair fall free on my shoulders.

NURSE   Quiet, child, quiet! Do not so restlessly
           keep tossing to and fro! It's easier
           to bear an illness if you have some patience;

you are a lady nobly born: remember
the spirit of a lady nobly born.
We all must suffer sometimes: we are mortal.

PHAED.   O,
       if I could only draw from the dewy spring
       a draught of fresh spring water!
       If I could only lie beneath the poplars,
       in the tufted meadow and find my rest there!

NURSE   Child, why do you rave so? There are others here.
       Cease tossing out these wild demented words
       whose driver is madness.

PHAED.   Bring me to the mountains! I *will* go to the mountains!
       Among the pine trees where the huntsmen's pack
       trails spotted stags and hangs upon their heels.
       God, how I long to set the hounds on, shouting!
       And poise the Thessalian javelin drawing it back,—
       here where my fair hair hangs above the ear,—
       I would hold in my hand a spear with a steel point!

NURSE   What ails you, child? What is this love of hunting,
       and you a lady! Draught of fresh spring water!
       Here, beside the tower there is a sloping ridge
       with springs enough to satisfy your thirst.

PHAED.   Artemis Mistress of the Salty Lake
       mistress of the ring echoing to the racers' hoofs
       if only I could gallop your level stretches,
       and break Venetian colts!

NURSE   This is sheer madness,
       that prompts such whirling frenzied senseless words.
       Here at one moment you're afire with longing
       to hunt wild beasts and you'd go to the hills,
       and then again all your desire is horses,
       horses on the sands beyond the reach of the breakers.
       Indeed it would need to be a mighty prophet
       to tell which of the gods mischievously
       jerks you from your true course and thwarts your wits!

PHAED.   O, I am miserable! What is this I've done?
Where have I strayed from the highway of good sense?
I was mad. It was the madness sent from some god
that caused my fall.
I am unhappy, so unhappy! Nurse,
cover my face again. I am ashamed
of what I said. Cover me up. The tears
are flowing and my face is turned to shame.
Rightness of judgment is bitterness to the heart.
Madness is terrible. It is better then,
that I should die and know no more of anything.

NURSE   There now, you are covered up. But my own body
when will death cover that? I have learned much
from my long life. The mixing bowl of friendship,
the love of one for the other must be tempered.
Love must not touch the marrow of the soul.
Our affections must be breakable chains that we
can cast them off or tighten them.
That one soul so for two should be in travail
as I for her, that is a heavy burden.
The practices of life most deep and true
trip us up more, they say, than bring us joy.
They're enemies to health. So I praise less
the extreme than temperance in everything.
The wise will bear me out.

LEADER   Old woman, you are Phaedra's faithful nurse.
We can see that she is in trouble but the cause
that ails her is black mystery to us.
We would like to hear you tell us what is the matter.

NURSE   I have asked and know no more. She will not tell me.

LEADER   Not even what began it?

NURSE   And my answer
Is still the same: of all this she will not speak.

LEADER   But see how ill she is, and how her body
is wracked and wasted!

NURSE	Yes, she has eaten nothing for two days now.
LEADER	Is this the scourge of madness? Or can it be . . . that death is what she seeks?
NURSE	Aye, death. She is starving herself to death.
LEADER	I wonder that her husband suffers this.
NURSE	She hides her troubles, swears that she isn't sick.
LEADER	But does he not look into her face and see a witness that disproves her?
NURSE	No, he is gone. He is away from home, in foreign lands.
LEADER	Why, you must force her then to find the cause of this mind-wandering sickness!
NURSE	Every means I have tried and still have won no foot of ground. But I'll not give up trying, even now. You are here and can in person bear me witness that I am loyal to my masters always even in misfortune's hour.

[*She approaches* PHAEDRA, *who has been lying mute
under the coverlet and speaks coaxingly.*

Dear child, let us both forget our former words.
Be kinder, you: unknit that ugly frown.
For my part I will leave this track of thought:
I cannot understand you there. I'll take
another and a better argument.

If you are sick and it is some secret sickness,
here are women standing at your side to help.
But if your troubles may be told to men,
speak, that a doctor may pronounce upon it.
So, not a word! O, why will you not speak?
There is no remedy in silence, child.

Either I am wrong and then you should correct me:
or right, and you should yield to what I say.
Say something! Look at me!

Women, I have tried and tried and all for nothing.
We are as far as ever from our goal.
It was the same before. She was not melted
by anything I said. She would not obey me.

But this you shall know, though to my reasoning
you are more dumbly obstinate than the sea:
If you die, you will be a traitor to your children.
They will never know their share in a father's palace.
No, by the Amazon Queen, the mighty rider
who bore a master for your children, one
bastard in birth but true born son in mind
you know him well—Hippolytus . . .
                               So that has touched you?

PHAED. You have killed me, nurse. For God's sake, I entreat you,
        never again speak that man's name to me.

NURSE   You see? You have come to your senses, yet despite that
        you will not make your children happy nor
        save your own life besides.

PHAED.   I love my children.
        It is another storm of fate that batters me.

NURSE   Your hands are clean,—there is no stain on them?

PHAED. My hands are clean: the stain is in my heart.

NURSE   The hurt comes from outside? Some enemy?

PHAED. One I love destroys me. Neither of us wills it.

NURSE   Has Theseus sinned a sin against you then?

PHAED. God keep me equally guiltless in his sight!

NURSE   What is this terror urging you to death?

PHAED. Leave me to my sins. My sins are not against you.

NURSE	Not of my will, but yours, you cast me off.
PHAED.	Would you force confession, my hand-clasping suppliant?
NURSE	Your knees too,—and my hands will never free you.
PHAED.	Sorrow, nurse, sorrow, you will find my secret.
NURSE	Can I know greater sorrow than losing you?
PHAED.	Entreat to death! My honor lies in silence.
NURSE	And then you will hide this honor, though I beseech you?
PHAED.	Yes, for I seek to win good out of shame.
NURSE	Where honor is, speech will make you more honorable.
PHAED.	O, God, let go my hand and go away!
NURSE	No, for you have not given me what you should.
PHAED.	I yield. Your suppliant hand compels my reverence.
NURSE	I will say no more. Yours is the word from now.
PHAED.	Unhappy mother, what a love was yours!
NURSE	It is her love for the bull you mean, dear child?
PHAED.	Unhappy sister, bride of Dionysus!
NURSE	Why these ill-boding words about your kin?
PHAED.	And I the unlucky third, see how I end!
NURSE	Your words are wounds. Where will your tale conclude?
PHAED.	Mine is an inherited curse. It is not new.
NURSE	I have not yet heard what I most want to know.
PHAED.	If you could say for me what I must say for myself.
NURSE	I am no prophet to know your hidden secrets.
PHAED.	What is this thing, this love, of which they speak?
NURSE	Sweetest and bitterest, both in one, at once.
PHAED.	One of the two, the bitterness, I've known.

NURSE   Are you in love, my child? And who is he?

PHAED.   There is a man, . . . his mother was an Amazon . . .

NURSE   You mean Hippolytus?

PHAED.   **You**
have spoken it, not I.

NURSE   What do you mean? This is my death.
Women, this is past bearing. I'll not bear
life after this. A curse upon the daylight!
A curse upon this shining sun above us!
I'll throw myself from a cliff, throw myself headlong!
I'll be rid of life somehow, I'll die somehow!
Farewell to all of you! This is the end for me.

The chaste, they love not vice of their own will,
but yet they love it. Cypris, you are no god.
You are something stronger than God if that can be.
You have ruined her and me and all this house.

                                [The NURSE *goes off.*

        [The CHORUS *forms into two* HALF-CHORUSES.

F.H.C.   Did you hear, did you hear
the queen crying aloud,
telling of a calamity
which no ear should hear?

S.H.C.   I would rather die
than think such thoughts as hers.

F.H.C.   I am sorry for her trouble.

S.H.C.   Trouble nourishes mankind.

                             [Turning to PHAEDRA.

F.H.C.   You are dead, you yourself
have dragged your ruin to the light
what can happen now in the long
dragging stretch of the rest of your days?

[United.

CHORUS We know now, we know now
    how your love will end,
    poor unhappy Cretan girl!

PHAED. Hear me, you women of Troezen who live
    in this extremity of land, this anteroom to Argos.
    Many a time in night's long empty spaces
    I have pondered on the causes of a life's shipwreck.
    I think that our lives are worse than the mind's quality
    would warrant. There are many who know virtue.
    We know the good, we apprehend it clearly.
    But we can't bring it to achievement. Some
    are betrayed by their own laziness, and others
    value some other pleasure above virtue.
    There are many pleasures in a woman's life—
    long gossiping talks and leisure, that sweet curse.
    Then there is shame that thwarts us. Shame is of two kinds.
    The one is harmless, but the other a plague.
    For clarity's sake, we should not talk of 'shame,'
    a single word for two quite different things.
    These then are my thoughts. Nothing can now seduce me
    to the opposite opinion. I will tell you
    in my own case the track which my mind followed.

    At first when love had struck me I reflected
    how best to bear it. Silence was my first plan.
    Silence and concealment. For the tongue
    is not to be trusted: it can criticize
    another's faults, but on its own possessor
    it brings a thousand troubles.
    Then I believed that I could conquer love,
    conquer it with discretion and good sense.
    And when that too failed me, I resolved to die.
    And death is the best plan of them all. Let none of you
    dispute that.
    It would always be my choice
    to have my virtues known and honored. So
    when I do wrong I could not endure to see

a circle of condemning witnesses.
I know what I have done: I know the scandal:
and all too well I know that I am a woman.

I could wish
the hatred of the world and a cruel death
upon the wife who herself plays the tempter
and stains her loyalty to her husband's bed
by dalliance with strangers. In the wives
of noble houses first this taint begins:
when wickedness approves itself to those
of noble birth, it will surely be approved
by their inferiors. Truly too I hate
lip-worshippers of chastity who own
a lecherous daring when they have privacy.

O Cypris, sea-born goddess, how can they
look frankly in the faces of their husbands
and never shiver with fear lest their accomplice,
old darkness, and the rafters of the house
take voice and cry aloud?

This then, my friends, is my destruction:
I cannot bear that I should be discovered
a traitor to my husband and my children.
God grant them rich and glorious life in Athens,—
our famous Athens,—freedom in word and deed,
and from their mother an honorable name.
It makes the stoutest hearted man a slave
if in his soul he knows his parents' shame.

The proverb runs: 'There is one thing alone
that stands the brunt of life throughout its course,
a quiet conscience,' . . . a just and quiet conscience
whoever can attain it.
Time is as diligent with his looking glass
as a young girl. He holds it up to us
and sometimes as occasion falls, he shows us

the ugly rogues of the world. I would not wish
that I should be seen among them.

LEADER   How virtue is held lovely everywhere,
and harvests a good name among mankind!

[*The* NURSE *returns.*

NURSE   Mistress, the trouble you have lately told me,
coming on me so suddenly, frightened me
but now I realize that I was foolish.
In this world second thoughts, it seems, are best.
Your case is not so extraordinary,
beyond thought or reason. The Goddess in her anger
has smitten you, and you are in love. What wonder
is this? There are many thousands suffer with you.
So, you will die for love! And all the others,
who love, and who will love, must they die, too?
How will that profit them? The tide of love,
at its full surge, is not withstandable.
Upon the yielding spirit she comes gently,
but to the proud and fanatic heart
she is a torturer with the brand of shame.
She wings her way through the air: she is in the sea,
in its foaming billows: from her everything,
that is, is born. For she engenders us,
and sows the seed of desire whereof we're born,
all we her children, living on the earth.

He who has read the writings of the ancients
and has lived much in books, he knows
that Zeus once loved the lovely Semele;
he knows that Dawn, the bright light of the world,
once ravished Cephalus hence to the gods' company
for love's sake. Yet all these dwell in heaven.
They are content, I am sure, to be subdued
by the stroke of love.
But you, you won't submit! Why, you should certainly
have had your father beget you on fixed terms

or with other gods for masters, if you don't like
the laws that rule this world. Tell me, how many
of the wise ones of the earth do you suppose
see with averted eyes their wives turned faithless;
how many erring sons have fathers helped
with secret loves? It is the wise man's part
to leave in darkness everything that is ugly.

We should not in the conduct of our lives
be too exacting. Look, see this roof here,—
these overarching beams that span your house,—
could builders with all their skill lay them dead straight?
You've fallen into the great sea of love
and with your puny swimming would escape!
If in the sum you have more good luck than ill,
count yourself fortunate,—for you are mortal.

Come, dear, give up your discontented mood.
Give up your railing. It's only insolent pride
to wish to be superior to the gods.
Endure your love. The gods have willed it so.
You are sick. Then try to find some subtle means
to turn your sickness into health again.
There are magic love charms, spells of enchantment;
we'll find some remedy for your love-sickness.
Men would take long to hunt devices out,
if we the women did not find them first.

LEADER   Phaedra, indeed she speaks more usefully
for today's troubles. But it is you I praise,
and yet my praise brings with it more discomfort
than her rebuke: it is bitterer to the ear.

PHAED.   This is the deadly thing which devastates
well-ordered cities and the homes of men,—
that's it, this art of over subtle words.
It's not the words ringing delight in the ear
that one should speak, but those that have the power
to save their hearer's honorable name.

NURSE   This is high moralizing! What you want
is not fine words, but the man! Come, let's be done.
And tell your story frankly and directly.
For if there were no danger to your life,
as now there is,—or if you could be prudent,
I never would have led you on so far,
merely to please your fancy or your lust.
But now a great prize hangs on our endeavors,
and that's the saving of a life,—yours, Phaedra,
there's none can blame us for our actions now.

PHAED.   What you say is wicked, wicked! Hold your tongue!
I will not hear such shameful words again.

NURSE   O, they are shameful! But they are better than
your noble sounding moral sentiments.
'The deed' is better if it saves your life:
than your 'good name' in which you die exulting.

PHAED.   For God's sake, do not press me any further!
What you say is true, but terrible!
My very soul is subdued by my love
and if you plead the cause of wrong so well
I shall fall into the abyss
from which I now am flying.

NURSE   If that is what you think, you should be virtuous.
But if you are not, obey me: that is next best.
It has just come to my mind, I have at home
some magic love charms. They will end your trouble
they'll never harm your honor nor your mind.
they'll end your trouble, . . . only you must be brave.

PHAED.   Is this a poison ointment or a drink?

NURSE   I don't know. Don't be overanxious, child,
to find out what it is. Accept its benefits.

PHAED.   I am afraid of you: I am afraid
that you will be too clever for my good.

NURSE   You are afraid of everything. What is it?

PHAED.   You surely will not tell this to Hippolytus?

NURSE   Come, let that be: I will arrange all well.
          Only, my lady Cypris of the Sea,
          be my helper you. The other plans I have
          I'll tell to those we love within the house;
          that will suffice.

CHORUS   Love distills desire upon the eyes,   [STROPHE
          love brings bewitching grace into the heart
          of those he would destroy.
          I pray that love may never come to me
          with murderous intent,
          in rhythms measureless and wild.
          Not fire nor stars have stronger bolts
          than those of Aphrodite sent
          by the hand of Eros, Zeus' child.

          In vain by Alpheus' stream,   [ANTISTROPHE
          in vain in the halls of Phoebus' Pythian shrine
          the land of Greece increases sacrifice.
          But Love the King of Men they honor not,
          although he keeps the keys
          of the temple of desire,
          although he goes destroying through the world
          author of dread calamities
          and ruin when he enters human hearts.

          The Oechalian maiden who had never known   [STROPHE
          the bed of love, known neither man nor marriage
          the Goddess Cypris gave to Heracles.
          She took her from the home of Eurytus,
          maiden unhappy in her marriage song,
          wild as a Naiad or a Bacchanal,
          with blood and fire, a murderous hymeneal!

          O holy walls of Thebes and Dirce's fountain   [ANTISTROPHE
          bear witness you, to Love's grim journeying:
          once you saw Love bring Semele to bed,

lull her to sleep, clasped in the arms of Death,
pregnant with Dionysus by the thunder king.
Love is like a flitting bee in the world's garden
and for its flowers, destruction is in his breath.

SCENE III

[PHAEDRA *is standing listening near the central door
of the palace.*

PHAED.   Women, be silent! (*She listens and then recoils.*)
O, I am destroyed forever.

LEADER   What is there terrible within the house?

PHAED.   Hush, let me hear the voices within!

LEADER   And I obey. But this is sorrow's prelude.

[*Cries out.*

PHAED.   O, I am the most miserable of women!

[*The* CHORUS LEADER *and the* CHORUS *babble excitedly
among themselves.*

LEADER   What does she mean by her cries?
Why does she scream?
Tell us the fear-winged word, Mistress, the fear-winged word,
rushing upon the heart.

PHAED.   I am lost. Go, women, stand and listen there yourselves
and hear the tumult that falls on the house.

LEADER   Mistress, you stand at the door.
It is you who can tell us best
what happens within the house.

PHAED. Only the son of the horse-loving Amazon,
        Hippolytus, cursing a servant maid.

LEADER My ears can catch a sound,
        but I can hear nothing clear.
        I can only hear a voice
        scolding in anger.

PHAED. It is plain enough. He cries aloud against
        the mischievous bawd who betrays her mistress' love.

LEADER Lady, you are betrayed!
        How can I help you?
        What is hidden is revealed.
        You are destroyed.
        Those you love have betrayed you.

PHAED. She loved me and she told him of my troubles,
        and so has ruined me. She was my doctor,
        but her cure has made my illness mortal now.

LEADER What will you do? There is no cure.

PHAED. I know of one, and only one,—quick death.
        That is the only cure for my disease.

[She retires into the palace through one of the side doors just
     as HIPPOLYTUS issues through the central door, dogged by
       the NURSE. PHAEDRA is conceived of as listening from
         behind her door during the entire conversation
           between the NURSE and HIPPOLYTUS.

HIPPOL. O Mother Earth! O Sun and open sky!
        What words I have heard from this accursed tongue!

NURSE Hush, son! Someone may hear you.

HIPPOL. You cannot
        expect that I hear horror and stay silent.

NURSE I beg of you, entreat you by your right hand,
        your strong right hand, . . . don't speak of this!

HIPPOL. Don't lay your hand on me! Let go my cloak!

NURSE   By your knees then, . . . don't destroy me!

HIPPOL.   What is this?
        Don't you declare that you have done nothing wrong?

NURSE   Yes, but the story, son, is not for everyone.

HIPPOL. Why not? A pleasant tale makes pleasanter telling,
        when there are many listeners.

NURSE   You will not break your oath to me, surely you will not?

HIPPOL. My tongue swore, but my mind was still unpledged.

NURSE   Son, what would you do?
        You'll not destroy your friends?

HIPPOL.   'Friends' you say!
        I spit the word away. None of the wicked
        are friends of mine.

NURSE   Then pardon, son. It's natural
        that we should sin, being human.

HIPPOL. Women! This coin which men find counterfeit!
        Why, why, Lord Zeus, did you put them in the world,
        in the light of the sun? If you were so determined
        to breed the race of man, the source of it
        should not have been women. Men might have dedicated
        in your own temples images of gold,
        silver, or weight of bronze, and thus have bought
        the seed of progeny, . . . to each been given
        his worth in sons according to the assessment
        of his gift's value. So we might have lived
        in houses free of the taint of women's presence.
        But now, to bring this plague into our homes
        we drain the fortunes of our homes. In this
        we have a proof how great a curse is woman.
        For the father who begets her, rears her up,
        must add a dowry gift to pack her off
        to another's house and thus be rid of the load.
        And he again that takes the cursed creature

rejoices and enriches his heart's jewel
with dear adornment, beauty heaped on vileness.
With lovely clothes the poor wretch tricks her out
spending the wealth that underprops his house.
That husband has the easiest life whose wife
is a mere nothingness, a simple fool
uselessly sitting by the fireside.
I hate a clever woman,—God forbid
that I should ever have a wife at home
with more than woman's wits! Lust breeds mischief
in the clever ones. The limits of their minds
deny the stupid lecherous delights.
We should not suffer servants to approach them,
but give them as companions voiceless beasts,
dumb, . . . but with teeth, that they might not converse,
and hear another voice in answer.
But now at home the mistress plots the mischief
and the maid carries it abroad. So you, vile woman,
came here to me to bargain and to traffic
in the sanctity of my father's marriage bed.
I'll go to a running stream and pour its waters
into my ear to purge away the filth.
Shall I who cannot even hear such impurity,
and feel myself untouched, . . . shall I turn sinner?
Woman, know this. It is my piety saves you.
Had you not caught me off my guard and bound
my lips with an oath by heaven I would not refrain
from telling this to my father.
Now I will go and leave this house until
Theseus returns from his foreign wanderings.
And I'll be silent. But I'll watch you close.
I'll walk with my father step by step and see
how you look at him, . . . you and your mistress both.
I have tasted of the daring of your infamy.
I'll know it for the future. Curses on you!
I'll hate you women, hate and hate and hate you,
and never have enough of hating. . . .

Some

say that I talk of this eternally,
yes, but eternal too is woman's wickedness.
Either let someone teach them to be chaste,
or suffer me to trample on them for ever.

[PHAEDRA *comes out from behind the door. Exit* HIPPOLYTUS.

PHAED.   Bitter indeed is woman's destiny!
I have failed. What trick is there now, what cunning plea
to loose the knot around my neck?
I have had justice. O earth and the warm sunlight!
Where shall I escape from my fate?
How shall I hide my trouble?
What God or man would appear
to bear hand or part in my crime?
There is a limit to all suffering and I have reached it.
I am the unhappiest of women.

CHORUS   Alas, mistress, all is over now
your servant's schemes have failed and you are ruined.

[*Enter the* NURSE.

PHAED.   This is fine service you have rendered me,
corrupted, damned seducer of your friends!
May Zeus, the father of my fathers' line,
blot you out utterly, raze you from the world
with thunderbolts! Did I not see your purpose,
did I not say to you, 'Breathe not a word of this'
which now overwhelms me with shame? But you,
you did not hold back. And therefore I must die
and die dishonored.

Enough of this. We have a new theme now.
The anger of Hippolytus is whetted.
He will tell his father all the story of your sin
to my disparagement. He will tell old Pittheus, too.
He will fill all the land with my dishonor.
May my curse

light upon you, on you and all the others
who eagerly help unwilling friends to ruin.

NURSE   Mistress, you may well blame my ill-success,
for sorrow's bite is master of your judgment.
But I have an answer to make if you will listen.
I reared you up. I am your loyal servant.
I sought a remedy for your love's sickness,
and found, . . . not what I sought.
Had I succeeded, I had been a wise one.
Our wisdom varies in proportion to
our failure or achievement.

PHAED.   So, that's enough
for me? Do I have justice if you deal me
my death blow and then say 'I was wrong: I grant it.'

NURSE   We talk too long. True I was not wise then.
But even from this desperate plight, my child,
you can escape.

PHAED.   You, speak no more to me.
You have given me dishonorable advice.
What you have tried has brought dishonor too.
Away with you!
Think of yourself. For me and my concerns
I will arrange all well.

                                        [Exit NURSE.

You noble ladies of Troezen, grant me this,
this one request, that what you have heard here
you wrap in silence.

LEADER   I swear by holy Artemis, child of Zeus,
never to bring your troubles to the daylight.

PHAED.   I thank you. I have found one single blessing
in this unhappy business, one alone,
that I can pass on to my children after me
life with an uncontaminated name,
and myself profit by the present throw
of Fortune's dice. For I will never shame you,

my Cretan home, nor will I go to face
Theseus, defendant on an ugly charge,
never,—for one life's sake.

LEADER What is the desperate deed you mean to do,
the deed past cure?

PHAED.   Death. But the way of it, that
is what I now must plan.

LEADER   O, do not speak of it!

PHAED. No, I'll not speak of it. But on this day
when I shake off the burden of this life
I shall delight the goddess who destroys me,
the goddess Cypris.
Bitter will have been the love that conquers me,
but in my death I shall at least bring sorrow,
upon another, too, that his high heart
may know no arrogant joy at my life's shipwreck;
he will have his share in this my mortal sickness
and learn of chastity in moderation.

CHORUS Would that I were under the cliffs, in the secret hiding-
   places of the rocks,   [STROPHE
that Zeus might change me to a winged bird
and set me among the feathered flocks.
I would rise and fly to where the sea
washes the Adriatic coast,
and to the waters of Eridanus.
Into that deep-blue tide,
where their father, the Sun, goes down,
the unhappy maidens weep
tears from their amber-gleaming eyes
in pity for Phaethon.

I would win my way to the coast,   [ANTISTROPHE
apple-bearing Hesperian coast,
of which the minstrels sing.
Where the Lord of the Ocean

denies the voyager further sailing,
and fixes the solemn limit of Heaven
which Giant Atlas upholds.
There the streams flow with ambrosia
by Zeus' bed of love,
and holy earth, the giver of life,
yields to the gods rich blessedness.

O Cretan ship with the white sails,   [STROPHE
from a happy home you brought her,
my mistress over the tossing foam, over the salty sea,
to bless her with a marriage unblest.
Black was the omen that sped her here,
black was the omen for both her lands,
for glorious Athens and her Cretan home,
as they bound to Munychia's pier
the cables' ends with their twisted strands
and stepped ashore on the continent.

The presage of the omen was true;   [ANTISTROPHE
Aphrodite has broken her spirit
with the terrible sickness of impious love.
The waves of destruction are over her head,
from the roof of her room with its marriage bed,
she is tying the twisted noose.
And now it is around her fair white neck!
The shame of her cruel fate has conquered.
She has chosen good name rather than life:
she is easing her heart of its bitter load of love.

                                                        [*Within.*

NURSE   Ho, there, help!
           You who are near the palace, help!
           My mistress, Theseus' wife, has hanged herself.

LEADER   It is done, she is hanged in the dangling rope.
           Our Queen is dead.

[*Within.*

NURSE   Quick! Someone bring a knife!
           Help me cut the knot around her neck.

                  [*The* CHORUS *talks among itself.*

1ST LA.   What shall we do, friends? Shall we cross the threshold,
           and take the Queen from the grip of the tight-drawn cords?

2ND LA.   Why should we? There are servants enough within
           for that. Where hands are over busy,
           there is no safety.

                                      [*Within.*

NURSE   Lay her out straight, poor lady.
           Bitter shall my lord find her housekeeping.

3RD LA.   From what I hear, the Queen is dead.
           They are already laying out the corpse.

⊓⊔⊓⊔⊓⊔⊓⊔⊓⊔⊓⊔⊓⊔⊓⊔⊓⊔⊓⊔⊓⊔⊓⊔⊓⊔⊓⊔⊓⊔⊓⊔⊓⊔

SCENE IV

[THESEUS *enters.*

THES.   Women, what is this crying in the house?
           I heard heavy wailing on the wind,
           as were servants, mourning. And my house
           deigns me no kindly welcome though I come
           crowned with good luck from Delphi.
           The doors are shut against me. Can it be
           something has happened to my father? He is old.
           His life has traveled a great journey,
           but bitter would be his passing from our house.

LEADER   King, it is not the old who claim your sorrow.
           Young is the dead and bitterly you'll grieve.

THES.   My children . . . has death snatched a life away?

LEADER   Your children live,—but sorrowfully, King.
             Their mother is dead.

THES.   It cannot be true, it cannot.
             My wife! How could she be dead?

LEADER   She herself tied the rope around her neck.

THES.   Was it grief and numbing loneliness drove her to it,
             or has there been some violence at work?

LEADER   I know no more than this. I, too, came lately
             to mourn for you and yours, King Theseus.

THES.   O,
             Why did I plait this coronal of leaves,
             and crown my head with garlands, I the envoy
             who find my journey end in misery?

                                             [*To the servants within.*

             Open the doors! Unbar the fastenings,
             that I may see this bitter sight, my wife
             who killed me when she killed herself.

             [*The doors are opened, and* THESEUS *goes inside. The
             * CHORUS *in the orchestra divide again into half-
             choruses and chant.*

F.H.C.   Woman unhappy, tortured,
             your suffering, your death,
             has shaken this house to its foundations.

S.H.C.   You were daring, you who died
             in violence and guilt.
             Here was a wrestling: your own hand against your life.
                                                        [*United.*

CHORUS   Who can have cast a shadow on your life?

SCENE V

[*Enter* THESEUS.

THES. O, city, city! Bitterness of sorrow!
Extremest sorrow that a man can suffer!
Fate, you have ground me and my house to dust,
fate in the form of some ineffable
pollution, some grim spirit of revenge.
The file has whittled away my life until
it is a life no more.
I am like a swimmer that falls into a great sea:
I cannot cross this towering wave I see before me.

My wife! I cannot think
of anything said or done to drive you to this horrible death.
You are like a bird that has vanished out of my hand.
You have made a quick leap out of my arms
into the land of Death.

It must be the sin of some of my ancestors in the dim past
God in his vengeance makes me pay now.

LEADER You are not the only one, King.
Many another as well as you
has lost a noble wife.

THES. Darkness beneath the earth, darkness beneath the earth!
How good to lie there and be dead,
now that I have lost you, my dearest comrade.
Your death is no less mine.

[*Turning furiously to the servants.*

Will any of you
Tell me what happened?
Or does the palace keep a flock of you for nothing?

God, the pain I saw in the house!
I cannot speak of it, I cannot bear it.
I cannot speak of it, I cannot bear it. I am a dead man.
My house is empty and my children orphaned.
You have left them, you
my loving wife,—
the best of wives
of all the sun looks down on or the blazing stars of the night.

CHORUS   Woe for the house! Such storms of ill assail it.
My eyes are wells of tears and overrun,
and still I fear the evil that shall come.

[*As the attendants are taking away the body,* THESEUS *stops
them. He has seen clenched in* PHAEDRA'S *hand a tablet
with writing on it. He takes and opens it.*

THES.   What can she wish to tell me?
Have you written begging me to care
for our children or, in dumb entreaty,
about another woman? Sad one, rest confident.
There is no woman in the world who shall come to this house
and sleep by my side.
Look, the familiar signet ring,
hers who was once my wife!

[*The* CHORUS OF TROEZENIAN LADIES *speak singly.*

1ST LA.   Surely some God
brings sorrow upon sorrow in succession.

2ND LA.   The house of our lords is destroyed: it is no more.

3RD LA.   God, if it so may be, hear my prayer.
Do not destroy this house utterly. I am a prophet:
I can see the omen of coming trouble.

LEADER   What is it? Tell us if we may share the story.

THES.   It cries aloud, this tablet, cries aloud,
and Death is its song!

LEADER   Prelude of ruin!

THES.   I shall no longer hold this secret prisoner
in the gates of my mouth. It is horrible,
yet I will speak.
Citizens,
Hippolytus has dared to rape my wife.
He has dishonored God's holy sunlight.

[*He turns in the direction of the sea.*

Father Poseidon, once you gave to me
three curses. . . . Now with one of these, I pray,
kill my son. Suffer him not to escape,
this very day, if you have promised truly.

LEADER   Call back your curses, King, call back your curses.
Else you will realize that you were wrong
another day, too late. I pray you, trust me.

THES.   I will not. And I now make this addition:
I banish him from this land's boundaries.
So fate shall strike him, one way or the other,
either Poseidon will respect my curse,
and send him dead into the House of Hades,
or exiled from this land, a beggar wandering,
on foreign soil, his life shall suck the dregs
of sorrow's cup.

LEADER   Here comes your son, and seasonably, King Theseus.
Give over your deadly anger. You will best
determine for the welfare of your house.

[*Enter* HIPPOLYTUS *with companions.*

HIPPOL.   I heard you crying, father, and came quickly.
I know no cause why you should be in mourning.
Tell me.

[*Suddenly he sees the body of* PHAEDRA.

O father, father,—Phaedra! Dead! She's dead!
I cannot believe it. But a few moments since
I left her. . . . And she is still so young.

But what could it be? How did she die, father?
I must hear the truth from you. Why won't you answer?

I always want to know of everything,
and when you are in trouble most of all.
You should not hide your troubles from your friends,
and, father, those who are closer than your friends.

THES. What fools men are! You work and work for nothing,
you teach ten thousand tasks to one another,
invent, discover everything. One thing only
you do not know: one thing you never hunt for:—
a way to teach fools wisdom.

HIPPOL. Clever indeed
would be the teacher able to compel
the stupid to be wise! This is no time
for such fine logic chopping.

                     I am afraid
your tongue runs wild through sorrow.

THES.   If there were
some token now, some mark to make the division
clear between friend and friend, the true and the false!
All men should have two voices, one the just voice,
and one as chance would have it. In this way
the treacherous scheming voice would be confuted
by the just, and we should never be deceived.

HIPPOL. Some friend has poisoned your ear with slanderous tales.
Am I suspected, then, for all my innocence?
I am amazed. I am amazed to hear
your words. They are distraught. They go indeed
far wide of the mark!

THES. The mind of man,—how far will it advance?
Where will its daring impudence find limits?
If human villainy and human life
shall wax in due proportion, if the son

shall always grow in wickedness past his father
the gods must add another world to this
that all the sinners may have space enough.

Look at this man! He was my son and he
dishonors my wife's bed! By the dead's testimony
he's clearly proved the vilest, falsest wretch.
Come,—you could stain your conscience with the impurity,—
show me your face; show it to me, your father.

You are the veritable holy man!
You walked with gods in chastity immaculate!
I'll not believe your boasts of gods' companionship:
the gods are not so simple nor so ignorant.
Go, boast that you eat no meat, that you have Orpheus
for your king. Read until you are demented
your great thick books whose substance is as smoke.
For I have found you out. I tell you all,
avoid such men as he. They hunt their prey
with holy-seeming words, but their designs
are black and ugly. 'She is dead' you thought,
'and that will save me.' Fool, it is chiefly that
which proves your guilt. What oath that you can swear,
what speech that you can make for your acquittal
outweighs this letter of hers? You'll say, to be sure,
she was your enemy and that the bastard son
is always hateful to the legitimate line.
Your words would argue her a foolish merchant
whose stock of merchandise was her own life
if she should throw away what she held dearest
to gratify her enmity for you.

Or you will tell me that this frantic folly
is inborn in a woman's nature; man
is different: but I know that young men
are no more to be trusted than a woman
when love disturbs the youthful blood in them.
The very male in them will make them false.

But why should I debate against you in words?
Here is the dead, surest of witnesses.
Get from this land with all the speed you can
to exile,—may you rot there! Never again
come to our city, god-built Athens, nor
to countries over which my spear is king.

If I should take this injury at your hands
and pardon you, then Sinis of the Isthmus
whom once I killed would vow I never killed him,
but only bragged of the deed. And Sciron's rocks
washed by the sea would call me liar when
I swore I was a terror to ill-doers.

LEADER   I cannot say of any man: he is happy.
See here how former happiness lies uprooted!

HIPPOL.   Your mind and intellect are subtle, father:
here you have a subject dressed in eloquent words;
but if you lay the matter bare of words
the matter is not eloquent. I am
no man to speak with vapid, precious skill
before a mob, although among my equals
and in a narrow circle I am held
not unaccomplished in the eloquent art.
That is as it should be. The demagogue
who charms a crowd is scorned by cultured experts.
But here in this necessity I must speak.
First I shall take the argument you first
urged as so irrefutable and deadly.
You see the earth and air about you, father?
In all of that there lives no man more chaste
than I, though you deny it.
It is my rule to honor the gods first
and then to have as friends only such men
as do no sin, nor offer wicked service
nor will consent to sin to serve a friend
as a return for kindness. I am no railer
at my companions. Those who are my friends

find me as much their friends when they are absent
as when we are together.

There is one thing that I have never done, the thing
of which you think that you convict me, father.
I am a virgin to this very day.
Save what I have heard or what I have seen in pictures
I'm ignorant of the deed. Nor do I wish
to see such things, for I've a maiden soul.
But say you disbelieve my chastity.
Then tell me how it was your wife seduced me:
was it because she was more beautiful
than all the other women in the world?
Or did I think, when I had taken her,
to win your place and kingdom for a dowry
and live in your own house? I would have been
a fool, a senseless fool, if I had dreamed it.
Was rule so sweet? Never, I tell you, Theseus,
for the wise. A man whom power has so enchanted
must be demented. I would wish to be
first in the contests of the Hellenic Games
but in the city I'd take second place
and an enduring happy life among
the best society who are my friends.
So one has time to work and danger's absence
has charms above the royal diadem.

But a word more and my defense is finished.
If I had one more witness to my character,
if I were tried when *she* still saw the light,
deeds would have helped you as you scanned your friends
to know the true from the false. But now I swear,
I swear to you by Zeus, the God of oaths,
by this deep rooted fundament of earth,
I never sinned against you with your wife
nor would have wished or thought of it.
If I have been a villain may I die
unfamed, unknown, a homeless stateless beggar,

an exile! May the earth and sea refuse
to give my body rest when I am dead!
Whether your wife took her own life because
she was afraid, I do not know. I may not speak
further than this.
Virtuous she was in deed although not virtuous:
I that have virtue used it to my ruin.

LEADER   You have rebutted the charge enough by your oath:
it is a great pledge you took in the god's name.

THES.   Why, here's a spell-binding magician for you!
He wrongs his father and then trusts his craft,
his smooth beguiling craft to lull my anger.

HIPPOL.   Father, I must wonder at this in you.
If I were father now, and you were son,
I would not have banished you to exile! I
would have killed you if I thought you touched my wife.

THES.   This speech is worthy of you: but you'll not die so.
You'll not prescribe your martyrdom to me.
A quick death is the easiest of ends
for miserable men. No, you'll go wandering
far from your fatherland and beg your way.
This is the payment of the impious man.

HIPPOL.   What will you do? You will not wait until
time's pointing finger proves me innocent.
Must I go at once to banishment?

THES.   Yes, and had I the power,
your place of banishment would be beyond
the limits of the world, the encircling sea
and the Atlantic Pillars.
That is the measure of my hate, my son.

HIPPOL.   Pledges, oaths and oracles,—you will not test them?
You will banish me from the kingdom without trial?

THES.   This letter here is proof without lot-casting.

The ominous birds may fly above my head:
they do not trouble me.

HIPPOL.   Eternal Gods!
Dare I speak out, since I am ruined now
through loyalty to the oath I took by you?
No, he would not believe who should believe
and I should be false to my oath for nothing.

THES.   This is more of your holy juggling!
I cannot stomach it. Away with you!
Get from this country,—and go quickly!

HIPPOL.   Where shall I turn? What friend will take me in,
when I am banished on a charge like this?

THES.   Doubtless some man who loves to entertain
his wife's seducers, welcoming them at the hearth.

HIPPOL.   That blow went home.
I am near crying when I think that I
am judged to be guilty and that it is you who are judge.

THES.   You might have sobbed and snivelled long ago,
and thought of that before when you resolved
to rape your father's wife.

HIPPOL.   House, speak for me!
Take voice and bear me witness if I have sinned.

THES.   You have a clever trick of citing witnesess,
Whose testimony is dumb. Here is your handiwork

[*Pointing to the body.*

It, too, can't speak,—but it convicts you.

HIPPOL.   If I could only find
another me to look me in the face
and see my tears and all that I am suffering!

THES.   Yes, in self-worship you are certainly practiced.
You are more at home there than in the other virtues,
justice, for instance, and duty towards a father.

HIPPOL.   Unhappy mother mine, and bitter birth-pangs,
when you gave me to the world! I would not wish
on any of my friends a bastard's birth.

                                     [*To the servants.*

THES.   Drag him away!
Did you not hear me, men, a long time since
proclaiming his decree of banishment?

HIPPOL.   Let one of them touch me at his peril! But you,
you drive me out yourself,—if you have the heart!

THES.   I'll do it, too, unless you go at once.
No, there is no chance that pity for your exile
will steal on my hard heart and make me change.

                                 [THESEUS *goes out.*

HIPPOL.   So, I'm condemned and there is no release.
I know the truth and dare not tell the truth.

                [*He turns to the statue of Artemis.*

    Daughter of Leto, dearest of the gods to me,
comrade and partner in the hunt, behold me,
banished from famous Athens.
Farewell, city! Farewell, Erechtheus' land!
Troezen, farewell! I had a happy boyhood
in your flat plains.
This is the last time I shall look upon you,
the last time I shall greet you.

                      [*To his companions.*

    Come friends, you are of my age and of this country,
say your farewells and set me on my way;
you will not see a man more innocent,—
innocent despite my judge!—condemned to banishment.

CHORUS   The care of God for us is a great thing,   [STROPHE
if a man believe it at heart:
it plucks the burden of sorrow from him.
So I have a secret hope

of someone, a god, who is wise and plans;
'but my hopes grow dim when I see
the deeds of men and their destinies.
For fortune is ever veering, and the currents of life are shifting
shifting, wandering for ever.

This is the lot in life I seek   [ANTISTROPHE
and I pray that God may grant it me,
luck and prosperity,
and a heart untroubled by anguish.
And a mind that is neither false clipped coin,
nor too clear eyed in sincerity,
that I may lightly change my ways,
my ways of today when tomorrow comes,
and so be happy all my life long.

My heart is no longer clear: [STROPHE
I have seen what I never dreamed,
I have seen the brightest star of Athens,
stricken by a father's wrath,
banished to an alien land.
Sands of the seashore!
Thicket of the mountain!
Where with his pacing hounds
he hunted wild beasts and killed
to the honor of holy Dictynna.

He will never again mount his car   [ANTISTROPHE
with its span of Venetian mares,
nor fill the ring of Limnae with the sound of horses' hoofs.
The music which never slept
on the strings of his lyre, shall be dumb,
shall be dumb in his father's house.
The haunts of the Goddess Maid
in the deep rich meadow shall want their crowns.
You are banished: there's an end
of the rivalry of maids for your love.

But my sorrow shall not die   [EPODE
still my eyes shall be wet with tears
for your heartless doom.
Sad mother, you bore him in vain:
I am angry against the gods.
Sister Graces, why did you let him go
guiltless, out of his native land,
out of his father's house?

SCENE VI

[Enter a MESSENGER, *one of* HIPPOLYTUS' *comrades.*

MESS.   Where shall I go to find King Theseus, women?
          If you know, tell me. Is he within doors?

CHORUS Here he is coming out.

MESS.   King Theseus,
          I bring you news worthy of much thought
          for you and all the citizens who live
          in Athens' walls and boundaries of Troezen.

THES.   What is it? Has some still newer disaster
          seized on the citizens of both my cities?

MESS.   Hippolytus is dead: I may almost say dead:
          he sees the light of day still, though the balance
          that holds him in this world is slight indeed.

THES.   Who killed him? I can guess that someone hated him,
          whose wife he raped, as he did mine, his father's.

MESS.   It was the horses of his own car that killed him,
          they, and the curses of your lips,

the curses you invoked against your son,
and prayed the Lord of Ocean to fulfill them.

THES.   O gods,—Poseidon, you are then truly
my father! You have heard my prayers.
How did he die? Tell me. How did the beam
of Justice's dead-fall strike him, my dishonored ....er?

MESS.   We were combing our horses' coats ...... beside the sea,
where the waves came ....ning to the shore. And we were
crying
for one had come and told us that our master,
Hippolytus should walk this land no more,
since you had laid hard banishment upon him.
Then he came himself down to the shore to us,
with the same refrain of tears,
and with him walked a countless company
of friends and young men his own age.

But at last he gave over crying and said:
'Why do I rave like this? It is my father
who has commanded and I must obey him.
Prepare my horses, men, and harness them.
This is no longer a city of mine.'
Then every man made haste. Before you could say the words,
there was the chariot ready before our master.
He put his feet into the driver's rings,
and took the reins from the rail into his hands.
But first he folded his hands like this and prayed:
'Zeus, let me die now, if I have been guilty!
Let my father know that he has done me wrong,
whether I live to see the day or not.'

With that, he took the goad and touched the horses.
And we his servants followed our master's car,
close by the horses' heads, on the straight road
that leads to Argos and to Epidaurus.
When we were entering the lonely country
the other side of the border, where the shore

goes down to the Saronic Gulf, a rumbling
deep in the earth, terrible to hear,
growled like the thunder of Father Zeus.
The horses raised their heads, pricked up their ears,
and gusty fear was on us all to know,
whence came the sound. As we looked towards the shore,
where the waves were beating, we saw a wave appear,
a miracle wave, lifting its crest to the sky,
so high that Sciron's coast was blotted out
from my eye's vision. And it hid the Isthmus
and the Asclepius Rock. To the shore it came,
swelling, boiling, crashing, casting its surf around,
to where the chariot stood.
But at the very moment when it broke,
the wave threw up a monstrous savage bull.
Its bellowing filled the land, and the land echoed it,
with shuddering emphasis. And sudden panic
fell on the horses in the car. But the master,—
he was used to horses' ways,—all his life long
he had been with horses—took a firm grip of the reins
and lashed the ends behind his back and pulled
like a sailor at the oar. The horses bolted:
their teeth were clenched upon the fire-forged bit.
They heeded neither the driver's hand nor harness
nor the jointed car. As often as he would turn them
with guiding hand to the soft sand of the shore,
the bull appeared in front to head them off,
maddening the team with terror.
But when in frenzy they charged towards the cliffs,
the bull came galloping beside the rail,
silently following until he brought disaster,
capsizing the car, striking the wheel on a rock.
Then all was in confusion. Axles of wheels
and lynch-pins flew up into the air,
and he the unlucky driver, tangled in the reins,
was dragged along in an inextricable
knot and his dear head pounded on the rocks,
his body bruised. He cried aloud and terrible

his voice rang in our ears: 'Stand, horses, stand!
You were fed in my stables. Do not kill me!
My father's curse! His curse! Will none of you
save me? I am innocent. Save me!'

Many of us had will enough, but all
were left behind in the race. Getting free of the reins
somehow he fell. There was still life in him.
But the horses vanished and that ill-omened monster,
somewhere, I know not where, in the rough cliffs.

I am only a slave in your household, King Theseus,
but I shall never be able to believe
that your son was guilty, not though the tribe of women
were hanged for it, not though the weight of tablets
of a high pine of Ida, filled with writing,
accused him,—for I know that he was good.

LEADER   It has been fulfilled, this bitter, new disaster,
for what is doomed and fated there is no quittance.

THES.   For hatred of the sufferer I was glad
at what you told me. Still, he was my son.
God sanctioned the tie which bound us and I reverence it.
I neither rejoice nor sorrow at this thing.

MESS.   What is your pleasure that we do with him?
Would you have him brought to you? If I might counsel,
you would not be harsh with your son,—for he is dying.

THES.   Bring him to me that I may see his face.
He swore that he had never wronged my wife.
I will refute him with God's punishing stroke.

CHORUS   Cypris, you guide men's hearts
and the inflexible
hearts of the gods and with you
comes Love with the flashing wings,
comes Love with the swiftest of wings.
Over the earth he flies

and the loud-echoing salt sea.
He bewitches and maddens the heart
of the victim he swoops upon.
He bewitches the race of the mountain haunting
lions and beasts of the sea,
and all the creatures that earth feeds,
and the blazing sun sees,—
and man, too,—
over all you hold kingly power,
Love, you are only ruler
over all these.

EPILOGUE

[*Enter* ARTEMIS.

ARTE.   I call on the noble king, the son of Aegeus,
to hear me! It is I, Artemis, child of Leto.

Miserable man, what joy have you in this?
you have murdered a son, you have broken nature's laws.
Dark indeed was the conclusion
you drew from your wife's lying accusations,
but plain for all to see is the destruction
to which they led you.
There is a hell beneath the earth: haste to it,
and hide your head there! Or will you take wings,
and choosing the life of a bird instead of man
keep your feet from destruction's path in which they tread?
Amongst good men, at least, you have no share in life.

Hear me tell you, Theseus, how these things came to pass.
I shall not better them, but I will give you pain.

I have come here for this,—to show you that your son's heart
was always just, so just that for his good name
he endured to die. I will show you, too,
the frenzied love that seized your wife, or I may call it,
a noble innocence. For that most hated goddess,
hated by all of us whose joy is virginity,
drove her with love's sharp prickings to desire
your son. She tried to overcome her love
with the mind's power, but at last against her will,
she fell by the nurse's stratagems,
the nurse, who told your son under oath her mistress loved
    him.
But he, just man, did not fall in with her
counsels, and even when reviled by you
refused to break the oath he had pledged.
Such was his piety. But your wife, fearing
lest she be proved the sinner, wrote a letter,
a letter full of lies; and so she killed
your son by treachery; but she convinced you.

THES.   Alas!

ARTE.   This is a bitter story, Theseus. Stay,
hear more that you may groan the more.

You know you had three curses from your father,
three, clear for you to use? One you have launched,
vile wretch, at your own son, when you might have
spent it upon an enemy. Your father,
King of the Sea, in loving kindness to you
gave you, by his bequest, all that he ought.
But you've been proved at fault both in his eyes
and mine in that you did not stay for oaths
nor voice of oracles, nor gave a thought
to what time might have shown; only too quickly
you hurled the curses at your son and killed him.

THES.   Mistress, I am destroyed.

ARTE.   You have sinned indeed, but yet you may win pardon.

For it was Cypris managed the thing this way
to gratify her anger against Hippolytus.
You know there is an understanding among the gods.
No one may fly in the face of another's wish:
we remain aloof and neutral. Else, I assure you,
had I not feared Zeus, I never would have endured
such shame as this,—my best friend among men
killed, and I could do nothing.
As for you, in the first place ignorance acquits you,
and then your wife, by her death, destroyed the proofs,
the verbal proofs which might have still convinced you.
You and I are the chief sufferers, Theseus.
Misfortune for you, grief for me.
The gods do not rejoice when pious worshippers die:
the wicked we destroy, children, house and all.

CHORUS   Here comes the suffering Hippolytus,
his fair young body and his golden head,
a battered wreck. O trouble of the house,
what double sorrow from the hand of God
has been fulfilled for this our royal palace!

HIPPOL.   A battered wreck of body! Unjust father,
and oracle unjust,—this is your work.
Woe for my fate!
My head is filled with shooting agony,
and in my brain there is a leaping fire.

Let me be!
For I would rest my weary frame awhile.

Curse on my team! How often have I fed you
from my own hand, you who have murdered me!

O, O!
In God's name touch my wounded body gently.

Who is this standing on the right of me?
Come lift me carefully, bear me easily,

a man unlucky, cursed by my own father
in bitter error. Zeus, do you see this,
see me that worshipped God in piety,
me that excelled all men in chastity,
see me now go to death which gapes before me;
all my life lost, and all for nothing now
labors of piety in the face of men?

O the pain, the pain that comes upon me!
Let me be, let me be, you wretches!

May death the healer come for me at last!
You kill me ten times over with this pain.
O for a spear with a keen cutting edge
to shear me apart,—and give me my last sleep!
Father, your deadly curse!
This evil comes from some manslaying of old,
some ancient tale of murder among my kin.
But why should it strike me who am clear of guilt?
What is there to say? How can I shake from me
this pitiless pain? O death, black night of death,
resistless death, come to me now the miserable,
and give me sleep!

ARTE.   Unhappy boy! You are yoked to a cruel fate.
         The nobility of your soul has proved your ruin.

HIPPOL. O divine fragrance! Even in my pain
         I sense it, and the suffering is lightened.
         The Goddess Artemis is near this place.

ARTE.   She is, the dearest of the gods to you.

HIPPOL. You see my suffering, mistress?

ARTE.   I see it. Heavenly law forbids my tears.

HIPPOL. Gone is your huntsman, gone your servant now.

ARTE.   Yes, truly: but you die beloved by me.

HIPPOL. Gone is your groom, gone your shrine's guardian.

ARTE.   Cypris, the worker of mischief, so contrived.

HIPPOL.   Alas, I know the goddess who destroyed me!

ARTE.   She blamed your disrespect, hated your chastity.

HIPPOL.   She claimed us three as victims then, did Cypris?

ARTE.   Your father, you, and me to make a third.

HIPPOL.   Yes, I am sorry for my father's suffering.

ARTE.   Cypris deceived him by her cunning snares.

HIPPOL.   O father, this is sorrow for you indeed!

THES.   I, too, am dead now. I have no more joy in life.

HIPPOL.   I sorrow for you in this more than myself.

THES.   Would that it were I who was dying instead of you!

HIPPOL.   Bitter were Poseidon's gifts, my father, bitter.

THES.   Would that they had never come into my mouth.

HIPPOL.   Even without them, you would have killed me,—
          you were so angry.

THES.   A god tripped up my judgment.

HIPPOL.   O, if only men might be a curse to gods!

ARTE.   Hush, that is enough! You shall not be unavenged,
          Cypris shall find the angry shafts she hurled
          against you for your piety and innocence
          shall cost her dear.
          I'll wait until she loves a mortal next time,
          and with this hand,—with these unerring arrows
          I'll punish him.

          To you, unfortunate Hippolytus,
          by way of compensation for these ills,
          I will give the greatest honors of Troezen.
          Unwedded maids before the day of marriage
          will cut their hair in your honor. You will reap

through the long cycle of time, a rich reward in tears.
And when young girls sing songs they will not forget you,
your name will not be left unmentioned,
nor Phaedra's love for you remain unsung.

[*To* THESEUS.

Son of old Aegeus, take your son
to your embrace. Draw him to you. Unknowing
you killed him. It is natural for men
to err when they are blinded by the gods.

[*To* HIPPOLYTUS.

Do not bear a grudge against your father.
It was fate that you should die so.
Farewell, I must not look upon the dead.
My eye must not be polluted by the last
gaspings for breath. I see you are near this.

HIPPOL.   Farewell to you too, holy maiden! Go in peace.
You can lightly leave a long companionship.
You bid me end my quarrel with my father,
and I obey. In the past too I obeyed you.

The darkness is upon my eyes already.

Father, lay hold on me and lift me up.

THES.   Alas, what are you doing to me, my son?

HIPPOL.   I am dying. I can see the gates of death.

THES.   And so you leave me, my hands stained with murder.

HIPPOL.   No, for I free you from all guilt in this.

THES.   You will acquit me of blood guiltiness?

HIPPOL.   So help me Artemis of the conquering bow!

THES.   Dear son, how noble you have proved to me!

HIPPOL.   Yes, pray to heaven for such legitimate sons.

THES.	Woe for your goodness, piety and virtue.
HIPPOL.	Farewell to you, too, father, a long farewell!
THES.	Dear son, bear up. Do not forsake me.
HIPPOL.	This is the end of what I have to bear. I'm gone. Cover my face up quickly.
THES.	Pallas Athene's famous city, What a man you have lost! Alas for me! Cypris, how many of your injuries I shall remember.
CHORUS	This is a common grief for all the city; it came unlooked for. There shall be a storm of multitudinous tears for this; the lamentable stories of great men prevail more than of humble folk.

Euripides

ALCESTIS

translated by
Dudley Fitts
and
Robert Fitzgerald

KATHERINÆ · ELEANORÆ · MARGARITÆ
plurima praestantibus referimus parvula

THE physician ASKLEPIOS, son of APOLLO, was killed by ZEUS for his arrogance in restoring the dead to life. APOLLO, in revenge, killed the CYCLOPES, ZEUS' armorers. He was accordingly banished to Earth and placed in the service of ADMETOS, son of PHERES, King of Pherae in Thessaly. ADMETOS had been warned by an oracle of his impending death; but APOLLO, in return for his master's generous hospitality, tricked the FATES into agreeing that ADMETOS might live out his normal life-span if a person could be found who would consent to die in his stead. ALCESTIS, his wife, offered to do so.

```
ппппппппппппппппппппппппппппп
```

DRAMATIS PERSONÆ:

APOLLO	HERACLES
DEATH	PHERES
ALCESTIS	A MAIDSERVANT
ADMETOS	A MANSERVANT
EUMELOS	CHORUS

ALCESTIS

SCENE: *Before the palace of* ADMETOS. *A central door and two lateral doors opening into the 'stage,' from which three steps lead down to the orchestra.*

The singing Chorus (CHORUS I) *is placed on both sides of the orchestra, extending from the platform or 'stage.' This Chorus remains in its position throughout the action, immobile, anonymous, darkly gowned, and as inconspicuous as possible. It sings (or chants, in the absence of music) the verses assigned to* CHORUS. *The dancing Chorus* (CHORUS II) *is composed of seven, twelve, or fifteen persons; their leader is the* CHORAGOS. *This Chorus dances and pantomimes the Odes.*

Masks are required for APOLLO, DEATH, *and* ALCESTIS. *The first two are wholly abstract. The third should be a slightly stylized representation of* ALCESTIS' *face.*

PROLOGUE

[*Enter from the palace* APOLLO, *clothed in white, masked, armed with a huge bow. He faces the house, and apostrophizes it in a declamatory tone.*

APOLLO   House of Admetos, where I lived so long,
Fed with the food of slaves and hired soldiers,
And I a god—!

301

[*Turning from the house and addressing the audience directly:*

Can I forget how Zeus
Stabbed my son with his lightning through the heart,
And I, raging,
Cut down old Wheeleyes, God's fire-forgers?
Or how for this the Father of Heaven bound me
Servant to death-bound man?

I came down into this country and served Admetos
As herdsman for his flock. I guarded his house,
I saved him even from death when I tricked the Three
Sisters of the frail thread, forcing
Their word for it that he need not go down
Into the dark land, if he found a friend
To take his place among the Dead.

A friend? He went to all his friends in turn,
To his father and his mother also; and he found
None but his wife who dared to die for him,
Dared to give up the sweet sunlight for him!
None but his wife: and now
They are comforting her in the house, for she is dying,
And I must leave the dear shelter of this place
That I be not stained with her death.
                              For see: already
Thánatos, priest of the dying, has come
To lead her down to the sad world under ground.

[*Enter, the figure of* DEATH, *shrouded in black, masked, holding a naked sword.* APOLLO *moves left, and stands there facing* DEATH. *The voice of* DEATH *should proceed from within the house, amplified by a megaphone located behind the* (closed) *central door. Keeping his position, until* APOLLO's *exit,* DEATH *mimes his speeches with a minimum of gesture.*

So you have come, Death. You have lost no time!

DEATH   Prince of Light,
         Have you come to quarrel with me in this house again?

Will you corrupt again those rights
That only Hell should use?
That you charmed the fatal Sisters, that your twisting
Slippery tricks delayed Admetos' death,
I know; but why you stand
Armed at the door, bright guardian of Alcestis!
I do not know. Has she not promised—
Tell me, Apollo—
Has she not promised to die?
Is not this the day?

APOLLO You need not be afraid of me, Death. I will not wrong you: only,
Admetos is my friend, and I suffer for him.

DEATH Yet you go armed, Apollo.

APOLLO   I go armed always.

DEATH And are always over-kind to Admetos' house.
Are you planning how to cheat me of this new death?

APOLLO Did I take Admetos from you by force?

DEATH   He walks
Above ground: why is he not beneath it?

APOLLO He has given you his wife—

DEATH   And I have come to take her.

APOLLO Take her, and go!
                —But stay, Death:
If any words of mine could move you—

DEATH   To what?
To kill a life that is forfeit? O Apollo,
You need not teach me my office.

APOLLO   No. I would have you
Postpone her death.

DEATH   I understand you. Well?

APOLLO Allow Alcestis to reach her old age!

DEATH   Never.
         My honor is mine, Apollo, as yours is yours.

APOLLO   Honor?
         What honor do you find in the death of one young woman?

DEATH   The prize is greater when the dead is young.

APOLLO   Let her die old, and her funeral will bring you riches.

DEATH   I leave you the riches, Apollo. You know what they are worth.
         Your rich men
         Can pay you well to buy them away from Death.

APOLLO   Who would ever have said Death had such wit!
         Then you will not grant me this?

DEATH   I can not. You
         Have measured me once before. You know what I am.

                                              [Violently.

APOLLO   I know you: the hatred of men, the loathing of the gods!

                                              [Calmly.

DEATH   Nevertheless, you shall not have everything that is not yours.

APOLLO   Death, Death, I say to you
         This day your bitterest cruelty is too weak!
         Listen: a man is coming,
         Here, to Pheræ: a man is coming,
         Stronger than all your strength. Here, in this house,
         Admetos will receive him, and honor him.
         And it is he, Death, who will wrestle with you and take
         Alcestis back from you at the door of Hell!
         For you must yield her, Death:
         And though you deny me now, you shall yield at last to my
            hate!

                                              [Exit APOLLO.

DEATH   This was a god of many words: but

Words are not enough, Apollo.

[DEATH *moves to the central door and touches it with*
the point of his sword. The door slowly begins
to open, while DEATH *turns and addresses the*
audience directly.

Today this woman must go down to Death.
My sword is ready.
The lock of hair, the sign of sacrifice
To the dark gods under ground,
Now it is mine to take.

[*The door is now open.* DEATH *very slowly turns and enters*
the house, the door closing softly behind him. Long
pause. Then a drum-beat begins, off stage, gently,
in the rhythm of the Parodos.

PARODOS

[*Enter* CHORUS. *During the opening speech of the* CHORAGOS,
the dancers group themselves in a circle facing the audi-
ence. The CHORAGOS *stands within the circle. The*
dancing begins with Strophe 1.

CHORAG.   I wonder what the silence means.
Why is the whole house so silent?

There is no one here to tell us
If we must mourn for our queen,
Or if she is alive still—
Alcestis, Pelias' daughter,
Surely the noblest of women,
The best of wives, surely.

[The Strophes are sung by CHORUS 1, *the lines assigned to*
HEMICHORI A *and* B *being spoken by isolated
voices in this group.*

CHORUS   Can anyone hear them weeping?   [STROPHE 1
                Is there beating of hands, or lamentation,
                Or any cry of death within there? Nothing,
                There is nothing. No sound.
                No servant stands at the door.—O Paian,
                Apollo, my God of Miracles,
                Stay the new storm of sorrow!

HEM. A   Would they be so quiet if she were dead?

HEM. B   She is surely dead.

HEM. A   One thing is sure: she has not been taken away.

HEM. B   Why is it sure? Tell me, why is it sure?

HEM. A   How could Admetos have given private burial
                To one who has been so loyal a wife?

CHORUS   I cannot see the urn at the door   [ANTISTROPHE 1
                With water in it, which is usual
                When a person is dead; nor any lock of hair
                Fallen, the sign of sorrow, at the threshold.
                There is no crying of girls,
                No sound of young women weeping
                For her who dies young.

HEM. A   Nevertheless, this is her day to die.

HEM. B   What are you whispering?

HEM. A   I said, 'Today she must go under ground.'

HEM. B   You have broken my heart.

HEM. A   Then be comforted: when a good man is hurt,
                All, who would be called good, must suffer with him.

CHORUS   There is no power in the world   [STROPHE 2
                To whom we could send to save her,

Neither in Lycia, nor in the desert
Where the dark temples of Ammon are.
Strong death comes down upon her.
I do not know what altars
We could make sacrifices on.

Only if Apollo's son were here,   [ANTISTROPHE 2
If his eyes opened to the light again,
He yet might save her from the dark,
From death's dark corridor. That God
Made men stand up, whom death had overthrown.
But God's thunder consumed him,
Him also. Then how shall we pray?

SCENE I

[*A* MAIDSERVANT *enters from the house.*

CHORAG.   Everything that could be done, the King has done:
             All the rites of funeral.
             On the altars of the gods the black blood
             Glows, the hopeless sacrifice . . .

[*To the* MAIDSERVANT.

             Of course you grieve
             If anything happens to your master, girl:
             We understand that.
             But tell us: the Queen—
             Is she alive, or dead?

MAID.   She is alive. And dead.

CHORAG.   How can that be?

MAID.   She is at the very brink of death. Her breath
           Is failing her.

CHORAG.   Oh, Admetos, Admetos!

MAID.   Let Admetos be:
           He will not understand, until she is gone.

CHORAG.   And can nothing be done for her?

MAID.   Nothing. This is her day.

CHORAG.   Oh, then her day is beyond praise! In all the world
           There is surely not her equal among women.

MAID.   Not in all the world . . .
           Where shall you ever find a greater love
           Than this, that a wife should die her husband's death?

                                   [With the utmost simplicity.

           But listen: I must tell you:
           Early this morning, when she saw that the day had come,
           She bathed her white body in fresh water from the stream,
           Took her fine things from the coffers of cedar
           And dressed herself becomingly; then stood
           Before the fire and prayed:
           'Hearth-goddess, now I am going into earth.
           'I shall not pray to you ever again.
           'Watch over my children when I am dead:
           'Give the boy a wife who will be dear to him,
           'And give the girl a good husband.
           'Do not let them die, like their mother, while they are young,
           'But grant that they may be fortunate.
           'Let them live happy lives in the land of their people.'
           Then she went from altar to altar in the house,
           Praying, and making wreaths for them all,
           Shearing off the leaves of young myrtle branches,
           Quietly, without a word, so still, so lovely,
           You would have said that no evil had ever touched her.
           But in her chamber,

Then there were tears: 'Dear bed,'
She cried, 'dear bridal bed, where first I lay
'Naked for him, and now I die for him . . . .
'You are no longer mine. I have loved you,
'And now I must go far away. And you,
'You will not miss me. Another woman
'Will sleep here, another, no more loving than I,—
'But, oh, may she be more fortunate!'
And she knelt and kissed it, weeping
Until there were no more tears. Then rose
And left the chamber,
Comforting her children, who clung to her crying. . . .
And all her servants came,
And she gave her right hand sweetly to each in turn:
Even the meanest blessed her, and was blessed.

[*A long pause.*

These are the sorrows of Admetos' house.

What has he gained?
If he had died, why, then he would have died:
But now his grief is so bitter that all his life
He never will escape it, never forget.

CHORAG.   What is he doing now?

[*Weeping.*

MAID.   Holding his wife in his arms,
Weeping. Begging her to stay.
All madness. . . .
For she is dying, her spirit is fainting,
And always her eyes are upon the moving sun,
As if she had never seen the sun before,
And now would say good-bye to it for ever. . . .

[*Pause.*

But I will tell Admetos that you have come:
Not everyone
Would have been so quick to share our master's burden,

But you are a good friend, and have been always:
You are welcome here.

[*Exit* MAIDSERVANT *into the house.*

ODE I

HEM. A	Is there no way, O God?	[STROPHE 1
	Must this terror come upon us?	
HEM. B	Is there no help, O God?	
	Must I go mourning for ever?	
CHORAG.	Dear friends, we must. But even so,	
	Pray to the gods: they have great power.	
CHORUS	O Lord Apollo, my god of healing,	
	Have mercy upon Admetos!	
	Grant it, oh, grant it!	
	As in the old time, now again	
	Save him from death:	
	Drive back the perilous King of the Dead.	
HEM. A	My tears are for you, Admetos.	[ANTISTROPHE 1
	How will you live when she is gone?	
HEM. B	A man could cut his throat	
	Or hang himself against Heaven for this.	
CHORAG.	She is not dear, but the dearest of all,	
	This woman who dies today.	
CHORUS	Look, she is coming out of her house,	
	And he is with her. Cry out,	
	Let all Pheræ mourn,	
	And earth itself cry out for her	

> Who goes now, fainting, frail,
> To the kingdoms under ground.

CHORAG.   Never say that marriage is more of joy than pain.
    I have seen many marriages. I have seen
    The fortune of my king.
    Lost is the loveliest, lost the dear wife:
    What can all his days bring,
    What pleasure is there in his life that is no life?

SCENE II

> [*Enter* ALCESTIS *from the house, supported by* ADMETOS, *leading* EUMELOS *by the hand. She stands before the central door with her eyes raised as though to the sun—* ALCESTIS *speaks remotely, almost in a chanting voice. The interpolations of* ADMETOS *are prosaic, wholly realistic.*

ALCES.   O Sun! O shining clear day,   [STROPHE 1
    And white clouds wheeling in the clear of heaven!

ADMET.   The sun looks upon us and sees that we are unhappy.
    How have we harmed him, or the other gods? Why should
     you die?

ALCES.   O Iôlkos, this ground that I stand on, this dear roof
    That sheltered me when I was married!

ADMET.   Pray to the gods: perhaps even now they
    may have pity on us both.

ALCES.   I see the dark lake,   [STROPHE 2
    The boat in shore,
    And Charon holding the double oar, calling,

'Why are you waiting, Alcestis? Come,
'You are holding us back. . . .'
Can you not hear him? Listen!
He is angry.

ADMET.   I hate this angry god and the voyage he is calling you for!
What a terrible thing this is for us both!

ALCES.   Someone is touching me—   [ANTISTROPHE 2
Do you see anyone?—
Someone, drawing me down to Death's house. . . .
It is Death himself with great wings, Death,
Frowning upon me—!
Such a strange journey, and I am so afraid!

ADMET.   This is a terrible thing for everyone who loves you, a terrible
thing for your husband and your children.

     [ALCESTIS seems to be aware of ADMETOS for the first time.

ALCES.   You need not hold me any more. Please,
Let me lie down. I have no strength to stand,
So near to death, and the dark
Creeps on my eyes like night.

Children, good-bye. You have no mother any more.
Be happy in the sweet sunlight.

ADMET.   Oh God, I'd rather die than hear you say these things! For my
sake, and for your children's sake, do not leave me now!
With you dead, I should be nothing at all: I live only in you
and for you.

                                            [Calmly.

ALCES.   Admetos, Admetos. . . .
You see what is happening to me now, and to you as well.
I have done this for you freely:
For though I am dying, I need not have died.
I could have had any man in Thessaly,
A prince even, like you,
And I might have lived with him in his splendid house.

But without you, with my children fatherless,
I could not live.
                    Yet this is no small thing,
For me to die. I am young, these years have been pleasant,
Your father and mother, who failed you,
Might have died for you, and it would have been noble:
For they had no other son, nor any hope
Of children after you. They might have saved you,
And you and I could have lived out all our days,
And you would not be left alone now
With these poor children.

But I suppose some god
Managed this thing to turn out as it has,
And so let it be.
                    But now, Admetos,
Promise me something in return: not so great a thing
(For nothing is more precious than life), but a thing
That I have surely deserved:
                            You love these children
As well as I do. Make them the masters here:
Do not marry again, do not set a woman above them:
Whoever she might be, sometimes she'd strike them—
And they are our children!

I beg you to promise me this.
A second wife is hateful to the children of the first.

The boy here has a strong friend in his father.
But, dearest daughter! . . .
                            how will it be with you
Growing up, if your father marries again?
Will she be kind to you? If only
She will bring no scandal upon you in your girlhood
And spoil your wedding day!
Dearest, your mother will never see your wedding,
Never hold your hand in childbirth, at that time

When there is no greater comfort than having her near
you . . .

But it is my fate to die,
Fate comes
Not tomorrow, or on the third day of the month, but
In only a moment: and I shall be counted
Among the dead.

Good-bye. You will be happy.

Admetos, you can be proud of a good wife.
Children, you can say that your mother was generous.

CHORAG. I will speak for Admetos:
As he is a true man, he will do this thing for you.

ADMET. I will speak for myself. . . .
It will be as you ask, believe me.
I have loved you in your life, love you now you are dying.
You are my only Queen.
No other woman in all Thessaly,
Shall ever take your place beside me here.
There is no other woman, however beautiful,
Who could change my heart in this.

And I pray the gods, who have given us both such pain,
That these children yet may have a little pleasure.
But until I die, this grief will remain with me,
And hatred for my parents, both my father and my mother:
Friends in words, but enemies in deed:
While you gave up your precious life to save my life.

Mourning?
I'll have mourning! I'll stop the dancing.
There will be no more flowers in my house,
No laughter, no music:
I'll never touch the strings of a harp again.
All my happiness goes away with you.

And listen:
I'll have wise carvers make your body's image
In ivory for our own bed; and I'll lie against it, dreaming
That when I clasp it and whisper your name
You are with me there . . .
                                 Cold comfort, surely! Yet
Often, I think, in sleep you will come to me:
A sweet thing,
To revisit in dreams the dear dead that we loved.

Oh, if I had Orpheus' voice and poetry
With which to move the Dark Maid and her Lord,
I'd call you back, dear love, from the world below.
I'd go down there for you. Charon or the grim
King's dog could not prevent me then
From carrying you up into the fields of light.

But you, down there, be patient: I am coming.
Make a place for me, that we may be together.
I'll be buried side by side with you,
And in my death I'll not be far from you,
My dearest, only faithful friend!

CHORAG.   Your grief will always be my grief, Admetos.
              She is worth more than both of us can give her.

ALCES.   Then you have promised.
              Children, you have heard your father promise.
              He will not marry another woman to trouble you:
              He will not dishonor my memory.

ADMET.   I swear it.

ALCES.   Then I leave you my children. Take them, love them.

ADMET.   A dear gift, from a dear hand!

ALCES.   Oh, my children! To think that I must die!

ADMET.   What shall I do when you are gone?

ALCES.   Why, nothing:
              Time will take care of that. The dead are nothing at all.

ADMET.   For God's sake, take me with you!

ALCES.   It seems enough that I am going—for you.

ADMET.   But you—that you should go and I should stay!

ALCES.   It is quite dark . . .

ADMET.   If you leave me, there is nothing left for me!

ALCES.   I am nothing. Speak of me as nothing. The dead are nothing.

ADMET.   Lift your head up! Look, your children!

ALCES.   Ah. . . .

[*With a tired gesture she slowly removes her mask, and holds
it before her in both hands.* ADMETOS *supports her until
the servants raise the litter behind her, upon which
she falls back. The litter is lowered to the ground.
The drumbeat begins, off stage, and continues
softly until the beginning of the Funeral Ode.*
ADMETOS *watches silently, as if dazed, until
the litter is lowered. Then he cries out
suddenly.*

ADMET.   What are you doing?
           What has happened?

                                           [*A long pause; then.*

           Oh, I am the most unhappy man that ever lived!

CHORAG.   She is dead.

[EUMELOS *throws himself across* ALCESTIS' *body;* ADMETOS
tries to comfort him. The CHORUS *surrounds the
group, momentarily shutting it off from the
sight of the audience.*

[*After a moment,* ADMETOS *leaves the group and moves
slowly up the steps toward the central door. The*
CHORAGOS *addresses him from the head
of the litter.*

CHORAG.   Admetos, you are not the first man to lose a dear wife,

Nor will you be the last. Have patience, then, and remember
That death comes to all of us.

> [Long pause. ADMETOS *stands at the door with his
> back to the audience.*

ADMET. That is true. . . .
For a long time I have been prepared for this: the blow fell
Not without warning.

> [*He turns, and addresses the* CHORUS *with cold formality:*

Thessalians, these are my orders for her funeral:
Every man subject to me shall share in my mourning:
Let every man clothe himself
In black. Let the horsemen and charioteers
Clip their horses' manes. For twelve full months
I forbid the sound of lyre or of flute throughout the city.

For never again shall I bury one more dear to me,
Or one more generous: for she, alone,
Has taken my place in death.

Meanwhile,
I command that you raise a paean to the King of the Dead.

> [*He goes into the house. During the singing of the Funeral
> Ode, the servants raise the litter and slowly carry
> ALCESTIS within. The door closes after them.
> Near the end of the Ode, the* MAIDSERVANT
> *comes out, places an urn beside the
> door, and retires within.*

ЛЛЛЛЛЛЛЛЛЛЛЛЛЛЛЛЛЛЛЛЛЛЛЛЛЛ

ODE II

CHORUS   Daughter of Pelias, our love goes with you   [STROPHE 1
Under dark earth where you must enter now,
Among the homes of death, the sunless houses.
Even that ancient and gloombearded god,
The guide of Death, bent to his sad oar,
Let him remember well: no braver woman
Crossed with him ever to the silent shore.

[ANTISTROPHE 1

Singers whom the Muse haunts, haunting music
Often shall make to praise you on their strings,
With lyreless chanting for your death's sorrow:
At Sparta in late summer when the moon
Glows all night long on nights of festival,
Or at rich Athens in the shining noon—
Such loveliness you leave them for their songs.

Would I could save you from the black water,   [STROPHE 2
Bring you to sunlight from that breathless dark!
Dear woman, alone dearest,
Yielding your spirit into death for him,
Light may the earth be over you, lightly rest.
If ever Admetos takes a bride again,
He shall be hateful to me and to his children.

[ANTISTROPHE 2

The old ones, grudging old bodies to the earth,
Mother and father, feared to save their son;
But you, who were beautiful,
Are gone now from the light: and you were young.
So dear a wife I wish might be my fortune,

So dear a thing, and rarest in the world:
Then I should pray she might stay with me ever.

SCENE III

[*Enter,* HERACLES. *As a good-humored stranger he
misunderstands and complicates the action;
as a benevolent hero he later provides
an ironic resolution.*

HERAC.	My good people of Pheræ, Is Admetos at home, and may I see him?
CHORAG.	He is at home, Heracles. But tell us: What brings you to Thessaly, and to our city here?
HERAC.	I am engaged on one of my labors for Eurystheus.

[*Not too hospitably.*

CHORAG.	Where are you bound? What is your journey this time?
HERAC.	To Thrace. Diomed's horses are what I'm after.
CHORAG.	How will you do it? Do you know Diomed?
HERAC.	Not at all. I have never been in that country.
CHORAG.	Then you've a fight on your hands to take those horses.
HERAC.	Possibly. But I can't avoid these things, you know.
CHORAG.	It's either kill Diomed or be killed yourself.
HERAC.	It will not be the first time I have fought like that.
CHORAG.	If you do overcome him, what will you gain by it?
HERAC.	Only the horses to drive back to the king.
CHORAG.	You'll not find it easy to get the bit into their mouths!

HERAC.   You think it will be so hard? Do they snort fire?

CHORAG.   That isn't it; they tear men apart with their jaws.

HERAC.   Come, we're discussing horses, friend, not lions.

CHORAG.   Wait till you see the blood trampled in their stalls.

HERAC.   The man that reared these beauties: who was his father?

CHORAG.   Arès, the war-god, lord of the golden shield.

HERAC.   Then this labor fits my destiny, always heavy:
A sheer cliff I keep climbing:
It seems that I must fight all the sons of Arès:
First with Lycaon, then with the Swan, so-called,
And now I go to wrestle with the third,
The master of these horses.
But I am Alcmena's son: no enemy
Shall ever see my hand tremble in battle.

[*Enter* ADMETOS *from the house.*

ADMET.   Heracles, son of Zeus, of Perseus' line,
You are welcome to my house.

HERAC.   Peace be with you, Admetos.

ADMET.   I wish it were! . . . But thank you, Heracles.

HERAC.   Why have you shorn your head? Are you in mourning?

[ADMETOS' *voice is low throughout this episode. He is
slow in his replies, yet deliberate and unembar-
rassed in his evasions.*

ADMET.   I have a burial to make today.

HERAC.   God keep all evil from your children!

ADMET.   They are alive. They are in their rooms now.

HERAC.   If it is your father, why, his time had come:
He dies in death's season.

ADMET.   He and my mother
Are both alive and well.

HERAC.   But the Queen—
Surely Alcestis is not dead? It is not your wife?

ADMET.   There are two answers I might make to that.

HERAC.   What do you mean?

ADMET.   She is alive, and yet she is not. It tortures me.

HERAC.   But these are riddles; what is their meaning?

ADMET.   Heracles, you know the death she was to die.

HERAC.   I know that she promised to die for you.

ADMET.   If that is true,
How could I say that she is really alive?

HERAC.   Ah. . . . But wait for her death, man: don't begin grieving
            now.

ADMET.   Whoever is doomed to death is already dead.

HERAC.   Being and not-being are thought to be different things.

ADMET.   Make the distinction if you like: I can not.

HERAC.   Why are you crying? What friend of yours is dead?

ADMET.   A woman. I have just been thinking of that woman.

HERAC.   Was she one of your family?

ADMET.   No; but there were ties between us.

HERAC.   How did she happen to die here in your house?

ADMET.   When her father died, she came here to live.

HERAC.   I am very sorry, Admetos.
I wish I might have come when you were not so troubled.

                                [HERACLES *turns to go.*

ADMET.   What do you mean? Where are you going, Heracles?

HERAC.   I must find lodging with another friend.

ADMET.   No, no, my Lord Heracles, that must never happen!

HERAC.   A guest is a burden in a house of mourning.

ADMET.   The dead are dead. Come now into my house.

HERAC.   It is shameful to force entertainment from sorrowing friends.
         I beg of you: please let me go. I shall be grateful.

ADMET.   You shall not go to·anyone else tonight.

                                        [*To a servant.*

         You will show our guest to his rooms.
         Open the private ones. Have the servants bring
         Dinner, and shut the doors to the main hall:
         He must not hear our weeping.

                                        [*Exit* HERACLES.

CHORAG. What are you thinking of, Admetos? Do you dare
         Give guests entertainment, after what has happened?

ADMET.   If I had turned this traveler away from my house,
         Would you approve of me more? Surely you would not.
         What good would it have done?
         My sorrow would be no less, and I should have
         One friend the less:
         And this would have been one more calamity,
         To have my house called inhospitable.
         This man is my good friend when I go to Argos.

CHORAG. If he is really your friend, as you have said,
         How could you keep from him the sorrow that is upon us?

ADMET.   He would not ever have stayed, if he had known. . . .
         I am aware that what I have done will be
         Misunderstood. . . .

                          [*Exit* ADMETOS *into the house. The drumbeat leads*
                                into the singing of the Ode.

ODE III

CHORUS	It is a gracious house and ever was,	[STROPHE 1

CHORUS   It is a gracious house and ever was,   [STROPHE 1
Friendly to strangers, and a home to friends;
The god of Heaven's music loved this place,
Herdsman and god, the god herdsman content,
Down gentle mountains piping
After his flock the bridal-songs of the hills.

So sweet his music, that the leopards came,   [ANTISTROPHE 1
And delicate lions prowled from the forest shadow,
Following where he led them, without harm;
And through a grove one time a spotted doe
Ventured on light hoofs, dancing,
As though it were for a chorus or a game.

Above the clear waves of this inland water,   [STROPHE 2
Our king has rich lands whitened by his flocks;
Plowland and plain he has: far off his borders,
Westward, where the sun goes down in cloud,
Where Phoebus reins his horses in bright air;
And on the east the sea: no harbors there.

                                                [ANTISTROPHE 2
Now he has thrown his doors wide for the stranger,
Weeping, his eyes wet, weeping the new dead;
Surely such kindness now is half insane!
Yet in all things a good man reckons best,
And bravery is set upon the mind
That man may act what truth he has divined.

꧀꧀꧀꧀꧀꧀꧀꧀꧀꧀꧀꧀꧀꧀꧀꧀꧀꧀꧀꧀꧀꧀

SCENE IV

[Enter ADMETOS *from the house, followed by servants bearing the corpse of* ALCESTIS *on a litter. This is placed facing the audience, with the head slightly higher than the feet, so that the face is clearly visible. The* CHORAGOS *stands at the head, facing the audience, throughout the following scene. During* ADMETOS' *first speech, the* CHORUS *groups itself in a semi- circle about the litter.*

ADMET. Friends, your courtesy gives me strength. There is only a little left for us to do now: my servants have prepared her for burial, and everything has been done in order. But before we take her away, I would have you salute her as is customary for one setting out on this last journey.

CHORAG. But look, Admetos: your father is coming, and slaves bringing funeral-ornaments for her. How old he seems, and how feeble!

[Enter PHERES, *slowly, leaning on his staff, followed by three servants carrying small gifts. His opening speech has been well rehearsed: an acceptable composition of cunning simplicity and customary rhetoric. He is no less sin- cere than the average eulogist, and is genuinely hurt by his son's brusque interruption.*

PHERES I have come to share your grief, son.
She was a good wife, and a wise one, and you have lost her.
Nevertheless, man was put on earth to suffer, and to endure,
Be the burden never so cruel.
                              Take then from me
These gifts that I have brought for her adorning,
And let her go in peace to the world below.
So, it is right to honor her, son:

She gave her life to save yours, she did not leave me
Childless, to drag out my dying day to its close.

*[He extends his right arm above the corpse, and
speaks a bit self-consciously.*

Honor of womankind!
Dear audacious girl!
Alcestis, daughter, saviour of my son
  (and of me also):
Even in the house of Death, farewell!

[Sententiously.

Believe me, son: such a marriage as yours has been
Is a blessed thing, a most profitable thing!
Why else should a man take a wife?

[Violently.

ADMET.   Were you invited here?
You dare to bring
Gifts for her?
Take your gifts! She needs no gifts of yours
To be lovely under ground.
You mourn for her?
Did I hear you snuffling for me when I was in danger?
Then, when I needed you, then—why then
The burden of dying was shoved off on a stranger, a woman!
You, squeaking back your old bones from the grave's door!
My father!
And now you dare come to cough out sobs at her funeral?
My father!
Or are you my father?
And she, that woman of yours,
Reputed by herself and by other authorities to be my
    mother—
Is she my mother? Or perhaps I was the brat of a slave girl,
And you graciously gave me your wife's pap to suck at!
Leave me, leave this place: you have shown what you are,
You, palsied at death's gate, afraid to die,
And with so little life left in you!

Have you never heard of a father's duty?
Is there no honor in you?

         . . . and we might have lived, she and I,
We might have lived together all the rest of her days,
And I should not now be crying. . . .

                 [Pause: then, with control.

What have you not had, that a man might have?
Power in your prime as king, and I to succeed you,
I, your son, in your own house.
You risked nothing, I think: you would not have died
Childless, leaving an empty house for strangers to ruin.
Or was I perhaps a bad son?
You will not say that I was a bad son, either:
I was good to you in your old age, both to you and my
    mother.
And for this, you and she have treated me so!

                         Go,
I tell you, go. Time is short, go, pump her full of more
    children!
You will need comforting on your death-bed, will you not?
And I will not bury you, this hand of mine
Will be no comfort to you.
For all you cared when I needed you, I am as good as dead.
For all I care now, die when you will:
I am no son of yours.

God, these old men! How they pray for death!
How heavy is their life in the slow drag of days!
And yet, when Death comes near them,
You will not find one who will rise and walk with him,
Not one whose years are still a burden to him!

                      [Sternly, sombrely.

CHORAG.   Let your father alone, Admetos.
              There is sorrow enough in this place.

     [A long pause emphasizes the indecency of this argument in
        the presence of the dead ALCESTIS. Then PHERES begins

> with a kind of hurt pomposity, which passes
> through a father-to-son reasonableness
> to a wearily furious irony.

PHERES Am I a Lydian slave, or perhaps a Phrygian slave, son,
That you should abuse me so? Or am I your father,
A Thessalian Thessalian-born, a king, and a free man?
Is it I who made you heir to my house,
Who gave you everything—is it I whose duty it is
To die for you as well? Does your father owe you that debt?
That is no law of the Greeks, my father told me of no such
law.

Dear boy, listen:
For happiness or unhappiness, every man is born for himself.
I gave you all you deserved, slaves, subjects, money,
And you'll soon have my lands, as I had them from my father.
Then how have I cheated you? How have I hurt you?
Die for you—?
Don't you die for me, and I'll not die for you.
You love the daylight: do you think your father does not?
Our stay in the world below will be long enough.
Life, I take it, is short: it is none the less agreeable.
And as for dying,—
Well, when it came to dying, did you not
Shudder away from it? Are you dead now?
Or did you not shove off the burden on your pretty wife?
'Coward!' You call me a coward? You,
Less brave than the girl who died for you? A cautious hero!

But you know best:
A gallant road you've found to Immortality!
Marry wife after wife, first making sure that they'll die for
you—
That's all. . . .

God, these young men! How they pray for life!

CHORAG.   Say no more, Pheres.
           Too much has been spoken on both sides.

ADMET.   Say as much as you like. I have spoken
           Only the truth.

PHERES   To have died for you would have been unfair to myself.

ADMET.   Is dying the same thing for a young man and an old?

PHERES   A man must live his own life, not another's.

ADMET.   Live on, then: live a longer life than God!

PHERES   You curse your father with a longer life than God's?

ADMET.   Because you whined for life when you might have died.

PHERES   I see a dead girl here: yet you are alive.

ADMET.   Then this dead girl is the proof of your shamelessness.

PHERES   Surely you will not say that I killed her?

ADMET.   I say only that some day you will need my help.

PHERES   Take a dozen wives, that a dozen may die for you!

ADMET.   Cowardly old fool! Afraid of death, afraid!

                        [Pause: then, with heartbreaking intensity.

PHERES   This daylight of God is sweet, I tell you, sweet!

           [Long pause. Within, the muffled drumbeat in the measure
           of the ensuing strophe. This continues until the sing-
           ing begins. ADMETOS turns momentarily towards the
           corpse, and then whirls furiously upon his father.
           PHERES is tired, and from this point his replies
           are in ironic contrast to ADMETOS' rage.

ADMET.   Your soul is a crawling thing, meaner than the meanest!

PHERES   You would find an old man's funeral laughable, then?

ADMET.   Oh, you will die, you will die some day, and die in dishonor!

PHERES   Dishonor will not much trouble me, once I am dead.

ADMET.   God, God, how shameless these old men are!

PHERES   She was not shameless, was she? Only demented.

ADMET.   For God's sake, go! Let me bury my wife in peace!

PHERES   Yes, I will go.
         You, being her murderer, should know the best way to bury
           her.

                    [*Exit* PHERES. ADMETOS *screams after him.*

ADMET.   Go back to your woman!
         Hurry back, childless old man, and grow older!
         You'll not come into my house again!

                              [*Pause: then, a bit foolishly.*

         If heralds and trumpets could cut you off from me,
         By God, I'd do it!

                                      [*Pause: recovery.*

         But, friends: our present grief:
         Come, let us bring her body to burial.

         [*The drumbeat has steadily increased in intensity. Now the
            first phrase is sung by the* CHORAGOS, *and taken up
               immediately by the* CHORUS, *following the
                 servants who are carrying out the litter
                    with the corpse of* ALCESTIS.

                                      [*Exit* ADMETOS.

CHORAG. Daughter of Pelias, Alcestis, Queen, farewell

CHORUS   Daughter of Pelias, Alcestis, Queen, farewell
         Even to Hades' gate!
         There, may Hermes greet you, a kindly Angel:
         There, may Death be gentle; and if great
         Souls, and fair, and generous, have favor
         Beneath the ground, you shall sit throned for ever
         The Bride of the Dark King.

                 [*The stage is empty. Enter a* MANSERVANT *angrily
                         from the house.*

MAN.   Never in all my life have I met a fellow so shameless as this stranger, whoever he is! And to think of all the people who have come to this house, and been entertained here! People from all over Greece,—and then this one! He must have known that Admetos was in trouble, but he insisted upon staying; and as though this were not enough, he grumbled at the food we set before him, and kept us running after more. . . . I can still see him hoisting up that wine-jug in both hands, and pouring it down, with not a drop of water in it, until he was roaring drunk: and then he had to crown himself with myrtle and bawl out his bawdy songs. A pretty bit of counterpoint *that* was! This man in there bellowing, with never a thought for all Admetos was suffering, and we in the next room mourning for our Queen. . . . But the King had told us not to let him see us with our eyes wet. . . . And so here I am, waiting on this guest, this ruffian—! And she is gone. The Queen is gone from her house. I could not follow her, I could not reach out my hand to her, or even say good-bye to her. She was my dear Lady, my mother, the mother of all of us. How often she saved us from a thousand punishments when Admetos was angry!—And now this stranger comes, bursting in on all our trouble!

[Enter HERACLES, *drunk, crowned with myrtle, holding a huge cup in both hands.*

HERAC.   Hello there. Why so
Solemn? Why do you look so
Grim?
Is this the correct way for a servant to act,
Staring at the guests he serves? It
Is not.
You should be trotting about with a
Smile, like a good
Fellow.
            Friend,
You behold in me your master's dearest friend.
And what do you do? You look, to say the least,
Bilious.

And all for the death of a woman you hardly knew.

Come over here. I've something to tell you.

[SERVANT *turns* away.

Do you understand the facts of this mortal life?
You do not. Of course not. Then listen to me:

[Chanting tunelessly.

All men have to die, and that's a fact:
There isn't one who knows when he'll get sacked.
Death isn't visible before he comes:
You can't predict your death by doing sums.

There you are, friend: straight from a first-class au-
Thority. Ponder, rejoice, and have a drink.
Today is today. Tomorrow will be
Tomorrow. And so on.
                              Listen:
Of all your gods and goddesses, your greater and lesser di-
Vinities, Cypris is the best for mortal man.
Honor Aphroditê, friend: she means well. And
Cheer up.
Forget whatever it is that's gnawing at you,
And remember what I've been telling you. You
Believe me, don't you? I hope so. Here, have a garland,
Have a drink, have another drink, have
another
little
drink

[As before.

O mortal man, think mortal thoughts,
And have a drink with me!
Wine's the best cure for sickly thoughts,
So have a drink with me!

Seriously, friend,
You should try to rise superior to these minor afflictions.

> By God, this wine would lift you!
> And as for all these sour-faced sigh-blasting belly-aching
>   fellows,
> What's life to them? Nothing but a catastrophe.
>
> [Bitterly.

MAN. I know all about that. But today
The house is in no mood for laughter.

HERAC. Whoever it is that's dead, she's a
Stranger, isn't she?
I see no reason for inordinate mourning,
Since your master and mistress are both well.

[Incredulously.

MAN. Both well? Is it possible that even now—

HERAC. Has Admetos lied to me?

MAN. Lied to you? No, he has been too good to you!

HERAC. Must I go without my dinner because a stranger has died?

MAN. A stranger. . . .

HERAC. Can Admetos have hidden a real sorrow from me?

MAN. Go back to your drinking. Leave the suffering to us.

HERAC. There's an uneasiness in your words—

MAN. At any other time we should not have minded your feasting.

HERAC. Can it be that Admetos has made a fool of me?

MAN. You came at the wrong time, that's all.
The house is in mourning. You can see for yourself.

HERAC. Who is it? One of the children? The old father?

MAN. It is Alcestis, man. The Queen is dead.

> [Long pause. HERACLES throws down his cup, and
>   slowly removes the garland from his head.

HERAC. O fool, fool, fool!
I knew it, I felt it: I saw his eyes red with weeping,

His hair clipped, his heavy motion:
And he told me it was all for a stranger, a casual death!
And I,
Drinking, rioting in the house of this excellent host,
And he crushed with grief!
Drinking, bawling, crowning my head with myrtle—!

But it was not wholly my fault.
You might have told me.

MAN. Admetos would never have sent a man away from his door.

HERAC. Where is he now? Where is he burying her?

MAN. Go straight along the Larissa road, and there,
Not far from the town, you will find the place.

[*Exit* SERVANT *into the house.*

HERAC. Now, my brave heart, my good hands scarred strong
By many labors,
Now is the greatest of all your trials! Today
It is yours to prove that Alcmena, Electryon's daughter,
Bore Zeus a son indeed.
                    For Admetos' sake
We must bring Alcestis back to her house from the dead.
I will follow the black god,
Old Thanatos, to her tomb: for there
I shall find him drinking the blood of the lustral victims.
And I will wrestle with Death,
I will crack his charnel body between my arms
Until he yields her up.
                    But if he is gone,
If he leaves the blood of offering untasted,
I will go down to the sad streets of the Dead,
To Persephone and the dim Lord of Hell, and there
Beg for her life.
                    And I
Will bring Alcestis back to the good sunlight,
Back to my friend who welcomed me to his house

In spite of his loss. Where in all Thessaly,
Where in all Greece should there be a kindlier host?
And he must never
Say that his goodness was wasted on a bad friend!

[Exit HERACLES.

⊓⊔⊓⊔⊓⊔⊓⊔⊓⊔⊓⊔⊓⊔⊓⊔⊓⊔⊓⊔⊓⊔⊓⊔⊓⊔⊓⊔

KOMMOS

[Enter ADMETOS, followed by the CHORUS. The procession
moves slowly across the stage towards the central door,
stopping for the chanting of each strophe
and antistrophe.

ADMET.   My mother was cursed the night she bore me,
And I am faint with envy of all the dead:
How clean they are, who are out of life for ever!
They are beautiful, and I would be with them.

For I shall never be warm in the thick sunlight,
Nor walk again as other men walk the earth:
She who was my life has been taken from me,
Stolen by Death for his still kingdom.

CHORUS   Go in to your house, Admetos: you must go in,   [STROPHE 1
Though you have reason to weep here. We know,
Today you have lived through a bitter time;
But all your bitterness cannot bring her back:
You will not see her ever again.

ADMET.   When you say that, my heart splits with the spearhead.
Better, oh, better if we had never married,
Never lived here together in this house!

Men who never marry, men who have no children,
Each of them has one life to live: his own;
And a man can endure the pain of a single life.
He will not see his children's sicknesses,
Their marriage-beds empty, cool with death:
All his life long he will be safe from this.

CHORUS   Fate is too strong for you: it is Fate's fall.   [ANTISTROPHE 1
Will you not see anything but sorrow?
Dark as your life may be, you must endure it,
Admetos: men have lost their wives before:
Images of disaster crush us all.

ADMET.   Mourning without end, and heartbreak here,
And the earth so heavy upon the ones we loved!
Why did you hold me back when I would have thrown myself
Into her grave? I would have lain dead with her,
And now the dark King of Hell would have us both,
Instead of only her.
Together we should have crossed the strange water.

CHORUS   I knew a man whose son died, a young man   [STROPHE 2
Full of promise: it was his only son.
Yet he endured this bravely:
Sorrow enough, yet he endured it bravely!
A childless old man, white-haired, and bent towards death.

ADMET.   How can I go into this house and live here now?
It is all changed.
I can see, as if from a great distance,
The evening I came in under the torches,
Holding her by the hand, and the music around us,
The singing and the great crowd following
To wish her, who is now dead, happiness;
And happiness to me: they said our marriage
Joined the magnificence of two lines of kings.
But now instead of songs there is only weeping;
Where there were white robes, these gray mourners
Beckon me in to sleep in an empty bed.

CHORUS   You were a stranger to sorrow: therefore Fate [ANTISTROPHE 2
     Has cursed you. Nevertheless, you have saved your life.
     The wife you loved is dead;
     But is this strange, that the wife you loved is dead?
     Death has dissolved many marriages before this.

ADMET.   Friends, Alcestis is happier than I,
     Whoever may think differently.
     Now she will feel no pain, no sorrow ever,
     No more distress: but peace; and her name is blessed.

     But as for me,
     I have no right to be living. I know that.
     My life is a death. My death is born today.

     How can I go on living in this house?
     Going and coming, and no one there at all,
     Only the emptiness where once she was:
     And the bed, and the chairs that were hers, and the floor
     Covered with dust; and her children
     Crying, coming to me day after day, crying,
     Asking for her. . . . And all her servants in tears,
     Thinking what a sweet mistress they have lost.
     And in the city there will be dinners and weddings,
     And I cannot go to them: how should I meet her friends?
     This one who hates me will whisper to another,
     'There is the man whose life is a daily shame,
     'The man who dared not die, whose cowardice
     'Let his own wife lay down her life for him.
     'What kind of man is he who hates his father
     'Because he himself was base?'

     You have said that I saved my life. What good, then,
     If I have lost everything, if I have lost my honor?

     [ADMETOS *has mounted the steps to the door. He stands
     facing it, his back to the audience, immobile, during
     the singing of the Ode.*

ODE IV

[*The* CHORAGOS *comes down stage and chants, or sings, directly to the audience.*

CHORAG.   I have found power in the mysteries of thought,   [STROPHE 1
In delicate chanting breathed by the rare Muses;
I have learned much in the curious books of men;
But Fate is stronger than anything I have known:
Nothing in mortal wisdom can subdue her,
Neither old prayers nor the skill Apollo taught.

[ANTISTROPHE 1
She has neither altar nor image, that we may kneel to her:
There are no temples where she might hear our prayers:
But let us pray to her now.

[*Here the* CHORAGOS *turns and the* CHORUS *joins him in the prayer.*

CHORUS   'O Goddess, Stranger,
'Be never more cruel than you have been this day:
'Though all that God wills you must bring to pass,
'And though your hand, were it shown, would crumple steel.'

[*The grouping of the* CHORUS, *hitherto random and disconsolate, centers on* ADMETOS *throughout the second
strophe, and reaches a final symmetry in the
antistrophe.*

Caught by her now, Admetos,   [STROPHE 2
Will you beat with your fists against her? Rest there, friend.
The dead will not hear you crying, you in the daylight:
The children of the gods, all the loud heroes,
Where is their bravery now? Thin, drained in night.

But she who was dearest among us when she lived,
Still shall be dearest of all among the dead.

And not as one dead for ever,   [ANTISTROPHE 2
We may not think of Alcestis as really dead:
Her tomb shall be a shrine that travelers love,
And turning at the roadside they shall say:
'This woman died for her husband in the old time,
'And now moves here, a gracious influence. Lady,
'Your blessing on mine!'—So shall they say for ever.

EXODOS

[Enter HERACLES, *followed by* ALCESTIS *holding her mask before her in both hands, as earlier. During the ensuing
dialogue she is motionless, as though in a trance,
until the moment when she replaces her mask.
This must be her only gesture. Nevertheless, her silence and immobility must
dominate the entire scene.*

HERAC.   Admetos, a man with a grievance against his friend
Should speak plainly.
When I came to your house, you were in trouble.
I would have helped you, as a friend should; but you,
Instead of telling me the nature of your sorrow,
Locked it up in your heart, and made me welcome
Here in your sad house.
How could I know? I crowned myself with myrtle,
And made the usual libations to the gods:
And all the time it was your wife who was dead!
It was wrong of you, Admetos! But enough of that.

Listen:

I have come back, and I must tell you why.
You see this woman here: take her; keep her for me
Until I come again.
For I must fight with Diomed, the King,
And win the Thracian horses. But if I fail,—
God forbid that I should fail, though!—keep her here,
Let her serve you in your house.
                              She was hard to win:
Not far from here I came on a public contest
For athletes, and she was the prize I took away.
Horses were given to the best runners and the jumpers,
And splendid cattle for the boxers and wrestling champions,
And then this woman.
Would you have had me pass by so worthy a prize? Then take
    her,
Care for her, I beg you. She is worth your trouble,
As she was worth all my trouble in winning her.

ADMET. I had no thought of wronging you, dear friend,
When I hid my wife's death from you. Do not think that.
Only, if you had gone to another's house
I should have been hurt twice over. It seemed enough
That I should mourn my wife.
                              But as for this woman—
Oh, Heracles, my friend and my lord! if you love me indeed,
Take her to some other man who has not suffered,
And have him keep her for you.

Pherae is full of your friends: you will find someone.

Please, do not remind me of what I have lost!
Seeing her here, in my own house,
My throat is hot again with tears; and I
Have suffered enough.
                      A young woman?
Where is there a place here for a young woman?
Here, living among these rough men,

Do you think she could walk safely among them? I tell you,
Youth is hot-blooded, youth is hard to restrain!

It is for your own good that I am telling you these things.

Or perhaps you would have me lead her
To my dead wife's chamber, and install her there?
Could I do that? give her that bed—!
Who would hate me more? the people of my own house,
Because I had defiled the memory of her who saved me,
Or Alcestis herself?

                                    [He turns to ALCESTIS. Strangely.

Woman, whoever you are, you are like Alcestis—
Did you know it?—the same height, the same bearing—

          [Turning aside and bursting into tears.

Heracles, Heracles!
For God's sake, take her away!
I am beaten: do not stand here torturing me!
I look at her, and it is Alcestis that I see!
I look at her, and my heart splits, my
Heart is an agony of weeping: Go,
Take her, go!

                              [A long pause. Then, almost boyishly.

I think that for the first time I know what unhappiness is.

                                    [Silence. Then, abstractedly.

CHORAG.   Nevertheless a man must take what God gives.

          [Silence. The drumbeat begins, very quietly and slowly, begin-
                ning to increase in intensity only after ALCESTIS has put
                on her mask, near the end of the scene.

HERAC.   If only I could have brought your wife to you, back from the
          dead!

ADMET.   I know. But why speak of it? The dead can never come back.

HERAC.   You are only hurting yourself: try to be brave.

ADMET.   It is easy to say 'be brave.' It is harder to do.

HERAC.   What good will it do you to mourn your wife for ever?

ADMET.   No good at all: but my grief is stronger than I.

HERAC.   Love of the dead is bitter, I know, and strong.

ADMET.   Heracles, I am nothing. . . .

HERAC.   No man can deny that you have lost a devoted wife.

ADMET.   And there is no more pleasure for me in anything.

HERAC.   Time will take care of that.

ADMET.   Yes, if Time is Death.

HERAC.   Perhaps a wife, perhaps another marriage—

ADMET.   Not another word! Are you a friend of mine?

HERAC.   An empty bed then? A widower for ever?

ADMET.   No woman in the whole world will ever sleep at my side!

HERAC.   Do you think that this attitude of yours is necessary?

ADMET.   Yes, to the dead. Wherever she is, I have promised her.

HERAC.   Good, very good. But some would say you're a fool.

ADMET.   Let them say it. But they will never call me a bridegroom.

HERAC.   In any case, I approve of your faithfulness.

ADMET.   And if I forget it, may I die the same death as she!

                [*Pause:* HERACLES *indicates* ALCESTIS.

HERAC.   And now, friend,
              Take this woman and keep her in your good house.

ADMET.   By the great God who is your Father, no! I beg of you!

HERAC.   You are wrong to deny me this, Admetos, you are wrong!

ADMET.   If I should do it, the shame would eat out my heart!

HERAC.   Come, come:
         In a little while you might even come to enjoy it.

ADMET.   God, why did you have to win *her* at the games?

HERAC.   It was my victory, of course; but also, your victory.

ADMET.   As you say. But let her go now, let her go!

HERAC.   She will go if she must; but, for the last time: must she?

ADMET.   She must. . . . Although I would not have you go away
         angry. . . .

HERAC.   You know how much this means to me, Admetos.

                                                   [*Pause.*

ADMET.   Very well then.
         You have won again. But you know what it is costing me.

HERAC.   Perhaps some day you will be glad of it. Take her.

                                              [*To the servants:*

ADMET.   Take her into the house, since she is going to live here.

HERAC.   No: I cannot have her turned over to your slaves.

ADMET.   Then take her inside yourself, if you feel that way.

HERAC.   No, I have given her to you. Here, take her hand.

ADMET.   I will not touch that woman! But let her go in:
         She is quite free.

HERAC.   I depend upon you alone.

ADMET.   You are my lord. I must do what you ask me.

HERAC.   Your hand, then:
         Give me your hand, and take this woman's hand.

         [ADMETOS *turns his head away from* ALCESTIS, *and gives his
             right hand to* HERACLES. *As he does so,* ALCESTIS *with
                  ineffable dignity replaces the mask of her living
                      face. From this point the drumbeat in-
                          creases steadily.*

[HERACLES, *smiling, joins the hands of* ALCESTIS *and* ADMETOS.
ADMETOS *resolutely keeps his eyes averted from her face.*

HERAC. Must you behave as though you had met the Gorgon?
There: you have her hand?

ADMET.   I have.

HERAC.   Then keep it well.
Some day you will know that I was a profitable guest.
Look at her, Admetos:

                                   [ADMETOS *slowly turns.*

As you have said, she is not unlike your wife.

ADMET. God, God, God,
A miracle, a ghost!
Alcestis! Are you really Alcestis?
Or is this the cruelest trick that God has ever played?

HERAC. No trick, Admetos:
It is really your wife, your own wife, brought back to you.

ADMET. Be careful. How do I know she is not a ghost from Hell?

HERAC. The guest you honored is not a dealer in ghosts.

ADMET. And this is my wife that I laid in her tomb myself?

HERAC. This is your wife. I understand your finding it strange.

ADMET. And I can touch her? Speak to her as though she were alive?

HERAC. She is alive. Speak to her, man, speak to her.

ADMET. Alcestis, Alcestis! my dear, my dearest wife!
It is you, your face, your body, mine again!
Mine, and I had thought you lost for ever!

HERAC. Yours. And I pray that your happiness bring down
No envious curse from the gods, Admetos.

ADMET. O Friend,
Great-hearted Son of the mighty Zeus! May God
Keep you and guard you for ever! You alone,

You, Heracles, have saved me and my house!
But tell me: how did you bring her back from the dead?

HERAC.   I wrestled with the God who was her master.

ADMET.   Where did you meet with Death? Where did you fight him?

HERAC.   I found him hiding near her tomb, and threw him.

ADMET.   But why is she silent? Can she not speak again?

HERAC.   It is not permitted you to hear her voice
For three days longer; then she will have washed away
The stain of death and memory of Hell.
So take her, Admetos, my good friend,
And think that this is the reward of a generous host.
But now, good-bye. I have work to do.

ADMET.   Stay with us, Heracles. All my house is yours.

HERAC.   Another day, perhaps. Now I must go.

[*Exit* HERACLES.

ADMET.   May every kind of happiness go with you,
And may you soon come back to us.
                          Friends,
I command these things to the whole city, and
The Assembly of the Four Quarters: let groups of dancers
Be formed to celebrate the glory of this day;
Let the flesh of oxen smoke on every altar
To propitiate the gods. For in one day
The old life has changed for the new. And now I say
That I am the happiest of all men.

[*Exit into the house, leading* ALCESTIS.

[*The* CHORAGOS *advances and speaks directly to the audience.*

CHORAG.   Destiny has many forms, and Heaven
Works in the dark with riddles and confusion.
If the expected happens, who can say,
'I knew that this would be, and in this fashion?'
God's way is unexpected, odd or even.

This is the meaning of all you have watched today.

Sophocles

KING OEDIPUS

translated by

William Butler Yeats

LAIUS, King of Thebes, learned from prophecies that he would be killed by his own son, and consequently he had the newly born OEDIPUS exposed on the slope of Mount Cithaeron. The baby was rescued and brought to POLYBUS, King of Corinth, who brought him up as his own son. When OEDIPUS was of age, he consulted the oracle at Delphi and was told that it was his fate to kill his father and marry his mother. In horror he left his supposed parents in Corinth and journeyed to Thebes, hoping in this way to outwit the oracle. He encountered LAIUS and killed him in a crossroads dispute, unaware of his victim's identity. At Thebes he married the Queen, his own mother, and by her had four children: ANTIGONE, ISMENE, POLYNEICES, and ETEOCLES.

DRAMATIS PERSONÆ:

OEDIPUS, *King of Thebes*

JOCASTA, *wife of* OEDIPUS

ANTIGONE, *daughter of* OEDIPUS

ISMENE, *daughter of* OEDIPUS

CREON, *brother-in-law of* OEDIPUS

TIRESIAS, *a seer*

A PRIEST

MESSENGERS

A HERDSMAN

CHORUS

KING OEDIPUS

The action takes place in Thebes, before the palace of Oedipus. (Ed.)

OEDIP.   Children, descendants of old Cadmus, why do you come before me, why do you carry the branches of suppliants, while the city smokes with incense and murmurs with prayer and lamentation? I would not learn from any mouth but yours, old man, therefore I question you myself. Do you know of anything that I can do and have not done? How can I, being the man I am, being King Oedipus, do other than all I know? I were indeed hard of heart did I not pity such suppliants.

PRIEST   Oedipus, King of my country, we who stand before your door are of all ages, some too young to have walked so many miles, some—priests of Zeus such as I—too old. Among us stand the pick of the young men, and behind in the market-places the people throng, carrying suppliant branches. We all stand here because the city stumbles towards death, hardly able to raise up its head. A blight has fallen upon the fruitful blossoms of the land, a blight upon flock and field and upon the bed of marriage—plague ravages the city. Oedipus, King, not God but foremost of living men, seeing that when you first came to this town of Thebes you freed us from that harsh singer, the riddling Sphinx, we beseech you, all we suppliants, to find some help; whether you find it by your power as a man, or because, being near the Gods, a God has whispered you. Uplift our State; think upon your fame; your coming brought us luck, be lucky to us still; remember that it is better to rule over men than over a waste place, since neither walled town nor ship is anything if it be empty and no man within it.

OEDIP.   My unhappy children! I know well what need has brought

349

you, what suffering you endure; yet, sufferers though you be, there is not a single one whose suffering is as mine—each mourns himself, but my soul mourns the city, myself, and you. It is not therefore as if you came to arouse a sleeping man. No! Be certain that I have wept many tears and searched hither and thither for some remedy. I have already done the only thing that came into my head for all my search. I have sent the son of Menoeceus, Creon, my own wife's brother, to the Pythian House of Phoebus, to hear if deed or word of mine may yet deliver this town. I am troubled, for he is a long time away—a longer time than should be—but when he comes I shall not be an honest man unless I do whatever the God commands.

PRIEST   You have spoken at the right time. They have just signalled to us that Creon has arrived.

OEDIP.   O King Apollo, may he bring brighter fortune, for his face is shining!

PRIEST   He brings good news, for he is crowned with bay.

OEDIP.   We shall know soon. Brother-in-law, Menoeceus' son, what news from the God?

CREON   Good news; for pain turns to pleasure when we have set the crooked straight.

OEDIP.   But what is the oracle?—so far the news is neither good nor bad.

CREON   If you would hear it with all these about you, I am ready to speak. Or do we go within?

OEDIP.   Speak before all. The sorrow I endure is less for my own life than these.

CREON   Then, with your leave, I speak. Our lord Phoebus bids us drive out a defiling thing that has been cherished in this land.

OEDIP.   By what purification?

CREON   King Laius was our King before you came to pilot us.

OEDIP.   I know—but not of my own knowledge, for I never saw him.

CREON   He was killed; and the God now bids us revenge it on his murderers, whoever they be.

OEDIP.   Where shall we come upon their track after all these years? Did he meet his death in house or field, at home or in some foreign land?

CREON   In a foreign land: he was journeying to Delphi.

OEDIP.   Did no fellow-traveller see the deed? Was there none there who could be questioned?

CREON   All perished but one man who fled in terror and could tell for certain but one thing of all he had seen.

OEDIP.   One thing might be a clue to many things.

CREON   He said that they were fallen upon by a great troop of robbers.

OEDIP.   What robbers would be so daring unless bribed from here?

CREON   Such things were indeed guessed at, but Laius once dead no avenger arose. We were amid our troubles.

OEDIP.   But when royalty had fallen what troubles could have hindered search?

CREON   The riddling Sphinx put those dark things out of our thoughts —we thought of what had come to our own doors.

OEDIP.   But I will start afresh and make the dark things plain. In doing right by Laius I protect myself, for whoever slew Laius might turn a hand against me. Come, my children, rise up from the altar steps; lift up these suppliant boughs and let all the children of Cadmus be called hither that I may search out everything and find for all happiness or misery as God wills.

PRIEST   May Phoebus, sender of the oracle, come with it and be our saviour and deliverer!

[*The* CHORUS *enters.*

CHORUS   What message comes to famous Thebes from the Golden House?

What message of disaster from that sweet-throated Zeus?
What monstrous thing our fathers saw do the seasons bring?
Or what that no man ever saw, what new monstrous thing?
Trembling in every limb I raise my loud importunate cry,
And in a sacred terror wait the Delian God's reply.

Apollo chase the God of Death that leads no shouting men,
Bears no rattling shield and yet consumes this form with pain.
Famine takes what the plague spares, and all the crops are
    lost;
No new life fills the empty place—ghost flits after ghost
To that God-trodden western shore, as flit benighted birds.
Sorrow speaks to sorrow, but no comfort finds in words.

Hurry him from the land of Thebes with a fair wind behind
Out onto that formless deep where not a man can find
Hold for an anchor-fluke, for all is world-enfolding sea;
Master of the thunder-cloud, set the lightning free,
And add the thunder-stone to that and fling them on his head,
For death is all the fashion now, till even Death be dead.

We call against the pallid face of this God-hated God
The springing heel of Artemis in the hunting sandal shod,
The tousel-headed Maenads, blown torch and drunken sound,
The stately Lysian king himself with golden fillet crowned,
And in his hands the golden bow and the stretched golden
    string,
And Bacchus' wine-ensanguined face that all the Maenads
    sing.

OEDIP. You are praying, and it may be that your prayer will be answered; that if you hear my words and do my bidding you
may find help out of all your trouble. This is my proclamation, children of Cadmus. Whoever among you knows by
what man Laius, son of Labdacus, was killed, must tell all he
knows. If he fear for himself and being guilty denounce himself, he shall be in the less danger, suffering no worse thing
than banishment. If on the other hand there be one that

knows that a foreigner did the deed, let him speak, and I shall give him a reward and my thanks: but if any man keep silent from fear or to screen a friend, hear all what I will do to that man. No one in this land shall speak to him, nor offer sacrifice beside him; but he shall be driven from their homes as if he himself had done the deed. And in this I am the ally of the Pythian God and of the murdered man, and I pray that the murderer's life may, should he be so hidden and screened, drop from him and perish away, whoever he may be, whether he did the deed with others or by himself alone: and on you I lay it to make—so far as man may—these words good, for my sake, and for the God's sake, and for the sake of this land. And even if the God had not spurred us to it, it were a wrong to leave the guilt unpurged, when one so noble, and he your King, had perished; and all have sinned that could have searched it out and did not: and now since it is I who hold the power which he held once, and have his wife for wife—she who would have borne him heirs had he but lived—I take up this cause even as I would were it that of my own father. And if there be any who do not obey me in it, I pray that the Gods send them neither harvest of the earth nor fruit of the womb; but let them be wasted by this plague, or by one more dreadful still. But may all be blessed for ever who hear my words and do my will!

CHORUS   We do not know the murderer, and it were indeed more fitting that Phoebus, who laid the task upon us, should name the man.

OEDIP.   No man can make the Gods speak against their will.

CHORUS   Then I will say what seems the next best thing.

OEDIP.   If there is a third course, show it.

CHORUS   I know that our lord Tiresias is the seer most like to our lord Phoebus, and through him we may unravel all.

OEDIP.   So I was advised by Creon, and twice already have I sent to bring him.

CHORUS   If we lack his help we have nothing but vague and ancient rumors.

OEDIP.   What rumors are they? I would examine every story.

CHORUS   Certain wayfarers were said to have killed the King.

OEDIP.   I know, I know. But who was there that saw it?

CHORUS   If there is such a man, and terror can move him, he will not keep silence when they have told him of your curses.

OEDIP.   He that such a deed did not terrify will not be terrified because of a word.

CHORUS   But there is one who shall convict him. For the blind prophet comes at last—in whom alone of all men the truth lives.

                                          [*Enter* TIRESIAS, *led by a boy.*

OEDIP.   Tiresias, master of all knowledge, whatever may be spoken, whatever is unspeakable, whatever omens of earth and sky reveal, the plague is among us, and from that plague, Great Prophet, protect us and save us. Phoebus in answer to our question says that it will not leave us till we have found the murderers of Laius, and driven them into exile or put them to death. Do you therefore neglect neither the voice of birds, nor any other sort of wisdom, but rescue yourself, rescue the State, rescue me, rescue all that are defiled by the deed. For we are in your hands, and what greater task falls to a man than to help other men with all he knows and has?

TIR.   Aye, and what worse task than to be wise and suffer for it? I know this well; it slipped out of mind, or I would never have come.

OEDIP.   What now?

TIR.   Let me go home. You will bear your burden to the end more easily, and I bear mine—if you but give me leave for that.

OEDIP.   Your words are strange and unkind to the State that bred you.

TIR.   I see that you, on your part, keep your lips tight shut, and therefore I have shut mine that I may come to no misfortune.

OEDIP.	For God's love do not turn away—if you have knowledge. We suppliants implore you on our knees.
TIR.	You are fools—I will bring misfortune neither upon you nor upon myself.
OEDIP.	What is this? You know all and will say nothing? You are minded to betray me and Thebes?
TIR.	Why do you ask these things? You will not learn them from me.
OEDIP.	What! Basest of the base! You would enrage the very stones. Will you never speak out? Cannot anything touch you?
TIR.	The future will come of itself though I keep silent.
OEDIP.	Then seeing that come it must, you had best speak out.
TIR.	I will speak no further. Rage if you have a mind to; bring out all the fierceness that is in your heart.
OEDIP.	That will I. I will not spare to speak my thoughts. Listen to what I have to say. It seems to me that you have helped to plot the deed; and, short of doing it with your own hands, have done the deed yourself. Had you eyesight I would declare that you alone had done it.
TIR.	So that is what you say? I charge you to obey the decree that you yourself have made, and from this day out to speak neither to these nor to me. You are the defiler of this land.
OEDIP.	So brazen in your impudence? How do you hope to escape punishment?
TIR.	I have escaped; my strength is in my truth.
OEDIP.	Who taught you this? You never got it by your art.
TIR.	You, because you have spurred me to speech against my will.
OEDIP.	What speech? Speak it again that I may learn it better.
TIR.	You are but tempting me—you understood me well enough.
OEDIP.	No; not so that I can say I know it; speak it again.

TIR.   I say that you are yourself the murderer that you seek.

OEDIP.   You shall rue it for having spoken twice such outrageous words.

TIR.   Would you that I say more that you may be still angrier?

OEDIP.   Say what you will. I will not let it move me.

TIR.   I say that you are living with your next of kin in unimagined shame.

OEDIP.   Do you think you can say such things and never smart for it?

TIR.   Yes, if there be strength in truth.

OEDIP.   There is; yes—for everyone but you. But not for you that are maimed in ear and in eye and in wit.

TIR.   You are but a poor wretch flinging taunts that in a little while everyone shall fling at you.

OEDIP.   Night, endless night has covered you up so that you can neither hurt me nor any man that looks upon the sun.

TIR.   Your doom is not to fall by me. Apollo is enough: it is his business to work out your doom.

OEDIP.   Was it Creon that planned this or you yourself?

TIR.   Creon is not your enemy; you are your own enemy.

OEDIP.   Power, ability, position, you bear all burdens, and yet what envy you create! Great must that envy be if envy of my power in this town—a power put into my hands unsought—has made trusty Creon, my old friend Creon, secretly long to take that power from me; if he has suborned this scheming juggler, this quack and trickster, this man with eyes for his gains and blindness in his art. Come, come, where did you prove yourself a seer? Why did you say nothing to set the townsmen free when the riddling Sphinx was here? Yet that riddle was not for the first-comer to read; it needed the skill of a seer. And none such had you! Neither found by help of birds, nor straight from any god. No, I came; I silenced her, I the ignorant Oedipus, it was I that found the answer in my mother-wit, untaught by any birds. And it is I that you would pluck out of my place, thinking to stand close to Creon's throne. But you and the plotter of all this shall mourn despite your zeal to purge the land. Were you not an old man, you had already learnt how bold you are and learnt it to your cost.

CHORUS   Both this man's words and yours, Oedipus, have been said in anger. Such words cannot help us here, nor any but those that teach us to obey the oracle.

TIR.   King though you are, the right to answer when attacked belongs to both alike. I am not subject to you, but to Loxias; and therefore I shall never be Creon's subject. And I tell you, since you have taunted me with blindness, that though you have your sight, you cannot see in what misery you stand, nor where you are living, nor with whom, unknowing what you do—for you do not know the stock you come of—you have been your own kin's enemy be they living or be they dead. And one day a mother's curse and father's curse alike shall drive you from this land in dreadful haste with darkness upon those eyes. Therefore, heap your scorn on Creon and on my message if you have a mind to; for no one of living men shall be crushed as you shall be crushed.

OEDIP.   Begone this instant! Away, away! Get you from these doors!

TIR.   I had never come but that you sent for me.

OEDIP.   I did not know you were mad.

TIR.   I may seem mad to you, but your parents thought me sane.

OEDIP.   My parents! Stop! Who was my father?

TIR.   This day shall you know your birth; and it will ruin you.

OEDIP.   What dark words you always speak!

TIR.   But are you not most skillful in the unravelling of dark words?

OEDIP.   You mock me for that which made me great?

TIR.   It was that fortune that undid you.

OEDIP.   What do I care? For I delivered all this town.

TIR.   Then I will go: boy, lead me out of this.

OEDIP.   Yes, let him lead you. You take vexation with you.

TIR.   I will go: but first I will do my errand. For frown though you may you cannot destroy me. The man for whom you look, the man you have been threatening in all the proclamations about the death of Laius, that man is here. He seems, so far as looks go, an alien; yet he shall be found a native Theban and shall nowise be glad of that fortune. A blind man, though now he has his sight; a beggar, though now he is most rich; he shall go forth feeling the ground before him with his stick; so you go in and think on that, and if you find I am in fault say that I have no skill in prophecy.

[TIRESIAS *is led out by the boy.* OEDIPUS *enters the palace.*

CHORUS   The Delphian rock has spoken out, now must a wicked mind,
Planner of things I dare not speak and of this bloody wrack,
Pray for feet that are as fast as the four hoofs of the wind:
Cloudy Parnassus and the Fates thunder at his back.

That sacred crossing-place of lines upon Parnassus' head,
Lines that have run through North and South, and run
   through West and East,
That navel of the world bids all men search the mountain
   wood,
The solitary cavern, till they have found that infamous beast.

[CREON *enters from the house.*

CREON   Fellow-citizens, having heard that King Oedipus accuses me of dreadful things, I come in my indignation. Does he think that he has suffered wrong from me in these present troubles, or anything that could lead to wrong, whether in word or deed? How can I live under blame like that? What life would be worth having if by you here, and by my nearest friends, called a traitor through the town?

CHORUS   He said it in anger, and not from his heart out.

CREON   He said it was I put up the seer to speak those falsehoods.

CHORUS   Such things were said.

CREON   And had he his right mind saying it?

CHORUS   I do not know—I do not know what my masters do.

                              [OEDIPUS *enters.*

OEDIP.   What brought you here? Have you a face so brazen that you come to my house—you, the proved assassin of its master—the certain robber of my crown? Come, tell me in the face of the gods what cowardice, or folly, did you discover in me that you plotted this? Did you think that I would not see what you were at till you had crept upon me, or seeing it would not ward it off? What madness to seek a throne, having neither friends nor followers!

CREON   Now, listen, hear my answer, and then you may with knowledge judge between us.

OEDIP.   You are plausible, but waste words now that I know you.

CREON   Hear what I have to say. I can explain it all.

OEDIP.   One thing you will not explain away—that you are my enemy.

CREON   You are a fool to imagine that senseless stubbornness sits well upon you.

OEDIP.   And you to imagine that you can wrong a kinsman and escape the penalty.

CREON   That is justly said, I grant you; but what is this wrong that you complain of?

OEDIP.   Did you advise, or not, that I should send for that notorious prophet?

CREON   And I am of the same mind still.

OEDIP.   How long is it, then, since Laius—

CREON   What, what about him?

OEDIP.	Since Laius was killed by an unknown hand?
CREON	That was many years ago.
OEDIP.	Was this prophet at his trade in those days?
CREON	Yes; skilled as now and in equal honor.
OEDIP.	Did he ever speak of me?
CREON	Never certainly when I was within earshot.
OEDIP.	And did you inquire into the murder?
CREON	We did inquire but learnt nothing.
OEDIP.	And why did he not tell out his story then?
CREON	I do not know. When I know nothing I say nothing.
OEDIP.	This much at least you know and can say out.
CREON	What is that? If I know it I will say it.
OEDIP.	That if he had not consulted you he would never have said that it was I who killed Laius.
CREON	You know best what he said; but now, question for question.
OEDIP.	Question your fill—I cannot be proved guilty of that blood.
CREON	Answer me then. Are you not married to my sister?
OEDIP.	That cannot be denied.
CREON	And do you not rule as she does? And with a like power?
OEDIP.	I give her all she asks for.
CREON	And am not I the equal of you both?
OEDIP.	Yes: and that is why you are so false a friend.
CREON	Not so; reason this out as I reason it, and first weigh this: who would prefer to lie awake amid terrors rather than to sleep in peace, granting that his power is equal in both cases? Neither I nor any sober-minded man. You give me what I ask and let me do what I want, but were I King I would have

to do things I did not want to do. Is not influence and no trouble with it better than any throne, am I such a fool as to hunger after unprofitable honors? Now all are glad to see me, every one wishes me well, all that want a favor from you ask speech of me—finding in that their hope. Why should I give up these things and take those? No wise mind is treacherous. I am no contriver of plots, and if another took to them he would not come to me for help. And in proof of this go to the Pythian Oracle, and ask if I have truly told what the gods said: and after that, if you have found that I have plotted with the Soothsayer, take me and kill me; not by the sentence of one mouth only—but of two mouths, yours and my own. But do not condemn me in a corner, upon some fancy and without proof. What right have you to declare a good man bad or a bad good? It is as bad a thing to cast off a true friend as it is for a man to cast away his own life—but you will learn these things with certainty when the time comes; for time alone shows a just man; though a day can show a knave.

CHORUS   King! He has spoken well, he gives himself time to think; a headlong talker does not know what he is saying.

OEDIP.   The plotter is at his work, and I must counterplot headlong, or he will get his ends and I miss mine.

CREON   What will you do then? Drive me from the land?

OEDIP.   Not so; I do not desire your banishment—but your death.

CREON   You are not sane.

OEDIP.   I am sane at least in my own interest.

CREON   You should be in mine also.

OEDIP.   No, for you are false.

CREON   But if you understand nothing?

OEDIP.   Yet I must rule.

CREON   Not if you rule badly.

OEDIP.   Hear him, O Thebes!

CREON	Thebes is for me also, not for you alone.
CHORUS	Cease, princes: I see Jocasta coming out of the house; she comes just in time to quench the quarrel.

[JOCASTA *enters.*

JOCAS.	Unhappy men! Why have you made this crazy uproar? Are you not ashamed to quarrel about your own affairs when the whole country is in trouble? Go back into the palace, Oedipus, and you, Creon, to your own house. Stop making all this noise about some petty thing.
CREON	Your husband is about to kill me—or to drive me from the land of my fathers.
OEDIP.	Yes: for I have convicted him of treachery against me.
CREON	Now may I perish accursed if I have done such a thing!
JOCAS.	For God's love believe it, Oedipus. First, for the sake of his oath, and then for my sake, and for the sake of these people here.
CHORUS	[*all*]. King, do what she asks.
OEDIP.	What would you have me do?
CHORUS	Not to make a dishonorable charge, with no more evidence than rumor, against a friend who has bound himself with an oath.
OEDIP.	Do you desire my exile or my death?
CHORUS	No, by Helios, by the first of all the gods, may I die abandoned by Heaven and earth if I have that thought! What breaks my heart is that our public griefs should be increased by your quarrels.
OEDIP.	Then let him go, though I am doomed thereby to death or to be thrust dishonored from the land; it is your lips, not his, that move me to compassion; wherever he goes my hatred follows him.
CREON	You are as sullen in yielding as you were vehement in anger, but such natures are their own heaviest burden.

OEDIP.   Why will you not leave me in peace and begone?

CREON   I will go away; what is your hatred to me? In the eyes of all here I am a just man.

[He goes.

CHORUS   Lady, why do you not take your man in to the house?

JOCAS.   I will do so when I have learnt what has happened.

CHORUS   The half of it was blind suspicion bred of talk; the rest the wounds left by injustice.

JOCAS.   It was on both sides?

CHORUS   Yes.

JOCAS.   What was it?

CHORUS   Our land is vexed enough. Let the thing alone now that it is over.

[Exit leader of CHORUS.

JOCAS.   In the name of the gods, King, what put you in this anger?

OEDIP.   I will tell you; for I honor you more than these men do. The cause is Creon and his plots against me.

JOCAS.   Speak on, if you can tell clearly how this quarrel arose.

OEDIP.   He says that I am guilty of the blood of Laius.

JOCAS.   On his own knowledge, or on hearsay?

OEDIP.   He has made a rascal of a seer his mouthpiece.

JOCAS.   Do not fear that there is truth in what he says. Listen to me, and learn to your comfort that nothing born of woman can know what is to come. I will give you proof of that. An oracle came to Laius once, I will not say from Phoebus, but from his ministers, that he was doomed to die by the hand of his own child sprung from him and me. When his child was but three days old, Laius bound its feet together and had it thrown by sure hands upon a trackless mountain; and when Laius was murdered at the place where three highways meet, it was, or so at least the rumor says, by foreign robbers. So Apollo did not bring it about that the child should kill its father, nor did Laius die in the dreadful way he feared by his child's hand. Yet that was how the message of the seers mapped out the future. Pay no attention to such things. What the God would show he will need no help to show it, but bring it to light himself.

OEDIP.   What restlessness of soul, lady, has come upon me since I heard you speak, what a tumult of the mind!

JOCAS.   What is this new anxiety? What has startled you?

OEDIP.   You said that Laius was killed where three highways meet.

JOCAS.   Yes: that was the story.

OEDIP.   And where is the place?

JOCAS.   In Phocis where the road divides branching off to Delphi and to Daulis.

OEDIP.   And when did it happen? How many years ago?

JOCAS.   News was published in this town just before you came into power.

OEDIP.   O Zeus! What have you planned to do unto me?

JOCAS.   He was tall; the silver had just come into his hair; and in shape not greatly unlike to you.

OEDIP.   Unhappy that I am! It seems that I have laid a dreadful curse upon myself, and did not know it.

JOCAS.   What do you say? I tremble when I look on you, my King.

OEDIP.   And I have a misgiving that the seer can see indeed. But I will know it all more clearly, if you tell me one thing more.

JOCAS.   Indeed, though I tremble I will answer whatever you ask.

OEDIP.   Had he but a small troop with him; or did he travel like a great man with many followers?

JOCAS.   There were but five in all—one of them a herald; and there was one carriage with Laius in it.

OEDIP.   Alas! It is now clear indeed. Who was it brought the news, lady?

JOCAS.   A servant—the one survivor.

OEDIP.   Is he by chance in the house now?

JOCAS.   No; for when he found you reigning instead of Laius he besought me, his hand clasped in mine, to send him to the fields among the cattle that he might be far from the sight of this town; and I sent him. He was a worthy man for a slave and might have asked a bigger thing.

OEDIP.   I would have him return to us without delay.

JOCAS.   Oedipus, it is easy. But why do you ask this?

OEDIP.   I fear that I have said too much, and therefore I would question him.

JOCAS.   He shall come, but I too have a right to know what lies so heavy upon your heart, my King.

OEDIP.   Yes: and it shall not be kept from you now that my fear has grown so heavy. Nobody is more to me than you, nobody has the same right to learn my good or evil luck. My father was Polybus of Corinth, my mother the Dorian Merope, and I was held the foremost man in all that town until a thing happened—a thing to startle a man, though not to make him angry as it made me. We were sitting at the table, and a man who had drunk too much cried out that I was not my father's son—and I, though angry, restrained my anger for that day; but the next day went to my father and my mother and questioned them. They were indignant at the taunt and that comforted me—and yet the man's words rankled, for they had spread a rumor through the town. Without consulting my father or my mother I went to Delphi, but Phoebus told me nothing of the thing for which I came, but much of other things—things of sorrow and of terror: that I should live in incest with my mother, and beget a brood that men would shudder to look upon; that I should be my father's murderer. Hearing those words I fled out of Corinth, and from that day have but known where it lies when I have found its direction by the stars. I sought where I might escape those infamous things—the doom that was laid upon me. I came in my flight to that very spot where you tell me this king perished. Now, lady, I will tell you the truth. When I had come close up to those three roads, I came upon a herald, and a man like him you have described seated in a carriage. The man who held the reins and the old man himself would not give me room, but thought to force me from the path, and I struck the driver in my anger. The old man, seeing what I had done, waited till I was passing him and then struck me upon the head. I paid him back in full, for I knocked him out of the carriage with a blow of my stick. He rolled on his back, and after that I killed them all. If this stranger were indeed Laius, is there a more miserable man in the world than the man before you? Is there a man more hated of Heaven? No stranger, no citizen, may receive him into his house, not a soul may speak to him, and no mouth but my own mouth has laid this curse upon me. Am I not wretched? May I be swept from this world before I have endured this doom!

CHORUS   These things, O King, fill us with terror; yet hope till you speak with him that saw the deed, and have learnt all.

OEDIP.   Till I have learnt all, I may hope. I await the man that is coming from the pastures.

JOCAS.   What is it that you hope to learn?

OEDIP.   I will tell you. If his tale agrees with yours, then I am clear.

JOCAS.   What tale of mine?

OEDIP.   He told you that Laius met his death from robbers; if he keeps to that tale now and speaks of several slayers, I am not the slayer. But if he says one lonely wayfarer, then beyond a doubt the scale dips to me.

JOCAS.   Be certain of this much at least, his first tale was of robbers. He cannot revoke that tale—the city heard it and not I alone. Yet, if he should somewhat change his story, King, at least he cannot make the murder of Laius square with prophecy; for Loxias plainly said of Laius that he would die by the hand of my child. That poor innocent did not kill him, for it died before him. Therefore from this out I would not, for all divination can do, so much as look to my right hand or to my left hand, or fear at all.

OEDIP. You have judged well; and yet for all that, send and bring this peasant to me.

JOCAS. I will send without delay. I will do all that you would have of me—but let us come in to the house.

[*They go into the house.*

CHORUS For this one thing above all I would be praised as a man,
That in my words and my deeds I have kept those laws in
  mind
Olympian Zeus, and that high clear Empyrean,
Fashioned, and not some man or people of mankind,
Even those sacred laws nor age nor sleep can blind.

A man becomes a tyrant out of insolence,
He climbs and climbs, until all people call him great,
He seems upon the summit, and God flings him thence;
Yet an ambitious man may lift up a whole State,
And in his death be blessed, in his life fortunate.

And all men honor such; but should a man forget
The holy images, the Delphian Sibyl's trance,
And the world's navel-stone, and not be punished for it
And seem most fortunate, or even blessed perchance,
Why should we honor the gods, or join the sacred dance?

[JOCASTA *enters from the palace.*

JOCAS. It has come into my head, citizens of Thebes, to visit every altar of the Gods, a wreath in my hand and a dish of incense. For all manner of alarms trouble the soul of Oedipus, who instead of weighing new oracles by old, like a man of sense, is at the mercy of every mouth that speaks terror. Seeing that my words are nothing to him, I cry to you, Lycian Apollo, whose altar is the first I meet: I come, a suppliant, bearing symbols of prayer; O, make us clean, for now we are all afraid, seeing him afraid, even as they who see the helmsman afraid.

[*Enter* MESSENGER.

MESS. May I learn from you, strangers, where is the home of King Oedipus? Or better still, tell me where he himself is, if you know.

CHORUS This is his house, and he himself, stranger, is within it, and this lady is the mother of his children.

MESS. Then I call a blessing upon her, seeing what man she has married.

JOCAS. May God reward those words with a like blessing, stranger! But what have you come to seek or to tell?

MESS. Good news for your house, Lady, and for your husband.

JOCAS. What news? From whence have you come?

MESS. From Corinth, and you will rejoice at the message I am about to give you; yet, maybe, it will grieve you.

JOCAS. What is it? How can it have this double power?

MESS. The people of Corinth, they say, will take him for king.

JOCAS. How then? Is old Polybus no longer on the throne?

MESS. No. He is in his tomb.

JOCAS. What do you say? Is Polybus dead, old man?

MESS. May I drop dead if it is not the truth.

JOCAS. Away! Hurry to your master with this news. O oracle of the gods, where are you now? This is the man whom Oedipus feared and shunned lest he should murder him, and now this man has died a natural death, and not by the hand of Oedipus.

[*Enter* OEDIPUS.

OEDIP.	Jocasta, dearest wife, why have you called me from the house?
JOCAS.	Listen to this man, and judge to what the oracles of the gods have come.
OEDIP.	And he—who may he be? And what news has he?
JOCAS.	He has come from Corinth to tell you that your father, Polybus, is dead.
OEDIP.	How, stranger? Let me have it from your own mouth.
MESS.	If I am to tell the story, the first thing is that he is dead and gone.
OEDIP.	By some sickness or by treachery?
MESS.	A little thing can bring the aged to their rest.
OEDIP.	Ah! He died, it seems, from sickness?
MESS.	Yes; and of old age.
OEDIP.	Alas! Alas! Why, indeed, my wife, should one look to that Pythian seer, or to the birds that scream above our heads? For they would have it that I was doomed to kill my father. And now he is dead—hid already beneath the earth. And here am I—who had no part in it, unless indeed he died from longing for me. If that were so, I may have caused his death; but Polybus has carried the oracles with him into Hades—the oracles as men have understood them—and they are worth nothing.
JOCAS.	Did I not tell you so, long since?
OEDIP.	You did, but fear misled me.
JOCAS.	Put this trouble from you.
OEDIP.	Those bold words would sound better, were not my mother living. But as it is—I have some grounds for fear; yet you have said well.
JOCAS.	Yet your father's death is a sign that all is well.
OEDIP.	I know that: but I fear because of her who lives.

MESS.	Who is this woman who makes you afraid?
OEDIP.	Merope, old man, the wife of Polybus.
MESS.	What is there in her to make you afraid?
OEDIP.	A dreadful oracle sent from Heaven, stranger.
MESS.	Is it a secret, or can you speak it out?
OEDIP.	Loxias said that I was doomed to marry my own mother, and to shed my father's blood. For that reason I fled from my house in Corinth; and I did right, though there is great comfort in familiar faces.
MESS.	Was it indeed for that reason that you went into exile?
OEDIP.	I did not wish, old man, to shed my father's blood.
MESS.	King, have I not freed you from that fear?
OEDIP.	You shall be fittingly rewarded.
MESS.	Indeed, to tell the truth, it was for that I came; to bring you home and be the better for it—
OEDIP.	No! I will never go to my parents' home.
MESS.	Ah, my son, it is plain enough, you do not know what you do.
OEDIP.	How, old man? For God's love, tell me.
MESS.	If for these reasons you shrink from going home.
OEDIP.	I am afraid lest Phoebus has spoken true.
MESS.	You are afraid of being made guilty through Merope?
OEDIP.	That is my constant fear.
MESS.	A vain fear.
OEDIP.	How so, if I was born of that father and mother?
MESS.	Because they were nothing to you in blood.
OEDIP.	What do you say? Was Polybus not my father?
MESS.	No more nor less than myself.

OEDIP.   How can my father be no more to me than you who are nothing to me?

MESS.   He did not beget you any more than I.

OEDIP.   No? Then why did he call me his son?

MESS.   He took you as a gift from these hands of mine.

OEDIP.   How could he love so dearly what came from another's hands?

MESS.   He had been childless.

OEDIP.   If I am not your son, where did you get me?

MESS.   In a wooded valley of Cithaeron.

OEDIP.   What brought you wandering there?

MESS.   I was in charge of mountain sheep.

OEDIP.   A shepherd—a wandering, hired man.

MESS.   A hired man who came just in time.

OEDIP.   Just in time—had it come to that?

MESS.   Have not the cords left their marks upon your ankles?

OEDIP.   Yes, that is an old trouble.

MESS.   I took your feet out of the spancel.

OEDIP.   I have had those marks from the cradle.

MESS.   They have given you the name you bear.

OEDIP.   Tell me, for God's sake, was that deed my mother's or my father's?

MESS.   I do not know—he who gave you to me knows more of that than I.

OEDIP.   What? You had me from another? You did not chance on me yourself?

MESS.   No. Another shepherd gave you to me.

OEDIP.   Who was he? Can you tell me who he was?

MESS.	I think that he was said to be of Laius' household.
OEDIP.	The king who ruled this country long ago?
MESS.	The same—the man was herdsman in his service.
OEDIP.	Is he alive, that I might speak with him?
MESS.	You people of this country should know that.
OEDIP.	Is there any one here present who knows the herd he speaks of? Any one who has seen him in the town pastures? The hour has come when all must be made clear.
CHORUS	I think he is the very herd you sent for but now; Jocasta can tell you better than I.
JOCAS.	Why ask about that man? Why think about him? Why waste a thought on what this man has said? What he has said is of no account.
OEDIP.	What, with a clue like that in my hands and fail to find out my birth?
JOCAS.	For God's sake, if you set any value upon your life, give up this search—my misery is enough.
OEDIP.	Though I be proved the son of a slave, yes, even of three generations of slaves, you cannot be made base-born.
JOCAS.	Yet, hear me, I implore you. Give up this search.
OEDIP.	I will not hear of anything but searching the whole thing out.
JOCAS.	I am only thinking of your good—I have advised you for the best.
OEDIP.	Your advice makes me impatient.
JOCAS.	May you never come to know who you are, unhappy man!
OEDIP.	Go, some one, bring the herdsman here—and let that woman glory in her noble blood.
JOCAS.	Alas, alas, miserable man! Miserable! That is all that I can call you now or for ever.

[*She goes out.*

CHORUS   Why has the lady gone, Oedipus, in such a transport of despair? Out of this silence will burst a storm of sorrows.

OEDIP.   Let come what will. However lowly my origin I will discover it. That woman, with all a woman's pride, grows red with shame at my base birth. I think myself the child of Good Luck, and that the years are my foster-brothers. Sometimes they have set me up, and sometimes thrown me down, but he that has Good Luck for mother can suffer no dishonor. That is my origin, nothing can change it, so why should I renounce this search into my birth?

CHORUS   Oedipus' nurse, mountain of many a hidden glen,
Be honored among men;
A famous man, deep-thoughted, and his body strong;
Be honored in dance and song.
Who met in the hidden glen? Who let his fancy run
Upon nymph of Helicon?
Lord Pan or Lord Apollo or the mountain lord
By the Bacchantes adored?

OEDIP.   If I, who have never met the man, may venture to say so, I think that the herdsman we await approaches; his venerable age matches with this stranger's, and I recognize as servants of mine those who bring him. But you, if you have seen the man before, will know the man better than I.

CHORUS   Yes, I know the man who is coming; he was indeed in Laius' service, and is still the most trusted of the herdsmen.

OEDIP.   I ask you first, Corinthian stranger, is this the man you mean?

MESS.   He is the very man.

OEDIP.   Look at me, old man! Answer my questions. Were you once in Laius' service?

HERD.   I was: not a bought slave, but reared up in the house.

OEDIP.   What was your work—your manner of life?

HERD.   For the best part of my life I have tended flocks.

OEDIP.   Where, mainly?

HERD.   Cithaeron or its neighborhood.

OEDIP.   Do you remember meeting with this man there?

HERD.   What man do you mean?

OEDIP.   This man. Did you ever meet him?

HERD.   I cannot recall him to mind.

MESS.   No wonder in that, master; but I will bring back his memory.
            He and I lived side by side upon Cithaeron. I had but one
            flock and he had two. Three full half-years we lived there,
            from spring to autumn, and every winter I drove my flock to
            my own fold, while he drove his to the fold of Laius. Is that
            right? Was it not so?

HERD.   True enough; though it was long ago.

MESS.   Come, tell me now—do you remember giving me a boy to
            rear as my own foster-son?

HERD.   What are you saying? Why do you ask me that?

MESS.   Look at that man, my friend, he is the child you gave me.

HERD.   A plague upon you! Cannot you hold your tongue?

OEDIP.   Do not blame him, old man; your own words are more
            blamable.

HERD.   And how have I offended, master?

OEDIP.   In not telling of that boy he asks of.

HERD.   He speaks from ignorance, and does not know what he is
            saying.

OEDIP.   If you will not speak with a good grace you shall be made
            to speak.

HERD.   Do not hurt me for the love of God, I am an old man.

OEDIP.   Some one there, tie his hands behind his back.

HERD.   Alas! Wherefore! What more would you learn?

OEDIP.	Did you give this man the child he speaks of?
HERD.	I did: would I had died that day!
OEDIP.	Well, you may come to that unless you speak the truth.
HERD.	Much more am I lost if I speak it.
OEDIP.	What! Would the fellow make more delay?
HERD.	No, no. I said before that I gave it to him.
OEDIP.	Where did you come by it? Your own child, or another?
HERD.	It was not my own child—I had it from another.
OEDIP.	From any of those here? From what house?
HERD.	Do not ask any more, master; for the love of God do not ask.
OEDIP.	You are lost if I have to question you again.
HERD.	It was a child from the house of Laius.
OEDIP.	A slave? Or one of his own race?
HERD.	Alas! I am on the edge of dreadful words.
OEDIP.	And I of hearing: yet hear I must.
HERD.	It was said to have been his own child. But your lady within can tell you of these things best.
OEDIP.	How? It was she who gave it to you?
HERD.	Yes, King.
OEDIP.	To what end?
HERD.	That I should make away with it.
OEDIP.	Her own child?
HERD.	Yes: from fear of evil prophecies.
OEDIP.	What prophecies?
HERD.	That he should kill his father.
OEDIP.	Why, then, did you give him up to this old man?
HERD.	Through pity, master, believing that he would carry him to

whatever land he had himself come from—but he saved him for dreadful misery; for if you are what this man says, you are the most miserable of all men.

OEDIP. O! O! All brought to pass! All truth! Now O light, may I look my last upon you, having been found accursed in bloodshed, accursed in marriage, and in my coming into the world accursed!

[*He rushes into the palace.*

CHORUS What can the shadow-like generations of man attain
But build up a dazzling mockery of delight that under their
   touch dissolves again?
Oedipus seemed blessed, but there is no man blessed amongst
   men.

Oedipus overcame the woman-breasted Fate;
He seemed like a strong tower against Death and first among
   the fortunate;
He sat upon the ancient throne of Thebes, and all men called
   him great.

But, looking for a marriage-bed, he found the bed of his
   birth,
Tilled the field his father had tilled, cast seed into the same
   abounding earth;
Entered through the door that had sent him wailing forth.

Begetter and begot as one! How could that be hid?
What darkness cover up that marriage-bed? Time watches,
   he is eagle-eyed,
And all the works of man are known and every soul is tried.

Would you had never come to Thebes, nor to this house,
Nor riddled with the woman-breasted Fate, beaten off Death
   and succored us,
That I had never raised this song, heartbroken Oedipus!

[SECOND MESSENGER *coming from the house.*

Friends and kinsmen of this house! What deeds must you look upon, what burden of sorrow bear, if true to race you still love the House of Labdacus. For not Ister nor Phasis could wash this house clean, so many misfortunes have been brought upon it, so many has it brought upon itself, and those misfortunes are always the worst that a man brings upon himself.

CHORUS   Great already are the misfortunes of this house, and you bring us a new tale.

S. MESS.   A short tale in the telling: Jocasta, our Queen, is dead.

CHORUS   Alas, miserable woman, how did she die?

S. MESS.   By her own hand. It cannot be as terrible to you as to one that saw it with his eyes, yet so far as words can serve, you shall see it. When she had come into the vestibule, she ran half crazed towards her marriage-bed, clutching at her hair with the fingers of both hands, and once within the chamber dashed the doors together behind her. Then called upon the name of Laius, long since dead, remembering that son who killed the father and upon the mother begot an accursed race. And wailed because of that marriage wherein she had borne a twofold race—husband by husband, children by her child. Then Oedipus with a shriek burst in and running here and there asked for a sword, asked where he would find the wife that was no wife but a mother who had borne his children and himself. Nobody answered him, we all stood dumb; but supernatural power helped him, for, with a dreadful shriek, as though beckoned, he sprang at the double doors, drove them in, burst the bolts out of their sockets, and ran into the room. There we saw the woman hanging in a swinging halter, and with a terrible cry he loosened the halter from her neck. When that unhappiest woman lay stretched upon the ground, we saw another dreadful sight. He dragged the golden brooches from her dress and lifting them struck them upon his eyeballs, crying out, 'You have looked enough upon those you ought never to have looked upon, failed long enough to know those that you should have known; henceforth you shall be dark.' He struck his eyes, not once, but many times, lifting his hands and speaking such or like words. The blood poured down and not with a few slow drops, but all at once over his beard in a dark shower as it were hail.

[*The* CHORUS *wails and he steps further on to the stage.*

Such evils have come forth from the deeds of those two and fallen not on one alone but upon husband and wife. They inherited much happiness, much good fortune; but today, ruin, shame, death, and loud crying, all evils that can be counted up, all, all are theirs.

CHORUS   Is he any quieter?

S. MESS. He cries for some one to unbar the gates and to show to all the men of Thebes his father's murderer, his mother's—the unholy word must not be spoken. It is his purpose to cast himself out of the land that he may not bring all this house under his curse. But he has not the strength to do it. He must be supported and led away. The curtain is parting; you are going to look upon a sight which even those who shudder must pity.

[*Enter* OEDIPUS.

OEDIP.   Woe, woe, is me! Miserable, miserable that I am? Where am I? Where am I going? Where am I cast away? Who hears my words?

CHORUS   Cast away indeed, dreadful to the sight of the eye, dreadful to the ear.

OEDIP.   Ah, friend, the only friend left to me, friend still faithful to the blind man! I know that you are there; blind though I am, I recognize your voice.

CHORUS   Where did you get the courage to put out your eyes? What unearthly power drove you to that?

OEDIP.   Apollo, friends, Apollo, but it was my own hand alone, wretched that I am, that quenched these eyes.

CHORUS   You were better dead than blind.

OEDIP.   No, it is better to be blind. What sight is there that could give me joy? How could I have looked into the face of my father when I came among the dead, aye, or on my miserable mother, since against them both I sinned such things that no halter can punish? And what to me this spectacle, town, statue, wall, and what to me this people, since I, thrice wretched, I, noblest of Theban men, have doomed myself to banishment, doomed myself when I commanded all to thrust out the unclean thing?

CHORUS   It had indeed been better if that herdsman had never taken your feet out of the spancel or brought you back to life.

OEDIP.   O three roads, O secret glen; O coppice and narrow way where three roads met; you that drank up the blood I spilt, the blood that was my own, my father's blood: remember what deeds I wrought for you to look upon, and then, when I had come hither, the new deeds that I wrought. O marriage-bed that gave me birth and after that gave children to your child, creating an incestuous kindred of fathers, brothers, sons, wives, and mothers. Yes, all the shame and the uncleanness that I have wrought among men.

CHORUS   For all my pity I shudder and turn away.

OEDIP.   Come near, condescend to lay your hands upon a wretched man; listen, do not fear. My plague can touch no man but me. Hide me somewhere out of this land for God's sake, or kill me, or throw me into the sea where you shall never look upon me more.

                        [*Enter* CREON *and attendants.*

CHORUS   Here Creon comes at a fit moment; you can ask of him what you will, help or counsel, for he is now in your place. He is King.

OEDIP.   What can I say to him? What can I claim, having been altogether unjust to him?

CREON   I have not come in mockery, Oedipus, nor to reproach you.
         Lead him in to the house as quickly as you can. Do not let
         him display his misery before strangers.

OEDIP.   I must obey, but first, since you have come in so noble a
         spirit, you will hear me.

CREON   Say what you will.

OEDIP.   I know that you will give her that lies within such a tomb
         as befits your own blood, but there is something more, Creon.
         My sons are men and can take care of themselves, but my
         daughters, my two unhappy daughters, that have ever eaten
         at my own table and shared my food, watch over my daugh-
         ters, Creon. If it is lawful, let me touch them with my hands.
         Grant it, Prince, grant it, noble heart. I would believe, could
         I touch them, that I still saw them.

                    [ISMENE *and* ANTIGONE *are led in by attendants.*

         But do I hear them sobbing? Has Creon pitied me and sent
         my children, my darlings? Has he done this?

CREON   Yes, I ordered it, for I know how greatly you have always
         loved them.

OEDIP.   Then may you be blessed, and may Heaven be kinder to you
         than it has been to me! My children, where are you? Come
         hither—hither—come to the hands of him whose mother
         was your mother; the hands that put out your father's eyes,
         eyes once as bright as your own; his who, understanding
         nothing, seeing nothing, became your father by her that bore
         him. I weep when I think of the bitter life that men will
         make you live, and the days that are to come. Into what com-
         pany dare you go, to what festival, but that you shall return
         home from it not sharing in the joys, but bathed in tears?
         When you are old enough to be married, what man dare face
         the reproach that must cling to you and to your children?
         What misery is there lacking? Your father killed his father,
         he begat you at the spring of his own being, offspring of her

that bore him. That is the taunt that would be cast upon you and on the man that you should marry. That man is not alive; my children, you must wither away in barrenness. Ah, son of Menoeceus, listen. Seeing that you are the only father now left to them, for we their parents are lost, both of us lost, do not let them wander in beggary—are they not your own kindred?—do not let them sink down into my misery. No, pity them, seeing them utterly wretched in helpless childhood if you do not protect them. Show me that you promise, generous man, by touching me with your hand.

[CREON *touches him.*

My children, there is much advice that I would give you were you but old enough to understand, but all I can do now is bid you pray that you may live wherever you are let live, and that your life be happier than your father's.

CREON	Enough of tears. Pass into the house.
OEDIP.	I will obey, though upon conditions.
CREON	Conditions?
OEDIP.	Banish me from this country. I know that nothing can destroy me, for I wait some incredible fate; yet cast me upon Cithaeron, chosen by my father and my mother for my tomb.
CREON	Only the gods can say yes or no to that.
OEDIP.	No, for I am hateful to the gods.
CREON	If that be so you will get your wish the quicker. They will banish that which they hate.
OEDIP.	Are you certain of that?
CREON	I would not say it if I did not mean it.
OEDIP.	Then it is time to lead me within.
CREON	Come, but let your children go.
OEDIP.	No, do not take them from me.

CREON   Do not seek to be master; you won the mastery but could not
keep it to the end.

> [*He leads* OEDIPUS *into the palace, followed by* ISMENE,
> ANTIGONE, *and attendants.*

CHORUS   Make way for Oedipus. All people said,
'That is a fortunate man';
And now what storms are beating on his head!
Call no man fortunate that is not dead.
The dead are free from pain.

Sophocles

OEDIPUS AT COLONUS

translated by
Robert Fitzgerald

TO THE MEMORY OF
MILMAN PARRY

'Nous vivons éternellement, non dans les écoles de
pointilleurs de syllabes, mais dans le cercle des sages
où l'on ne discute pas sur la mère d'Andromaque ou
les fils de Niobé, mais où l'on s'entretient des
origines profondes des choses divines et humaines.'

Long after he had left Thebes, the blinded OEDIPUS came with ANTIGONE to the Attic deme of COLONUS, where the oracle of Apollo had prophesied that he was to die.

‍‍‍‍‍‍‍‍‍‍‍‍‍‍‍‍‍‍‍‍‍‍‍‍‍‍‍‍‍‍‍‍‍‍

DRAMATIS PERSONÆ:

OEDIPUS	ISMENE
ANTIGONE	THESEUS
A STRANGER	CREON

POLYNEICES

A MESSENGER

CHORUS

OEDIPUS AT COLONUS

Scene, like the theatre, is in the open air. In the background is the
grove of the Furies at Colonus in Attica, about a mile northwest
of Athens. A statue or stele of Colonus, a legendary horseman and
hero, can be seen stage left. Stage right, a flat rock jutting out
among the trees of the grove. Downstage, center, another ridge
of rock.

Time: early afternoon of a day about twenty years after the action of
King Oedipus.

SCENE I

> [OEDIPUS, *old, blind, bearded and ragged, but carrying*
> *himself well, enters stage right, led by* ANTIGONE.

OEDIP.   My daughter—daughter of the blind old man—
Where, I wonder, have we come to now?
What place is this, Antigone? What people?
Who will be kind to Oedipus this evening
And give the wanderer charity?

Though he ask little and receive still less,
It is sufficient:
              Suffering and time,
Vast time, have been instructors in contentment,
Which kingliness teaches too.

But now, child,
If you can see a place where we might rest,
Some public place or consecrated park,
Let me stop and sit down there.
And then let us inquire where we may be.
As foreigners and strangers we must learn
From the local people, and do as they direct.

ANTIG.   Father, poor tired Oedipus, the towers
That crown the city still seem far away;
As for this place, it is clearly a holy one,
Shady with vines and olive trees and laurel;
Within the grove the gray-winged nightingales
Make a sweet music.

Rest on this rough stone.
It was a long road for an old man to travel.

OEDIP.   Help me sit down; take care of the blind man.

ANTIG.   After so long, you need not tell me, father.

OEDIP.   And now have you any idea where we are?

ANTIG.   This place I do not know; the city is Athens.

OEDIP.   Yes, everyone we met has told us that.

ANTIG.   Then shall I go and ask?

OEDIP.   Do, child, if there is any life near-by.

ANTIG.   Oh, but indeed there is; I need not leave you;
I see a man, now, not far away from us.

OEDIP.   Is he coming this way? Has he started towards us?

[The STRANGER enters, left.

ANTIG.   Here he is now.

Say what seems best to you,
Father; the man is here.

OEDIP.   Friend, my daughter's eyes serve for my own.
She tells me we are fortunate enough to meet you,
And no doubt you will inform us—

STRANG.   Do not go on;
         First move from where you sit; the place is holy;
         It is forbidden to walk upon that ground.

OEDIP.   What ground is this? What god is honored here?

STRANG. It is not to be touched, no one may live upon it;
         Most dreadful are its divinities, most feared,
         Daughters of darkness and mysterious earth.

OEDIP.   Under what solemn name shall I invoke them?

STRANG. The people here prefer to address them as Gentle
         All-seeing Ones; elsewhere there are other names.

OEDIP.   Then may they be gentle to me.
         For I shall never leave this resting place.

STRANG. What is the meaning of this?

OEDIP.   It was ordained;
         I recognize it now.

STRANG.   Without authority
         From the city government I dare not move you;
         First I must show them what it is you are doing.

OEDIP.   Friend, in the name of God, bear with me now!
         I turn to you for light; answer the wanderer.

STRANG. Speak. You will not find me discourteous.

OEDIP.   What is this region into which I've come?

STRANG. Whatever I can tell you, I will tell.
         This country, all of it, is blessed ground;
         The god of ocean loves it; in it the firecarrier
         Prometheus has his influence; in particular
         That spot you rest on has been called this earth's
         Doorsill of Brass, and buttress of great Athens.
         All men of this land claim descent from him
         Whose statue stands near-by: Colonus the horseman,
         And bear his name in common with their own.

That is this country, stranger: honored less
In histories than in the hearts of the people.

OEDIP.   Then people live in the land?

STRANG.   Yes, certainly,
The clan of those descended from that hero.

OEDIP.   Ruled by a king? Or do the people rule?

STRANG.   The land is governed from Athens, by Athens' king.

OEDIP.   And who is he whose word has power here?

STRANG.   Theseus, son of Aegeus, the king before him.

OEDIP.   Ah. Would someone then go to this king for me?

STRANG.   To tell him what? Perhaps to urge his coming?

OEDIP.   To tell him a small favor will gain him much.

STRANG.   What service can a blind man render him?

OEDIP.   All I shall say will be clear-sighted indeed.

STRANG.   Listen, stranger: I wish you no injury;
You seem well-born, though obviously unlucky;
Stay where you are, exactly where I found you,
And I'll inform the people of what you say—
Not in the town, but here—it rests with them
To decide if you should stay or must move on.

                                    [*Exit* STRANGER, *left.*

OEDIP.   Child, has he gone?

ANTIG.   Yes, father. Now you may speak tranquilly,
For only I am with you.

                                    [*Praying.*

OEDIP.   Ladies whose eyes
Are terrible: Spirits: upon your sacred ground
I have first bent my knees in this new land;
Therefore be mindful of me and of Apollo,
For when his riddler prophesied my ruin,

He also spoke of this:
                    A resting place,
After long years, in the last country, where
I should find home among the powers of justice:
That there I might round out my bitter life,
Conferring benefit on those who received me,
A curse on those who have driven me away.

Portents, he said, would make me sure of this:
Earthquake, thunder, or God's smiling lightning;
But I am sure of it now, sure that you guided me
With feathery influence upon this road,
And led me here into your hallowed wood.

How otherwise could I, in my wandering,
Have sat down first with you in all this land,
I who drink not, with you who love not wine?

How otherwise had I found this chair of stone?
Grant me then, goddesses, passage from life at last,
And consummation, as the unearthly voice foretold;
Unless indeed I seem not worth your grace:
Slave as I am to such unending pain
As no man had before.
                    O hear my prayer,
Sweet children of original Darkness! Hear me,
Athens, city named for great Athena,
Honored above all cities in the world!
Pity a man's poor carcase and his ghost,
For Oedipus is not the strength he was.

ANTIG. Be still. Some elderly men are coming this way,
        Looking for the place where you are seated.

OEDIP. I shall be still. You get me clear of the path,
        And hide me in the wood, so I may hear
        What they are saying. If we know their temper
        We shall be better able to act with prudence.

        [OEDIPUS *and* ANTIGONE *withdraw into the grove.*

ᒣᒪᒣᒪᒣᒪᒣᒪᒣᒪᒣᒪᒣᒪᒣᒪᒣᒪᒣᒪᒣᒪᒣᒪᒣᒪᒣᒪᒣᒪᒣ

CHORAL DIALOGUE

[*The* CHORUS *enters from the left. Here, and throughout the play, its lines may be taken by various members as seems suitable.*

CHORUS   Look for him. Who could he be? Where
Is he? Where has he scuttled?
Impious, blasphemous, shameless!
Use your eyes, search him out!
Cover the ground and uncover him!
     Vagabond!
The old man must be a vagabond,
Not of our land, for he'd never
Otherwise dare to go in there,
In the inviolate thicket
Of those whom it's futile to fight,
Those whom we tremble to name.
When we pass we avert our eyes—
     Close our eyes!—
In silence, without conversation,
Shaping our prayers with our lips.
But now, if the story is credible,
Some alien fool has profaned it;
Yet I have looked over all the grove and
     Still cannot see him;
Cannot say where he has hidden.

[OEDIPUS *comes forward from the wood.*

OEDIP.   That stranger is I. As they say of the blind,
Sounds are the things I see.

CHORUS   Ah!
His face is dreadful! His voice is dreadful!

OEDIP.   Do not regard me, please, as a law-breaker.

CHORUS   Merciful heaven, who is this old man?

OEDIP.   One whose fate is not quite to be envied,
    O my masters, and men of this land;
    That must be evident: why, otherwise,
        Should I need this girl
    To lead me, her frailty to put my weight on?

CHORUS   Ah! His eyes are blind!
    And were you brought into the world so?
    Unhappy life—and so long!
    Well, not if I can help it,
    Will you have this curse besides.—
        Stranger! you
    Trespass there! But beyond there,
    In the glade where the grass is still,
    Where the honeyed libations drip
    In the rill from the brimming spring,
    You must not step! O stranger,
    It is well to be careful about it!
        Most careful!
    Stand aside and come down then!
    There is too much space between us!
    Say, wanderer, can you hear?
    If you have a mind to tell us
    Your business, or wish to converse with our council,
        Come down from that place!
    Only speak where it's proper to do so!

OEDIP.   Now, daughter, what is the way of wisdom?

ANTIG.   We must do just as they do here, father;
    We should give in now, and listen to them.

OEDIP.   Stretch out your hand to me.

ANTIG.   There, I am near you.

OEDIP.   Sirs, let there be no injustice done me,
          Once I have trusted you, and left my refuge.

                              [*Led by* ANTIGONE, *he starts downstage.*

CHORUS   Never, never, will anyone drive you away
          From rest in this land, old man!

OEDIP.   Shall I come further?

CHORUS   Yes, further.

OEDIP.   And now?

CHORUS   You must guide him, girl;
          You can see how much further to come.

ANTIG.   Come with your blind step, father;
          This way; come where I lead you.

CHORUS   Though the land is strange, newcomer,
          You've weathered much; take heart;
          What the state has long held hateful,
          Hate, and respect what it loves.

OEDIP.   Lead me on, then, child,
          To where we may speak or listen respectfully;
          Let us not fight necessity.

CHORUS   Now! Go no further than that platform there,
          Formed of the natural rock.

OEDIP.   This?

CHORUS   Far enough; you can hear us.

OEDIP.   Shall I sit down?

CHORUS   Yes, sit there
          To the left on the ridge of the rock.

ANTIG.   Father, this is where I can help you;
          You must keep step with me; gently now.

OEDIP.   Ah, me!

ANTIG.	Lean your old body on my arm; It is I who love you; let yourself down.
OEDIP.	How bitter blindness is!

[*He is seated on the rock downstage, center.*

CHORUS	Now that you are at rest, poor man, Tell us, what is your name? Who are you, wanderer? What is the land of your ancestors?
OEDIP.	I am an exile, friends; but do not ask me . . .
CHORUS	What is it you fear to say, old man?
OEDIP.	No, no, no! Do not go on Questioning me! Do not ask my name!
CHORUS	Why not?
OEDIP.	My star was unspeakable.
CHORUS	Speak!
OEDIP.	My child, what can I say to them?
CHORUS	Answer us, stranger; what is your race, Who was your father?
OEDIP.	God help me, what will become of me, child?
ANTIG.	Tell them; there is no other way.
OEDIP.	I suppose I must; I cannot conceal it.
CHORUS	Between you, you greatly delay. Speak up!
OEDIP.	Have you heard of Laius' family?
CHORUS	Ah!
OEDIP.	Of the race of Labdacidae?
CHORUS	Ah, God!
OEDIP.	And ruined Oedipus?
CHORUS	You are he!

OEDIP.   Do not take fright from what I say—

CHORUS   Oh, dreadful!

OEDIP.   I am accursed.

CHORUS   Oh, fearful!

OEDIP.   Antigone, what will happen now?

CHORUS   Away with you! Out with you! Leave our country!

OEDIP.   And what of the promises you made me?

CHORUS   God will not punish the man
Who makes return for an injury:
Deceivers may be deceived:
They play a game that ends
In grief, and not in pleasure.
Leave this grove at once!
Our country is not for you!
Wind no further
Your clinging evil upon us!

ANTIG.   O men of reverent mind!
Since you will not suffer my father,
Old man though he is,
And though you know his story—
He never knew what he did—
Take pity still on my unhappiness,
And let me intercede with you for him.
Not with lost eyes, but looking in your eyes
As if I were a child of yours, I beg
Mercy for him, the beaten man! O hear me!
We are thrown upon your mercy as on God's;
    Be kinder than you seem!
By all you have and own that is dear to you:
Children, wives, possessions, gods, I pray you!
For you will never see in all the world
    A man whom God has led
    Escape his destiny!

· SCENE II

CHORUS   Child of Oedipus, indeed we pity you,
Just as we pity him for his misfortune;
But we tremble to think of what the gods may do;
We could not dare to speak more generously!

OEDIP.   What use is reputation then? What good
Comes of a noble name? A noble fiction!
For Athens, so they say, excels in piety;
Has power to save the wretched of other lands;
Can give them refuge; is unique in this.
Yet, when it comes to me, where is her refuge?
You pluck me from these rocks and cast me out,
All for fear of a name!
                      Or do you dread
My strength? my actions? I think not, indeed,
Since all I have done was suffering, not action,
As I might show if it were fitting here
To tell my father's and my mother's story . . .
For which you fear me, as I know too well.

And yet, how was I evil in myself?
I had been wronged, I retaliated; even had I
Known what I was doing, was that evil?
Then, knowing nothing, I went on. Went on.
But those who wronged me knew, and ruined me.

Therefore I beg you in God's name
For the same cause that made you move me—
In reverence of your gods—give me this shelter,
And thus accord those powers what is theirs.
Think: their eyes are fixed upon the just,
Fixed on the unjust, too; no impious man

Can twist away from them forever.
Now, in their presence, do not blot your city's
Luster by bending to unholy action;
As you would receive an honest petitioner,
Give me, too, sanctuary; though my face
Be dreadful in its look, yet honor me!

For I come here as one endowed with grace
By those who are over Nature; and I bring
Advantage to this race, as you may learn
More fully when some lord of yours is here.
Meanwhile be careful to be just.

CHORUS   Old man,
This argument of yours compels our wonder.
It was not feebly worded. I am content
That higher authorities should judge this matter.

OEDIP.   And where is he who rules the land, strangers?

CHORUS   In his father's city; but the messenger
Who sent us here has gone to fetch him also.

OEDIP.   Do you think a blind man will so interest him
As to bring him such a distance?

CHORUS   I do, indeed, when he has heard your name.

OEDIP.   But who will tell him that?

CHORUS   It is a long road, and the rumors of travellers
Have a way of wandering. He will have word of them;
Take heart—he will be here. Old man, your name
Has gone over all the earth; though he may be
At rest when the news comes, he will come quickly.

OEDIP.   Then may he come with luck for his own city,
As well as for me . . . The good befriend themselves.

ANTIG.   O God! What shall I say? How interpret this?

OEDIP.   Antigone, my dear child, what is it?

ANTIG.   A woman
Riding a pony and drawing nearer to us;
She is wearing a wide hat that shades her face;
I don't know!
Is it or isn't it? Or am I dreaming?
I think so; yes!—No. I can't be sure . . .

Ah, poor child,
It is no one else but she! And she is smiling
Now as she comes! It is my dear Ismene!

OEDIP.   What did you say, child?

                                    [ISMENE *enters, with one* ATTENDANT.

ANTIG.   That I see your daughter!
My sister! Now you can tell her by her voice.

ISMENE   O father and sister together! Dearest voices!
Now I have found you—how, I scarcely know—
I don't know how I shall see you through my tears!

OEDIP.   Child, you have come?

ISMENE   Father, how old you seem!

OEDIP.   Child, are you here?

ISMENE   And such a time I had!

OEDIP.   Touch me, little one.

ISMENE   I shall hold you both!

OEDIP.   My children . . . and sisters.

ISMENE   Oh, unhappy people!

OEDIP.   She and I?

ISMENE   And I with you, unhappy.

OEDIP.   But, child, why have you come?

ISMENE   For your sake, father.

OEDIP.   You missed me?

ISMENE   Yes; and I have news for you.
I came with the one person I could trust.

OEDIP.   Why, where are your brothers? Could they not do it?

ISMENE   They are—where they are. It is a hard time for them.

OEDIP.   Ah! They behave as if they were Egyptians,
Bred the Egyptian way! Down there, the men
Sit indoors all day long, weaving;
The women go out and attend to business.
Just so your brothers, who should have done this work
Sit by the fire like home-loving girls,
And you two, in their place, must bear my hardships.

One, since her childhood ended and her body
Gained its power, has wandered ever with me,
An old man's governess; often in the wild
Forest going without shoes, and hungry,
Beaten by many rains, tired by the sun;
Yet she rejected the sweet life of home
So that her father should have sustenance.

And you, my daughter, once before came out,
Unknown to Thebes, bringing me news of all
The oracle had said concerning me;
And you remained my faithful outpost there,
When I was driven from that land.
                           But now,
What news, Ismene, do you bring your father?
Why have you left your house to make this journey?
You came for no light reason, I know that;
It must be something serious for me.

ISMENE   I will pass over the troubles I have had
Searching for your whereabouts, father.
They were hard enough to bear; and I will not
Go through it all again in telling of them.
In any case, it is your sons' troubles
That I have come to tell you.

First it was their desire, as it was Creon's,
That the throne should pass to him; that thus the city
Should be defiled no longer: such was their reasoning
When they considered our people's ancient curse
And how it enthralled your pitiful family.
But then some fury put it in their hearts—
O pitiful again!—to itch for power:
For seizure of prerogative and throne;
And it was the younger and the less mature
Who stripped his elder brother, Polyneices,
Of place and kingship, and then banished him.

But now the people hear he has gone to Argos,
Into the valley land, has joined that nation,
And is enlisting friends among its warriors,
Telling them Argos shall honorably win
Thebes and her plain, or else eternal glory.

This is not a mere recital, father;
But terrible truth!
              How long will it be, I wonder,
Before the gods take pity on your distress?

OEDIP.   You have some hope then that they are concerned
          With my deliverance?

ISMENE   I have, father.
          The latest sentences of the oracle . . .

OEDIP.   How are they worded? What do they prophesy?

ISMENE   That you shall be much solicited by our people
          Before your death—and after—for their welfare.

OEDIP.   And what could anyone hope from such as I?

ISMENE   The riddler has it that their strength's in you—

OEDIP.   When I am finished, I suppose I am strong!

ISMENE   For the gods who threw you down sustain you now.

OEDIP.	Slight favor, now I am old! My doom was early.
ISMENE	The proof of it is that Creon is coming to you For that same reason, and soon: not by and by.
OEDIP.	To do what, daughter? Tell me about this.
ISMENE	To settle you near the land of Thebes, and so Have you at hand; but you may not cross the border.
OEDIP.	What good am I to them outside the country?
ISMENE	It is merely that if your burial were unlucky, That would be perilous for them.
OEDIP.	Ah, then! No god's assistance is needed in comprehending.
ISMENE	Therefore they want to keep you somewhere near, Just at the border, where you'll not be free.
OEDIP.	And will they compose my shade with Theban dust?
ISMENE	Ah, father! No. Your father's blood forbids it.
OEDIP.	Then they shall never hold me in their power!
ISMENE	If so, some day it will be bitter for them.
OEDIP.	How will that be, my child?
ISMENE	When they shall stand Where you are buried, and feel your anger there.
OEDIP.	What you have said—from whom did you hear it, child?
ISMENE	The envoys told me when they returned from Delphi.
OEDIP.	Then all this about me was spoken there?
ISMENE	According to those men, just come to Thebes.
OEDIP.	Has either of my sons had word of this?
ISMENE	They both have, and they understand it well.
OEDIP.	The scoundrels! So they knew all this, and yet Would not give up the throne to have me back?

ISMENE   It hurts me to hear it, but I can't deny it.

OEDIP.   Gods!
Put not their fires of ambition out!
Let the last word be mine upon this battle
They are about to join, with the spears lifting!
I'd see that the one who holds the sceptre now
Would not have power long, nor would the other,
The banished one, return!
                            These were the two
Who saw me in disgrace and banishment
And never lifted a hand for me. They heard me
Howled from the country, heard the thing proclaimed!

And will they say I wanted exile then,
An appropriate clemency, granted by the state?
That is all false! The truth is that at first
My mind was a boiling caldron; nothing so sweet
As death, death by stoning, could have been given me;
Yet no one there would grant me that desire.
It was only later, when my madness cooled,
And I had begun to think my rage excessive,
My punishment too great for what I had done;
Then it was that the city—in its good time!—
Decided to be harsh, and drove me out.
They could have helped me then; they could have
Helped him who begot them! Would they do it?
For lack of a little word from those two gentlemen
Out I went, like a beggar, to wander forever!
Only by grace of these two girls, unaided,
Have I got food or shelter or devotion;
The others held their father of less worth
Than sitting on a throne and being king.

Well, they shall never win me in their fight!
Nor will they profit from the rule of Thebes.
I am sure of that; I have heard the prophecies
Brought by this girl; I think they fit those others
Spoken so long ago, and now fulfilled.

> So let Creon be sent to find me: Creon,
> Or any other of influence in the state.
> If you men here consent—as do those powers
> Holy and awful, the spirits of this place—
> To give me refuge, then shall this city have
> A great savior; and woe to my enemies!

CHORUS   Oedipus: you are surely worth our pity:
You, and your children, too. And since you claim
Also to be a savior of our land,
I'd like to give you counsel for good luck.

OEDIP.   Most generous friend! I'll do whatever you say.

CHORUS   Make expiation to these divinities
Whose ground you violated when you came.

OEDIP.   In what way shall I do so? Tell me, friends.

CHORUS   First you must bring libations from the spring
That runs forever; and bring them with clean hands.

OEDIP.   And when I have that holy water, then?

CHORUS   There are some bowls there, by a skillful potter;
Put chaplets round the brims, over the handles.

OEDIP.   Of myrtle sprigs, or woolen stuff, or what?

CHORUS   Take the fleeces cropped from a young lamb.

OEDIP.   Just so; then how must I perform the rite?

CHORUS   Facing the quarter of the morning light,
Pour your libations out.

OEDIP.   Am I to pour them from the bowls you speak of?

CHORUS   In three streams, yes; the last one, empty it.

OEDIP.   With what should it be filled? Tell me this, too.

CHORUS   With water and honey; but with no wine added.

OEDIP.   And when the leaf-dark earth receives it?

CHORUS	Lay three times nine young shoots of olive on it With both your hands; meanwhile repeat this prayer:
OEDIP.	This I am eager to hear: it has great power.
CHORUS	That as we call them Eumenides, Which means the gentle of heart, May they accept with gentleness The suppliant and his wish.
	So you, or he who prays for you, address them;
	But do not speak aloud or raise a cry; Then come away, and do not turn again. If you will do all this, I shall take heart And stand up for you; otherwise, O stranger, I should be seriously afraid for you.
OEDIP.	Children, you hear the words of these good people?
ANTIG.	Yes; now tell us what we ought to do.
OEDIP.	It need not be performed by me; I'm far From having the strength or sight for it—I have neither. Let one of you go and carry out the ritual. One soul, I think, often can make atonement For many others, if it be sincere. Now do it quickly.—Yet do not leave me alone! I could not move without the help of someone.
ISMENE	I'll go and do it. But where am I to go? Where shall I find the holy place, I wonder?
CHORUS	On the other side of the wood, girl. If you need it, You may get help from the attendant there.
ISMENE	I am going now. Antigone, you'll stay And care for father. Even if it were hard, I should not think it so, since it is for him.

[ISMENE *goes out, right. The* CHORUS *draws nearer
to* OEDIPUS.

⎍⎍⎍⎍⎍⎍⎍⎍⎍⎍⎍⎍⎍⎍⎍⎍⎍⎍⎍⎍⎍⎍⎍⎍

CHORAL DIALOGUE

CHORUS   What evil things have slept since long ago
            It is not sweet to awaken;
            And yet I long to be told—

OEDIP.   What?

CHORUS   Of that heartbreak for which there was no help,
            The pain you have had to suffer.

OEDIP.   For kindness' sake, do not open
            My old wound, and my shame.

CHORUS   It is told everywhere, and never dies;
            I only want to hear it truly told.

OEDIP.   God! God!

CHORUS   Consent I beg you;
    Give me my wish, and I shall give you yours.

OEDIP.   I had to face a thing most terrible,
            Not willed by me, I swear;
            I would have abhorred it all.

CHORUS   So?

OEDIP.   Though I did not know, Thebes married me to evil;
            Fate and I were joined there.

CHORUS   Then it was indeed your mother
         With whom the thing was done?

OEDIP.   O God! It is worse than death to have to hear it!
    Strangers! Yes: and these two girls of mine . . .

CHORUS   Go on—

OEDIP.   These luckless two
    Were given birth by her who gave birth to me.

CHORUS   These then are daughters; they are also—

OEDIP.   Sisters: yes, their father's sisters . . .

CHORUS   Ah, pity!

OEDIP.   Pity, indeed. What throngs
Of pities come into my mind!

CHORUS   You suffered—

OEDIP.   Yes, unspeakably.

CHORUS   You sinned—

OEDIP.   No, I did not sin!

CHORUS   How not?

OEDIP.   I thought
Of her as my reward. Would God I had never won it!
Would God I had never served the State that day!

CHORUS   Unhappy man—and you also killed—

OEDIP.   What is it now? What are you after?

CHORUS   Killed your father!

OEDIP.   God in heaven!
You strike again where I am hurt.

CHORUS   You killed him.

OEDIP.   Killed him. Yet, there is—

CHORUS   What more.

OEDIP.   A just extenuation.
                                   This:
I did not know him; and he wished to murder me.
Before the law—before God—I am innocent!

[The CHORUS turns at the approach of THESEUS.

SCENE III

CHORUS   The king is coming! Aegeus' eldest son,
        Theseus: news of you has brought him here.

                     [THESEUS *enters with soldiers, left.*

THES.   In the old time I often heard men tell
        Of the bloody extinction of your eyes.
        Even if on my way I were not informed,
        I'd recognize you, son of Laius.
        The garments and the tortured face
        Make plain your identity. I am sorry for you.
        And I should like to know what favor here
        You hope for from the city and from me:
        Both you and your unfortunate companion.
        Tell me. It would be something dire indeed
        To make me leave you comfortless; for I
        Too was an exile. I grew up abroad,
        And in strange lands I fought as few men have
        With danger and with death.
        Therefore no wanderer shall come, as you do,
        And be denied my audience or aid.
        I know I am only a man; I have no more
        To hope for in the end than you have.

OEDIP.   Theseus, in those few words your nobility
        Is plain to me. I need not speak at length;
        You have named me and my father accurately,
        Spoken with knowledge of my land and exile.
        There is, then, nothing left for me to tell
        But my desire; and then the tale is ended.

THES.   Tell me your wish, then; let me hear it now.

OEDIP.   I come to give you something, and the gift

Is my own beaten self: no feast for the eyes;
Yet in me is a more lasting grace than beauty.

THES.   What grace is this you say you bring to us?

OEDIP.   In time you'll learn, but not immediately.

THES.   How long, then, must we wait to be enlightened?

OEDIP.   Until I am dead, and you have buried me.

THES.   Your wish is burial? What of your life meanwhile?
Have you forgotten that?—or do you care?

OEDIP.   It is all implicated in my burial.

THES.   But this is a brief favor you ask of me.

OEDIP.   See to it, nevertheless! It is not simple.

THES.   You mean I shall have trouble with your sons?

OEDIP.   Those people want to take me back there now.

THES.   Will you not go? Is exile admirable?

OEDIP.   No. When I would have returned, they would not have it.

THES.   What childishness! You are surely in no position—

OEDIP.   When you know me, rebuke me; not till then!

THES.   Well, tell me more. I must not speak in ignorance.

OEDIP.   Theseus, I have been wounded more than once.

THES.   Is it your family's curse that you refer to?

OEDIP.   Not merely that; for all Greece buzzes with it.

THES.   Then what is the wound that is so pitiless?

OEDIP.   Think how it is with me. I was expelled
From my own land by my own sons; and now,
As a parricide, my return is not allowed.

THES.   How can they summon you, if this is so?

OEDIP.   The oracle of God compels them to.

THES.   They fear some punishment from his forebodings?

OEDIP.   They fear they will be struck down in this land!

THES.   And how could war arise between these nations?

OEDIP.   Most gentle son of Aegeus! The immortal
Gods alone have neither age nor death!
All other things almighty Time disquiets.
Earth wastes away; the body wastes away;
Faith dies; distrust is born.
And imperceptibly the spirit changes
Between a man and his friend, or between two cities.
For some men soon, for others in later time,
Their pleasure sickens; or love comes again.
And so with you and Thebes: the sweet season
Holds between you now; but time goes on,
Unmeasured Time, fathering numberless
Nights, unnumbered days: and on one day
They'll break apart with spears this harmony—
All for a trivial word.
And then my sleeping and long-hidden corpse,
Cold in the earth, will drink hot blood of theirs,
If God endures; if his son's word is true . . .

However: there's no felicity in speaking
Of hidden things. Let me come back to this:
Be careful that you keep your word to me;
For if you do you'll never say of Oedipus
That he was given refuge uselessly—
Or if you say it, then the gods have lied.

CHORUS   My lord: before you came this man gave promise
Of having power to make his words come true.

THES.   Who would reject his friendship? Is he not
One who would have, in any case, an ally's
Right to our hospitality?
Moreover he has asked grace of our deities,
And offers no small favor in return.

As I value that favor, I shall not refuse
This man's desire; I declare him a citizen.

And if it should please our friend to remain here,
I direct you to take care of him;
Or else he may come with me.
Whatever you choose,
Oedipus, we shall be happy to accord.
You know your own needs best; I accede to them.

OEDIP.   May God bless men like these!

THES.   What do you say then? Shall it be my house?

OEDIP.   If it were right for me. But the place is here . . .

THES.   And what will you do here?—Not that I oppose you.

OEDIP.   Here I shall prevail over those who banished me.

THES.   Your presence, as you say, is a great blessing.

OEDIP.   If you are firm in doing what you promise.

THES.   You can be sure of me; I'll not betray you.

OEDIP.   I'll not ask pledges, as I would of scoundrels.

THES.   You'd get no more assurance than by my word.

OEDIP.   I wonder how you will behave?

THES.   You fear?

OEDIP.   That men will come—

THES.   These men will attend to them.

OEDIP.   Look: when you leave me—

THES.   I know what to do!

OEDIP.   I am oppressed by fear!

THES.   I feel no fear.

OEDIP.   You do not know the menace!

THES.   I do know
    No man is going to take you against my will.
    Angry men are liberal with threats
    And bluster generally. When the mind
    Is master of itself, threats are no matter.
    These people may have dared to talk quite fiercely
    Of taking you; perhaps, as I rather think,
    They'll find a sea of troubles in the way.
    Therefore I should advise you to take heart.
    Even aside from me and my intentions,
    Did not Apollo send and guide you here?
    However it may be, I can assure you,
    While I'm away, my name will be your shield.

[*Exit* THESEUS *and soldiers. The* CHORUS *turns to
the audience.*

CHORAL POEM

CHORUS   The land beloved of horsemen, fair
    Colonus takes a guest;
    He shall not seek another home,
    For this, in all the earth and air,
    Is most secure and loveliest.

    In the god's untrodden vale
    Where leaves and berries throng,
    And wine-dark ivy climbs the bough,
    The sweet, sojourning nightingale
    Murmurs all day long.

    No sun nor wind may enter there
    Nor the winter's rain;

But ever through the shadow goes
Dionysus reveler,
Immortal maenads in his train.

Here with drops of heaven's dews
At daybreak all the year,
The clusters of narcissus bloom,
Time-hallowed garlands for the brows
Of those great ladies whom we fear.

The crocus like a little sun
Blooms with its yellow ray;
The river's fountains are awake,
And his nomadic streams that run
Unthinned forever, and never stay;

But like perpetual lovers move
On the maternal land.
And here the choiring Muses come,
And the divinity of love
With the gold reins in her hand.

[*The* CHORUS *may now shift its grouping or otherwise
indicate a change of theme.*

CHORUS   And our land has a thing unknown
On Asia's sounding coast
Or in the sea-surrounded west
Where Agamemnon's race has sway:
The olive, fertile and self-sown,
The terror of our enemies
That no hand tames nor tears away—
The blessed tree that never dies!—
But it will mock the swordsman in his rage.

Ah, how it flourishes in every field,
Most beautifully here!
The gray-leafed tree, the children's nourisher!
No young man nor one partnered by his age

Knows how to root it out nor make
Barren its yield;
For God the Father smiles on it with sage
Eyes that forever are awake,
And Pallas watches with her sea-pale eyes.

Last and grandest praise I sing
To Athens, nurse of men,
For her great pride and for the splendor
Destiny has conferred on her.
Land from which fine horses spring!
Land where foals are beautiful!
Land of the sea and the sea-farer!
Upon whose lovely littoral
The god of ocean moves, the son of Time.

That lover of our land I praise again,
Who found our horsemen fit
For first bestowal of the curb and bit,
To discipline the stallion in his prime;
And strokes to which our oarsmen sing,
Well-fitted, oak and men,
Whose long sea-oars in wondrous rhyme
Flash from the salt foam, following
The hundred-footed sea-wind and the gull.

[*At the conclusion of this,* ANTIGONE *is standing stage
right, looking off-stage attentively.*

SCENE IV

ANTIG.   Land so well spoken of and praised so much!
Now is the time to show those words are true.

OEDIP. What now, my child?

[*Returning to him.*

ANTIG. A man is coming towards us,
And it is Creon—not unaccompanied, father.

OEDIP. Most kindly friends! I hope you may give proof,
And soon, of your ability to protect me!

CHORUS Don't be afraid: you'll see. I may be old,
But the nation's strength has not grown old.

[*Enter* CREON, *right, with guards.*

CREON Gentlemen, and citizens of this land:
I can see from your eyes that my arrival
Has been a cause of sudden fear to you;
Do not be fearful. And say nothing hostile!
I have not come for any hostile action,
For I am old, and know this city has
Power, if any city in Hellas has.

But for this man here: I was sent to tell him
To follow me back to the land of Thebes.
This is not one man's mission, but was ordered
By the whole Theban people. I am their emissary
Because it fell to me as a relative
To mourn his troubles more than anyone.

So, now, poor Oedipus, come home.
You have heard my message. The people of the city
Are right in summoning you—I most of all,
For most of all, unless I am worst of men,
I grieve for your unhappiness, old man.
I see you ravaged as you are, a stranger
Everywhere, never at rest,
With only a girl to serve you in your need.—
I never thought she'd fall to such indignity,
Poor child! And yet she has;
Forever tending you, leading a beggar's

Life with you; a grown-up girl who knows
Nothing of marriage; whoever comes can take her . . .

Is not this a disgrace? I weep to see it!
Disgrace for you, for me, for all our people!
We cannot hide what is so palpable,
But you, if you will listen to me, Oedipus—
And in the name of your father's gods, listen!—
Bury the whole thing now; agree with me
To go back to your city and your home!

Take friendly leave of Athens, for she deserves it;
But you should have more reverence for Thebes,
Since long ago she was your kindly nurse.

OEDIP.   You brazen rascal! Playing your rascal's tricks
In righteous speeches, as you always would!
Why do you try it? How can you think to take me
Into that snare I should so hate if taken?

That time when I was sick with my private
Agony: when I would lightly have left the earth—
You had no mind to give me what I wanted!
But when at long last I had had my fill
Of rage and grief, and in my quiet house
Began to find some comfort: that was the time
You chose to rout me out.
How precious was this kinship to you then?
It is the same thing now: you see this city
And all its people being kind to me,
So you attempt to coax me away from them!
A cruel thing, for all your soothing words.

What pleasure is there in being amiable
To those who do not want your amiability?

Suppose that when you wanted something terribly
A man should neither grant it you nor give

Sympathy even; but later when you were glutted
With all your heart's desire, should give it then,
When charity was no charity at all?
Would you not think the kindness somewhat hollow?
That is the sort of kindness you offer me:
Generous in words, but in reality evil.

Now I will tell these men, and prove you evil.
You come to take me, but not to take me home;
Rather to settle me outside the city
So that the city may escape my curse,
Escape from punishment by Athens.
                                                    Yes;
But you'll not have it. What you'll have is this:
My vengeance active in that land forever;
And what my sons will have of my old kingdom
Is just so much room as they need to die in!

Now who knows better the destiny of Thebes?
I do, for I have had the best informants:
Apollo, and God himself who is his father.
And yet you come here with your fraudulent speech
All whetted up! The more you talk, the more
Harm, not good, you'll get by it!—
However, I know you'll never believe that.—

Only leave us! Let us live here in peace!
Is it a bad life, if it gives us pleasure?

CREON   Which of us do you consider is more injured
        By talk like this? You hurt only yourself.

OEDIP. I am perfectly content, so long as you
        Can neither wheedle me nor fool these others.

CREON   Unhappy man! Shall it be plain that time
        Brings you no wisdom? that you shame your age?

OEDIP. What repartee! I know no honest man
        Able to speak so well under all conditions!

CREON   To speak much is one thing; to speak to the point's another!

OEDIP.   As if you spoke so little but so fittingly!

CREON   No, not fittingly for a mind like yours!

OEDIP.   Go away! I speak for these men also!
Stop busybodying here where I must live!

CREON   I call on these—not you!—as witnesses
Of what rejoinder you have made to friends.—
If I ever take you—

OEDIP.   With these men fighting for me,
Who is going to take me by violence?

CREON   You'll have pain enough without that, I promise you!

OEDIP.   What are you up to? What is behind that brag?

CREON   Your two daughters: one of them I have just now
Had seized and carried off, and I'll take this one!

OEDIP.   Ah!

CREON   You'll soon have better reason to groan about it!

OEDIP.   You have my child?

CREON   And this one in a moment!

OEDIP.   Ah, friends! What will you do? Will you betray me?
Are you not going to drive this thief away?

CHORUS   Go, stranger! Off with you! You have no right
To do what you are doing, or what you have done!

                                     [*To* GUARDS:

CREON   You there: it would be well to take her now,
Whether she wants to go with you or not.

                       [*Two* GUARDS *approach* ANTIGONE.

ANTIG.   Oh, God, where shall I run? What help is there
From gods or men?

CHORUS   What are you doing, stranger?

CREON	I will not touch this man; only her who is mine.
OEDIP.	O masters of this land!
CHORUS	This is unjust!
CREON	No, just!
CHORUS	Why so?
CREON	I take what belongs to me!
OEDIP.	O Athens!

[The GUARDS *pinion* ANTIGONE'S *arms.*

CHORUS	What are you doing, stranger? Will you Let her go? Must we have a test of strength?
CREON	Hold off!
CHORUS	Not while you persist in doing this!
CREON	Your city will have war if you hurt me!
OEDIP.	Did I not proclaim this?

[To the GUARDS:

CHORUS	Take your hands Off the child at once!
CREON	What you cannot enforce, Do not command!
CHORUS	I tell you, let go!
CREON	And I tell you—on your way!

[The GUARDS *pull* ANTIGONE *toward the right.*

CHORUS	Help! Here, men of Colonus! Help! Help! The city, my city, is pillaged! Hurry! Help, ho!
ANTIG.	They drag me away. How wretched! O friends, friends!

[*Groping.*

OEDIP.   Where are you, child?

ANTIG.   They have overpowered me!

OEDIP.   Give me your hands, little one!

ANTIG.   I cannot do it!

[*To* GUARDS:

CREON   Will you get on with her?

[*They go out, right.*

OEDIP.   God help me now!

CREON   With these two sticks at any rate you'll never
         Guide yourself again! But since you wish
         To conquer your own people—by whose command,
         Though I am royal, I have performed this act—
         Go on and conquer! Later, I think, you'll learn
         That now as before you have done yourself no good
         By gratifying your temper against your friends!
         Anger has always been your greatest sin!

[*Approaching* CREON.

CHORUS   Control yourself, stranger!

CREON   Don't touch me, I say!

CHORUS   I'll not release you! Those two girls were stolen!

CREON   By God, I'll have more booty in a moment
         To bring my city! I'll not stop with them!

CHORUS   Now what are you about?

CREON   I'll take him, too!

CHORUS   A terrible thing to say!

CREON   It will be done!

CHORUS   Not if the ruler of our land can help it!

OEDIP.   Voice of shamelessness! Will you touch me?

CREON   Silence, I say!

OEDIP.   No! May the powers here
Not make me silent until I say this curse:
You scoundrel, who have cruelly taken her
Who served my naked eyepits as their eyes!
On you and yours forever may the sun god,
Watcher of all the world, confer such days
As I have had, and such an age as mine!

CREON   Do you see this, citizens of this country?

OEDIP.   They see both me and you; and they see also
That when I am hurt I have only words to avenge it!

CREON   I'll not stand for it longer! Alone as I am,
And slow with age, I'll try my strength to take him!

                        [CREON *goes slowly toward* OEDIPUS.

OEDIP.   Oh, God!

CHORUS   You are a bold man, friend,
If you think you can do this!

CREON   I do think so!

CHORUS   If you could do it, our city would be finished!

CREON   In a just cause the weak will beat the strong!

OEDIP.   You hear his talk?

CHORUS   By God, he shall not do it!

CREON   God may determine that, but you will not.

CHORUS   Is this not arrogance!

                        [*Laying hold of* OEDIPUS.

CREON   If so, you'll bear it!

CHORUS   Ho, everyone! Captains, ho!
Hurry up! Come on the run!
They are well on their way by now!

[THESEUS *enters, left, with armed men.*

THES.	Why do you shout? What is the matter here?
	Of what are you afraid?
	You have interrupted me as I was sacrificing
	To the great ocean god, Colonus's patron.
	Tell me everything, so I may know;
	I do not care to make such haste for nothing.
OEDIP.	O dearest friend—I recognize your voice—
	A despicable thing has just been done to me!
THES.	What is it? Who is the man who did it? Tell me.
OEDIP.	Creon, here, has abducted my two children.
THES.	What's that you say?
OEDIP.	Yes; now you know my loss.

[To his men:

THES.	One of you will please go on the double
	To the altar place and rouse the people there;
	Make them leave the sacrifice at once
	And run full speed, both foot and cavalry
	As hard as they can gallop, for the place
	Where the two highways come together.
	The girls must not be permitted to pass there,
	Or I will be a laughing-stock to this fellow,
	As if I were a man to be handled roughly!
	Go on, do as I tell you! Quick!

[*Exit* SOLDIER, *left.*

This fellow—
If I should act in anger, as he deserves,
I wouldn't let him go without chastisement;
But he shall be subject to the sort of laws
He has himself imported here.—

[To CREON:

You: you shall never leave this land of Attica
Until you produce those girls here in my presence;

For your behavior is an affront to me,
A shame to your own people and your nation.

You come to a city-state that practices justice,
A state that rules by law, and by law only;
And yet you cast aside her authority,
Take what you please, and worse, by violence,
As if you thought there were no men among us,
Or only slaves; and as if I were nobody.

I doubt that Thebes is responsible for you:
She has no propensity for breeding rascals.
And Thebes would not applaud you if she knew
You tried to trick me and to rob the gods
By dragging helpless people from their sanctuary!

Were I a visitor in your country—
No matter how immaculate my claims—
Without consent from him who ruled the land,
Whoever he might be, I'd touch nothing.
I think I have some notion of the conduct
Proper to one who visits a friendly city.
You bring disgrace upon an honorable
Land—your own land, too; a long life
Seems to have left you witless as you are old.

I said it once and say it now again:
Someone had better bring those girls here quickly,
Unless you wish to prolong your stay with us
Under close guard, and not much liking it.
This is not just a speech; I mean it, friend.

CHORUS   Now do you see where you stand? Thebes is just,
But you are adjudged to have acted wickedly.

CREON   It was not that I thought this state unmanly,
Son of Aegeus; nor ill-governed, either;
Rather I did this thing in the opinion
That no one here would love my citizens

So tenderly as to keep them against my will . . .
And surely, I thought, no one would give welcome
To an unholy man, a parricide,
A man with whom his mother had been found!
Such at least was my estimate of the wisdom
Native to the Areopagus; I thought
Athens was not a home for such exiles.
In that belief I considered him my prize.
Even so, I'd not have touched him had he not
Called down curses on my race and me;
That was an injury that deserved reprisal.
There is no old age for a man's anger,
Only death; the dead cannot be hurt.

You'll do whatever you wish in this affair,
For even though my case is right and just,
I am weak, without support. Nevertheless,
Old as I am, I'll try to hold you answerable.

OEDIP.   O arrogance unashamed! Whose age do you
Think you are insulting, mine or yours?
The bloody deaths, the incest, the calamities
You speak so glibly of: I suffered them,
By fate, against my will! It was God's pleasure,
And perhaps our race had angered him long ago.
In me myself you could not find such evil
As would have made me sin against my own.
And tell me this: if there were prophecies
Repeated by the oracles of the gods,
That father's death should come through his own son,
How could you justly blame it upon me?
On me, who was yet unborn, yet unconceived,
Not yet existent for my father and mother?
If then I came into the world—as I did come—
In wretchedness, and met my father in fight,
And knocked him down, not knowing that I killed him
Nor whom I killed—again, how could you find
Guilt in that unmeditated act?

As for my mother—damn you, you have no shame,
Though you are her own brother, in forcing me
To speak of that unspeakable marriage;
But I shall speak, I'll not be silent now
After you've let your foul talk go so far!
Yes, she gave me birth—incredible fate!—
But neither of us knew the truth; and she
Bore my children also—and then her shame.
But one thing I do know: you are content
To slander her as well as me for that;
While I would not have married her willingly
Nor willingly would I ever speak of it.

No: I shall not be judged an evil man,
Neither in that marriage nor in that death
Which you forever charge me with so bitterly.—
Just answer me one thing:
If someone tried to kill you here and now,
You righteous gentleman, what would you do,
Inquire first if the stranger was your father?
Or would you not first try to defend yourself?
I think that since you like to be alive
You'd treat him as the threat required; not
Look around for assurance that you were right.
Well, that was the sort of danger I was in,
Forced into it by the gods. My father's soul,
Were it on earth, I know would bear me out.

You, however, being a knave—and since you
Think it fair to say anything you choose,
And speak of what should not be spoken of—
Accuse me of all this before these people.
You also think it clever to flatter Theseus,
And Athens—her exemplary government;
But in your flattery you have forgotten this:
If any country comprehends the honors
Due to the gods, this country knows them best;
Yet you would steal me from Athens in my age

And in my time of prayer; indeed, you seized me,
And you have taken and carried off my daughters.

Now for that profanation I make my prayer,
Calling on the divinities of the grove
That they shall give me aid and fight for me;
So you may know what men defend this town.

CHORUS My lord, our friend is worthy; he has had
Disastrous fortune; yet he deserves our comfort.

THES. Enough of speeches. While the perpetrators
Flee, we who were injured loiter here.

CREON What will you have me do?—since I am worthless.

THES. You lead us on the way. You can be my escort.
If you are holding the children in this neighborhood
You yourself will uncover them to me.
If your retainers have taken them in flight,
The chase is not ours; others are after them.
And they will never have cause to thank their gods
For getting free out of this country.
All right. Move on. And remember that the captor
Is now the captive; the hunter is in the snare.
What was won by stealth will not be kept.

In this you'll not have others to assist you;
And I know well you had them, for you'd never
Dare to go so far in your insolence
Were you without sufficient accomplices.
You must have had a reason for your confidence,
And I must reckon with it. The whole city
Must not seem overpowered by one man.
Do you understand at all? Or do you think
That what I say is still without importance?

CREON To what you say I make no objection here.
At home we, too, shall determine what to do.

THES. If you must threaten, do so on the way.
Oedipus, you stay here, and rest assured

That unless I perish first I'll not draw breath
Until I put your children in your hands.

OEDIP.   Bless you for your noble heart, Theseus!
And good luck to you in what you do for us!

[*Two* SOLDIERS *take* CREON *by the arms and march him out,
right, followed by* THESEUS *and the rest of his men.
The* CHORUS *follows a short way and stands
gazing after them.*

CHORAL POEM

CHORUS   Ah, God, to be where the pillagers make stand!
To hear the shout and brazen sound of war!
Or maybe on Apollo's sacred strand,
Or by that torchlit Eleusinian shore

Where pilgrims come, whose lips the golden key
Of sweet-voiced ministers has rendered still,
To cherish there with grave Persephone
Consummate rest from death and mortal ill;

For even to those shades the warrior king
Will press the fighting on—until he take
The virgin sisters from the foemen's ring,
Within his country, for his country's sake!

It may be they will get beyond the plain
And reach the snowy mountain's western side,
If their light chariots have the racing rein,
If they have ponies, and if they can ride;

Yet they'll be taken: for the god they fear
Fights for our land, and Theseus sends forth
His breakneck cavalry with all its gear
Flashing like mountain lightning to the north.

These are the riders of Athens, conquered never;
They honor her whose glory all men know,
And honor the ocean god, who loves forever
The feminine earth that bore him long ago.

> [A shift of grouping, and the four following stanzas
> taken each by a separate voice.

CHORUS   Has the fight begun? May it begin!
The presentiment enchants my mind
That they shall soon give in!
And free the daughters of the blind
From hurt by their own kind!

*For God will see some noble thing
Before this day is over.*

Forevisioning the fight, and proud,
Would God I were a soaring dove
Circling the tall cloud;
So might I gaze down from above
On the mêlée I love.

*For God will see some noble thing
Before this day is over.*

All highest of immortals! Hail,
Great God who sees all things below!
Let not our troopers fail;
But give them luck to snare and throw
And bring the quarry low!

*And you shall see some noble thing
Before this day is over.*

Stern Pallas, hear us! Apollo, hear!
Hunter and sister who give chase
To the swift and dappled deer:
Be our protectors! Lend your grace
To our land and our race!

And you shall see some noble thing
Before this day is over.

[There is a long pause, and then the CHORUS turns
to OEDIPUS in joy.

SCENE V

CHORUS   O wanderer! You will not say I lied;
I who kept lookout for you!
I see them now—the two girls—here they come
With our armed men around them!

OEDIP.   Ah, where? Do you really mean it?

[THESEUS comes in leading by the hand ANTIGONE and
ISMENE, followed by SOLDIERS.

ANTIG.   Father, father!
I wish some god would give you eyes to see
The noble prince who brings us back to you!

OEDIP.   Ah, child! You are really here?

ANTIG.   Yes, for the strength
Of Theseus and his kind followers saved us.

OEDIP.   Come to your father, child, and let me touch you
Whom I had thought never to touch again!

ANTIG.   It shall be as you ask; I wish it as much as you.

OEDIP.	Where are you?
ANTIG.	We are coming to you together.
OEDIP.	My sweet children!
ANTIG.	To our father, sweet indeed.
OEDIP.	My staff and my support!
ANTIG.	And partners in sorrow.

OEDIP.   I have what is dearest to me in the world.
To die, now, would not be so terrible,
Since you are near me.
            Press close to me, child,
Be rooted in your father's arms; rest now
From the cruel separation, the going and coming;
And tell me the story as briefly as you can:
A little talk is enough for girls so tired.

ANTIG.   Theseus saved us: he is the one to tell you;
Neither you nor I had much to do with it!

OEDIP.   Dear friend: don't be put out at my continuing
To talk to these two children overlong;
I had scarce thought they would be seen again!
Be sure I understand that you alone
Made this joy possible for me.
You are the one that saved them, no one else.
And may the gods give you such destiny
As I desire for you: and for your country.
For I have found you truly reverent,
Decent, and straight in speech: you only
Of all mankind.
I know it, and I thank you with these words.
All that I have I owe to your courtesy;—
Now give me your right hand, my lord,
And if it be permitted, let me kiss you. . . .

What am I saying? How can a wretch like me
Desire to touch a man who has no stain

Of evil in him? No, no; I will not do it;
And neither shall you touch me. The only ones
Fit to be fellow sufferers of mine
Are those with such experience as I have.
Receive my salutation where you are.
And for the rest, be kindly to me still
As you have been up to now.

THES.   That you should talk a long time to your children
In joy at seeing them—why, that's no wonder!
Or that you should address them before me—
There's no offense in that. It is not in words
That I should wish my life to be distinguished,
But rather in things done.
Have I not shown that? I was not a liar
In what I swore I'd do for you, old man.
I am here; and I have brought them back
Alive and safe, for all they were threatened with.
As to how I found them, how I took them, why
Brag of it? You will surely learn from them.

However, there is a matter that just now
Came to my attention on my way here—
A trivial thing to speak of, and yet puzzling;
I want your opinion on it.
It is best for a man not to neglect such things.

OEDIP.   What is it, son of Aegeus? Tell me,
So I may know on what you desire counsel.

THES.   They say some man is here who claims to be
A relative of yours, though not of Thebes;
For some reason he has thrown himself in prayer
Before Poseidon's altar, where I was making
Sacrifice before I came.

OEDIP.   What is his country? What is he praying for?

THES.   All I know is this: he asks, they tell me,
A brief interview with you, and nothing more.

| OEDIP. | What about, I wonder?
It can't be a slight matter, if he is praying. |
| THES. | They say he only asks to speak to you
And then to depart safely by the same road. |
| OEDIP. | Who could it be who would come here to pray? |
| THES. | Think: have you any relative in Argos
Who might desire this favor of you? |
| OEDIP. | Dear friend!
Say no more! |
THES.	What is the matter with you?
OEDIP.	No more!
THES.	But: what is the matter? Tell me.
OEDIP.	When I heard 'Argos' I knew the petitioner.
THES.	And who is he whom I must prepare to dislike?
OEDIP.	A son of mine, my lord, and a hated one.
Nothing could be more painful than to listen to him.
THES.	But why? Is it not possible to listen
Without doing anything you need not do?
Why should it annoy you so to hear him?
OEDIP.	My lord, even his voice is hateful to me.
Don't beat me down; don't make me yield in this!
THES.	But now consider if you are not obliged
To do so by his supplication here:
Perhaps you have a duty to the god.
ANTIG.	Father: listen to me, even if I am young.
Allow this man to satisfy his conscience
And give the gods whatever he thinks their due.
And let our brother come here, for my sake.
Don't be afraid: he will not throw you off
In your resolve, nor speak offensively.
What is the harm in hearing what he says?

If he has ill intentions, he'll betray them.
You sired him; even had he wronged you, father,
And wronged you impiously, still you could not
Rightfully wrong him in return!
Do let him come!

                   Other men have bad sons,
And other men are swift to anger; yet
They will accept advice, they will be swayed
By their friends' pleading, even against their nature.
Reflect, not on the present, but on the past;
Think of your mother's and your father's fate
And what you suffered through them! If you do,
I think you'll see how terrible an end
Terrible wrath may have.
You have, I think, a permanent reminder
In your lost, irrecoverable eyes . . .
Ah, yield to us! If our request is just,
We need not, surely, be importunate;
And you, to whom I have not yet been hard,
Should not be obdurate with me!

OEDIP.   Child, your talk wins you a pleasure
That will be pain for me. If you have set
Your heart on it, so be it.

Only, Theseus: if he is to come here,
Let no one have power over my life!

THES.   That is the sort of thing I need hear only
Once, not twice, old man. I do not boast,
But you should know your life is safe while mine is.

    [THESEUS *goes out, left, with his* SOLDIERS, *leaving two on
guard. The* CHORUS *turns to address the audience.*

CHORAL POEM

CHORUS   Though he has watched a decent age pass by,
A man will sometimes still desire the world.
I swear I see no wisdom in that man.
The endless hours pile up a drift of pain
More unrelieved each day; and as for pleasure,
When he is sunken in excessive age,
You will not see his pleasure anywhere.
The last attendant is the same for all,
Old men and young alike, as in its season
Man's heritage of underworld appears:
There being then no epithalamion,
No music and no dance. Death is the finish.

Not to be born beats all philosophy.
The second best is to have seen the light
And then to go back quickly whence we came.
The feathery follies of his youth once over,
What trouble is beyond the range of man?
What heavy burden will he not endure?
Jealousy, faction, quarreling, and battle—
The bloodiness of war, the grief of war.
And in the end he comes to strengthless age,
Abhorred by all men, without company,
Unfriended in that uttermost twilight
Where he must live with every bitter thing.

This is the truth, not for me only,
But for this blind and ruined man.
Think of some shore in the north the
Concussive waves make stream
This way and that in the gales of winter:
It is like that with him:

The wild wrack breaking over him
From head to foot, and coming on forever;
Now from the plunging down of the sun,
Now from the sunrise quarter,
Now from where the noonday gleams,
Now from the night and the north.

> [ANTIGONE *and* ISMENE *have been looking off-stage, left.*
> ANTIGONE *turns.*

SCENE VI

ANTIG. I think I see the stranger near us now,
And no men with him, father; but his eyes
Swollen with weeping as he comes.

> [POLYNEICES *enters, left.*

OEDIP.   Who comes?

ANTIG. The one whom we have had so long in mind;
It is he who stands here: it is Polyneices.

POLY. Ah, now what shall I do? Sisters, shall I
Weep for my misfortunes or for those
I see in the old man, my father,
Whom I have found here in an alien land,
With you two girls, an outcast for so long,
And with such garments! The abominable
Filth grown old with him, rotting his sides!
And on his sightless face the ragged hair
Streams in the wind. There's the same quality
In the food he carries for his thin old belly.
All this I learn too late.

And I swear now that I have been villainous
In not supporting you! You need not wait
To hear it said by others!
                Only, think:
Compassion limits even the power of God;
So may there be a limit for you, father!
For all that has gone wrong may still be healed,
And surely the worst is over!

Why are you silent?

Speak to me, father! Don't turn away from me!
Will you not answer me at all? Will you
Send me away without a word?
                   Not even
Tell me why you are enraged against me?

Daughters of Oedipus, my own sisters,
Try to move your so implacable father;
Do not let him reject me in such contempt!
Make him reply!
              I am here on pilgrimage . . .

ANTIG.   Poor brother: you yourself must tell him why.
As men speak on they may sometimes give pleasure,
Sometimes annoy, or sometimes touch the heart;
And so somehow provide the mute with voices.

POLY.   I will speak out then; your advice is fair.
First, however, I must claim the help
Of that same god of ocean from whose altars
The governor of this land has lifted me
And sent me here, giving me leave to speak
And to await response, and a safe passage.
These are the favors I desire from you,
Strangers, and from my sisters and my father.

And now, father, I will tell you why I came.

I am a fugitive, driven from my country,
Because I thought fit, as the eldest born,
To take my seat upon your sovereign throne.
For that, Eteocles, the younger of us,
Banished me—but not by a decision
In argument or ability or arms;
Merely because he won the city over.
Of this I believe the Furies that pursue you
Were indeed the cause: and so I hear
From clairvoyants whom I afterwards consulted . . .

Then, when I went into the Dorian land,
I took Adrastus as my father-in-law,
And bound to me by oath whatever men
Were known as leaders or as fighters there;
My purpose being to form an expedition
Of seven troops of spearmen against Thebes.—
With which enlistment may I die for justice
Or else expel the men who exiled me!

So it is. Then why should I come here now?
Father, my prayers must be made to you!
Mine and those of all who fight with me!
Their seven columns under seven captains
Even now complete the encirclement of Thebes:
Men like Amphiareus, the hard spear thrower,
Expert in spears and in the ways of eagles;
Second is Tydeus, the Aetolian,
Son of Oineus; third is Eteoclus,
Born in Argos; fourth is Hippomedon
(His father, Talaus, sent him); Capaneus,
The fifth, has sworn he'll raze the town of Thebes
With fire-brands; and sixth is Parthenopaeus,
An Arcadian who roused himself to war—
Son of that virgin famous in the old time
Who long years afterward conceived and bore him—
Parthenopaeus, Atalanta's son.
And it is I, your son—or if I am not

Truly your son, since evil fathered me,
At least I am called your son—it is I who lead
The fearless troops of Argos against Thebes.

Now in the name of these two children, father,
And for your own soul's sake, we all implore
And beg you to give up your heavy wrath
Against me! I go forth to punish him,
The brother who robbed me of my fatherland!
If we can put any trust in oracles,
They say that those you bless shall come to power.

Now by the gods and fountains of our people,
I pray you, listen and comply! Are we not beggars
Both of us, and exiles, you and I?
We live by paying court to other men;
The same fate follows us.
But as for him—how insupportable!—
He lords it in our house, luxuriates there,
Laughs at us both!

If you will stand by me in my resolve,
I'll waste no time or trouble whipping him;
And then I'll re-establish you at home,
And settle there myself, and throw him out.
If your will is the same as mine, it's possible
To promise this. If not, I can't be saved.

CHORUS   For the sake of the one who sent him, Oedipus,
Speak to this man before you send him back.

OEDIP.   Yes, gentlemen: but were it not Theseus,
The sovereign of your land, who sent him here,
Thinking it right that he should have an answer,
You never would have heard a sound from me.

Well: he has asked for it. He shall hear from me
A kind of answer that will not overjoy him.

You scoundrel!
              When it was you who held
Throne and authority—as your brother now
Holds them in Thebes—you drove me into exile:
Me, your own father: made me a homeless man,
Insuring me these rags you blubber over
When you behold them now—now that you, too,
Have fallen on evil days and are in exile.

Weeping is no good now. However long
My life may last, I have to see it through;
But I regard you as a murderer!
For you reduced me to this misery,
You made me an alien. Because of you
I have begged my daily bread from other men.
If I had not these children to sustain me,
I might have lived or died for all your interest.
But they have saved me, they are my support,
And are not girls, but men, in faithfulness.
As for you two, you are no sons of mine!

And so it is that there are eyes that watch you
Even now; though not as they shall watch
If those troops are in fact marching on Thebes.
You cannot take that city. You'll go down
All bloody, and your brother, too.
                    For I
Have placed that curse upon you before this,
And now I invoke that curse to fight for me,
That you may see a reason to respect
Your parents, though your birth was as it was;
And though I am blind, not to dishonor me.
These girls did not.

And so your supplication and your throne
Are overmastered surely,—if accepted
Justice still has place in the laws of God.

Now go! For I abominate and disown you!
You utter scoundrel! Go with the malediction
I here pronounce for you: that you shall never
Master your native land by force of arms,
Nor ever see your home again in Argos,
The land below the hills; but you shall die
By your own brother's hand, and you shall kill
The brother who banished you. For this I pray.
And I cry out to the hated underworld
That it may take you home; cry out to those
Powers indwelling here; and to that Power
Of furious War that filled your hearts with hate!

Now you have heard me. Go: tell it to Thebes,
Tell all the Thebans; tell your faithful fighting
Friends what sort of honors
Oedipus has divided among his sons!

CHORUS   Polyneices, your coming here has given me
No joy at all. Now go away at once.

POLY.   Ah, what a journey! What a failure!
My poor companions! See the finish now
Of all we marched from Argos for! See me . . .
For I can neither speak of this to anyone
Among my friends, nor lead them back again;
I must go silently to meet this doom.

O sisters—daughters of his, sisters of mine!
You heard the hard curse of our father:
For God's sweet sake, if father's curse comes true,
And if you find some way to return home,
Do not, at least, dishonor me in death!
But give me a grave and what will quiet me.
Then you shall have, besides the praise he now
Gives you for serving him, an equal praise
For offices you shall have paid my ghost.

ANTIG.   Polyneices, I beseech you, listen to me!

POLY.   Dearest—what is it? Tell me, Antigone.

ANTIG. Withdraw your troops to Argos as soon as you can.
        Do not go to your own death and your city's!

POLY.   But that is impossible. How could I command
        That army, even backward, once I faltered?

ANTIG. Now why, boy, must your anger rise again?
        What is the good of laying waste your homeland?

POLY.   It is shameful to run; and it is also shameful
        To be a laughing-stock to a younger brother.

ANTIG. But see how you fulfill his prophecies!
        Did he not cry that you should kill each other?

POLY.   He wishes that. But I cannot agree.

ANTIG. Ah, I am desolate! But who will dare
        Go with you, after hearing the prophecies?

POLY.   I'll not report this trifle. A good commander
        Tells what is encouraging, not what is not.

ANTIG. Then you have made up your mind to this, my brother?

POLY.   Yes. And do not try to hold me back.
        The dark road is before me; I must take it,
        Doomed by my father and his avenging Furies.
        God bless you if you do what I have asked:
        It is only in death that you can help me now.
        Now let me go. Good-bye! You will not ever
        Look in my eyes again.

ANTIG.   You break my heart!

POLY.   Do not grieve for me.

ANTIG.   Who would not grieve for you,
        Sweet brother! You go with open eyes to death!

POLY.   Death, if that must be.

ANTIG.	No! Do as I ask!
POLY.	You ask the impossible.
ANTIG.	Then I am lost, If I must be deprived of you!
POLY.	All that Rests with the powers that are over us,— Whether it must be so or otherwise. You two—I pray no evil comes to you, For all men know you merit no more pain.

[POLYNEICES *goes out, left. There is a dead silence; then the* CHORUS *meditates.*

╷╷╷╷╷╷╷╷╷╷╷╷╷╷╷╷╷╷╷╷╷╷╷╷╷╷

CHORAL POEM AND DIALOGUE

CHORUS	So in this new event we see New forms of terror working through the blind, Or else inscrutable destiny. I am not one to say 'This is in vain' Of anything allotted to mankind. Though some must fall, or fall to rise again, Time watches all things steadily—

[A *terrific peal of thunder.*

Ah, God! Heaven's height has cracked!

[*Thunder and lightning.*

OEDIP.	O my child, my child! Could someone here— Could someone bring the hero, Theseus?
ANTIG.	Father, what is your reason for calling him?

OEDIP. God's beating thunder, any moment now,
        Will clap me underground: send for him quickly!

                              [*Thunder and lightning.*

CHORUS Hear it cascading down the air!
        The God-thrown, the gigantic, holy sound!
        Terror crawls to the tips of my hair!
        My guts shrink!
                        There the lightning flames again!
        What heavenly marvel is it bringing 'round?
        I fear it, for it never comes in vain,
        But for man's luck or his despair . . .

                              [*Another terrific peal.*

        Ah, God! Majestic heaven!

OEDIP. My children, the appointed end has come;
        I can no longer turn away from it.

ANTIG. How do you know? What is the sign that tells you?

OEDIP. I know it clearly now. Let someone quickly
        Send for the king and bring him here to me!

                              [*Thunder and lightning.*

CHORUS Hear the wild thunder fall!
        Towering Nature is transfixed!
        Be merciful, great spirit, if you run
        This sword of darkness through our mother land;
        Come not for our confusion,
        And deal no blows to me,
        Though your tireless Furies stand
        By him whom I have looked upon.
        Great God, I make my prayer to thee!

OEDIP. Is the king near by? Will he come in time
        To find me still alive, my mind still clear?

ANTIG. Tell me what it is you have in mind!

OEDIP. To give him now, in return for his great kindness,
        The blessing that I promised I would give.

                                            [Thunder.

CHORUS O noble son, return!
        No matter if you still descend
        In the deep fastness of the sea god's grove,
        To make pure offering at his altar fire:
        Come back quickly, for God's love!
        Receive from this strange man
        Whatever may be his heart's desire
        That you and I and Athens are worthy of.
        My lord, come quickly as you can!

            [*The thunder continues, until it stops abruptly with
                the entrance of* THESEUS, *left.*

SCENE VII

THES.   Now why do you all together
        Set up this shout once more?
        I see it comes from you, as from our friend.
        Is it a lightning bolt from God? a squall
        Of rattling hail? Those are familiar things
        When such a tempest rages over heaven.

OEDIP. My lord, I longed for you to come! This is
        God's work, your lucky coming.

THES.   Now, what new
        Circumstance has arisen, son of Laius?

OEDIP. My life sinks in the scale: I would not die
        Without fulfilling what I promised Athens.

THES.　What proof have you that your hour has come?

OEDIP.　The great, incessant thunder and continuous
　　　　Flashes of lightning from the hand of God.

THES.　I believe you. I have seen you prophesy
　　　　Many things, none falsely. What must be done?

OEDIP.　I shall disclose to you, O son of Aegeus,
　　　　What is appointed for you and for your city:
　　　　A thing that age will never wear away.
　　　　Presently now, without a soul to guide me,
　　　　I'll lead you to the place where I must die;
　　　　But you must never tell it to any man,
　　　　Not even the neighborhood in which it lies.
　　　　If you obey, this will count more for you
　　　　Than many shields and many neighbors' spears.
　　　　These things are mysteries, not to be explained;
　　　　But you will understand when you come there
　　　　Alone. Alone, because I cannot disclose it
　　　　To any of your men or to my children,
　　　　Much as I love and cherish them. But you
　　　　Keep it secret always, and when you come
　　　　To the end of life, then you must hand it on
　　　　To your most cherished son, and he in turn
　　　　Must teach it to his heir, and so forever.
　　　　That way you shall forever hold this city
　　　　Safe from the men of Thebes, the dragon's sons.

　　　　For every nation that lives peaceably,
　　　　There will be many others to grow hard
　　　　And push their arrogance to extremes: the gods
　　　　Attend to these things slowly. But they attend
　　　　To those who put off God and turn to madness!
　　　　You have no mind for that, child of Aegeus;
　　　　Indeed, you know already all that I teach.

　　　　Let us proceed then to that place
　　　　And hesitate no longer; I am driven

By an insistent voice that comes from God.
Children, follow me this way: see, now,
I have become your guide, as you were mine!
Come: do not touch me: let me alone discover
The holy and funereal ground where I
Must take this fated earth to be my shroud.

This way, O come! The angel of the dead,
Hermes, and veiled Persephone lead me on!

[*He leads them, firmly and slowly, to the left.*

O sunlight of no light! Once you were mine!
This is the last my flesh will feel of you;
For now I go to shade my ending day
In the dark underworld. Most cherished friend!
I pray that you and this your land and all
Your people may be blessed: remember me,
Be mindful of my death, and be
Fortunate in all the time to come!

[OEDIPUS *goes out, followed by his children and by* THESEUS
with his SOLDIERS. *The* CHORUS *lifts its arms to pray.*

CHORAL POEM

CHORUS   If I may dare to adore that Lady
The living never see,
And pray to the master of spirits plunged in night,
Who of vast Hell has sovereignty;
Let not our friend go down in grief and weariness
To that all-shrouding cold,
The dead men's plain, the house that has no light.

Because his sufferings were great, unmerited and untold,
Let some just god relieve him from distress!

O powers under the earth, and tameless
Beast in the passage way,
Rumbler who lie at the gate of the strange hosts,
Their guard forever, the legends say:
I pray you, even Death, offspring of Earth and Hell,
To let the descent be clear
As Oedipus goes down among the ghosts
On those dim fields of underground that all men living fear.
Eternal sleep, let Oedipus sleep well!

[*A long pause. A* MESSENGER *comes in, left.*

ЛЛЛЛЛЛЛЛЛЛЛЛЛЛЛЛЛЛЛЛЛЛЛЛЛЛЛЛЛЛ

SCENE VIII

MESS.   Citizens, the briefest way to tell you
         Would be to say that Oedipus is no more;
         But what has happened cannot be told so simply—
         It was no simple thing.

CHORUS   He is gone, poor man?

MESS.   You may be sure that he has left this world.

CHORUS   By God's mercy, was his death a painless one?

MESS.   That is the thing that seems so marvelous.

         You know, for you were witnesses, how he
         Left this place with no friend leading him,
         Acting, himself, as guide for all of us.
         Well, when he came to the steep place in the road,

The embankment there, secured with steps of brass,
He stopped in one of the many branching paths.

This was not far from the stone bowl that marks
Theseus' and Pirithous' covenant.

Half-way between that place of stone
With its hollow pear tree, and the marble tomb,
He sat down and undid his filthy garments;
Then he called his daughters and commanded
That they should bring him water from a fountain
For bathing and libation to the dead.
From there they could see the hill of Demeter,
Freshener of all things: so they ascended it
And soon came back with water for their father;
Then helped him properly to bathe and dress.

When everything was finished to his pleasure,
And no command of his remained undone,
Then the earth groaned with thunder from the god below;
And as they heard the sound, the girls shuddered,
And dropped to their father's knees, and began wailing,
Beating their breasts and weeping as if heartbroken.
And hearing them cry out so bitterly,
He put his arms around them, and said to them:

'Children, this day your father is gone from you.
All that was mine is gone. You shall no longer
Bear the burden of taking care of me—
I know it was hard, my children.—And yet one word
Makes all those difficulties disappear:
That word is love. You never shall have more
From any man than you have had from me.
And now you must spend the rest of life without me.'

That was the way of it. They clung together
And wept, all three. But when they finally stopped,
And no more sobs were heard, then there was

Silence, and in the silence suddenly
A voice cried out to him—of such a kind
It made our hair stand up in panic fear:
Again and again the call came from the god:
'Oedipus! Oedipus! Why are we waiting?
You delay too long; you delay too long to go!'

Then, knowing himself summoned by the spirit,
He asked that the lord Theseus come to him;
And when he had come, said: 'O beloved one,
Give your right hand now as a binding pledge
To my two daughters; children, give him your hands.
Promise that you will never willingly
Betray them, but will carry out in kindness
Whatever is best for them in the days to come.'

And Theseus swore to do it for his friend,
With such restraint as fits a noble king.
And when he had done so, Oedipus at once
Laid his blind hands upon his daughters, saying:
'Children, you must show your nobility,
And have the courage now to leave this spot.
You must not wish to see what is forbidden,
Or hear what may not afterward be told.
But go—go quickly. Only the lord Theseus
May stay to see the thing that now begins.'

This much every one of us heard him say,
And then we came away with the sobbing girls.
But after a little while as we withdrew
We turned around—and nowhere saw that man,
But only the king, his hands before his face,
Shading his eyes as if from something awful,
Fearful and unendurable to see.
Then very quickly we saw him do reverence
To Earth and to the powers of the air,
With one address to both.
                              But in what manner

Oedipus perished, no one of mortal men
Could tell but Theseus. It was not lightning,
Bearing its fire from God, that took him off;
No hurricane was blowing.
But some attendant from the train of Heaven
Came for him; or else the underworld
Opened in love the unlit door of earth.
For he was taken without lamentation,
Illness or suffering; indeed his end
Was wonderful if mortal's ever was.

Should someone think I speak intemperately,
I make no apology to him who thinks so.

CHORUS But where are his children and the others with them?

MESS. They are not far away; the sound of weeping
Should tell you now that they are coming here.

[ANTIGONE *and* ISMENE *enter together.*

CHORAL DIALOGUE

ANTIG. Now we may weep, indeed.
Now, if ever, we may cry
In bitter grief against our fate,
Our heritage still unappeased.
In other days we stood up under it,
Endured it for his sake,
The unrelenting horror. Now the finish
Comes, and we know only
In all that we have seen and done
Bewildering mystery.

CHORUS What happened?

ANTIG.   We can only guess, my friends.

CHORUS   He has gone?

ANTIG.   He has; as one could wish him to.
Why not? It was not war
Nor the deep sea that overtook him,
But something invisible and strange
Caught him up—or down—
Into a space unseen.
But we are lost. A deathly
Night is ahead of us.
For how, in some far country wandering,
Or on the lifting seas,
Shall we eke out our lives?

ISMENE   I have no notion. As for me
I wish that charnel Hell would take me
In one death with our father.
This is such desolation
I cannot go on living.

CHORUS   Most admirable sisters:
Whatever God has brought about
Is to be borne with courage.
You must not feed the flames of grief.
No blame can come to you.

ANTIG.   One may long for the past
Though at the time indeed it seemed
Nothing but wretchedness and evil.
Life was not sweet, yet I found it so
When I could put my arms around my father.
O father! O my dear!
Now you are shrouded in eternal darkness,
Even in that absence
You shall not lack our love,
Mine and my sister's love.

CHORUS   He lived his life.

ANTIG.   He did as he had wished!

CHORUS	What do you mean?
ANTIG.	In this land among strangers

ANTIG. (continued)
He died where he chose to die.
He has his eternal bed well shaded,
And in his death is not unmourned.
My eyes are blind with tears
From crying for you, father.
The terror and the loss
Cannot be quieted.
I know you wished to die in a strange country,
Yet your death was so lonely!
Why could I not be with you?

ISMENE	O pity! What is left for me?

What destiny awaits us both
Now we have lost our father?

CHORUS	Dear children, remember

That his last hour was free and blessed.
So make an end of grieving!
Is anyone in all the world
Safe from unhappiness?

ANTIG.	Let us run back there!
ISMENE	Why, what shall we do?
ANTIG.	I am carried away with longing—
ISMENE	For what,—tell me!
ANTIG.	To see the resting place in the earth—
ISMENE	Of whom?
ANTIG.	Oh, father's! O dear God, I am so unhappy!
ISMENE	But that is not permitted. Do you not see?
ANTIG.	Do not rebuke me!
ISMENE	—And remember, too—
ANTIG.	Oh, what?

ISMENE	He had no tomb, there was no one near!
ANTIG.	Take me there and you can kill me, too!
ISMENE	Ah! God! I am truly lost! Helpless and so forsaken! Where shall I go and how shall I live?
CHORUS	Don't be afraid, now.
ANTIG.	Yes, but where is a refuge?
CHORUS	A refuge has been found—
ANTIG.	Where do you mean?
CHORUS	A place where you will be unharmed!
ANTIG.	No . . .
CHORUS	What are you thinking?
ANTIG.	I think there is no way For me to get home again.
CHORUS	Do not go home!
ANTIG.	My home is in trouble.
CHORUS	So it has been before.
ANTIG.	There was no help for it then: but now it is worse.
CHORUS	Indeed your misfortunes do seem limitless.
ANTIG.	Great God! What way is there? Do the powers that rule our lives Still press me on to hope at all?

[THESEUS *comes in, with attendants.*

THES.	Mourn no more, children. Those to whom The night of earth gives benediction Should not be mourned. Retribution comes.
ANTIG.	Theseus: we fall on our knees to you!
THES.	What is it that you desire, children?

ANTIG.   We wish to see the place ourselves
            In which our father rests.

THES.   No, no.
            It is not permissible to go there.

ANTIG.   My lord and ruler of Athens, why?

THES.   Because your father told me, children,
            That no one should go near the spot,
            No mortal man should tell of it,
            Since it is holy, and is his.
            And if I kept this pledge, he said,
            I should preserve my land from its enemies.
            I swore I would, and the god heard me:
            The oathkeeper who keeps track of all.

ANTIG.   If this was our father's cherished wish,
            We must be satisfied.
            Send us back, then, to ancient Thebes,
            And we may stop the bloody war
            From coming between our brothers!

THES.   I will do that, and whatever else
            I am able to do for your happiness,
            For his sake who has gone just now
            Beneath the earth. I must not fail.

CHORUS   Now let the weeping cease;
            Let no one mourn again.
            These things are in the hands of God.

Sophocles

ANTIGONE

translated by
Dudley Fitts
and
Robert Fitzgerald

TO HORACE GREGORY

πολλὰ γάρ σε θεσπίζονθ' ὁρῶ κοὐ ψευδόφημα

Reprinted from The Antigone of Sophocles, an English Version by Dudley Fitts and Robert Fitzgerald
by permission of Harcourt, Brace and Company, Inc.

Because of the curse that their father had laid upon them, ETEOCLES and POLYNEICES quarreled about the royal power, and POLYNEICES was finally driven from Thebes. He took refuge in Argos and married the daughter of KING ADRASTOS; then, as one of seven captains whose commander was ADRASTOS, he marched upon Thebes to recover his throne. In the assault, ETEOCLES and POLYNEICES met at the Seventh Gate and killed each other in combat. CREON became king, and his first official act was to forbid, on pain of death, the burial of POLYNEICES.

DRAMATIS PERSONÆ:

ANTIGONE	CREON
ISMENE	HAIMON
EURYDICE	TEIRESIAS

A SENTRY

A MESSENGER

CHORUS

ANTIGONE

SCENE: *Before the palace of* CREON, *King of Thebes. A central double door, and two lateral doors. A platform extends the length of the façade, and from this platform three steps lead down into the orchestra, or chorus-ground. Time: dawn of the day after the repulse of the Argive army from the assault on Thebes.*

PROLOGUE

[ANTIGONE *and* ISMENE *enter from the central door of the Palace.*

ANTIG. Ismenê, dear sister,
You would think that we had already suffered enough
For the curse on Oedipus:
I cannot imagine any grief
That you and I have not gone through. And now—
Have they told you the new decree of our King Creon?

ISMENE I have heard nothing: I know
That two sisters lost two brothers, a double death
In a single hour; and I know that the Argive army
Fled in the night; but beyond this, nothing.

ANTIG. I thought so. And that is why I wanted you
To come out here with me. There is something we must do.

ISMENE Why do you speak so strangely?

459

ANTIG.   Listen, Ismenê:
Creon buried our brother Eteoclês
With military honours, gave him a soldier's funeral,
And it was right that he should; but Polyneicês,
Who fought as bravely and died as miserably,—
They say that Creon has sworn
No one shall bury him, no one mourn for him,
But his body must lie in the fields, a sweet treasure
For carrion birds to find as they search for food.
That is what they say, and our good Creon is coming here
To announce it publicly; and the penalty—
Stoning to death in the public square!

                                  There it is,
And now you can prove what you are:
A true sister, or a traitor to your family.

ISMENE   Antigonê, you are mad! What could I possibly do?

ANTIG.   You must decide whether you will help me or not.

ISMENE   I do not understand you. Help you in what?

ANTIG.   Ismenê, I am going to bury him. Will you come?

ISMENE   Bury him! You have just said the new law forbids it.

ANTIG.   He is my brother. And he is your brother, too.

ISMENE   But think of the danger! Think what Creon will do!

ANTIG.   Creon is not strong enough to stand in my way.

ISMENE   Ah sister!
Oedipus died, everyone hating him
For what his own search brought to light, his eyes
Ripped out by his own hand; and Iocastê died,
His mother and wife at once: she twisted the cords
That strangled her life; and our two brothers died,
Each killed by the other's sword. And we are left:
But oh, Antigonê,
Think how much more terrible than these
Our own death would be if we should go against Creon

And do what he has forbidden! We are only women,
We cannot fight with men, Antigonê!
The law is strong, we must give in to the law
In this thing, and in worse. I beg the Dead
To forgive me, but I am helpless: I must yield
To those in authority. And I think it is dangerous business
To be always meddling.

ANTIG.   If that is what you think,
I should not want you, even if you asked to come.
You have made your choice, you can be what you want to be.
But I will bury him; and if I must die,
I say that this crime is holy: I shall lie down
With him in death, and I shall be as dear
To him as he to me.

                    It is the dead,
Not the living, who make the longest demands:
We die for ever . . .

                    You may do as you like,
Since apparently the laws of the gods mean nothing to you.

ISMENE   They mean a great deal to me; but I have no strength
To break laws that were made for the public good.

ANTIG.   That must be your excuse, I suppose. But as for me,
I will bury the brother I love.

ISMENE   Antigonê,
I am so afraid for you!

ANTIG.   You need not be:
You have yourself to consider, after all.

ISMENE   But no one must hear of this, you must tell no one!
I will keep it a secret, I promise!

ANTIG.   Oh tell it! Tell everyone!
Think how they'll hate you when it all comes out
If they learn that you knew about it all the time!

ISMENE   So fiery! You should be cold with fear.

ANTIG.   Perhaps. But I am doing only what I must.

ISMENE But can you do it? I say that you cannot.

ANTIG. Very well: when my strength gives out, I shall do no more.

ISMENE Impossible things should not be tried at all.

ANTIG. Go away, Ismenê:
I shall be hating you soon, and the dead will too,
For your words are hateful. Leave me my foolish plan:
I am not afraid of the danger; if it means death,
It will not be the worst of deaths—death without honour.

ISMENE Go then, if you feel that you must.
You are unwise,
But a loyal friend indeed to those who love you.

[*Exit into the Palace.* ANTIGONE *goes off,* L. *Enters the* CHORUS.

PARODOS

CHORUS Now the long blade of the sun, lying [STROPHE 1
Level east to west, touches with glory
Thebes of the Seven Gates. Open, unlidded
Eye of golden day! O marching light
Across the eddy and rush of Dircê's stream,
Striking the white shields of the enemy
Thrown headlong backward from the blaze of morning!

CHORAG. Polyneicês their commander
Roused them with windy phrases,
He the wild eagle screaming
Insults above our land,
His wings their shields of snow,
His crest their marshalled helms.

CHORUS   Against our seven gates in a yawning ring   [ANTISTROPHE 1
          The famished spears came onward in the night;
          But before his jaws were sated with our blood,
          Or pinefire took the garland of our towers,
          He was thrown back; and as he turned, great Thebes—
          No tender victim for his noisy power—
          Rose like a dragon behind him, shouting war.

CHORAG.   For God hates utterly
          The bray of bragging tongues;
          And when he beheld their smiling,
          Their swagger of golden helms,
          The frown of his thunder blasted
          Their first man from our walls.

CHORUS   We heard his shout of triumph high in the air   [STROPHE 2
          Turn to a scream; far out in a flaming arc
          He fell with his windy torch, and the earth struck him.
          And others storming in fury no less than his
          Found shock of death in the dusty joy of battle.

CHORAG.   Seven captains at seven gates
          Yielded their clanging arms to the god
          That bends the battle-line and breaks it.
          These two only, brothers in blood,
          Face to face in matchless rage,
          Mirroring each the other's death,
          Clashed in long combat.

CHORUS   But now in the beautiful morning of victory   [ANTISTROPHE 2
          Let Thebes of the many chariots sing for joy!
          With hearts for dancing we'll take leave of war:
          Our temples shall be sweet with hymns of praise,
          And the long night shall echo with our chorus.

SCENE I

CHORAG. But now at last our new King is coming:
Creon of Thebes, Menoiceus' son.
In this auspicious dawn of his reign
What are the new complexities
That shifting Fate has woven for him?
What is his counsel? Why has he summoned
The old men to hear him?

[*Enter* CREON *from the Palace. He addresses the* CHORUS *from the top step.*

CREON Gentlemen: I have the honour to inform you that our Ship of State, which recent storms have threatened to destroy, has come safely to harbour at last, guided by the merciful wisdom of Heaven. I have summoned you here this morning because I know that I can depend upon you: your devotion to King Laïos was absolute; you never hesitated in your duty to our late ruler Oedipus; and when Oedipus died, your loyalty was transferred to his children. Unfortunately, as you know, his two sons, the princes Eteoclês and Polyneicês, have killed each other in battle; and I, as the next in blood, have succeeded to the full power of the throne.

I am aware, of course, that no Ruler can expect complete loyalty from his subjects until he has been tested in office. Nevertheless, I say to you at the very outset that I have nothing but contempt for the kind of Governor who is afraid, for whatever reason, to follow the course that he knows is best for the State; and as for the man who sets private friendship above the public welfare,—I have no use for him, either. I call God to witness that if I saw my country headed for ruin, I should not be afraid to speak out plainly; and I need hardly remind you that I would never have any dealings with an enemy of the people. No one values friendship more highly than I; but we must remember that friends made at the risk of wrecking our Ship are not real friends at all.

These are my principles, at any rate, and that is why I have made the following decision concerning the sons of Oedipus: Eteoclês, who died as a man should die, fighting for his country, is to be buried with full military honours, with all the ceremony that is usual when the greatest heroes die; but his brother Polyneicês, who broke his exile to come back with fire and sword against his native city and the shrines of his fathers' gods, whose one idea was to spill the blood of his blood and sell his own people into slavery—Polyneicês, I say, is to have no burial: no man is to touch him or say the least prayer for him; he shall lie on the plain, unburied; and the birds and the scavenging dogs can do with him whatever they like.

This is my command, and you can see the wisdom behind it. As long as I am King, no traitor is going to be honoured with the loyal man. But whoever shows by word and deed that he is on the side of the State,—he shall have my respect while he is living, and my reverence when he is dead.

CHORAG.	If that is your will, Creon son of Menoiceus, You have the right to enforce it: we are yours.
CREON	That is my will. Take care that you do your part.
CHORAG.	We are old men: let the younger ones carry it out.
CREON	I do not mean that: the sentries have been appointed.
CHORAG.	Then what is it that you would have us do?
CREON	You will give no support to whoever breaks this law.
CHORAG.	Only a crazy man is in love with death!
CREON	And death it is; yet money talks, and the wisest Have sometimes been known to count a few coins too many.

[*Enter* SENTRY.

SENTRY   I'll not say that I'm out of breath from running, King, be-
          cause every time I stopped to think about what I have to
          tell you, I felt like going back. And all the time a voice kept
          saying, 'You fool, don't you know you're walking straight
          into trouble?'; and then another voice: 'Yes, but if you let
          somebody else get the news to Creon first, it will be even
          worse than that for you!' But good sense won out, at least I
          hope it was good sense, and here I am with a story that makes
          no sense at all; but I'll tell it anyhow, because, as they say,
          what's going to happen's going to happen, and—

CREON   Come to the point. What have you to say?

SENTRY   I did not do it. I did not see who did it. You must not punish
          me for what someone else has done.

CREON   A comprehensive defence! More effective, perhaps,
          If I knew its purpose. Come: what is it?

SENTRY   A dreadful thing . . . I don't know how to put it—

CREON   Out with it!

SENTRY   Well, then;
          The dead man—
                    Polyneicês—

[*Pause. The* SENTRY *is overcome, fumbles for words.* CREON
                    waits impassively.

                    out there—
                              someone,—
          New dust on the slimy flesh!

                              [*Pause. No sign from* CREON.

          Someone has given it burial that way, and
          Gone . . .

              [*Long pause.* CREON *finally speaks with deadly control:*

CREON   And the man who dared do this?

SENTRY   I swear I
       Do not know! You must believe me!
                                        Listen:
       The ground was dry, not a sign of digging, no,
       Not a wheeltrack in the dust, no trace of anyone.
       It was when they relieved us this morning: and one of them,
       The corporal, pointed to it.
                              There it was,
       The strangest—
                   Look:
       The body, just mounded over with light dust: you see?
       Not buried really, but as if they'd covered it
       Just enough for the ghost's peace. And no sign
       Of dogs or any wild animal that had been there.

       And then what a scene there was! Every man of us
       Accusing the other: we all proved the other man did it,
       We all had proof that we could not have done it.
       We were ready to take hot iron in our hands,
       Walk through fire, swear by all the gods,
       It was not I!
       I do not know who it was, but it was not I!

       [CREON's *rage has been mounting steadily, but the* SENTRY *is
                    too intent upon his story to notice it.*

       And then, when this came to nothing, someone said
       A thing that silenced us and made us stare
       Down at the ground: you had to be told the news,
       And one of us had to do it! We threw the dice,
       And the bad luck fell to me. So here I am,
       No happier to be here than you are to have me:
       Nobody likes the man who brings bad news.

CHORAG.   I have been wondering, King: can it be that the gods have
          done this?

                              [*Furiously.*

CREON   Stop!
          Must you doddering wrecks

Go out of your heads entirely? 'The gods!'
Intolerable!
The gods favour this corpse? Why? How had he served them?
Tried to loot their temples, burn their images,
Yes, and the whole State, and its laws with it!
Is it your senile opinion that the gods love to honour bad
    men?
A pious thought!—
                 No, from the very beginning
There have been those who have whispered together,
Stiff-necked anarchists, putting their heads together,
Scheming against me in alleys. These are the men,
And they have bribed my own guard to do this thing.

                                     [*Sententiously.*

Money!
There's nothing in the world so demoralising as money.
Down go your cities,
Homes gone, men gone, honest hearts corrupted,
Crookedness of all kinds, and all for money!

                   [*To* SENTRY:

                              But you—!
I swear by God and by the throne of God,
The man who has done this thing shall pay for it!
Find that man, bring him here to me, or your death
Will be the least of your problems: I'll string you up
Alive, and there will be certain ways to make you
Discover your employer before you die;
And the process may teach you a lesson you seem to have
    missed:
The dearest profit is sometimes all too dear.
That depends on the source. Do you understand me?
A fortune won is often misfortune.

SENTRY   King, may I speak?

CREON   Your very voice distresses me.

SENTRY   Are you sure that it is my voice, and not your conscience?

CREON	By God, he wants to analyse me now!
SENTRY	It is not what I say, but what has been done, that hurts you.
CREON	You talk too much.
SENTRY	Maybe; but I've done nothing.
CREON	Sold your soul for some silver: that's all you've done.
SENTRY	How dreadful it is when the right judge judges wrong!
CREON	Your figures of speech May entertain you now; but unless you bring me the man, You will get little profit from them in the end.

[*Exit* CREON *into the Palace.*

SENTRY	'Bring me the man'—! I'd like nothing better than bringing him the man! But bring him or not, you have seen the last of me here. At any rate, I am safe!

[*Exit* SENTRY.

ODE I

CHORUS	Numberless are the world's wonders, but none [STROPHE 1 More wonderful than man; the stormgrey sea Yields to his prows, the huge crests bear him high; Earth, holy and inexhaustible, is graven With shining furrows where his plows have gone Year after year, the timeless labour of stallions.

[ANTISTROPHE 1

The lightboned birds and beasts that cling to cover,
The lithe fish lighting their reaches of dim water,

All are taken, tamed in the net of his mind;
The lion on the hill, the wild horse windy-maned,
Resign to him; and his blunt yoke has broken
The sultry shoulders of the mountain bull.

Words also, and thought as rapid as air,   [STROPHE 2
He fashions to his good use; statecraft is his,
And his the skill that deflects the arrows of snow,
The spears of winter rain: from every wind
He has made himself secure—from all but one:
In the late wind of death he cannot stand.

O clear intelligence, force beyond all measure! [ANTISTROPHE 2
O fate of man, working both good and evil!
When the laws are kept, how proudly his city stands!
When the laws are broken, what of his city then?
Never may the anarchic man find rest at my hearth,
Never be it said that my thoughts are his thoughts.

SCENE II

[Re-enter SENTRY leading ANTIGONE.

CHORAG.   What does this mean? Surely this captive woman
          Is the Princess, Antigonê. Why should she be taken?

SENTRY   Here is the one who did it! We caught her
          In the very act of burying him.—Where is Creon?

CHORAG.   Just coming from the house.

                                        [Enter CREON, C.

CREON   What has happened?
          Why have you come back so soon?

[*Expansively.*

SENTRY O King,
A man should never be too sure of anything:
I would have sworn
That you'd not see me here again: your anger
Frightened me so, and the things you threatened me with;
But how could I tell then
That I'd be able to solve the case so soon?

No dice-throwing this time: I was only too glad to come!

Here is this woman. She is the guilty one:
We found her trying to bury him.

Take her, then; question her; judge her as you will.
I am through with the whole thing now, and glad of it.

CREON But this is Antigonê! Why have you brought her here?

SENTRY She was burying him, I tell you!

[*Severely.*

CREON Is this the truth?

SENTRY I saw her with my own eyes. Can I say more?

CREON The details: come, tell me quickly!

SENTRY It was like this:
After those terrible threats of yours, King,
We went back and brushed the dust away from the body.
The flesh was soft by now, and stinking,
So we sat on a hill to windward and kept guard.
No napping this time! We kept each other awake.
But nothing happened until the white round sun
Whirled in the centre of the round sky over us:
Then, suddenly,
A storm of dust roared up from the earth, and the sky
Went out, the plain vanished with all its trees
In the stinging dark. We closed our eyes and endured it.
The whirlwind lasted a long time, but it passed;
And then we looked, and there was Antigonê!

I have seen
A mother bird come back to a stripped nest, heard
Her crying bitterly a broken note or two
For the young ones stolen. Just so, when this girl
Found the bare corpse, and all her love's work wasted,
She wept, and cried on heaven to damn the hands
That had done this thing

And then she brought more dust
And sprinkled wine three times for her brother's ghost.

We ran and took her at once. She was not afraid,
Not even when we charged her with what she had done.
She denied nothing.

And this was a comfort to me,
And some uneasiness: for it is a good thing
To escape from death, but it is no great pleasure
To bring death to a friend.

Yet I always say
There is nothing so comfortable as your own safe skin!

[*Slowly, dangerously.*

CREON   And you, Antigonê,
           You with your head hanging,—do you confess this thing?

ANTIG.   I do. I deny nothing.

[*To* SENTRY:

CREON   You may go.

[*Exit* SENTRY.

[*To* ANTIGONE:

           Tell me, tell me briefly:
           Had you heard my proclamation touching this matter?

ANTIG.   It was public. Could I help hearing it?

CREON   And yet you dared defy the law.

ANTIG.   I dared.
It was not God's proclamation. That final Justice
That rules the world below makes no such laws.

Your edict, King, was strong,
But all your strength is weakness itself against
The immortal unrecorded laws of God.
They are not merely now: they were, and shall be,
Operative for ever, beyond man utterly.

I knew I must die, even without your decree:
I am only mortal. And if I must die
Now, before it is my time to die,
Surely this is no hardship: can anyone
Living, as I live, with evil all about me,
Think Death less than a friend? This death of mine
Is of no importance; but if I had left my brother
Lying in death unburied, I should have suffered.
Now I do not.
                    You smile at me. Ah Creon,
Think me a fool, if you like; but it may well be
That a fool convicts me of folly.

CHORAG.   Like father, like daughter: both headstrong, deaf to reason!
She has never learned to yield.

CREON   She has much to learn.
The inflexible heart breaks first, the toughest iron
Cracks first, and the wildest horses bend their necks
At the pull of the smallest curb.
                                    Pride? In a slave?
This girl is guilty of a double insolence,
Breaking the given laws and boasting of it.
Who is the man here,
She or I, if this crime goes unpunished?
Sister's child, or more than sister's child,
Or closer yet in blood—she and her sister
Win bitter death for this!

                              [*To servants:*

                             Go, some of you,
Arrest Ismenê. I accuse her equally.
Bring her: you will find her sniffling in the house there.

Her mind's a traitor: crimes kept in the dark
Cry for light, and the guardian brain shudders;
But how much worse than this
Is brazen boasting of barefaced anarchy!

ANTIG.   Creon, what more do you want than my death?

CREON   Nothing.
That gives me everything.

ANTIG.   Then I beg you: kill me.
This talking is a great weariness: your words
Are distasteful to me, and I am sure that mine
Seem so to you. And yet they should not seem so:
I should have praise and honour for what I have done.
All these men here would praise me
Were their lips not frozen shut with fear of you.

                                       [Bitterly.

Ah the good fortune of kings,
Licensed to say and do whatever they please!

CREON   You are alone here in that opinion.

ANTIG.   No, they are with me. But they keep their tongues in leash.

CREON   Maybe. But you are guilty, and they are not.

ANTIG.   There is no guilt in reverence for the dead.

CREON   But Eteoclês—was he not your brother too?

ANTIG.   My brother too.

CREON   And you insult his memory?

                                       [Softly.

ANTIG.   The dead man would not say that I insult it.

CREON   He would: for you honour a traitor as much as him.

ANTIG.   His own brother, traitor or not, and equal in blood.

CREON   He made war on his country. Eteoclês defended it.

ANTIG.   Nevertheless, there are honours due all the dead.

CREON   But not the same for the wicked as for the just.

ANTIG.   Ah Creon, Creon,
Which of us can say what the gods hold wicked?

CREON   An enemy is an enemy, even dead.

ANTIG.   It is my nature to join in love, not hate.

> [*Finally losing patience.*

CREON   Go join them, then; if you must have your love,
Find it in hell!

CHORAG.   But see, Ismenê comes:

> [*Enter* ISMENE, *guarded.*

Those tears are sisterly, the cloud
That shadows her eyes rains down gentle sorrow.

CREON   You too, Ismenê,
Snake in my ordered house, sucking my blood
Stealthily—and all the time I never knew
That these two sisters were aiming at my throne!

> Ismenê,

Do you confess your share in this crime, or deny it?
Answer me.

ISMENE   Yes, if she will let me say so. I am guilty.

> [*Coldly.*

ANTIG.   No, Ismenê. You have no right to say so.
You would not help me, and I will not have you help me.

ISMENE   But now I know what you meant; and I am here
To join you, to take my share of punishment.

ANTIG.   The dead man and the gods who rule the dead
Know whose act this was. Words are not friends.

ISMENE	Do you refuse me, Antigonê? I want to die with you: I too have a duty that I must discharge to the dead.
ANTIG.	You shall not lessen my death by sharing it.
ISMENE	What do I care for life when you are dead?
ANTIG.	Ask Creon. You're always hanging on his opinions.
ISMENE	You are laughing at me. Why, Antigonê?
ANTIG.	It's a joyless laughter, Ismenê.
ISMENE	But can I do nothing?
ANTIG.	Yes. Save yourself. I shall not envy you. There are those who will praise you; I shall have honour, too.
ISMENE	But we are equally guilty!
ANTIG.	No, more, Ismenê. You are alive, but I belong to Death.
CREON	[*To the* CHORUS: Gentlemen, I beg you to observe these girls: One has just now lost her mind; the other It seems, has never had a mind at all.
ISMENE	Grief teaches the steadiest minds to waver, King.
CREON	Yours certainly did, when you assumed guilt with the guilty!
ISMENE	But how could I go on living without her?
CREON	You are. She is already dead.
ISMENE	But your own son's bride!
CREON	There are places enough for him to push his plow. I want no wicked women for my sons!
ISMENE	O dearest Haimon, how your father wrongs you!
CREON	I've had enough of your childish talk of marriage!
CHORAG.	Do you really intend to steal this girl from your son?

CREON   No; Death will do that for me.

CHORAG.   Then she must die?

CREON   You dazzle me.
                      —But enough of this talk!

[To GUARDS:

You, there, take them away and guard them well:
For they are but women, and even brave men run
When they see Death coming.

[*Exeunt* ISMENE, ANTIGONE, *and* GUARDS.

ᒛᒋᒛᒋᒛᒋᒛᒋᒛᒋᒛᒋᒛᒋᒛᒋᒛᒋᒛᒋᒛᒋᒛᒋᒛᒋᒛᒋᒛᒋᒛ

ODE II

[STROPHE 1

CHORUS   Fortunate is the man who has never tasted God's vengeance!
Where once the anger of heaven has struck, that house is shaken
For ever: damnation rises behind each child
Like a wave cresting out of the black northeast,
When the long darkness under sea roars up
And bursts drumming death upon the windwhipped sand.

[ANTISTROPHE 1

I have seen this gathering sorrow from time long past
Loom upon Oedipus' children: generation from generation
Takes the compulsive rage of the enemy god.
So lately this last flower of Oedipus' line
Drank the sunlight! but now a passionate word
And a handful of dust have closed up all its beauty.

What mortal arrogance   [STROPHE 2
Transcends the wrath of Zeus?
Sleep cannot lull him, nor the effortless long months
Of the timeless gods: but he is young for ever,
And his house is the shining day of high Olympos.
    All that is and shall be,
    And all the past, is his.
No pride on earth is free of the curse of heaven.

The straying dreams of men   [ANTISTROPHE 2
May bring them ghosts of joy:
But as they drowse, the waking embers burn them;
Or they walk with fixed eyes, as blind men walk.
But the ancient wisdom speaks for our own time:
    Fate works most for woe
    With Folly's fairest show.
Man's little pleasure is the spring of sorrow.

SCENE III

CHORAG.   But here is Haimon, King, the last of all your sons.
        Is it grief for Antigonê that brings him here,
        And bitterness at being robbed of his bride?

                                      [Enter HAIMON.

CREON   We shall soon see, and no need of diviners.
                                   —Son,
        You have heard my final judgment on that girl:
        Have you come here hating me, or have you come
        With deference and with love, whatever I do?

HAIMON I am your son, father. You are my guide.
You make things clear for me, and I obey you.
No marriage means more to me than your continuing wisdom.

CREON Good. That is the way to behave: subordinate
Everything else, my son, to your father's will.
This is what a man prays for, that he may get
Sons attentive and dutiful in his house,
Each one hating his father's enemies,
Honouring his father's friends. But if his sons
Fail him, if they turn out unprofitably,
What has he fathered but trouble for himself
And amusement for the malicious?
                                    So you are right
Not to lose your head over this woman.
Your pleasure with her would soon grow cold, Haimon,
And then you'd have a hellcat in bed and elsewhere.
Let her find her husband in Hell!
Of all the people in this city, only she
Has had contempt for my law and broken it.

Do you want me to show myself weak before the people?
Or to break my sworn word? No, and I will not.
The woman dies.

I suppose she'll plead 'family ties.' Well, let her.
If I permit my own family to rebel,
How shall I earn the world's obedience?
Show me the man who keeps his house in hand,
He's fit for public authority.
                                    I'll have no dealings
With law-breakers, critics of the government:
Whoever is chosen to govern should be obeyed—
Must be obeyed, in all things, great and small,
Just and unjust! O Haimon,
The man who knows how to obey, and that man only,
Knows how to give commands when the time comes.

You can depend on him, no matter how fast
The spears come: he's a good soldier, he'll stick it out.

Anarchy, anarchy! Show me a greater evil!
This is why cities tumble and the great houses rain down,
This is what scatters armies!

No, no: good lives are made so by discipline.
We keep the laws then, and the lawmakers,
And no woman shall seduce us. If we must lose,
Let's lose to a man, at least! Is a woman stronger than we?

CHORAG. Unless time has rusted my wits,
What you say, King, is said with point and dignity.

[Boyishly earnest.

HAIMON Father:
Reason is God's crowning gift to man, and you are right
To warn me against losing mine. I cannot say—
I hope that I shall never want to say!—that you
Have reasoned badly. Yet there are other men
Who can reason, too; and their opinions might be helpful.
You are not in a position to know everything
That people say or do, or what they feel:
Your temper terrifies them—everyone
Will tell you only what you like to hear.
But I, at any rate, can listen; and I have heard them
Muttering and whispering in the dark about this girl.
They say no woman has ever, so unreasonably,
Died so shameful a death for a generous act:
'She covered her brother's body. Is this indecent?
'She kept him from dogs and vultures. Is this a crime?
'Death?—She should have all the honour that we can give
    her!'

This is the way they talk out there in the city.

You must believe me:
Nothing is closer to me than your happiness.

What could be closer? Must not any son
Value his father's fortune as his father does his?
I beg you, do not be unchangeable:
Do not believe that you alone can be right.
The man who thinks that,
The man who maintains that only he has the power
To reason correctly, the gift to speak, the soul—
A man like that, when you know him, turns out empty.

It is not reason never to yield to reason!

In flood time you can see how some trees bend,
And because they bend, even their twigs are safe,
While stubborn trees are torn up, roots and all.
And the same thing happens in sailing:
Make your sheet fast, never slacken,—and over you go,
Head over heels and under: and there's your voyage.
Forget you are angry! Let yourself be moved!
I know I am young; but please let me say this:
The ideal condition
Would be, I admit, that men should be right by instinct;
But since we are all too likely to go astray,
The reasonable thing is to learn from those who can teach.

CHORAG.   You will do well to listen to him, King,
          If what he says is sensible. And you, Haimon,
          Must listen to your father.—Both speak well.

CREON   You consider it right for a man of my years and experience
          To go to school to a boy?

HAIMON   It is not right
          If I am wrong. But if I am young, and right,
          What does my age matter?

CREON   You think it right to stand up for an anarchist?

HAIMON   Not at all. I pay no respect to criminals.

CREON   Then she is not a criminal?

HAIMON   The City would deny it, to a man.

CREON	And the City proposes to teach me how to rule?
HAIMON	Ah. Who is it that's talking like a boy now?
CREON	My voice is the one voice giving orders in this City!
HAIMON	It is no City if it takes orders from one voice.
CREON	The State is the King!
HAIMON	Yes, if the State is a desert.

[*Pause.*

CREON	This boy, it seems, has sold out to a woman.
HAIMON	If you are a woman: my concern is only for you.
CREON	So? Your 'concern'! In a public brawl with your father!
HAIMON	How about you, in a public brawl with justice?
CREON	With justice, when all that I do is within my rights?
HAIMON	You have no right to trample on God's right.

[*Completely out of control.*

CREON	Fool, adolescent fool! Taken in by a woman!
HAIMON	You'll never see me taken in by anything vile.
CREON	Every word you say is for her!

[*Quietly, darkly.*

HAIMON	And for you. And for me. And for the gods under the earth.
CREON	You'll never marry her while she lives.
HAIMON	Then she must die.—But her death will cause another.
CREON	Another? Have you lost your senses? Is this an open threat?
HAIMON	There is no threat in speaking to emptiness.
CREON	I swear you'll regret this superior tone of yours! You are the empty one!

HAIMON   If you were not my father,
I'd say you were perverse.

CREON   You girlstruck fool, don't play at words with me!

HAIMON   I am sorry. You prefer silence.

CREON   Now, by God—!
I swear, by all the gods in heaven above us,
You'll watch it, I swear you shall!

                               [To the SERVANTS.

                       Bring her out!
Bring the woman out! Let her die before his eyes,
Here, this instant, with her bridegroom beside her!

HAIMON   Not here, no; she will not die here, King.
And you will never see my face again.
Go on raving as long as you've a friend to endure you.

                               [Exit HAIMON.

CHORAG.   Gone, gone.
Creon, a young man in a rage is dangerous!

CREON   Let him do, or dream to do, more than a man can.
He shall not save these girls from death.

CHORAG.   These girls?
You have sentenced them both?

CREON   No, you are right.
I will not kill the one whose hands are clean.

CHORAG.   But Antigonê?

                               [Sombrely.

CREON   I will carry her far away
Out there in the wilderness, and lock her
Living in a vault of stone. She shall have food,
As the custom is, to absolve the State of her death.
And there let her pray to the gods of Hell:
They are her only gods:

Perhaps they will show her an escape from death,
Or she may learn,

> though late,

That piety shown the dead is pity in vain.

[Exit CREON.

ODE III

CHORUS   Love, unconquerable   [STROPHE
Waster of rich men, keeper
Of warm lights and all-night vigil
In the soft face of a girl:
Sea-wanderer, forest-visitor!
Even the pure Immortals cannot escape you,
And mortal man, in his one day's dusk,
Trembles before your glory.

Surely you swerve upon ruin   [ANTISTROPHE
The just man's consenting heart,
As here you have made bright anger
Strike between father and son—
And none has conquered but Love!
A girl's glance working the will of heaven:
Pleasure to her alone who mocks us,
Merciless Aphroditê.

SCENE IV

[As ANTIGONE enters guarded.

CHORAG. But I can no longer stand in awe of this,
Nor, seeing what I see, keep back my tears.
Here is Antigonê, passing to that chamber
Where all find sleep at last.

ANTIG. Look upon me, friends, and pity me   [STROPHE 1
Turning back at the night's edge to say
Good-bye to the sun that shines for me no longer;
Now sleepy Death
Summons me down to Acheron, that cold shore:
There is no bridesong there, nor any music.

CHORUS Yet not unpraised, not without a kind of honour,
You walk at last into the underworld;
Untouched by sickness, broken by no sword.
What woman has ever found your way to death?

ANTIG. How often I have heard the story of Niobê,   [ANTISTROPHE 1
Tantalos' wretched daughter, how the stone
Clung fast about her, ivy-close: and they say
The rain falls endlessly
And sifting soft snow; her tears are never done.
I feel the loneliness of her death in mine.

CHORUS But she was born of heaven, and you
Are woman, woman-born. If her death is yours,
A mortal woman's, is this not for you
Glory in our world and in the world beyond?

ANTIG. You laugh at me. Ah, friends, friends,   [STROPHE 2
Can you not wait until I am dead? O Thebes,
O men many-charioted, in love with Fortune,
Dear springs of Dircê, sacred Theban grove,

Be witnesses for me, denied all pity,
Unjustly judged! and think a word of love
For her whose path turns
Under dark earth, where there are no more tears.

CHORUS You have passed beyond human daring and come at last
Into a place of stone where Justice sits.
I cannot tell
What shape of your father's guilt appears in this.

ANTIG. You have touched it at last: that bridal bed   [ANTISTROPHE 2
Unspeakable, horror of son and mother mingling:
Their crime, infection of all our family!
O Oedipus, father and brother!
Your marriage strikes from the grave to murder mine.
I have been a stranger here in my own land:
All my life
The blasphemy of my birth has followed me.

CHORUS Reverence is a virtue, but strength
Lives in established law: that must prevail.
You have made your choice,
Your death is the doing of your conscious hand.

ANTIG. Then let me go, since all your words are bitter,   [EPODE
And the very light of the sun is cold to me.
Lead me to my vigil, where I must have
Neither love nor lamentation; no song, but silence.

[CREON *interrupts impatiently.*

CREON If dirges and planned lamentations could put off death,
Men would be singing for ever.

[*To the* SERVANTS.

Take her, go!
You know your orders: take her to the vault
And leave her alone there. And if she lives or dies,
That's her affair, not ours: our hands are clean.

ANTIG. O tomb, vaulted bride-bed in eternal rock,
Soon I shall be with my own again

Where Persephonê welcomes the thin ghosts underground:
And I shall see my father again, and you, mother,
And dearest Polyneicês—
                                        dearest indeed
To me, since it was my hand
That washed him clean and poured the ritual wine:
And my reward is death before my time!

And yet, as men's hearts know, I have done no wrong,
I have not sinned before God. Or if I have,
I shall know the truth in death. But if the guilt
Lies upon Creon who judged me, then, I pray,
May his punishment equal my own.

CHORAG.   O passionate heart,
Unyielding, tormented still by the same winds!

CREON   Her guards shall have good cause to regret their delaying.

ANTIG.   Ah! That voice is like the voice of death!

CREON   I can give you no reason to think you are mistaken.

ANTIG.   Thebes, and you my fathers' gods,
And rulers of Thebes, you see me now, the last
Unhappy daughter of a line of kings,
Your kings, led away to death. You will remember
What things I suffer, and at what men's hands,
Because I would not transgress the laws of heaven.

                                        [To the GUARDS, simply.

Come: let us wait no longer.

                                        [Exit ANTIGONE, L., guarded.

ODE IV

CHORUS   All Danaê's beauty was locked away   [STROPHE 1
         In a brazen cell where the sunlight could not come:
         A small room, still as any grave, enclosed her.
         Yet she was a princess too,
         And Zeus in a rain of gold poured love upon her.
         O child, child,
         No power in wealth or war
         Or tough sea-blackened ships
         Can prevail against untiring Destiny!

         And Dryas' son also, that furious king,   [ANTISTROPHE 1
         Bore the god's prisoning anger for his pride:
         Sealed up by Dionysos in deaf stone,
         His madness died among echoes.
         So at the last he learned what dreadful power
         His tongue had mocked:
         For he had profaned the revels,
         And fired the wrath of the nine
         Implacable Sisters that love the sound of the flute.

         And old men tell a half-remembered tale   [STROPHE 2
         Of horror done where a dark ledge splits the sea
         And a double surf beats on the grey shores:
         How a king's new woman, sick
         With hatred for the queen he had imprisoned,
         Ripped out his two sons' eyes with her bloody hands
         While grinning Arês watched the shuttle plunge
         Four times: four blind wounds crying for revenge,

                                                    [ANTISTROPHE 2
         Crying, tears and blood mingled.—Piteously born,
         Those sons whose mother was of heavenly birth!

Her father was the god of the North Wind
And she was cradled by gales,
She raced with young colts on the glittering hills
And walked untrammeled in the open light:
But in her marriage deathless Fate found means
To build a tomb like yours for all her joy.

SCENE V

[Enter blind TEIRESIAS, *led by a boy. The opening speeches
of* TEIRESIAS *should be in singsong contrast to the
realistic lines of* CREON.

TEIRES. This is the way the blind man comes, Princes, Princes,
Lock-step, two heads lit by the eyes of one.

CREON What new thing have you to tell us, old Teiresias?

TEIRES. I have much to tell you: listen to the prophet, Creon.

CREON I am not aware that I have ever failed to listen.

TEIRES. Then you have done wisely, King, and ruled well.

CREON I admit my debt to you. But what have you to say?

TEIRES. This, Creon: you stand once more on the edge of fate.

CREON What do you mean? Your words are a kind of dread.

TEIRES. Listen, Creon:
I was sitting in my chair of augury, at the place
Where the birds gather about me. They were all a-chatter,
As is their habit, when suddenly I heard
A strange note in their jangling, a scream, a
Whirring fury; I knew that they were fighting,
Tearing each other, dying

In a whirlwind of wings clashing. And I· was afraid.
I began the rites of burnt-offering at the altar,
But Hephaistos failed me: instead of bright flame,
There was only the sputtering slime of the fat thigh-flesh
Melting: the entrails dissolved in grey smoke,
The bare bone burst from the welter. And no blaze!

This was a sign from heaven. My boy described it,
Seeing for me as I see for others.

I tell you, Creon, you yourself have brought
This new calamity upon us. Our hearths and altars
Are stained with the corruption of dogs and carrion birds
That glut themselves on the corpse of Oedipus' son.
The gods are deaf when we pray to them, their fire
Recoils from our offering, their birds of omen
Have no cry of comfort, for they are gorged
With the thick blood of the dead.

                                  O my son,
These are no trifles! Think: all men make mistakes,
But a good man yields when he knows his course is wrong,
And repairs the evil. The only crime is pride.

Give in to the dead man, then: do not fight with a corpse—
What glory is it to kill a man who is dead?
Think, I beg you:
It is for your own good that I speak as I do.
You should be able to yield for your own good.

CREON   It seems that prophets have made me their especial province.
All my life long
I have been a kind of butt for the dull arrows
Of doddering fortune-tellers!

                            No, Teiresias:
If your birds—if the great eagles of God himself
Should carry him stinking bit by bit to heaven,
I would not yield. I am not afraid of pollution:
No man can defile the gods.

>   Do what you will,
> Go into business, make money, speculate
> In India gold or that synthetic gold from Sardis,
> Get rich otherwise than by my consent to bury him.
> Teiresias, it is a sorry thing when a wise man
> Sells his wisdom, lets out his words for hire!

TEIRES.   Ah Creon! Is there no man left in the world—

CREON   To do what?—Come, let's have the aphorism!

TEIRES.   No man who knows that wisdom outweighs any wealth?

CREON   As surely as bribes are baser than any baseness.

TEIRES.   You are sick, Creon! You are deathly sick!

CREON   As you say: it is not my place to challenge a prophet.

TEIRES.   Yet you have said my prophecy is for sale.

CREON   The generation of prophets has always loved gold.

TEIRES.   The generation of kings has always loved brass.

CREON   You forget yourself! You are speaking to your King.

TEIRES.   I know it. You are a king because of me.

CREON   You have a certain skill; but you have sold out.

TEIRES.   King, you will drive me to words that—

CREON   Say them, say them!
Only remember: I will not pay you for them.

TEIRES.   No, you will find them too costly.

CREON   No doubt. Speak:
Whatever you say, you will not change my will.

TEIRES.   Then take this, and take it to heart!
The time is not far off when you shall pay back
Corpse for corpse, flesh of your own flesh.
You have thrust the child of this world into living night,
You have kept from the gods below the child that is theirs:
The one in a grave before her death, the other,

Dead, denied the grave. This is your crime:
And the Furies and the dark gods of Hell
Are swift with terrible punishment for you.

Do you want to buy me now, Creon?

                            Not many days,
And your house will be full of men and women weeping,
And curses will be hurled at you from far
Cities grieving for sons unburied, left to rot before the walls
   of Thebes.

These are my arrows, Creon: they are all for you.

                                    [*To* boy:

But come, child: lead me home.
Let him waste his fine anger upon younger men.
Maybe he will learn at last
To control a wiser tongue in a better head.

                                    [*Exit* TEIRESIAS.

CHORAG.   The old man has gone, King, but his words
Remain to plague us. I am old, too,
But I can not remember that he was ever false.

CREON   That is true. . . . It troubles me.
Oh it is hard to give in! but it is worse
To risk everything for stubborn pride.

CHORAG.   Creon: take my advice.

CREON   What shall I do?

CHORAG.   Go quickly: free Antigonê from her vault
And build a tomb for the body of Polyneicês.

CREON   You would have me do this?

CHORAG.   Creon, yes!
And it must be done at once: God moves
Swiftly to cancel the folly of stubborn men.

CREON   It is hard to deny the heart! But I
               Will do it: I will not fight with destiny.

CHORAG.   You must go yourself, you cannot leave it to others.

CREON   I will go.
               —Bring axes, servants:
               Come with me to the tomb. I buried her, I
               Will set her free.
                         Oh quickly!
               My mind misgives—
               The laws of the gods are mighty, and a man must serve them
               To the last day of his life!

                                       [*Exit* CREON.

PÆAN

CHORAG.   God of many names   [STROPHE 1

CHORUS   O Iacchos
                               son
        of Cadmeian Sémelê
                      O born of the Thunder!
        Guardian of the West
                  Regent
        of Eleusis' plain
                 O Prince of mænad Thebes
        and the Dragon Field by rippling Ismenos:

CHORAG.   God of many names   [ANTISTROPHE 1

CHORUS   the flame of torches
        flares on our hills
                 the nymphs of Iacchos

dance at the spring of Castalia:

from the vine-close mountain
                              come ah come in ivy:
Evohé evohé! sings through the streets of Thebes

CHORAG.   God of many names   [STROPHE 2

CHORUS   Iacchos of Thebes
heavenly Child
                    of Sémelê bride of the Thunderer!
The shadow of plague is upon us:
                                        come
with clement feet
                    oh come from Parnasos
down the long slopes
                    across the lamenting water

CHORAG.   Iô Fire! Chorister of the throbbing stars!   [ANTISTROPHE 2
O purest among the voices of the night!
Thou son of God, blaze for us!

CHORUS   Come with choric rapture of circling Mænads
Who cry Iô Iacche!

             God of many names!

EXODOS

[Enter MESSENGER.

MESS.   Men of the line of Cadmos, you who live
Near Amphion's citadel:
                        I cannot say
Of any condition of human life 'This is fixed,

This is clearly good, or bad.' Fate raises up,
And Fate casts down the happy and unhappy alike:
No man can foretell his Fate.
                              Take the case of Creon:
Creon was happy once, as I count happiness:
Victorious in battle, sole governor of the land,
Fortunate father of children nobly born.
And now it has all gone from him! Who can say
That a man is still alive when his life's joy fails?
He is a walking dead man. Grant him rich,
Let him live like a king in his great house:
If his pleasure is gone, I would not give
So much as the shadow of smoke for all he owns.

CHORAG.   Your words hint at sorrow: what is your news for us?

MESS.   They are dead. The living are guilty of their death.

CHORAG.   Who is guilty? Who is dead? Speak!

MESS.   Haimon.
Haimon is dead; and the hand that killed him
Is his own hand.

CHORAG.   His father's? or his own?

MESS.   His own, driven mad by the murder his father had done.

CHORAG.   Teiresias, Teiresias, how clearly you saw it all!

MESS.   This is my news: you must draw what conclusions you can
            from it.

CHORAG.   But look: Eurydicê, our Queen:
            Has she overheard us?

                    [Enter EURYDICE from the Palace, C.

EURYD.   I have heard something, friends:
            As I was unlocking the gate of Pallas' shrine,
            For I needed her help today, I heard a voice
            Telling of some new sorrow. And I fainted
            There at the temple with all my maidens about me.

But speak again: whatever it is, I can bear it:
Grief and I are no strangers.

MESS.   Dearest Lady,
I will tell you plainly all that I have seen.
I shall not try to comfort you: what is the use,
Since comfort could lie only in what is not true?
The truth is always best.

                              I went with Creon
To the outer plain where Polyneicês was lying,
No friend to pity him, his body shredded by dogs.
We made our prayers in that place to Hecatê
And Pluto, that they would be merciful. And we bathed
The corpse with holy water, and we brought
Fresh-broken branches to burn what was left of it,
And upon the urn we heaped up a towering barrow
Of the earth of his own land.

                              When we were done, we ran
To the vault where Antigonê lay on her couch of stone.
One of the servants had gone ahead,
And while he was yet far off he heard a voice
Grieving within the chamber, and he came back
And told Creon. And as the King went closer,
The air was full of wailing, the words lost,
And he begged us to make all haste. 'Am I a prophet?'
He said, weeping, 'And must I walk this road,
'The saddest of all that I have gone before?
'My son's voice calls me on. Oh quickly, quickly!
'Look through the crevice there, and tell me
'If it is Haimon, or some deception of the gods!'

We obeyed; and in the cavern's farthest corner
We saw her lying:
She had made a noose of her fine linen veil
And hanged herself. Haimon lay beside her,
His arms about her waist, lamenting her,
His love lost under ground, crying out
That his father had stolen her away from him.

When Creon saw him the tears rushed to his eyes
And he called to him: 'What have you done, child? Speak
   to me.
'What are you thinking that makes your eyes so strange?
'O my son, my son, I come to you on my knees!'
But Haimon spat in his face. He said not a word,
Staring—
        And suddenly drew his sword
And lunged. Creon shrank back, the blade missed; and the
   boy,
Desperate against himself, drove it half its length
Into his own side, and fell. And as he died
He gathered Antigonê close in his arms again,
Choking, his blood bright red on her white cheek.
And now he lies dead with the dead, and she is his
At last, his bride in the houses of the dead.

                [Exit EURYDICE into the Palace.

CHORAG.   She has left us without a word. What can this mean?

MESS.   It troubles me, too; yet she knows what is best,
Her grief is too great for public lamentation,
And doubtless she has gone to her chamber to weep
For her dead son, leading her maidens in his dirge.

CHORAG.   It may be so: but I fear this deep silence.

                [Pause.

MESS.   I will see what she is doing. I will go in.

          [Exit MESSENGER into the Palace.

    [Enter CREON with attendants, bearing HAIMON's body.

CHORAG.   But here is the King himself: oh look at him,
Bearing his own damnation in his arms.

CREON   Nothing you say can touch me any more.
My own blind heart has brought me
From darkness to final darkness. Here you see
The father murdering, the murdered son—
And all my civic wisdom!

Haimon my son, so young, so young to die,
I was the fool, not you; and you died for me.

CHORAG.   That is the truth; but you were late in learning it.

CREON   This truth is hard to bear. Surely a god
Has crushed me beneath the hugest weight of heaven,
And driven me headlong a barbaric way
To trample out the thing I held most dear.

The pains that men will take to come to pain!

[*Enter* MESSENGER *from the Palace.*

MESS.   The burden you carry in your hands is heavy,
But it is not all: you will find more in your house.

CREON   What burden worse than this shall I find there?

MESS.   The Queen is dead.

CREON   O port of death, deaf world,
Is there no pity for me? And you, Angel of evil,
I was dead, and your words are death again.
Is it true, boy? Can it be true?
Is my wife dead? Has death bred death?

MESS.   You can see for yourself.

[*The doors are opened, and the body of* EURYDICE *is
disclosed within.*

CREON   Oh pity!
All true, all true, and more than I can bear!
O my wife, my son!

MESS.   She stood before the altar, and her heart
Welcomed the knife her own hand guided,
And a great cry burst from her lips for Megareus dead,
And for Haimon dead, her sons; and her last breath
Was a curse for their father, the murderer of her sons.
And she fell, and the dark flowed in through her closing eyes.

CREON   O God, I am sick with fear.
                 Are there no swords here? Has no one a blow for me?

MESS.   Her curse is upon you for the deaths of both.

CREON   It is right that it should be. I alone am guilty.
                 I know it, and I say it. Lead me in,
                 Quickly, friends.
                 I have neither life nor substance. Lead me in.

CHORAG.   You are right, if there can be right in so much wrong.
                 The briefest way is best in a world of sorrow.

CREON   Let it come,
                 Let death come quickly, and be kind to me.
                 I would not ever see the sun again.

CHORAG.   All that will come when it will; but we, meanwhile,
                 Have much to do. Leave the future to itself.

CREON   All my heart was in that prayer!

CHORAG.   Then do not pray any more: the sky is deaf.

CREON   Lead me away. I have been rash and foolish.
                 I have killed my son and my wife.
                 I look for comfort; my comfort lies here dead.
                 Whatever my hands have touched has come to nothing.
                 Fate has brought all my pride to a thought of dust.

> [As CREON *is being led into the house, the* CHORAGOS
> *advances and speaks directly to the audience.*

CHORAG.   There is no happiness where there is no wisdom;
                 No wisdom but in submission to the gods.
                 Big words are always punished,
                 And proud men in old age learn to be wise.

CREON: O God, I am sick with fear.
Are there no swords here? Has no one a blow for me?

MESS: Her curse is upon you for the deaths of both.

CREON: It is right that it should be. I alone am guilty.
I know it, and I say it. Lead me in,
Quickly, friends.
I have neither life nor substance. Lead me in.

CHORAGOS: You are right, if there can be right in so much wrong.
The briefest way is best in a world of sorrow.

CREON: Let it come,
Let death come quickly, and be kind to me.
I would not ever see the sun again.

CHORAGOS: All that will come when it will; but we, meanwhile,
Have much to do. Leave the future to itself.

CREON: All my heart was in that prayer!

CHORAGOS: Then do not pray any more: the sky is deaf.

CREON: Lead me away. I have been rash and foolish.
I have killed my son and my wife.
I look for comfort; my comfort lies here dead.
Whatever my hands have touched has come to nothing.
Fate has brought all my pride to a thought of dust.

[As Creon is being led into the house, the Choragos
advances and speaks directly to the audience.]

CHORAGOS: There is no happiness where there is no wisdom;
No wisdom but in submission to the gods.
Big words are always punished,
And proud men in old age learn to be wise.

Aeschylus

PROMETHEUS BOUND

translated by

Edith Hamilton

After ZEUS, in the struggle between the gods and the Titans, had overthrown his father KRONOS and seized for himself the supreme power of heaven and earth, the Titan PROMETHEUS (who had sided with ZEUS in the combat) incurred the victor's disfavor. ZEUS had planned to destroy the existing race of man and to fashion another; but PROMETHEUS, out of pity, stole fire from heaven and brought it to earth, thus inaugurating human civilization. As punishment, ZEUS decreed that he should be bound to a rock in the Scythian wilderness and there tormented forever.

DRAMATIS PERSONÆ:

HEPHESTUS	PROMETHEUS
FORCE	OCEAN
VIOLENCE	IO
HERMES	
CHORUS OF OCEANIDES	

PROMETHEUS BOUND

SCENE: PROMETHEUS *by tradition was fastened to a peak of the Caucasus.*

FORCE   Far have we come to this far spot of earth,
this narrow Scythian land, a desert all untrodden.
God of the forge and fire, yours the task
the Father laid upon you.
To this high-piercing, head-long rock
in adamantine chains that none can break
bind him—him here, who dared all things.
Your flaming flower he stole to give to men,
fire, the master craftsman, through whose power
all things are wrought, and for such error now
he must repay the gods; be taught to yield
to Zeus' lordship and to cease
from his man-loving way.

HEPHES.   Force, Violence, what Zeus enjoined on you
has here an end. Your task is done.
But as for me, I am not bold to bind
a god, a kinsman, to this stormy crag.
Yet I must needs be bold.
His load is heavy who dares disobey the Father's word.
O high-souled child of Justice, the wise counselor,
against my will as against yours I nail you fast
in brazen fetters never to be loosed
to this rock peak, where no man ever comes,
where never voice or face of mortal you will see.
The shining splendor of the sun shall wither you.
Welcome to you will be the night

when with her mantle star-inwrought*
she hides the light of day.
And welcome then in turn the sun
to melt the frost the dawn has left behind.
Forever shall the intolerable present grind you down,
and he who will release you is not born.
Such fruit you reap for your man-loving way.
A god yourself, you did not dread God's anger,
but gave to mortals honor not their due,
and therefore you must guard this joyless rock—
no rest, no sleep, no moment's respite.
Groans shall your speech be, lamentation
your only words—all uselessly.
Zeus has no mind to pity. He is harsh,
like upstarts always.

FORCE   Well then, why this delay and foolish talk?
         A god whom gods hate is abominable.

HEPHES. The tie of blood has a strange power,
         and old acquaintance too.

FORCE   And so say I—but don't you think
         that disobedience to the Father's words
         might have still stranger power?

HEPHES. You're rough, as always. Pity is not in you.

FORCE   Much good is pity here. Why all this pother
         that helps him not a whit?

HEPHES. O skill of hand now hateful to me.

FORCE   Why blame your skill? These troubles here
         were never caused by it. That's simple truth.

HEPHES. Yet would it were another's and not mine.

FORCE   Trouble is everywhere except in heaven.
         No one is free but Zeus.

* Shelley's adjective is the perfect translation. Anything else would be
less exact and less like Aeschylus.

HEPHES.	I know—I've not a word to say.
FORCE	Come then. Make haste. On with his fetters. What if the Father sees you lingering?
HEPHES.	The chains are ready here if he should look.
FORCE	Seize his hands and master him. Now to your hammer. Pin him to the rocks.
HEPHES.	All done, and quick work too.
FORCE	Still harder. Tighter. Never loose your hold. For he is good at finding a way out where there is none.
HEPHES.	This arm at least he will not ever free.
FORCE	Buckle the other fast, and let him learn with all his cunning he's a fool to Zeus.
HEPHES.	No one but he, poor wretch, can blame my work.
FORCE	Drive stoutly now your wedge straight through his breast, the stubborn jaw of steel that cannot break.
HEPHES.	Alas, Prometheus, I grieve for your pain.
FORCE	You shirk your task and grieve for those Zeus hates? Take care; you may need pity for yourself.
HEPHES.	You see a sight eyes should not look upon.
FORCE	I see one who has got what he deserves. But come. The girdle now around his waist.
HEPHES.	What must be shall be done. No need to urge me.
FORCE	I will and louder too. Down with you now. Make fast his legs in rings. Use all your strength.
HEPHES.	Done and small trouble.
FORCE	Now for his feet. Drive the nails through the flesh. The judge is stern who passes on our work.
HEPHES.	Your tongue and face match well.

FORCE   Why, you poor weakling. Are you one to cast
         a savage temper in another's face?

HEPHES.   Oh, let us go. Chains hold him, hand and foot.

FORCE   Run riot now, you there upon the rocks.
         Go steal from gods to give their goods to men—
         to men whose life is but a little day.
         What will they do to lift these woes from you?
         Forethought your name means, falsely named.
         Forethought you lack and need now for yourself
         if you would slip through fetters wrought like these.

                           [*Exeunt* FORCE, VIOLENCE, HEPHESTUS.

PROM.   O air of heaven and swift-winged winds,
         O running river waters,
         O never numbered laughter of sea waves,
         Earth, mother of all, Eye of the sun, all seeing,
         on you I call.
         Behold what I, a god, endure from gods.
         See in what tortures I must struggle
         through countless years of time.
         This shame, these bonds, are put upon me
         by the new ruler of the gods.
         Sorrow enough in what is here and what is still to come.
         It wrings groans from me.
         When shall the end be, the appointed end?
         And yet why ask?
         All, all I knew before,
         all that should be.
         Nothing, no pang of pain
         that I did not foresee.
         Bear without struggle what must be.
         Necessity is strong and ends our strife.
         But silence is intolerable here.
         So too is speech.
         I am fast bound, I must endure.
         I gave to mortals gifts.
         I hunted out the secret source of fire.

I filled a reed therewith,
fire, the teacher of all arts to men,
the great way through.
These are the crimes that I must pay for,
pinned to a rock beneath the open sky.

But what is here? What comes?
What sound, what fragrance, brushed me with faint wings,
of deities or mortals or of both? *
Has someone found a way to this far peak
to view my agony? What else?
Look at me then, in chains, a god who failed,
the enemy of Zeus, whom all gods hate,
all that go in and out of Zeus' hall.
The reason is that I loved men too well.
Oh, birds are moving near me. The air murmurs
with swift and sweeping wings.
Whatever comes to me is terrible.

[Enter CHORUS. They are SEA NYMPHS. It is clear from what
    follows that a winged car brings them on to the stage.

LEADER   Oh, be not terrified, for friends are here,
each eager to be first,
on swift wings flying to your rock.
I prayed my father long
before he let me come.
The rushing winds have sped me on.
A noise of ringing brass went through the sea-caves,
and for all a maiden's fears it drove me forth,
so swift, I did not put my sandals on,
but in my winged car I came to you.

PROM.   To see this sight—
Daughters of fertile Tethys,
children of Ocean who forever flows
unresting round earth's shores,
behold me, and my bonds

    * This line of Keats is the exact translation.

> that bind me fast upon the rocky height
> of this cleft mountain side,
> keeping my watch of pain.

SEA NY. I look upon you and a mist of tears,
of grief and terror, rises as I see
your body withering upon the rocks,
in shameful fetters.
For a new helmsman steers Olympus.
By new laws Zeus is ruling without law.
He has put down the mighty ones of old.

PROM. Oh, had I been sent deep, deep into earth,
to that black boundless place where go the dead,
though cruel chains should hold me fast forever,
I should be hid from sight of gods and men.
But now I am a plaything for the winds.
My enemies exult—and I endure.

AN. NY. What god so hard of heart to look on these things gladly?
Who, but Zeus only, would not suffer with you?
He is malignant always and his mind
unbending. All the sons of heaven
he drives beneath his yoke.
Nor will he make an end
until his heart is sated or until
someone, somehow, shall seize his sovereignty—
if that could be.

PROM. And yet—and yet—all tortured though I am,
fast fettered here,
he shall have need of me, the lord of heaven,
to show to him the strange design
by which he shall be stripped of throne and sceptre.
But he will never win me over
with honeyed spell of soft, persuading words,
nor will I ever cower beneath his threats
to tell him what he seeks.
First he must free me from this savage prison
and pay for all my pain.

AN. NY.   Oh, you are bold. In bitter agony
          you will not yield.
          These are such words as only free men speak.
          Piercing terror stings my heart.
          I fear because of what has come to you.
          Where are you fated to put in to shore
          and find a haven from this troubled sea?
          Prayers cannot move,
          persuasions cannot turn,
          the heart of Kronos' son.

PROM.   I know that he is savage.
          He keeps his righteousness at home.
          But yet some time he shall be mild of mood,
          when he is broken.
          He will smooth his stubborn temper,
          and run to meet me.
          Then peace will come and love between us two.

LEADER   Reveal the whole to us. Tell us your tale.
          What guilt does Zeus impute
          to torture you in shame and bitterness?
          Teach us, if you may speak.

PROM.   To speak is pain, but silence too is pain,
          and everywhere is wretchedness.
          When first the gods began to quarrel
          and faction rose among them,
          some wishing to throw Kronos out of heaven,
          that Zeus, Zeus, mark you, should be lord,
          others opposed, pressing the opposite,
          that Zeus should never rule the gods,
          then I, giving wise counsel to the Titans,
          children of Earth and Heaven, could not prevail.
          My way out was a shrewd one, they despised it,
          and in their arrogant minds they thought to conquer
          with ease, by their own strength.
          But Justice, she who is my mother, told me—
          Earth she is sometimes called,

whose form is one, whose name is many—
she told me, and not once alone,
the future, how it should be brought to pass,
that neither violence nor strength of arm
but only subtle craft could win.
I made all clear to them.
They scorned to look my way.
The best then left me was to stand with Zeus
in all good will, my mother with me,
and, through my counsel, the black underworld
covered, and hides within its secret depths
Kronos the aged and his host.
Such good the ruler of the gods had from me,
and with such evil he has paid me back.
There is a sickness that infects all tyrants,
they cannot trust their friends.
But you have asked a question I would answer:
What is my crime that I am tortured for?
Zeus had no sooner seized his father's throne
than he was giving to each god a post
and ordering his kingdom,
but mortals in their misery
he took no thought for.
His wish was they should perish
and he would then beget another race.
And there were none to cross his will save I.
I dared it, I saved men.
Therefore I am bowed down in torment,
grievous to suffer, pitiful to see.
I pitied mortals,
I never thought to meet with this.
Ruthlessly punished here I am
an infamy to Zeus.

LEADER   Iron of heart or wrought from rock is he
who does not suffer in your misery.
Oh, that these eyes had never looked upon it.
I see it and my heart is wrung.

PROM.	A friend must feel I am a thing to pity.
LEADER	Did you perhaps go even further still?
PROM.	I made men cease to live with death in sight.
LEADER	What potion did you find to cure this sickness?
PROM.	Blind hopes I caused to dwell in them.
AN. NY.	Great good to men that gift.
PROM.	To it I added the good gift of fire.
AN. NY.	And now the creatures of a day have flaming fire?
PROM.	Yes, and learn many crafts therefrom.
LEADER	For deeds like these Zeus holds you guilty, and tortures you with never ease from pain? Is no end to your anguish set before you?
PROM.	None other except when it pleases him.
LEADER	It pleases him? What hope there? You must see you missed your mark. I tell you this with pain to give you pain. But let that pass. Seek your deliverance.
PROM.	Your feet are free. Chains bind mine fast. Advice is easy for the fortunate. All that has come I knew full well. Of my own will I shot the arrow that fell short, of my own will. Nothing do I deny. I helped men and found trouble for myself. I knew—and yet not all. I did not think to waste away hung high in air upon a lonely rock. But now, I pray you, no more pity for what I suffer here. Come, leave your car, and learn the fate that steals upon me,

all, to the very end.
Hear me, oh, hear me. Share my pain. Remember,
trouble may wander far and wide
but it is always near.

LEADER   You cry to willing ears, Prometheus.
Lightly I leave my swiftly speeding car
and the pure ways of air where go the birds.
I stand upon this stony ground.
I ask to hear your troubles to the end.

[Enter OCEAN *riding on a four-footed bird. The* CHORUS
draws back, and he does not see them.

OCEAN   Well, here at last, an end to a long journey.
I've made my way to you, Prometheus.
This bird of mine is swift of wing
but I can guide him by my will,
without a bridle.
Now you must know, I'm grieved at your misfortunes.
Of course I must be, I'm your kinsman.
And that apart, there's no one I think more of.
And you'll find out the truth of what I'm saying.
It isn't in me to talk flattery.
Come: tell me just what must be done to help you,
and never say that you've a firmer friend
than you will find in me.

PROM.   Oho! What's here? You? Come to see my troubles?
How did you dare to leave your ocean river,
your rock caves hollowed by the sea,
and stand upon the iron mother earth?
Was it to see what has befallen me,
because you grieve with me?
Then see this sight: here is the friend of Zeus,
who helped to make him master.
This twisted body is his handiwork.

OCEAN   I see, Prometheus. I do wish
You'd take some good advice.

I know you're very clever,
but real self-knowledge—that you haven't got.
New fashions have come in with this new ruler.
Why can't you change your own to suit?
Don't talk like that—so rude and irritating.
Zeus isn't so far off but he might hear,
and what would happen then would make these troubles
seem child's play.
You're miserable. Then do control your temper
and find some remedy.
Of course you think you know all that I'm saying.
You certainly should know the harm
that blustering has brought you.
But you're not humbled yet. You won't give in.
You're looking for more trouble.
Just learn one thing from me:
Don't kick against the pricks.
You see he's savage—why not? He's a tyrant.
He doesn't have to hand in his accounts.
Well, now I'm going straight to try
if I can free you from this wretched business.
Do you keep still. No more of this rash talking.
Haven't you yet learned with all your wisdom
the mischief that a foolish tongue can make?

PROM.   Wisdom? The praise for that is yours alone,
who shared and dared with me and yet were able
to shun all blame.
But—let be now. Give not a thought more to me.
You never would persuade him.
He is not easy to win over.
Be cautious. Keep a sharp lookout,
or on your way back you may come to harm.

OCEAN   You counsel others better than yourself,
to judge by what I hear and what I see.
But I won't let you turn me off.
I really want to serve you.
And I am proud, yes, proud to say

I know that Zeus will let you go
just as a favor done to me.

PROM. I thank you for the good will you would show me.
But spare your pains. Your trouble would be wasted.
The effort, if indeed you wish to make it,
could never help me.
Now you are out of harm's way. Stay there.
Because I am unfortunate myself
I would not wish that others too should be.
Not so. Even here the lot of Atlas, of my brother,
weighs on me. In the western country
he stands, and on his shoulders is the pillar
that holds apart the earth and sky,
a load not easy to be borne.
Pity too filled my heart when once I saw
swift Typhon overpowered.
Child of the Earth was he, who lived
in caves in the Cilician land,
a flaming monster with a hundred heads,
who rose up against all the gods.
Death whistled from his fearful jaws.
His eyes flashed glaring fire.
I thought he would have wrecked God's sovereignty.
But to him came the sleepless bolt of Zeus,
down from the sky, thunder with breath of flame,
and all his high boasts were struck dumb.
Into his very heart the fire burned.
His strength was turned to ashes.
And now he lies a useless thing,
a sprawling body, near the narrow sea-way
by Aetna, underneath the mountain's roots.
High on the peak the god of fire sits,
welding the molten iron in his forge,
whence sometimes there will burst
rivers red hot, consuming with fierce jaws
the level fields of Sicily,
lovely with fruits.

And that is Typhon's anger boiling up,
his darts of flame none may abide,
of fire-breathing spray,
scorched to a cinder though he is
by Zeus' bolt.
But you are no man's fool; you have no need
to learn from me. Keep yourself safe,
as you well know the way.
And I will drain my cup to the last drop,
until Zeus shall abate his insolence of rage.

OCEAN   And yet you know the saying,
        when anger reaches fever heat
        wise words are a physician.

PROM.   Not when the heart is full to bursting.
        Wait for the crisis; then the balm will soothe.

OCEAN   But if one were discreet as well as daring—?
        You don't see danger then? Advise me.

PROM.   I see your trouble wasted,
        and you good-natured to the point of folly.

OCEAN   That's a complaint I don't mind catching.
        Let be: I'll choose to seem a fool
        if I can be a loyal friend.

PROM.   But he will lay to me all that you do.

OCEAN   There you have said what needs must send me home.

PROM.   Just so. All your lamenting over me
        will not have got you then an enemy.

OCEAN   Meaning—the new possessor of the throne?

PROM.   Be on your guard. See that you do not vex him.

OCEAN   Your case, Prometheus, may well teach me—

PROM.   Off with you. Go—and keep your present mind.

OCEAN   You urge one who is eager to be gone.
        For my four-footed bird is restless

to skim with wings the level ways of air.
He'll be well pleased to rest in his home stable.

[*Exit* OCEAN. *The* CHORUS *now come forward.*

CHORUS I mourn for you, Prometheus.
Desolation is upon you.
My face is wet with weeping.
Tears fall as waters which run continually.
The floods overflow me.
Terrible are the deeds of Zeus.
He rules by laws that are his own.
High is his spear above the others,
turned against the gods of old.
All the land now groans aloud,
mourning for the honor of the heroes of your race.
Stately were they, honored ever in the days of long ago.
Holy Asia is hard by.
Those that dwell there suffer in your trouble, great and sore.
In the Colchian land maidens live,
fearless in fight.
Scythia has a battle throng,
the farthest place of earth is theirs,
where marsh grass grows around Maeotis lake.
Arabia's flower is a warrior host;
high on a cliff their fortress stands,
Caucasus towers near;
men fierce as the fire, like the roar of the fire
they shout when the sharp spears clash.
All suffer with you in your trouble, great and sore.
Another Titan too, Earth mourns,
bound in shame and iron bonds.
I saw him, Atlas the god.
He bears on his back forever
the cruel strength of the crushing world
and the vault of the sky.
He groans beneath them.
The foaming sea-surge roars in answer,
the deep laments,

the black place of death far down in earth is moved exceed-
    ingly,
and the pure-flowing river waters grieve for him in his piteous
    pain.

PROM.   Neither in insolence nor yet in stubbornness
have I kept silence.
It is thought that eats my heart,
seeing myself thus outraged.
Who else but I, but I myself,
gave these new gods their honors?
Enough of that. I speak to you who know.
Hear rather all that mortals suffered.
Once they were fools. I gave them power to think.
Through me they won their minds.
I have no blame for them. All I would tell you
is my good will and my good gifts to them.
Seeing they did not see, nor hearing hear.
Like dreams they led a random life.
They had no houses built to face the sun,
of bricks or well-wrought wood,
but like the tiny ant who has her home
in sunless crannies deep down in the earth,
they lived in caverns.
The signs that speak of winter's coming,
of flower-faced spring, of summer's heat
with mellowing fruits,
were all unknown to them.
From me they learned the stars that tell the seasons,
their risings and their settings hard to mark.
And number, that most excellent device,
I taught to them, and letters joined in words.
I gave to them the mother of all arts,
hard working memory.
I, too, first brought beneath the yoke
great beasts to serve the plow,
to toil in mortals' stead.
Up to the chariot I led the horse that loves the rein,

the glory of the rich man in his pride.
None else but I first found
the seaman's car, sail-winged, sea-driven.
Such ways to help I showed them, I who have
no wisdom now to help myself.

LEADER   You suffer shame as a physician must
who cannot heal himself.
You who cured others now are all astray,
distraught of mind and faint of heart,
and find no medicine to soothe your sickness.

PROM.   Listen, and you shall find more cause for wonder.
Best of all gifts I gave them was the gift of healing.
For if one fell into a malady
there was no drug to cure, no draught, or soothing ointment.
For want of these men wasted to a shadow
until I showed them how to use
the kindly herbs that keep from us disease.
The ways of divination I marked out for them,
and they are many; how to know
the waking vision from the idle dream;
to read the sounds hard to discern;
the signs met on the road; the flight of birds,
eagles and vultures,
those that bring good or ill luck in their kind,
their way of life, their loves and hates
and council meetings.
And of those inward parts that tell the future,
the smoothness and the color and fair shape
that please the gods.
And how to wrap the flesh in fat
and the long thigh bone, for the altar fire
in honor to the gods.
So did I lead them on to knowledge
of the dark and riddling art.
The fire omens, too, were dim to them
until I made them see.
Deep within the earth are hidden

precious things for men,
brass and iron, gold and silver.
Would any say he brought these forth to light
until I showed the way?
No one, except to make an idle boast.
All arts, all goods, have come to men from me.

LEADER Do not care now for mortals
but take thought for yourself, O evil-fated.
I have good hope that still loosed from your bonds
you shall be strong as Zeus.

PROM. Not thus—not yet—is fate's appointed end,
fate that brings all to pass.
I must be bowed by age-long pain and grief.
So only will my bonds be loosed.
All skill, all cunning, is as foolishness
before necessity.

SEA NY. Who is the helmsman of necessity?

PROM. Fate, threefold, Retribution, unforgetting.

AN. NY. And Zeus is not so strong?

PROM. He cannot shun what is foredoomed.

AN. NY. And is he not foredoomed to rule forever?

PROM. No word of that. Ask me no further.

AN. NY. Some solemn secret hides behind your silence.

PROM. Think of another theme. It is not yet
the time to speak of this.
It must be wrapped in darkness, so alone
I shall some time be saved
from shame and grief and bondage.

CHORUS Zeus orders all things.
May he never set his might against purpose of mine,
like a wrestler in the match.
May I ever be found where feast the holy gods,

and the oxen are slain,
where ceaselessly flows the pathway
of Ocean, my father.
May the words of my lips forever
be free from sin.
May this abide with me and not depart
like melting snow.
Long life is sweet when there is hope
and hope is confident.
And it is sweet when glad thoughts make the heart grow
strong,
and there is joy.
But you, crushed by a thousand griefs,
I look upon you and I shudder.
You did not tremble before Zeus.
You gave your worship where you would, to men,
a gift too great for mortals,
a thankless favor.
What help for you there? What defense in those
whose life is but from morning unto evening?
Have you not seen?
Their little strength is feebleness,
fast bound in darkness,
like a dream.
The will of man shall never break
the harmony of God.
This I have learned beholding your destruction.
Once I spoke different words to you
from those now on my lips.
A song flew to me.
I stood beside your bridal bed,
I sang the wedding hymn,
glad in your marriage.
And with fair gifts persuading her,
you led to share your couch,
Hesione, child of the sea.

[Enter IO.

10   What land—what creatures here?
      This, that I see—
      A form storm-beaten,
      bound to the rock.
      Did you do wrong?
      Is this your punishment?
      You perish here.
      Where am I?
      Speak to a wretched wanderer.
      Oh! Oh! he stings again—
      the gadfly—oh, miserable!
      But you must know he's not a gadfly.
      He's Argus, son of Earth, the herdsman.
      He has a thousand eyes.
      I see him. Off! Keep him away!
      No, he comes on.
      His eyes can see all ways at once.
      He's dead but no grave holds him.
      He comes straight up from hell.
      He is the huntsman,
      and I his wretched quarry.
      He drives me all along the long sea strand.
      I may not stop for food or drink.
      He has a shepherd's pipe,
      a reed with beeswax joined.
      Its sound is like the locust's shrilling,
      a drowsy note—that will not let me sleep.
      Oh, misery. Oh, misery.
      Where is it leading me,
      my wandering—far wandering.
      What ever did I do,
      how ever did I sin,
      that you have yoked me to calamity,
      O son of Kronos,
      that you madden a wretched woman
      driven mad by the gadfly of fear?
      Oh, burn me in fire or hide me in earth
      or fling me as food to the beasts of the sea.

Master, grant me my prayer.
Enough—I have been tried enough—
my wandering—long wandering.
Yet I have found no place
to leave my misery.
—I am a girl who speaks to you,
but horns are on my head.

PROM.   Like one caught in an eddy, whirling round and round,
the gadfly drives you.
I know you, girl. You are Inachus' daughter.
You made the god's heart hot with love,
and Hera hates you. She it is
who drives you on this flight that never stops.

IO   How is it that you speak my father's name?
Who are you? Tell me for my misery.
Who are you, sufferer, that speak the truth
to one who suffers?
You know the sickness God has put upon me,
that stings and maddens me and drives me on
and wastes my life away.
I am a beast, a starving beast,
that frenzied runs with clumsy leaps and bounds,
oh, shame,
mastered by Hera's malice.
Who among the wretched
suffer as I do?
Give me a sign, you there.
Tell to me clearly
the pain still before me.
Is help to be found?
A medicine to cure me?
Speak, if you know.

PROM.   I will and in plain words,
as friend should talk to friend.
—You see Prometheus, who gave mortals fire.

IO   You, he who succored the whole race of men?

You, that Prometheus, the daring, the enduring?
Why do you suffer here?

PROM. Just now I told the tale—

IO But will you not still give to me a boon?

PROM. Ask what you will. I know all you would learn.

IO Then tell me who has bound you to this rock.

PROM. Zeus was the mind that planned.
The hand that did the deed the god of fire.

IO What was the wrong that you are punished for?

PROM. No more. Enough of me.

IO But you will tell the term set to my wandering?
My misery is great. When shall it end?

PROM. Here not to know is best.

IO I ask you not to hide what I must suffer.

PROM. I do so in no grudging spirit.

IO Why then delay to tell me all?

PROM. Not through ill will. I would not terrify you.

IO Spare me not more than I would spare myself.

PROM. If you constrain me I must speak. Hear then—

LEADER Not yet. Yield to my pleasure too.
For I would hear from her own lips
what is the deadly fate, the sickness
that is upon her. Let her say—then teach her
the trials still to come.

PROM. If you would please these maidens, Io—
they are your father's sisters,
and when the heart is sorrowful, to speak
to those who will let fall a tear
is time well spent.

10   I do not know how to distrust you.
You shall hear all. And yet—
I am ashamed to speak,
to tell of that god-driven storm
that struck me, changed me, ruined me.
How shall I tell you who it was?
How ever to my maiden chamber
visions came by night,
persuading me with gentle words:
'Oh happy, happy girl,
Why are you all too long a maid
when you might marry with the highest?
The arrow of desire has pierced Zeus.
For you he is on fire.
With you it is his will to capture love.
Would you, child, fly from Zeus' bed?
Go forth to Lerna, to the meadows deep in grass.
There is a sheep-fold there,
an ox-stall, too, that holds your father's oxen—
so shall Zeus find release from his desire.'
Always, each night, such dreams possessed me.
I was unhappy and at last I dared
to tell my father of these visions.
He sent to Pytho and far Dodona
man after man to ask the oracle
what he must say or do to please the gods.
But all brought answers back of shifting meaning,
hard to discern, like golden coins unmarked.
At last a clear word came. It fell upon him
like lightning from the sky. It told him
to thrust me from his house and from his country,
to wander to the farthest bounds of earth
like some poor dumb beast set apart
for sacrifice, whom no man will restrain.
And if my father would not, Zeus would send
his thunderbolt with eyes of flame to end
his race, all, everyone.
He could not but obey such words

from the dark oracle. He drove me out.
He shut his doors to me—against his will
as against mine. Zeus had him bridled.
He drove him as he would.
Straightway I was distorted, mind and body.
A beast—with horns—look at me—
stung by a fly, who madly leaps and bounds.
And so I ran and found myself beside
the waters, sweet to drink, of Kerchneia
and Lerna's well-spring.
Beside me went the herdsman Argus,
the violent of heart, the earth-born,
watching my footsteps with his hundred eyes.
But death came to him, swift and unforeseen.
Plagued by a gadfly then, the scourge of God,
I am driven on from land to land.
So for what has been. But what still remains
of anguish for me, tell me.
Do not in pity soothe me with false tales.
Words strung together by a lie
are like a foul disease.

LEADER   Oh, shame. Oh, tale of shame.
Never, oh never, would I have believed that my ears
would hear words such as these, of strange meaning.
Evil to see and evil to hear,
misery, defilement, and terror.
They pierce my heart with a two-edged sword.
A fate like that—
I shudder to look upon Io.

PROM.   You are too ready with your tears and fears.
Wait for the end.

LEADER   Speak. Tell us, for when one lies sick,
to face with clear eyes all the pain to come
is sweet.

PROM.   What first you asked was granted easily,
to hear from her own lips her trials.

But for the rest, learn now the sufferings
she still must suffer, this young creature,
at Hera's hands. Child of Inachus,
keep in your heart my words, so you shall know
where the road ends. First to the sunrise,
over furrows never plowed, where wandering Scythians
live in huts of wattles made, raised high
on wheels smooth-rolling. Bows they have,
and they shoot far. Turn from them.
Keep to the shore washed by the moaning sea.
Off to the left live the Chalybians,
workers of iron. There be on your guard.
A rough people they, who like not strangers.
Here rolls a river called the Insolent,
true to its name. You cannot find a ford
until you reach the Caucasus itself,
highest of mountains. From beneath its brow
the mighty river rushes. You must cross
the summit, neighbor to the stars.
Then by the southward road, until you reach
the warring Amazons, men-haters, who one day
will found a city by the Thermodon,
where Salmydessus thrusts
a fierce jaw out into the sea that sailors hate,
stepmother of ships.
And they will bring you on your way right gladly
to the Cimmerian isthmus, by a shallow lake,
Maeotis, at the narrows.
Here you must cross with courage.
And men shall tell forever of your passing.
The strait shall be named for you, Bosporus,
Ford of the Cow. There leave the plains of Europe,
and enter Asia, the great Continent.
—Now does he seem to you, this ruler of the gods,
evil, to all, in all things?
A god desired a mortal—drove her forth
to wander thus.
A bitter lover you have found, O girl,

	for all that I have told you is not yet the prelude even.
IO	O, wretched, wretched.
PROM.	You cry aloud for this? What then when you have learned the rest?
LEADER	You will not tell her of more trouble?
PROM.	A storm-swept sea of grief and ruin.
IO	What gain to me is life? Oh, now to fling myself down from this rock peak to the earth below, and find release there from my trouble. Better to die once than to suffer through all the days of life.
PROM.	Hardly would you endure my trial, whose fate it is not ever to find death that ends all pain. For me there is no end until Zeus falls from power.
IO	Zeus fall from power?
PROM.	You would rejoice, I think, to see that happen?
IO	How could I not, who suffer at his hands?
PROM.	Know then that it shall surely be.
IO	But who will strip the tyrant of his scepter?
PROM.	He will himself and his own empty mind.
IO	How? Tell me, if it is not wrong to ask.
PROM.	He will make a marriage that will vex him.
IO	Goddess or mortal, if it may be spoken?
PROM.	It may not be. Seek not to know.
IO	His wife shall drive him from his throne?
PROM.	Her child shall be more than his father's match.
IO	And is there no way of escape for him?

PROM.	No way indeed, unless my bonds are loosed.
IO	But who can loose them against Zeus' will?
PROM.	A son of yours—so fate decrees.
IO	What words are these? A child of mine shall free you?
PROM.	Ten generations first must pass and then three more.
IO	Your prophecy grows dim through generations.
PROM.	So let it be. Seek not to know your trials.
IO	Do not hold out a boon and then withdraw it.
PROM.	One boon of two I will bestow upon you.
IO	And they are? Speak. Give me the choice.
PROM.	I give it you: the hardships still before you, or his name who shall free me. Choose.
LEADER	Of these give one to her, but give to me a grace as well—I am not quite unworthy. Tell her where she must wander, and to me tell who shall free you. It is my heart's desire.
PROM.	And to your eagerness I yield. Hear, Io, first, of your far-driven journey. And bear in mind my words, inscribe them upon the tablets of your heart. When you have crossed the stream that bounds the continents, turn to the East where flame the footsteps of the sun, and pass along the sounding sea to Cisthene. Here on the plain live Phorcys' children, three, all maidens, very old, and shaped like swans, who have one eye and one tooth to the three. No ray of sun looks ever on that country, nor ever moon by night. Here too their sisters dwell. And they are three, the Gorgons, winged, with hair of snakes, hateful to mortals, whom no man shall behold and draw again

the breath of life. They garrison that place.
And yet another evil sight, the hounds of Zeus,
who never bark, griffins with beaks like birds.
The one-eyed Arimaspi too, the riders,
who live beside a stream that flows with gold,
a way of wealth. From all these turn aside.
Far off there is a land where black men live,
close to the sources of the sun, whence springs
a sun-scorched river. When you reach it,
go with all care along the banks up to
the great descent, where from the mountains
the holy Nile pours forth its waters
pleasant to drink from. It will be your guide
to the Nile land, the Delta. A long exile
is fated for you and your children here.
If what I speak seems dark and hard to know,
ask me again and learn all clearly.
For I have time to spare and more
than I could wish.

LEADER   If in your story of her fatal journey
there is yet somewhat left to tell her,
speak now. If not, give then to us
the grace we asked. You will remember.

PROM.   The whole term of her roaming has been told.
But I will show she has not heard in vain,
and tell her what she suffered coming hither,
in proof my words are true.
A moving multitude of sorrows were there,
too many to recount, but at the end
you came to where the levels of Molossa
surround the lofty ridge of Dodona,
seat of God's oracle.
A wonder past belief is there, oak trees that speak.
They spoke, not darkly but in shining words,
calling you Zeus' glorious spouse.
The frenzy seized you then. You fled
along the sea-road washed by the great inlet,

named for God's mother. Up and down you wandered,
storm-tossed. And in the time to come that sea
shall have its name from you, Ionian,
that men shall not forget your journey.
This is my proof to you my mind can see
farther than meets the eye.
From here the tale I tell is for you all,
and of the future, leaving now the past.
There is a city, Canobus, at the land's end,
where the Nile empties, on new river soil.
There Zeus at last shall make you sane again,
stroking you with a hand you will not fear.
And from this touch alone you will conceive
and bear a son, a swarthy man,
whose harvest shall be reaped on many fields,
all that are washed by the wide-watered Nile.
In the fifth generation from him, fifty sisters
will fly from marriage with their near of kin,
who, hawks in close pursuit of doves, aquiver
with passionate desire, shall find that death
waits for the hunters on the wedding night.
God will refuse to them the virgin bodies.
Argos will be the maidens' refuge, to their suitors
a slaughter dealt by women's hands,
bold in the watches of the night.
The wife shall kill her husband,
dipping her two-edged sword in blood.
O Cyprian goddess, thus may you come to my foes.
One girl, bound by love's spell, will change
her purpose, and she will not kill
the man she lay beside, but choose the name
of coward rather than be stained with blood.
In Argos she will bear a kingly child—
a story overlong if all were told.
Know this, that from that seed will spring
one glorious with the bow, bold-hearted,
and he shall set me free.
This is the oracle my mother told me,

Justice, who is of old, Earth's daughter.
But how and where would be too long a tale,
nor would you profit.

IO   Oh, misery. Oh, misery.
A frenzy tears me.
Madness strikes my mind.
I burn. A frantic sting—
an arrow never forged with fire.
My heart is beating at its walls in terror.
My eyes are whirling wheels.
Away. Away. A raging wind of fury
sweeps through me.
My tongue has lost its power.
My words are like a turbid stream,
wild waves that dash against a surging sea,
the black sea of madness.

                                           [*Exit* IO.

CHORUS   Wise, wise was he,
who first weighed this in thought
and gave it utterance:
Marriage within one's own degree is best,
not with one whom wealth has spoiled,
nor yet with one made arrogant by birth.
Such as these he must not seek
who lives upon the labor of his hands.
Fate, dread deity,
may you never, oh, never behold me
sharing the bed of Zeus.
May none of the dwellers in heaven
draw near to me ever.
Terrors take hold of me
seeing her maidenhood
turning from love of man,
torn by Hera's hate,
driven in misery.
For me, I would not shun marriage nor fear it,

so it were with my equal.
But the love of the greater gods,
from whose eyes none can hide,
may that never be mine.
To war with a god-lover is not war,
it is despair.
For what could I do,
or where could I fly
from the cunning of Zeus?

PROM. In very truth shall Zeus, for all his stubborn pride,
be humbled, such a marriage he will make
to cast him down from throne and power.
And he shall be no more remembered.
The curse his father put on him
shall be fulfilled.
The curse that he cursed him with as he fell
from his age-long throne.
The way from such trouble no one of the gods
can show him save I.
These things I know and how they shall come to pass.
So let him sit enthroned in confidence,
trust to his crashing thunder high in air,
shake in his hands his fire-breathing dart.
Surely these shall be no defense,
but he will fall, in shame unbearable.
Even now he makes ready against himself
one who shall wrestle with him and prevail,
a wonder of wonders, who will find
a flame that is swifter than lightning,
a crash to silence the thunder,
who will break into pieces the sea-god's spear,
the bane of the ocean that shakes the earth.
Before this evil Zeus shall be bowed down.
He will learn how far apart are a king and a slave.

LEADER These words of menace on your tongue
speak surely only your desire.

PROM.	They speak that which shall surely be— and also my desire.
LEADER	And we must look to see Zeus mastered?
PROM.	Yes, and beneath a yoke more cruel than this I bear.
LEADER	You have no fear to utter words like these?
PROM.	I am immortal—and I have no fear.
SEA NY.	But agony still worse he might inflict—
PROM.	So let him do. All that must come I know.
AN. NY.	The wise bow to the inescapable.
PROM.	Be wise then. Worship power. Cringe before each who wields it. To me Zeus counts as less than nothing. Let him work his will, show forth his power for his brief day, his little moment of lording it in heaven. —But see. There comes a courier from Zeus, a lackey in his new lord's livery. Some curious news is surely on his lips.

[*Enter* HERMES.

HERMES	You trickster there, you biter bitten,
	sinner against the gods, man-lover, thief of fire,
	my message is to you.
	The great father gives you here his orders:
	Reveal this marriage that you boast of,
	by which he shall be hurled from power.
	And, mark you, not in riddles, each fact clearly.
	—Don't make me take a double journey, Prometheus.
	    You can see Zeus isn't going to be made kinder
	    by this sort of thing.

PROM.	Big words and insolent. They well become you, O lackey of the gods. Young—young—your thrones just won,

you think you live in citadels grief cannot reach.
Two dynasties I have seen fall from heaven,
and I shall see the third fall fastest,
most shamefully of all.
Is it your thought to see me tremble
and crouch before your upstart gods?
Not so—not such a one am I.
Make your way back. You will not learn from me.

HERMES   Ah, so? Still stubborn? Yet this willfulness
has anchored you fast in these troubled waters.

PROM.   And yet I would not change my lot
with yours, O lackey.

HERMES   Better no doubt to be slave to a rock
than be the father's trusted herald.

PROM.   I must be insolent when I must speak to insolence.

HERMES   You are proud, it seems, of what has come to you.

PROM.   I proud? May such pride be
the portion of my foes.—I count you of them.

HERMES   You blame me also for your sufferings?

PROM.   In one word, all gods are my enemies.
They had good from me. They return me evil.

HERMES   I heard you were quite mad.

PROM.   Yes, I am mad, if to abhor such foes is madness.

HERMES   You would be insufferable, Prometheus, if you were not so
wretched.

PROM.   Alas!

HERMES   Alas? That is a word Zeus does not understand.

PROM.   Time shall teach it him, gray time,
that teaches all things.

HERMES   It has not taught you wisdom yet.

PROM.	No, or I had not wrangled with a slave.
HERMES	It seems that you will tell the Father nothing.
PROM.	Paying the debt of kindness that I owe him?
HERMES	You mock at me as though I were a child.

PROM.
A child you are or what else has less sense
if you expect to learn from me.
There is no torture and no trick of skill,
there is no force, which can compel my speech,
until Zeus wills to loose these deadly bonds.
So let him hurl his blazing bolt,
and with the white wings of the snow,
with thunder and with earthquake,
confound the reeling world.
None of all this will bend my will
to tell him at whose hands he needs must fall.

HERMES
I urge you, pause and think if this will help you.

PROM.
I thought long since of all. I planned for all.

HERMES
Submit, you fool. Submit. In agony learn wisdom.

PROM.
Go and persuade the sea wave not to break.
You will persuade me no more easily.
I am no frightened woman, terrified
at Zeus' purpose. Do you think to see me
ape women's ways, stretch out my hands
to him I hate, and pray him for release?
A world apart am I from prayer for pity.

HERMES
Then all I say is said in vain.
Nothing will move you, no entreaty
soften your heart.
Like a young colt new-bridled,
you have the bit between your teeth,
and rear and fight against the rein.
But all this vehemence is feeble bombast.
A fool, bankrupt of all but obstinacy,

is the poorest thing on earth.
Oh, if you will not hear me, yet consider
the storm that threatens you from which
you cannot fly, a great third wave of evil.
Thunder and flame of lightning will rend
this jagged peak. You shall be buried deep,
held by a splintered rock.
After long length of time you will return
to see the light, but Zeus' winged hound,
an eagle red with blood,
shall come a guest unbidden to your banquet.
All day long he will tear to rags your body,
great rents within the flesh,
feasting in fury on the blackened liver.
Look for no ending to this agony
until a god will freely suffer for you,
will take on him your pain, and in your stead
descend to where the sun is turned to darkness,
the black depths of death.
Take thought: this is no empty boast
but utter truth. Zeus does not lie.
Each word shall be fulfilled.
Pause and consider. Never think
self-will is better than wise counsel.

LEADER   To us the words he speaks are not amiss.
He bids you let your self-will go and seek
good counsel. Yield.
For to the wise a failure is disgrace.

PROM.   These tidings that the fellow shouts at me
were known to me long since.
A foe to suffer at the hands of foes
is nothing shameful.
Then let the twisting flame of forked fire
be hurled upon me. Let the very air
be rent by thunder-crash.
Savage winds convulse the sky,
hurricanes shake the earth from its foundations,

the waves of the sea rise up and drown the stars,
and let me be swept down to hell,
caught in the cruel whirlpool of necessity.
He cannot kill me.

HERMES   Why, these are ravings you may hear from madmen.
His case is clear. Frenzy can go no further.
You maids who pity him, depart, be swift.
The thunder peals and it is merciless.
Would you too be struck down?

LEADER   Speak other words, another counsel,
if you would win me to obey.
Now, in this place, to urge
that I should be a coward is intolerable.
I choose with him to suffer what must be.
Not to stand by a friend—there is no evil
I count more hateful.
I spit it from my mouth.

HERMES   Remember well I warned you,
when you are swept away in utter ruin.
Blame then yourselves, not fate, nor ever say
that Zeus delivered you
to a hurt you had not thought to see.
With open eyes,
not suddenly, not secretly,
into the net of utter ruin
whence there is no escape,
you fall by your own folly.

[*Exit* HERMES.

PROM.   An end to words. Deeds now.
The world is shaken.
The deep and secret way of thunder
is rent apart.
Fiery wreaths of lightning flash.
Whirlwinds toss the swirling dust.
The blasts of all the winds are battling in the air,

and sky and sea are one.
On me the tempest falls.
It does not make me tremble.
O holy Mother Earth, O air and sun,
behold me. I am wronged.

APPENDIX: COMMENTARIES

ELECTRA

PREFATORY NOTE: This version of Sophocles' *Electra* is intended primarily to convey the dramatic value of the original. I have tried to write from the point of view of the actor, and to make the English words and rhythms of speech spring from the feeling of the particular character in the particular situation. A Sophoclean tragedy is a very unified "imitation of an action and of life," and its language can best be understood as only one expression of the fundamental theatrical idea.

Another aim has been to keep the language as simply intelligible as possible, in order to give an audience in a theatre the actual meaning of the original. I have not (intentionally at least) changed or adapted the literal meaning, except in the effort to get idiomatic English; but I have omitted some of the mythological references which would not be understood, and some of the cries of woe, some of the "me miserable's" and "wretched me's," which do not have the desired effect in English. I have also cut two or three lines from each of the following speeches: Orestes, page 64; Paidagogos, page 80; Electra, page 87.

NOTES ON PRODUCTION: The following notes were suggested by the production of *Electra* with a danced epilogue by the Bennington Theater Studio in June, 1937:

GREEK CONVENTIONS OF WRITING FOR THE STAGE: The form of a Sophoclean tragedy is so unlike most contemporary writing for the stage, that one is in danger of thinking it is not "theatrical," or of simply dismissing it by remarking that "we aren't interested in those ideas any more." The long speeches, for instance, sometimes running to two pages, in which the troubles of the House of Atreus are minutely rationalized, might be expected to bore an audience with no interest in Atreus and his troubles. But it is doubtful if Sophocles himself cared much about the story, already dubious and dim in his day. What is certain is that he used the long speeches as frames for action, to show people full of hatred and aspirations, engaged in the perennially dramatic struggle for life. If one can show the character through the speech, trying to outwit an adversary, to encourage himself, to impress the chorus, one may hope to hold the audience through that spectacle. Thus the problem is one in the technique of acting to find the drive intended by Sophocles beneath the words. Only in that way will the author's dramaturgy be able to reveal itself.

The theatrical effectiveness of two clichés of Greek dramatic writing, the peripeteia and the recognition scene, became very clear in working on the production. The recognition scene in this play begins with Orestes' return (p. 91). It is also a peripeteia, or reversal of fortune, for the man who is first taken for the messenger confirming Orestes' death turns out to be Orestes himself, and when that is clear the main drive of the play is switched from mourning to wild rejoicing. When one reads the play there is time to be struck by the absurdity of Electra's long mourning while Orestes is standing by, and to wonder whether she could really fail to recognize him, even after ten or fifteen years. And one may fail to understand Orestes' unwillingness to make himself known, if one does not have the visible house, perhaps full of enemies, brooding over the scene. In production the theatrical intention becomes clear. For the main drive of the play ("to break through or dissolve the nightmare of the curse on the House") passes, so to speak, through the emotional extremes of this scene. The peripeteia and recognition constitute an unsurpassed mechanism for scenically presenting this drive in the whole emotional scale from success to failure. If the audience follows and sympathizes with the drive to break the nightmare, it will be more excited by the recognition scene than by anything else in the play except the murder. The whole device, traditional and artificial though it be, is justified scenically if only the acting is honest and correct.

THE STAGE: *Electra* was of course written for a particular stage, and if the intention (as in our production) is to play again Sophocles' dramatic idea, the usual modern stage, with its boxlike proscenium opening and its tradition of realistic illusion presents a difficult problem. It may be solved of course in many ways, and I wish here merely to mention what we found to be the inescapable requirements. We found that the action of the play moves both physically and emotionally between the house and the altar, and that we could not do without these traditional elements on the scene. The house must have a practicable door or curtain. There must be room for the chorus to dance; yet the stage space must be broken up in such a way as to allow the chorus to sink into the background when it is desired to focus on a passage of dialogue.

THE CHORUS: The question of what to do with the chorus is the most striking of all the questions connected with producing a Greek play. Cocteau in his versions of *Oedipus* and *Antigone* reduced the chorus to a single laconic voice from an invisible speaker, and so avoided some of the most embarrassing questions altogether. Mr. W. B. Yeats commanded the services of a choir trained in church chanting, which determined the style of delivery; and he moved the chorus very little. Academic productions of Greek plays will very often have the chorus parade, and perhaps engage in a little illustrative pantomime, but unless the performance is extremely good, such choruses are likely to slow the pace of the play unjustifiably. The operatic versions of Greek plays by Strauss, Honegger, Stravinsky and Milhaud are mines of suggestion for style and rhythmic effects, and sometimes for ways of using the voice; but since their principle is to carry the thing musically their usefulness is limited in a dramatic production.

The chorus in *Electra* is certainly a character with a stake in the struggle. Its stake is less than that of the other characters, and its role is less active. Moreover it is only a generalized or group personality, not a real being. The verse in which it speaks is closer to singing and farther from realistic speech than that of the dialogue. These considerations define the search for a convention of choral speaking: it must be close enough to ordinary speech to convey what the chorus feels about the actual situation, yet formal enough to be acceptable as the conventional voice of the group.

Similar considerations apply to the style of the choral movement. Like the speaking it must be based on the natural response to the situation on the stage, but this response is expressed not in natural movement but in dance.

What is to be the relation between the verse-speaking and the movement? The movements have no business to try to illustrate the metaphors in the verse pantomimically, and on the other hand the verse-speaking must not be allowed to degenerate into a beating of time for the dance. They should both spring from the one root dramatic conception. As for their mechanical relation, we varied it continually, sometimes moving and speaking in rhythm together, sometimes preparing emotionally for the speaking through movement; sometimes using half of the chorus as speakers while the other half danced. There are great possibilities (which will perhaps be explored as part of the new interest in poetic drama) in combining verse and dance. We found that, to be safe, one must be sure that everything expresses the main drive of the play.

MUSICAL AND SOUND EFFECTS: A Greek play calls for music of some kind, and music must have been all-important in the original productions. The sound accompaniment for this production was composed during rehearsals as an accompaniment to the acting and dancing. Various kinds of percussion instruments were used. The sound pattern was behind the entire play, dialogue as well as choruses, but often so faintly that it would hardly have been noticed except for the occasional silences. The purpose was to emphasize the rhythms of the performance, and to establish the mood of the whole play.

FRANCIS FERGUSSON.

EUMENIDES

1. The Furies

In the third play of the trilogy the fate of Orestes concerns us still, but with it is now bound up the future of humanity at large. The issue is not merely whether the matricide is to be punished or absolved, but whether mankind is to succeed in establishing a new order or to perish in the conflicts of the old.

The contending parties are Apollo and the Furies. Apollo is God of Light, and his dwelling is in Olympus. The Furies are daughters of the Night, and their dwelling is in Hades. It is therefore a struggle between Light and Darkness, Heaven and Hell. And it is more than that. Apollo is the Interpreter of Zeus (p. 111), and he claims that his testimony is incontrovertible, because it comes from Zeus (p. 130). This claim would have been readily conceded by an audience familiar with the doctrine of Delphic infallibility, and it is confirmed by Athena, who declares that Orestes has been supported by "the perfect witness of all-judging Jove" (p. 136).

What then of the Furies? If Apollo appeals to Zeus, his opponents appeal to the Fates, whose decrees they have been appointed to safe-guard (p. 123); in particular, they have been entrusted with the task of punishing those guilty of shedding kindred blood (p. 121). They contend therefore that, in opposing them, Apollo is destroying the authority of the Fates (p. 116), and they recall his conduct on another occasion, when he tried to cheat the Fates of a life which was their due. Thus, behind the feud between Apollo and the Furies there lies a deeper discord. Zeus and the Fates are at variance. At the end of the trilogy they will be reconciled.

In order to understand the issue between these rival divinities we must consider briefly the functions traditionally ascribed to the Furies: namely, the execution of the decrees of the Fates; the punishment of homicide between kinsmen, of perjury, sacrilege, unfilial conduct, and of violation of the rights of hospitality.

At the end of the *Choephoroe* the Furies were introduced to us as female monsters clothed in snakes. There can be little doubt that this conception was primitive. Indeed, it has been suggested with some probability that in origin the Furies were nothing but snakes[1]—ghosts of the tribal ancestors. As such, their function would have been to protect the taboos defining tribal custom; and if, as there is reason to believe, the divisions of labour which gave rise to these taboos lie at the root of the Greek conception of the Fates (Μοῖραι), then it would appear that this aspect of the Furies has survived, in a generalised form, in the first of the functions enumerated above. The sex of the Furies, as of the Fates, points to matrilineal descent.

Primitive society makes no provision for homicide within the group of kinsmen; and such offences are extremely rare. So long as the *gens* is based on collective ownership, the main cause of crime is absent. In the so-called heroic ages, however, they become common. Having burst the bonds of tribal custom, the ruling families embroil themselves in internecine struggles of inheritance and succession.[2] It was probably during this period that the association of the Furies with homicide acquired the special prominence which we find in the historical tradition.

The man who killed a kinsman was expelled from the community,

---

[1] J. E. Harrison *Prolegomena* p. 213-39. The belief that the dead assume the form of animals is of course fundamental in totemic religion; and the belief that they become snakes, which is found in various parts of the world (J. G. Frazer *Adonis* i. p. 82, R. Karsten *South American Indians* p. 289), is represented in Greek tradition by the fate of Cadmus and Harmonia (Apollod. iii. 5. 4): Farnell *Cults* i. p. 300 note c. The identification of ἐρινύς with the Sanskrit *saranyu* has little to commend it. Pausanias connected it with the Arcadian ἐρινύειν "to be angry" (viii. 25. 6).

[2] H. M. Chadwick *Heroic Age* p. 344-48, 359-61.

pursued by the curses of his kinsfolk, or, as they expressed it, by the avenging spirit of his victim. The curse and the avenging spirit were identical. That is why the Furies are "called Curses in the palaces of hell" (p. 124). In this capacity they persecute Orestes for the murder of his mother, just as they persecuted Alcmaeon for the murder of Eriphyle; and in the same way they were invoked by Althaea against her son for the murder of her brother.[3] These instances point to matrilineal descent, and in the *Eumenides* we are expressly told that the Furies did not persecute Clytemnestra for the murder of Agamemnon, because in that case offender and victim were not "of the same blood" (p. 129).

The issue between the Furies and Apollo is therefore this. The Furies stand for the tribal order of society, in which kinship, traced through the mother, is a closer bond than marriage. Apollo, on the other hand, whom the Athenians worshipped as "paternal" (πατρῷος), proclaims the sanctity of marriage and the precedence of the male. And the issue turns on the fate of Orestes. The dilemma in which he has been placed reflects the struggle of divided loyalties which must have been a feature of the time when descent was being shifted, for the sake of the accompanying inheritance, from the mother's to the father's side; and his acquittal will mark the inauguration of the new order which is to culminate in Athenian democracy.

With the dissolution of tribal society the conception of the Furies underwent a further transformation. They were invoked to punish offences created by new conditions—the development of law and of state-religion, the restriction of kinship obligations to the private family, and the beginnings of trade. At the same time, as man extended his control over nature, they ceased to roam the earth and receded into the other world.[4] Their anger was manifested indirectly by means of pestilence and famine.

These changes were eventually formulated in mystical religion as the three Unwritten Laws: Honour the Gods (a warning against perjury and sacrilege); Honour thy father and thy mother; Honour the stranger (the

---

[3] Apollod. iii, 7. 5, i. 8. 3, cf. *Il.* ix. 565-72. In the story of Oedipus, as treated by Aeschylus and Sophocles, the ἐρινύς is regarded as the embodiment of the curse inherited from Laius in the male line (Aesch. *Theb.* 710-12, 751, 770-1, 776, Soph. *O.C.* 1434, cf. Hdt. iv. 149); but according to Homer the Fury which afflicted Oedipus was his mother's (*Od.* xi. 279-80). See J. Bachofen *Mutterrecht* p. 35.

[4] The epic tradition hesitates between the punishment of perjury in this life (Hes. *Op.* 802-4) and in the life to come (*Il.* xix. 259-60); Solon says that the sinner is

rights of hospitality). These laws are described as of unknown authorship or made in heaven, as overriding the laws of man and protected by penalties exacted by the Gods themselves—that is, the Furies. These are the laws which Antigonê invoked and Oedipus doubly transgressed. In the Platonic Hades offenders of these three classes are consigned to eternal torment, and in the *Frogs* of Aristophanes we see them lying in the infernal mire.

In the *Eumenides*, these two conceptions of the Furies, derived from successive stages in their development, are dramatically combined. Orestes is to be hunted in this life and tormented in the next:

> Alive and wasted, I shall drag thee down
> To pay the full price of that terrible act of blood;
> And others shalt thou see in hell who did
> Evil to strangers, Gods,
> Or unto those dearest that gave them life,
> Each well requited with his just reward.
> For Hades is a stern inquisitor
> Of mankind below.
> All things are written down in that watchful heart.

In later literature we see the Furies standing beside the infernal judgment-seat waiting to carry off the sinner as soon as he has been condemned.[5] That is the fearful vision which lies behind the trial of Orestes at the Areopagus, where we see them standing in similar expectancy beside Athena's earthly judgment-seat.[6]

2. Prologue (p. 111), Parodos (p. 115) and First Episode (p. 116)

The scene is laid before the temple of Apollo at Delphi. According to the common tradition, the shrine had once belonged to the nether powers, from whom Apollo seized it by violence.[7] Here his priestess gives a different version. He received it as a birthday gift. By choosing the more gracious alternative Aeschylus prepares us for the reconciliation which is to come.

Having finished her prayers, the Priestess enters the temple, and

punished in his own person immediately or else his sin is visited on his children (1. 29-32); and according to the Orphic doctrine explained on *Cho.* 59-63 he is punished either in this life or the life to come.

[5] Lucian. i. 471, 644.

[6] This point has been developed by M. Tierney in *J.H.S.* lvii. p. 11-21. As he well says, all through the *Eumenides* there runs a "majestic comparison between the institutions of Athens and the eternal economy of the kosmos."

[7] See Frazer on Apollod. i. 4. 1.

immediately afterwards we hear a cry of horror. Though its meaning is as yet unknown to us, it falls on the ear like a note of destiny, startling and yet familiar. The three prologues of the trilogy have been designed according to a common plan.

Half-paralysed with terror, the Priestess returns and describes what she has seen. Then the interior of the temple is revealed: Orestes clinging to the sanctuary, the Furies asleep upon the thrones, and standing over them the commanding figure of Apollo.

On the west pediment of the temple of Zeus at Olympia is portrayed the battle of the Centaurs with the Lapithae. "It is a scene of wild riot and rapine. . . . And amidst all the heat and dust of that mad grapple of writhing bodies and clutching hands . . . with one arm stretched above the tumult stands Apollo, with the splendour of his immortal body, the calm of the Gods that know no mortal pain."[8] This pediment dates from very near the time when the Oresteia was first performed, and the spirit that animated the two artists is the same. Gazing at the statue at Olympia, we recover something of what contemporary Athenians must have felt at this spectacle of Apollo and the Furies, who to many of them were no doubt as real and terrifying as the demons of medieval Christianity:

> For evil born, even as the darkness where
> They dwell is evil.

Yet they are not wholly evil. Before the end of the trilogy they are destined to undergo a wonderful conversion.

Apollo assures his suppliant that he will keep faith with him and commands him to go to Athens. Escorted by Hermes, the pilgrim sets out upon his journey. Apollo remains, a silent witness to what follows.

The ghost of the murdered queen appears. She picks her steps among the prostrate Furies, recalling them with bitter reproaches to their forgotten purpose:

> I, Clytemnestra, call you now in dreams!

This is the woman who dreamt of victory at the fall of Troy and of retribution at the coming of Orestes; now, as her avenging spirits dream of her, they wake with whimpering cries and creep into the sunlight, only to find that their quarry has escaped. Then they catch sight of Apollo, and point accusing fingers at the thief.

In a speech of violent denunciation he commands them to depart. His attitude is natural, but too passionate to be final; and in contrast

[8] F. L. and P. Lucas *From Olympus to Styx* p. 313.

their own is impressive by its restraint: they do not denounce, they reason with him. And their reasoning is consistent. They are persecuting Orestes in virtue of the powers assigned to them; they did not persecute Clytemnestra because the blood she shed was not a kinsman's; and they have no concern with the sanctity of wedlock. Apollo's reply, on the other hand, is not consistent, being an attempt at compromise between two incompatible principles. He uses the law of retribution to condemn Clytemnestra, the law of purification to protect Orestes: but, if Clytemnestra forfeited her life by murdering Agamemnon, then by murdering her Orestes has forfeited his own. Apollo's attitude represents a period of transition. He has challenged the old order, but it is not for him to devise the new.

3. First Episode (p. 119) and First Stasimon (p. 120)

The scene changes, and we find ourselves at a shrine of Athena in the city of Athens. During the interval Orestes has travelled far and wide, and now, having served his term of exile, he claims that his penance is complete and seeks refuge with the goddess who is to decide his fate.

The Furies are still hot upon his trail. They gather round him and begin to dance and weave their magic spell:

> Hymn of hell to harp untuned,
> Chant to bind the soul in chains,
> Spell to parch the flesh to dust.

We remember the vision of Cassandra:

> *On yonder housetop ever abides a choir
> Of minstrels unmelodious, singing of ill;
> And deeply-drunk, to fortify their spirit,
> In human blood, those revellers yet abide,
> Whom none can banish, Furies congenital.

And the premonition of the Argive elders:

> Still I hear a strain of stringless music,
> Dissonant dirge of the Furies, a chant uninstructed
> Quired in this uneasy breast.

And the Watchman's cry:

> Hail, lamp of joy, whose gleam turns night to day,
> Hail, radiant sign of dances numberless
> In Argos for our happy state!

* This and the following two quotations from the *Agamemnon* are from the translation by George Thomson. (*The Oresteia of Aeschylus*, Cambridge University Press, 1938.)

Apart from the refrains, which form the magical element in the chant, the Furies expound once more the authority on which their powers rest. The decrees of everlasting Fate enjoined upon them when they first came into being the task of exacting vengeance from those who have shed the blood of kith and kin, and they conclude:

> What mortal then boweth not
> In fear and dread, while he hears
> The ordinance which Fate made ours, the gift of heaven too,
> A perfect power and privilege
> Of ancient ages? We
> Are not unhonoured, tho' deep in the earth the clime
> Set for us, sunk in sunless, everlasting gloom.

Orestes is prostrate with terror and fatigue, like a hare that cowers motionless while the hounds close in for the kill.

Athena, the daughter whom Zeus loved best, born of the father who begot her, was greater than Apollo. To the poets and sculptors of Periclean Athens she was the divine embodiment of their ideal, the pattern of all those qualities by which they strove to make their city glorious—bravery on the field of battle, skill in the arts of peace, and above all that wisdom, that gracious restraint (σωφροσύνη) by which passion is curbed, grief tempered, and joy made more profound. In sculpture this conception found its highest expression in the statue of Pheidias in gold and ivory, presenting her, as Aeschylus presents her now, fully armed with helmet, spear and aegis. Yet, for all her majesty, there was no remoteness in her character. The Athena at Frankfurt, also from Athens, has the grave, meditative beauty of a girl; and the mourning Athena on the tombstone of that name has the mysterious tenderness of an Italian Madonna. For Athena too was a mediator, and inspired among her worshippers a sense of almost personal intimacy such as still enters into the adoration of that other Virgin who eventually took her place on the Acropolis.

In Homer, it was she who checked Achilles when he drew his sword on Agamemnon, and who brought peace to Ithaca; in Sophocles, it was she, through her servant Odysseus, who brought the strife over the body of Ajax to an end. She represents that gift of clear, persuasive reason, which, in the view of the Athenians, is the vital condition of human civilisation. As Isocrates said: "It is by the power of persuading one another that we have emancipated ourselves from the life of the beasts, founded cities, laid down laws and discovered arts."[9] And again: "Finding the Greeks living without laws and dwelling in scattered communities, some oppressed by tyrannies, others perishing in anarchy, the city of Athena delivered them from these evils, either by taking them under her protection or by offering herself as an example; for she was the first to lay down laws and establish a polity. That is clear from the fact that those who preferred the earliest charges of homicide, desiring to compose their differences by reason instead of violence, tried their cases according to Athenian law."[10] It is in this spirit that Athena now addresses herself to the task of putting an end to barbarism on earth.

In the view of the Pythagoreans, the constitution of the universe rests on the supremacy of Mind over Necessity, effected by Persuasion. Translated into the language of mythology, these three principles are the Mind of Zeus, the Fates, and Athena. Accordingly, it is Athena who will now, without violence, impose on the agents of the Fates her Father's will.

She confronts them with serene and majestical reserve—very different from the passionate indignation of Apollo. She listens to their statement with courteous deference; only when they venture to argue their case does she adopt a sterner tone. The Furies accept the rebuke, and offer to submit to her decision. With the same impartiality she then turns to Orestes, who declares that he has sought her sanctuary as one already purified, and he too beseeches her to judge.

By consent of both parties the decision rests with her. She immediately declines it. The issue is too grave for mortal judgment, too fraught with passion for her own. The suppliant has a claim on her protection; yet, if his pursuers are frustrated, they will vent their displeasure on her chosen people:

> But be it so; since it is come to this,
> Judges I will appoint for homicide,
> A court set up in perpetuity.
> Meanwhile do you call proofs and witnesses
> As sworn supports of justice; then, having chosen
> The best of all my people, I shall come
> To pass true judgment on the present cause.

In these words she forecasts the institution of the Court of the Areopagus, which is to be the symbol of the new order; and of that order one feature

---

[9] xv. 254 ἐγγενομένου δ' ἡμῖν τοῦ πείθειν ἀλλήλους . . . οὐ μόνον τοῦ θηριωδῶς ζῆν ἀπηλλάγημεν ἀλλὰ καὶ συνελθόντες πόλεας ᾠκίσαμεν καὶ νόμους ἐθέμεθα καὶ τέχνας εὕρομεν.
[10] iv. 39-40, cf. Aelian. V.H. iii. 38.

is already clear. Hitherto the homicide has been punished summarily according to the penalties prescribed by divine sanction; henceforward he is to be tried before a jury of his fellow-men.

The task of these judges will of course be to try the case of Orestes; but Athena seems to have suggested that she hopes to find in them a means of solving the divine dispute as well—that the foundation of the new Court will have the *effect* of conciliating the Furies. We look to the sequel to see how this can be.

4. Second Stasimon (p. 126) and Second Episode (p. 127)

The origin of the Council of the Areopagus and the circumstances of the trial of Orestes were the subject of a mass of diverse traditions, as was natural in an ancient legend which concerned the history of separate communities.[11] From these variants Aeschylus has selected those which best serve his purpose. The Court was founded by Athena for the express purpose of trying Orestes, his accusers were the Furies and his judges a chosen committee of the Athenian people.

In other respects he found in the tradition an instrument ready to his hands. The Athenians claimed that their city was the first to establish laws; that of their laws those relating to homicide were the oldest and best; and that of all their legal institutions the Court of the Areopagus was the most venerable, distinctive and august. It was the "overseer of all things and guardian of the laws"; it had in its keeping "the secret depositions wherein lay the salvation of the city"; it was charged to uphold sobriety and good conduct; it kept watch upon the life of every man, with authority to pass judgment on the body and soul of each of the citizens, on the principle that good government depends not on a multiplicity of edicts but on the maintenance of justice within the hearts of men; it was grave, severe and incorruptible; and so far were evildoers from eluding its vigilance that even those intending to commit a crime were discovered before the act. The conservatives of a later generation counted it as one of the superior virtues of their fathers that they had

[11] Apollod. iii. 14. 1-2, *Marmor Parium* 40 sq., Hygin. *Fab.* 119, *Et.M. s.v.* αἰώρα, Paus. viii. 34. 4. The diversity of Greek tradition was a result of the political autonomy of the Greek city-states. The persistence side by side of alternative versions of the same events provided copious material for discrimination and analysis. Hence the general veracity of the Greek historical tradition as compared with the Roman, which was distorted from the outset by overriding imperial interests.

been slow to tamper with their ancestral traditions, deterred by their respect for the Council of the Areopagus.[12]

Such were the ideas traditionally associated with the Court which we are now to see established; and as such they would already have been called to mind by a contemporary audience. Let us too keep them in mind during the following stasimon.

The Furies predict that, if the matricide is acquitted, the result will be the overthrow of justice and good order. If the judgment goes against them, they will withdraw their influence. No longer will the sinner be visited with the wrath of these "watchers over men" (p. 126), no longer will there be any check on violence such as has been supplied by the fear which they inspire:

> Times there be when fear is well;
> Yea, it must continually
> Watch within the soul enthroned.
> Needful too straits to teach humility.
> Who of those that never nursed
> Healthy dread within the heart,
> Be they men or peoples, shall
> Show to Justice reverence?

Yet, in opposing anarchy, they are not pleading for despotism, but for the mean between the two:

> Choose a life despot-free,
> Yet restrained by rule of law. Thus and thus
> God doth administer, yet he appointeth the mean as the master in all things.

The Furies here profess that very attitude of vigilant severity which, as we have just seen, was associated with the Court of the Areopagus; and in pleading for the mean they take their stand on the fundamental principle of Athenian democracy. Can it be that Athena is designing her new court in order to satisfy their claims? Let us listen to her direction to the judges before they record their votes:

> People of Athens, hear my ordinance
> At this first trial for bloodshed. Evermore
> This great tribunal shall abide in power
> Among the sons of Aegeus. . . .
> > Here Reverence
> And inbred Fear enthroned among my people
> Shall hold their hands from evil night and day,
> Only let them not tamper with their laws. . . .

[12] Isocr. vii. 30.

I bid my people honour and uphold
The mean between the despot and the slave,
And not to banish terror utterly,
For what man shall be upright without fear?
And if you honour this high ordinance,
Then shall you have for land and commonweal
A stronghold of salvation. . . .
                                    I establish
This great tribunal to protect my people,
Grave, quick to anger, incorruptible,
And ever vigilant over those that sleep.

Not only has Athena expounded the character of the Court in accordance with the familiar tradition, but she has shown that it is exactly designed to allay the fears which the Furies have expressed. Their aims are identical with hers, and, so far from being in jeopardy, are safe for ever. Is it the intention of Athena to ask the Furies to vest their ancient powers in the new Court? As we begin to discern the poet's ulterior purpose, a new prospect opens before us, leading to the conclusion of the trilogy. But for the present we are preoccupied with the trial of Orestes.

Athena has returned, accompanied by her chosen judges, probably ten or twelve in number, who are followed by the citizens of Athens, eager to witness the first trial for homicide in the history of man; and presently Apollo appears to give evidence for the accused.

The procedure of the trial corresponds in its main features with the established procedure of historical times. We know that one of the court officials was a herald; that the judges listened to the pleas in silence; that the prosecutor spoke first, followed by the defendant; and that the Court was notoriously strict in ruling out of order appeals to irrelevant considerations, such as that of Apollo which prompts Athena to close the hearing.

The Furies begin by addressing to Orestes three questions, which again are probably designed with reference to the actual procedure of the Court. They ask whether he did what he is accused of doing, how and why.[13] This means that Athena's judges are going to consider, not

13 For the first question cf. Lys. x. 11 ὁ μὲν γὰρ διώκων ὡς ἔκτεινε διόμνυται, ὁ δὲ φεύγων ὡς οὐκ ἔκτεινεν, Plat. Euthyphro 4b εἴτε ἐν δίκῃ ἔκτεινεν ὁ κτείνας εἴτε μή. The archaic use of the simple verb in these passages shows that the formula was traditional. The τρία παλαίσματα of 592 are the three questions of which this is the first; and the reason for the assumption that two more questions are to follow seems to be that the second and third are also modelled on the actual procedure of the court.

merely the act itself, but the circumstances and the motive. That is the second feature of the new order. The fixed and absolute standards of primitive morality have been superseded by the more flexible instrument of human reason.

The examination advances rapidly to the point where the controversy was abandoned earlier in the play. Then, after a false step which will be retrieved later by Apollo, Orestes turns to his protector, beseeching him to pronounce whether his act was *just*. Apollo comes forward for his second encounter with the Furies and declares in bold and ringing tones that it was *just*.

He soon finds, however, that to defend this plea against the sharp wits of the Furies is not an easy matter. His first attempt, an appeal to the authority of Zeus, is abortive. Appeals to authority are useless when there is a conflict of authority. And so we are brought back to the dilemma with which the controversy began: Orestes has avenged his father by dishonouring his mother.

Apollo makes a second attempt. He contends that, since the murder of Agamemnon was a crime, the execution of the murderess was not. He seeks to discriminate between two acts similar in effect but different in motive: it is a plea of justifiable homicide. To this argument the Furies reply with the caustic comment that such a plea comes ill from the spokesman of the God who bound in chains his own father Kronos. Apollo indignantly retorts that chains can be loosed, whereas blood once shed is irrecoverable. But this, as the Furies are quick to point out, is the very crime of which Orestes is guilty.

By this time it is plain that no progress can be made until a solution has been found for the dilemma with which we have been confronted from the outset: to which parent does the son owe the prior duty? The Furies champion the mother; Apollo, on the other hand, who has already urged that the tie between mother and son is no more sacred than the ties between husband and wife, now declares that the son is more closely related to the father than to the mother.

This argument is not an improvisation; it is the Pythagorean doctrine of paternity. In this issue, now at last clearly stated, lies the crux of the whole matter.

Why then does Athena give her casting vote to Orestes? Because she grants precedence to the male, being herself "verily of the father." The reason could not have been more plainly stated, and it touches the crucial point at issue. On the question of paternity she endorses the attitude of Apollo, and so lays down the principle of the Attic law of inheritance. And not only is the plain interpretation of her words demanded by the nature of the issue, but it brings the trial to its full and proper conclusion. Some critics have been puzzled by a decision so out of keeping with modern ideas of the administration of the law; but, at the time when this crime was committed, there were no laws. What Athena has had to interpret are not laws but divine sanctions, diverse and incompatible; and her decision constitutes a ruling on the very point at which they were in conflict. So much for the past, but for the future all is changed. Such a case as this can never arise again, because henceforward the homicide will be tried before a court of justice. The reign of law has begun. As we followed the fortunes of Orestes, we were in effect watching the growth of law through successive stages of social evolution. Regarded originally as a tort, to be redressed by the kinsmen of the victim, and later as a pollution, to be expiated by the prescriptions of the aristocratic priesthood, the offence of homicide is now a crime to be submitted to the judgment of a legally appointed committee of the Athenian people. The conflict between tribal custom and aristocratic privilege has been resolved in democracy. So too the principle of male precedence, now formally ratified as the basis of democracy, is accompanied by the declaration that the wealth of the community is now equitably distributed. In the dispute between the Furies and Apollo over the fate of Orestes, and in the feud between Zeus and the Fates, who are now to be reconciled by Athena, we see as it were mirrored in heaven the terrestrial process that began with the primitive tribe and ended with the emergence of a state in which the common people had recovered in a new form the equality denied to them during the rule of the aristocracy.

5. Kommos (p. 135), Third Stasimon (p. 139) and Exodos

That Athena's decision is acceptable to Apollo goes without saying, but what of the Furies? The nature of the settlement proposed by Athena has already been indicated, but we have still to see how she will work it out.

Hitherto, as we have seen, the homicide has been punished in accordance with divine sanctions, but henceforward he is to be tried by a court of human judges. The control of public justice has been secularised. But, though these judges may be trusted to give true judgment on the pleas, there is still a danger that the facts of the case may be misrepresented to them. Here then is the proper place for appeals to divine sanction. At the Areopagus both prosecutor and defendant bound themselves to tell the truth by an oath in which, as the penalty of perjury, they called down destruction on themselves, their houses and their families, and this oath was taken in the name of the Awful Goddesses (Σεμναὶ Θεαί), who were worshipped in a cave on the slopes of the Aregopagus as the presiding deities of the Court.

At this point Aeschylus crowns our expectations with a surprise.[14] Under the influence of Athena the Furies actually become these Awful Goddesses, and in their new guise they will still be required in case of need to visit the perjurer with the penalties which have been theirs to inflict since the beginning of the world.

Athena's solution is in harmony with her character. The case of Orestes, which she declared to be too grave for mortals, and too passionate for her, to decide, has now been decided by a court of mortal judges with her assistance; and by placing the new Court under the supervision of the Furies the old order and the new are harmoniously blended and reconciled.

At first the Furies are blinded by pride and passion to the advantages of Athena's offer. But Athena is unrivalled in her power of persuasion:

> Let me persuade you from this passionate grief.
> You are not vanquished; the issue of the trial
> Has been determined by an equal vote.

Unmoved, the Furies repeat their maledictions. Still serene, Athena repeats her invitation:

> Calm the black humours of embittered rage,
> Reside with me, and share my majesty.

Menaces give place to impotent despair, and Athena speaks again:

> Nay, if Persuasion's holy majesty . . .
> Is aught to thee, why then, reside with me. . . .
> Since it is in thy power to own the soil
> Justly attended with the highest honours.

This is the spirit which tempted Agamemnon to commit the crime we

[14] There is no evidence of the identification before this date, but there may have been Orphics or Pythagoreans before Aeschylus who observed the affinity between the Ἐρινύες, the Σεμναί of Athens, and the Εὐμενίδες of Argos: see J. E. Harrison *Prolegomena* p. 253-6.

have seen visited on him and on his children; which tempted Paris to plunge the world in war; which was embodied in Helen and again in Clytemnestra, and was summoned to the support of Orestes when he plotted to kill his mother. Now the same spirit, embodied in Athena, brings the sufferings of three generations to an end:

> To the eye of Persuasion I give all praise,
> That with favour she looked on the breath of my lips
> As I strove to appease these powers that once
> Were averted in anger; but Zeus who is Lord
> Of the eloquent word hath prevailed, and at last
> In contention for blessings we conquer.

Versed from time immemorial only in the language of malediction, the Furies are at first at a loss for words to express their change of heart, and so these 'singers of ill' are taught a new song:

> A song of faultless victory: from earth and sea,
> From skies above may gentle breezes blow,
> And, breathing sunshine, float from shore to shore.

Quick to learn, the converts call down a shower of blessings on the people whom they have threatened to destroy. They pray that the people of Attica may be blessed by sun and earth, in allusion to the present reconciliation between the upper and nether powers; that the spring blossoms may be protected from the storms (p. 140), in allusion to the "Spirits who hush the winds" (Εὐδάνεμοι), worshipped on the slopes of the Acropolis, that flocks and herds may multiply by the grace of Pan, whose shrine may still be seen on the same hillside; that the precious metals of the earth, guarded by Plutus, God of subterranean wealth, may be brought to light by Hermes, God of treasure-trove, in allusion to the silver mines of Laurium and to the three deities worshipped with the Awful Goddesses in their sanctuary on the Areopagus, that husband and home may be found for each of the daughters of Athens, and that her sons, free from the curse of civil strife, may be brought up in unity and goodwill.

Their curses have melted into blessings; Athena has prevailed. But having prevailed, she introduces a note of warning, reminding her people that these divinities are still to be feared by the perjurer:

> He is led unto these to be judged, and the still
> Stroke of perdition
> In the dust shall stifle his proud boast.

When the Furies threatened, Athena sought to assuage; now, when the Furies bless, Athena warns. It is like a duet in which, after the bass has taken up the theme of the treble, the treble imitates the bass; and by this last austerity the joy of the conclusion is made the more profound.

Among the population of Attica, besides the native citizens, who alone enjoyed full civic rights, there was a class of resident aliens (μέτοικοι), whom it was the policy of the state to encourage, because the foreign trade of the country was largely in their hands. As foreigners, they were excluded from the ordinary ceremonies of the state religion, and were sometimes regarded by the full citizens with disfavour. In order to maintain mutual goodwill, once a year, at the national festival of the Panathenaea, the resident aliens were not only permitted to take part but were accorded special marks of honour. The climax of the festival came on the night of the anniversary of Athena's birth, when a robe of saffron, woven by the women of the city, was carried to the Acropolis in a torch-light procession, led by a band of young men chosen for the occasion and attended with cries of alleluia by all the citizens, men and women, old and young, and there hung on the statue of Athena Polias. In this procession, to mark the purpose of the festival, which was to proclaim peace and goodwill to all who dwelt under the protection of the goddess, the resident aliens were clothed in robes of crimson and attended by a special escort.

An outstanding feature of the genius of Aeschylus, and the secret of his constructive power, is his unique gift of conceiving and working out a parallel, thus heightening the significance of his dramatic moments. One of the main purposes of this introduction has been to expound and illustrate this quality; but what is perhaps its most splendid manifestation, and, after the parallel with the Eleusinian Mysteries, the most profound, is reserved for the concluding scene.

The Furies have consented to become co-residents with Athena, partakers and joint owners of the country; and accordingly they now assume the title of *resident aliens*, accepting the goodwill of the citizens and offering their own.

The dominant mood of the Panathenaic festival was rejoicing—not the wild transport of the Bacchant, but deep, restrained, almost solemn joy, the prize of grief and suffering. Accordingly the Furies sing:

> Joy to you, joy of your justly appointed riches,
> Joy to all the people, blest

> With the Virgin's love, who sits
> Next beside her Father's throne.
> Wisdom ye have learned at last.
> Folded under Pallas' wing,
> Yours at last the grace of Zeus.

At this point a company of women enters the orchestra, carrying lighted torches and crimson robes. Meanwhile Athena returns the greeting:

> Joy to you likewise! Walking before you,
> To the chambers appointed I show you the way,
> Led by the sacred lights of the escort.
> Come with me, come, and let solemn oblations
> Speed you in joy to your homes in the earth.

The Furies repeat their greeting, and again Athena thanks them:

> I thank you for these words of benison,
> And now with flames of torchlit splendour bright
> Escort you to your subterranean home,
> Attended by the wardens of my shrine,
> And justly so; for meet it is that all
> The eye of Theseus' people should come forth,
> This noble company of maidens fair,
> And women wed and venerable in years.
> Adorn them well in robes of crimson dye,
> And let these blazing torches lead the way,
> So that the goodwill of these residents
> Be proved in manly prowess of your sons.

At this point a band of young men, the flower of Athenian manhood, take their place at the head of the procession. The Furies put on their new robes; and in the light of the torches black gives place to crimson. This blaze of light and this feast of colour are both fitting symbols to mark the close of a spectacle in which again and again lights have been lit only to be quenched in deeper darkness and in which we have twice gazed in horror upon displays of bloodstained purple.

The procession begins to move away, and the women of the escort invite the Furies to accompany them:

> Gracious and kindly of heart to our people,
> Hither, O holy ones, hither in gladness,
> Follow the lamps that illumine the way.
> O sing at the end Alleluia!

This alleluia, first raised by Clytemnestra in answer to the Watchman, heard by Cassandra from the Furies on the housetop, raised again by Clytemnestra over her husband's dead body and by the friends of Orestes over her own—now, as it is heard for the last time, it signifies that the spirit of man has passed out of suffering into true and lasting joy; and in the closing words of the trilogy we are reminded of the new harmony in heaven in virtue of which these changes on earth have been effected:

> Peace to you, peace of a happy communion,
> People of Pallas. Zeus who beholdeth
> All with the Fates is at last reconciled.
> O sing at the end Alleluia!

By his introduction of the Panathenaic procession the poet has brought his story out of the darkness of remote antiquity into the brilliant light of the Athens of his day. It is as though at the end of the trilogy he invited his audience to rise from their seats and carry on the drama from the point where he has left it.

GEORGE THOMSON.

HIPPOLYTUS

It is a commonplace to say that any great play admits of many analyses, that by reason of its greatness it has a many-sided interpretation. Some of these analyses may represent more accurately the intention of the artist, and some more perceptively the aspects of the work which are of predominant importance at the time when it appears. Only a moderate certainty can be attained as to the artist's original purpose, but whatever certainty there is comes from the attempt to explain the play in the light of its internal structure. We must at all costs avoid an interpretation based on what we believe the artist should have wanted to express. It is with this in mind that I put forward an interpretation of the *Hippolytus* widely at variance with the traditional view in the never extensive criticism to which the play·has been subjected in the last sixty years.

This traditional criticism exhibits two main lines of agreement: (1) That the play is a symbolic conflict of two ideals, an austere chastity and the natural desires of the flesh. According to these critics, the manner in which the play is framed by the two goddesses, Aphrodite and Artemis, is significant. (2) That Hippolytus is the central figure. Phaedra, we are told, is merely the foil to Hippolytus—the means used to serve Aphrodite's vengeance. I believe it is possible to show that, first of all, the critics have misinterpreted the symbolism: it is a conflict, but not such a one as they envisaged; and, second, this conflict centers around Phaedra, not Hippolytus, and the rôle of the latter is secondary.

There is one slightly different point of view on the subject matter significant enough to merit notice. This agrees with tradition already mentioned in regarding the play as a symbolic conflict between chastity and desire but believes that for a Greek the character of Hippolytus would be nothing in itself admirable and stresses that the Greeks, being a healthy and "natural" folk, would readily conceive that Hippolytus was aiming at a degree of inhuman virtue which was in fact a sin. It was a blasphemy against the nature of man. Hippolytus is an offender against the principle of "nothing too much." Now it is true that Hippolytus does hold to the spiritual chastity of the ascetic. It is true that he is insolent both in his presumption in refusing to participate in the worship of Aphrodite and in his treatment of the old servant who gives him the advice of common sense. But it is equally true that his punishment does not arise from any action of his within the play's scope which can be regarded as typical of his ascetic regimen. A man may be quite normally unchaste and refuse to go to bed with his father's wife.

There is a strong analogy between this story and that of Bellerophon, and both in turn are comparable to the Joseph tale in the Old Testament. In all three cases chastity, however desirable in itself, is reinforced by another sanction. In the *Stheneboia* this sanction is the sacred duty of hospitality. The guest must not corrupt the wife of the man who has fed him and given him shelter. In the Joseph story the servant must not corrupt the wife of the master who has been kind to him. But the chastity of Hippolytus is tried in circumstances where sin is double sin of the most obnoxious kind. In the first place, yielding will involve a shameful breach of loyalty to his father, and that aspect of the offense is already enough to take it out of the category of venial slips which some believe to have been the hallmark of "humanism" among the Greeks. But, in addition, there is the unsavory nature of the relation to his father's wife. We have only to recall the case of Phoenix in the *Iliad* (ix 448), who was smitten with the curse of sterility for the much less heinous offense of violating his father's concubine. There were the most extenuating circumstances—he sinned at the request of his mother, in order to break Amyntor's attachment to the woman; but, nonetheless, his father called the Furies against him, and he was driven forth, condemned henceforth to childlessness. That the Furies are called on is highly significant. They are summoned as "upholders of the moral order and avengers of sins against the family" (Leaf). It is hardly hypercritical to suppose that the feeling which prompted Amyntor to curse his son was not only the wrath of outraged parenthood. Gen. 35:22 and 49:4 and the story of Absalom, who went in unto David's concubines in the sight of all Israel and thereby made these unhappy ladies to be regarded as permanently unclean, are other examples of the feeling awakened by this particular relation in the most various communities. Only fifteen years ago, in Eugene O'Neill's *Desire under the Elms*, we find the same theme treated again, and again there is the undertone of suppressed horror throughout the play.

Listen to what the Chorus (p. 258) says when they first hear of Phaedra's love. We notice the force of the adjective "unheard of" and the allusion to Phaedra's Cretan parentage. There is further proof if we look at the scene between the Nurse and Phaedra, where the latter is trying to express her unspeakable love. We find her making various indirect approaches to the subject: on page 257 she speaks of the tragic loves of the tragic Cretan household, beginning with Pasiphaë's unnatural passion for the bull.

All this is designed to lead the Nurse on to a correct guess at the frightfulness of the disclosure Phaedra is about to make concerning her own life. However, the Nurse is intentionally or unintentionally obtuse, and Phaedra tries another tack (p. 257).

PHAEDRA   What is this thing, this love, of which they speak?

NURSE   Sweetest and bitterest, both things in one, at once.

PHAEDRA   One of the two, the bitterness, I've known.

NURSE   Are you in love, child? And who is he?

PHAEDRA   There is a man, ... his mother was an Amazon. . . . .

NURSE   You mean *Hippolytus*?

PHAEDRA   You have spoken it, not I.

It is extremely important that there are no signs of any excessive horror on the part of the Nurse until Hippolytus' name is actually mentioned. Probably she is not exactly unused to affairs of this kind. What ultimately produces the outburst on page 258 is the appalling nature of the liaison. And, when the Nurse curses the daylight and the sun, we can be sure that this will be the reaction of almost any right-minded member

of the audience, if apprised of a similar monstrosity. Let us note Theseus'
reactions when he learns of the crime which he believes has been committed.

> p. 277 Hippolytus has dared to rape my wife.
> He has dishonoured God's holy sunlight.
> p. 279 Come, you could stain your conscience with the impurity.
> Show me your face, show it to me, your father.

Had Euripides wished to give us in Hippolytus a symbolic figure
whose efforts to achieve a superhuman virtue resulted in tragic disaster, it
would have been easy to shape another play like the *Bacchae* with ap-
plication to the sexual theme. Pentheus represents the cause of human
reason struggling against primitive mysticism. He is one of the tragic
fools of the world pitted hopelessly against the emotional forces which
lie in the hinterland of man's nature, a man who believes that the world
is run rationally as Euripides insists that it is not. But the essence of the
difference of the two ideals crystallizes in the conflict. If Pentheus had
permitted the establishment of the Dionysiac dances in Thebes and if he
had permitted his father and the seer to attend them without let or
hindrance, then there would have been no tragedy of Pentheus.
Pentheus possesses qualities of fair-mindedness and justice which his
opponent Dionysus signally lacks, but this is Euripides presenting the case
with the objectivity of a great artist. The fact remains that Pentheus'
tragedy is the direct result of his character exhibited in a typical aspect
by the play's action. Now let us look at Hippolytus. If the last view
mentioned above is right, we have to believe that the audience was bound
to survey Hippolytus' position with the feeling, "That is precisely the
attitude a wrong-headed fanatic like Hippolytus would assume." We
must believe that the audience would consider an alternative open to
him. Can we possibly imagine that any Greek would consider it a reasonable or natural action to consent to such a proposal as Phaedra makes to
Hippolytus?

Well, then, we say that he is doomed from the beginning of the play.
Yes, doomed, but doomed for what he is when the play opens. We assume Aphrodite's hatred as the dynamic force of the plot, and the rest
follows. The goddess destroys her enemy by a peculiarly cruel and malicious device. He, the supremely chaste, must meet his ruin through
suspicion of the greatest pollution. Nothing in his actions from the time
the play opens helps or hinders the fulfilment of that design. Aphrodite
has resolved to destroy him, and destroyed he is. And the moral sym-

bolism, what of that? The moral symbolism is that Aphrodite and Artemis, the spirit of lust and the spirit of virginity, are opposed. Like Horatio, we may say: "There needs no ghost come from the grave to tell us that." A symbolic play, a play symbolic of the conflict of ideals, must in its action show how these ideals come into conflict. You cannot postulate their conflict and then contemplate their incompatibility through five acts relieved by episodes in themselves interesting but irrelevant to the thesis of the piece.

Suppose, then, that we abandon the theory that the play is a piece of moral symbolism and take up the position that it is concerned with the tragedy of Hippolytus, without any conflict of moral values. We are now regarding Hippolytus, like Oedipus, as a character tragically doomed from the outset by reason of a flaw in himself or an accidental fault. But the tragedy of Oedipus is actually a prolonged recognition, *anagnorisis*, as Aristotle would call it. The entire play is concerned with the king's discovery of himself and the tragic consequences of that discovery. That is, every action of Oedipus within the play conduces directly to the final catastrophe. Oedipus is active throughout as the instrument of his own ruin. But Hippolytus is completely passive. Apart from his expressed contempt for Aphrodite—and that belongs as much to the antecedents of the play as the murder of Laius in the *Oedipus*—and his rejection of Phaedra, which we cannot regard as a symptom of Hippolytus' peculiar weakness, the only positive attitude taken by Hippolytus is in the matter of the oath. Of this, more later.

Let us turn to the respective importance of the two figures, Phaedra and Hippolytus. The first thing that must strike the impartial observer is the respective length of the two parts. Admittedly, this is not decisive. We are not trying to weigh tragedy like meat, as Aristophanes says. But investigation of the Phaedra scenes is convincing by more than the mere matter of dead weight. Let us make a brief survey of the play, with the object of illuminating the spiritual proportions of the two parts.

It may be claimed that the Prologue, by its statement of the plot, gives decisive evidence that Hippolytus is the center of the play. The goddess Aphrodite, in her exposé of the circumstances antecedent to the play's action and of its subsequent course, starts with the story of Hippolytus' sin. She is bent on his punishment, and we are led to infer that she is principally moved by jealousy of Artemis. She relates how Phaedra first met Hippolytus, and how she sickened with love for him. She stresses the misery of Phaedra and tells us its ultimate consequence in Hippolytus' death brought about by his father Theseus' curse. When she says, "Phaedra shall die gloriously, but die she must. I do not rate her death so high that I should let my enemies go free and pay me not the retribution which honor demands that I have," she is not assigning Phaedra an inferior role in the play. She is merely explaining why it is necessary that one who is guiltless should perish in the course of the punishment exacted from Hippolytus. I do not seek to prove that the legend did not stress Hippolytus' punishment but that Euripides, taking the legend—and this playbill Prologue is only a restatement of the legend—changes the emphasis from Hippolytus to Phaedra.

After the Prologue with which the play opens, there is the song of the hunters in honor of Artemis. The scene which introduces Hippolytus is poignant in its suppressions and tragic irony. The following dialogue between him and the old servant marks out clearly the contours of his personality. He is youthfully imperious, a mystic, and piously confident in his own righteousness. At this point Euripides undoubtedly focuses our attention on him. It is more than likely that the dramatist is thinking of many of his young contemporaries, intellectual mystics with leanings toward Orphism.

After the lyrical chorus comes the story of Phaedra's love for Hippolytus. For five hundred lines from page 250 Hippolytus does not appear. He is not even kept before our eyes by the dialogue between the Nurse and Phaedra, for these scenes are clinical in their concentration on the symptoms of love and philosophical in their general treatment of the problem. Except for the *Electra* later, Euripides has made no more brilliant analysis of a woman's emotions. His subject, however, is a woman's emotions, not a woman. A passage in a letter from D. H. Lawrence to Garnett illustrates what I mean:

Somehow that which is physic, non-human in humanity, is more interesting to me than the old-fashioned human element which causes one to conceive a character in a certain moral scheme and make him consistent. The certain moral scheme is what I object to. . . . When Marinetti writes: "It is the solidity of a blade of steel that is interesting in itself, that is the incomprehending and inhuman alliance of its molecules in resistance to, say, a bullet. The heat of a piece of wood or iron is a fact more passionate for us than the laughter or tears of a woman"—I know what he means. He is stupid as an artist for contrasting the heat of the iron and the laughter of a woman. Because what is interesting in the laughter of a woman is the same as the binding of the molecules of steel. It is the inhuman will, call it physiology, or, like Marinetti, physiology of matter if you like, which fascinates me. I do not care so much for what the woman feels in the ordinary sense of the word.

That presumes an ego to feel with. I only care what the woman *is*, inhumanly, physiologically, materially according to the use of the word.[1]

It is the physiology of matter that fascinates Euripides. Phaedra's guilty innocence is a true example of the driving force of Marinetti's "inhuman will." How applicable to Euripides' treatment of Phaedra are these words of Lawrence we can see by contrasting the play with Seneca's *Hippolytus* and Racine's *Phèdre*; both the Roman and the Frenchman are trying to conceive a character within a certain moral scheme. For Seneca it is the deathly conventionality of the literary heroine of tragedy, a conventionality bred of the rhetoric of the schools. For Racine it is the classic artificiality of the seventeenth century, with its cumbrous amorous and chivalrous pretensions. It is Euripides who cares about the "something that is physic, non-human in humanity."

In the scene from page 267 to page 269 we get a glimpse, a significant glimpse, of Hippolytus. It is his pathological antifeminist outburst. Apart from the revelation granted us of his horror at such a proposal as the Nurse has made him, the scene is indicative of a hopelessly neurotic mentality on the part of Hippolytus. Whether there are really any grounds for believing that this play was written at the time when Euripides was involved in domestic trouble we have no means of being sure. Aristophanes in the *Frogs* affirms that Euripides had such trouble in his life, and he mentions it directly after his criticism of the two plays, the *Stheneboia* and the *Hippolytus*. There is also a strong tradition in the scholia that the *Hippolytus* was composed at the moment of Euripides' bitterness. There seems, indeed, no very good reason for disregarding this story. However that may be, the passage from page 267 to page 268 is the final refutation, if another is needed, of the conception of Hippolytus as a man free from any abnormality. On pages 278-9 (in Theseus' indictment of his son) there are clear proofs that Hippolytus, so far from being the healthy hero of the drama, is someone haunted and tortured by an obsession. Homosexuality would have been no particular reproach for a young man like Hippolytus, but Euripides is searching to express something much deeper. It is the pathetic discontent, restlessness, and supreme unhappiness of an adolescent overintellectually developed.

After the disappearance of Phaedra, the individual part of the play is

[1] *Letters of D. H. Lawrence* (London: Heinemann, 1932), pp. 198-99. Acknowledgment is due to Mrs. Frieda Lawrence, William Heinemann, Ltd., and the Viking Press for permission to reprint this passage.

over. There remains the denouement of the plot, which is characterized by a certain stiff formality. The personal qualities which picked out the various shades in Hippolytus in the first scene are lost; and, in the charge and refutation scenes between him and Theseus, the matter and manner are mostly stock sophistic technique. Hippolytus' speech (p. 280) is all too evidently modeled on the speech of Creon in *Oedipus Rex*, a play written shortly before this, the second version of the *Hippolytus*. But Creon's speech in the *Oedipus* seems realistic and characteristic, because Sophocles has by minor hints prepared us for just such a speech from a man of Creon's temperament. Hippolytus is accused in a very complicated emotional situation. He is also by no means a hardheaded pragmatist like Creon in the Sophoclean play. The man who could utter the denunciation of woman in the scene on page 267 would have been quite incapable of reasoning with this pretty attention to arguments of first and second worth, when charged with a most heinous crime by a father he dearly loved. All this scene shows Euripides in his customary role of rhetorical speech-writer. And as in the *Andromache* and the *Hecuba*, the agon[2] is an abstract agon in which for convenience the characters bear the same labels as when we saw them earlier in the play. But of the character of Hippolytus, the hot-headed Hippolytus who is arrogant with a servant who gives him a word or two of good advice, of the passionate Hippolytus hissing the words of hate at the Nurse, of the intensely devotional Hippolytus devoured with the white heat of his adoration of Artemis, there is not one trace. The only particular as distinct from the general formal characteristics which distinguish this agon from the others is the audience' awareness that Hippolytus is sacrificing himself for the sake of his oath. Hippolytus swears to the Nurse that he will not reveal the secret she confides in him. Later, since he realizes that the oath was taken in ignorance, he is in doubt about the advisability of keeping it but sticks to his word and perishes. Now, is this the tragic element in his character? Is this the destruction of the noble man through his greatest nobility? I think that our answer lies in Hippolytus' own words. At the last moment, when he has heard his doom from

2 The agon is the technical term for the contest in a Greek tragedy. Sometimes this contest is a clash between the characters in a purely verbal way and sometimes it is accompanied with at least the threat of physical violence. It was a fixed feature of both Greek tragedy and comedy and perhaps is rooted in some primitive religious rite which was part of the ceremony out of which tragedy and comedy sprang.

Theseus, he speculates on the wisdom of renouncing his oath and clarifying the situation. "But no," he says, "he would not believe who should believe and I should be false to my oath and all for nothing." Surely it is plain that the oath is the creation of the second edition and is designed to meet a dramaturgical need. In the first edition,[3] where Phaedra made the proposition to Hippolytus herself and survived his death brought on him by her accusations, I doubt if there was this oath. Then the *agon* may well have been Phaedra and Hippolytus before Theseus. But when the tragedy demands that the truth should break on Theseus like a lightning bolt in the Epilogue, the oath which binds the lips of Hippolytus is the only device whereby this can be accomplished. For a modern dramatist there would be no need for such an oath. That one should not kiss and tell, or indeed should not even tell where one has not kissed, is our heritage from the Romantic age. But, like the oath imposed on the Chorus by Phaedra, Hippolytus' oath and his fidelity to it are of purely dramaturgical and not spiritual significance. It is a necessary condition of the plot.

What follows the end of the *Hippolytus agon* is also conventionally formal—a messenger's speech and the *theophaneia*. Here, then, we have our materials for forming a judgment on Hippolytus—two short opening scenes in which the dramatist adumbrates a character by sketching a few personal traits, Hippolytus' outburst against women, and one or two deductions to be made from Theseus' charges against him (pp. 278-9), e.g., that he was interested in Orphism; that he was spiritually arrogant; that he was a master of the supersophistical subtleties of argument. Can one, from such evidence as this, build either a picture of the ideal champion of chastity or the central figure of a great tragedy? It seems to me that it is Hippolytus who is the foil of Phaedra. Such personal traits as have been given him are designed to make of him a satire on the intellectuals of the fifth century.

What, then, at last shall we say is the theme of the *Hippolytus*? It is a play about the unchallengeable rule of love over the human animal and about the transformation which love can make in the human animal. In

---

[3] There were two editions of the *Hippolytus*. The first version, when acted, proved so unpalatable to the audience that they hissed it off the stage. Apparently, Euripides had allowed Phaedra to make her offer to Hippolytus herself and thus outraged the Athenians' sense of decency. In the second version the Nurse was introduced to perform this part, and it would seem that certain other minor changes, rather difficult to understand exactly, were also introduced. The evidence for this story is to be found in Aristophanes' *Frogs*.

Aphrodite, Euripides has made a composite figure out of two different aspects of the goddess. One is the Aphrodite of folk tale, the petulant, wilful goddess of the *Iliad*. The other is the primitive life-force. As the first she furnishes the machinery of the plot, and part of that machinery is her hatred of Hippolytus and her destruction of him. It is Aphrodite, the life-force, who gives inner significance to the drama. It is her supremacy that the play asserts, but over Phaedra primarily and only secondarily over Hippolytus. Phaedra is a normal, rather conventional woman metamorphosed into a neurotic sadist. She can cast aside the moral restraints of the society in which she lives and try to seduce her stepson. When she fails, she plans his murder and makes her suicide the guaranty of his guilt (p. 266). Yet, says Euripides, she is not really a criminal. Love is a frenzy of madness, and, when it strikes, the victim is not accountable in terms of her former personality or in terms of abstract rightness or wrongness. Thus, the general philosophical theme of the play, which centers around Phaedra, is crossed by the purely personal tragedy of Hippolytus. He, pathetically immature, unreal, and more than a little of a prig, is precisely a man born to be ill used by life in grotesque fashion. There is a grinning cynicism in the description of this pure, young idealist who knows nothing of love "save what I have heard or what I have seen in pictures" (p. 281). But the legend has all along identified him as Aphrodite's victim, and Euripides only needed to draw a verisimilar detail or two to finish off the picture. But the dramatist's own contribution (and one of his most masterly achievements in characterization and dramatic technique) is the study of Phaedra—this simple and cowardly woman transformed into an incestuous harlot and a murderess. On her he has spent the most pains and virtually all the dramatic tension of the play. If Phaedra and her tragedy are not his central interest, the artist has been guilty of an incredible preoccupation with the nonessential and an unintelligible concentration on irrelevant detail. Just as the sacrifice of Alcestis for her husband has been made the peg on which Euripides has hung a play about the complacent selfishness of Admetus, the Torvald Helmer of antiquity, so the story of Hippolytus done to death by Aphrodite is the formal scheme into which the study of Phaedra and her guilty innocence is fitted. Consider the following passages of the play and their context. They are indications of the poet's stress.

The Nurse, on learning of her mistress' passion for Hippolytus says (p. 258):

The chaste, they love not vice of their own will,
but yet they love it. Cypris, you are no God:
you are something stronger than God if that can be.
You have ruined her and me and all the house.

On page 261, when she is pleading with Phaedra for the gratification of love which otherwise threatens to destroy her life, she says:

The tide of love,
at its full surge, is not withstandable.
Upon the yielding spirit she comes gently,
but to the proud and fanatic heart
she is a torturer with the brand of shame.
She wings her way through the air: she is in the sea,
in its foaming billows: from her everything,
that is, is born. For she engenders us,
and sows the seed of desire whereof we're born,
all we her children, living on the earth.

In view of the general philosophical character of the Nurse's speeches (pp. 261 and 262), these two speeches have obviously more than dramaturgical importance.

On page 264, when the Nurse has won her case with Phaedra and Phaedra has yielded to her fatal pleading, the Chorus chants:

Love distills desire upon the eyes,
love brings bewitching grace into the heart
of those he would destroy.
I pray that Love may never come to me
with murderous intent,
in rhythms measureless and wild.
Not fire nor star have stronger bolts
than those of Aphrodite sent
by the hand of Eros, Zeus' child.

Finally, the Chorus sums up the action of the play before the *theophaneia* in the following lyric (p. 289):

Cypris, you guide men's hearts
and the inflexible
heart of the Gods and with you
comes Love with the flashing wings,
comes Love with the swiftest of wings.
Over the land he flies
and the land echoing salt sea.
He bewitches and maddens the heart
of the victim he swoops upon.
He bewitches the race of the mountain-haunting
lion and beasts of the sea,
and all the creatures that earth feeds,

and the blazing sun sees,—
and man, too,—
over all you hold kingly power,
Love, you are only ruler
over all these.

The two editions of the play give us a further indication of its author's interests. In the first, Phaedra makes the proposition to Hippolytus herself. That proved too much for the Athenian audience, so Euripides took it back and amended it. But he did not alter anything essential in the character of his main figure. He invented the Nurse as a go-between to carry out the ugly part of the affair. But there is no doubt whatever that Phaedra knows what is going on. That we can see from the conclusion of the scene between the Nurse and Phaedra (p. 263). Euripides wished to show that, given the most incriminating indictment of Phaedra possible, she is still innocent at the bar of human, if not divine, justice. Love working through Phaedra destroys Hippolytus. Such is the framework of the plot. But how does it work? With great dexterity the first Phaedra scene makes us feel all the subconscious stirrings of her mind before Phaedra herself is aware of them. Then the tentative approach to the step which will inevitably lead to her destruction. We are shown dramatically by the action in the first two scenes what Phaedra tells us explicitly later (pp. 257 and 259). Phaedra is guiltless, if by guilt we mean the conscious and deliberate choice of evil when the good is intellectually apprehended. But can we ever talk of a conscious decision of this kind when the chooser is under the influence of an essentially animal passion which carries him or her out and beyond the limits of reason? "I will show you," says Artemis to Theseus when she explains the machinery of the plot, "the frenzied love which seized your wife, or, I may call it, a noble innocence. For that most hated goddess, hated by all of us whose joy is virginity, drove her with love's sharp prickings to desire your son."

"Was the story I composed about Phaedra not true?" asks Euripides in the Frogs, where she is listed among his perverse creations along with Stheneboia. And the Athenian audience, as well as we, can answer as did Aeschylus: "By Zeus, most true," even if we do not continue with Aeschylus, "but the poet should conceal the vile, and not bring it on the boards. For children have the school master and the young men have the poets."

DAVID GRENE.

ALCESTIS

1. The Chorus

The original Chorus of the *Alcestis* was composed of fifteen old men, citizens of Pherae. The Maidservant describes the Choragos himself as an "old friend" of the house:

σὺ δ' εἶ παλαιὸς δεσπόταις ἐμοῖς φίλος.

Nevertheless, the tone of the Chorus throughout is sufficiently anonymous to have justified us in a step which we should have had to take in any event, since we were writing with a definite singing and dancing group in mind: the substitution of a Chorus of women. This step meant less violence to the text than might have been expected: in only one instance that we can remember is the thought definitely masculine (in the Second Ode, where the Chorus wishes for such wives as Alcestis), and even here the feeling is fairly impersonal. In short, we conceived the Chorus as being neither masculine nor feminine, but as being a neuter symbol of public opinion.

The Greek Choral Dance may or may not have been an athletic event, but experience has taught us that it is difficult to chant words effectively if the body is occupied at the same time with motion, however restrained. For this reason, we have created another Chorus, of singers only, to be placed antiphonally on the stage, where it should remain throughout the action. All the singing is to be done by this group, and from it speak the isolated voices of the Half-chorus. The *Choragos* is the only member of the dancing Chorus to speak or sing. In this way it is hoped that whatever the evolutions of the dance may be (and we urge a minimum of action), the words of the strophes will be intelligibly sung.

2. The Lament of Eumelos

We have not hesitated to suppress entirely the only verses assigned to the child Eumelos:[1] a lamentation in strophic form that follows immediately upon the death of Alcestis. The song is florid in versification, intolerably sententious and "cute" in diction. Whether it was actually sung by a trained choir-boy, or whether a child mimed it to singing behind the scene, we do not know. In our version we have reluctantly al-

---

[1] The name of Admetos' son is not given by Euripides, but is drawn from the mythographers.

lowed the presence of Eumelos on the stage, because the text demands it;[2] but we beg that he be as inconspicuous as possible.

For the curious, and in the interests of completeness, we append a restrained prose version of Small Eumelos' remarks:

[STROPHE.

EUMELOS   Ah! Mother is dead, gone under ground, dear Father! She is no longer in the sunlight. She has left her children orphans. See her eyes, her still hands! Listen, listen, dearest Mother! It is I, your own little bird, calling you, clinging to your lips.

ADMETOS   She neither hears us nor sees us: the calamity is intolerable.

[ANTISTROPHE.

EUMELOS   Father, I am so young to go on without a mother's guidance! And you, dear sister, sharing my grief!—Father, father, how useless was your marriage! You could not reach old age with her: she has died first, and your death, Mother, is the death of our house.

That, it seems to us, is enough.

3. The Mask of Alcestis

Traditionally, when Alcestis is brought back from the dead she is wearing a veil: she usually looks like a Decent Widow. Admetos' failure to recognize her must obviously be accounted for somehow, and since we both have an aversion to veils, we have ventured a trick of symbolism which we hope is not too precious to succeed.

At her first entrance, dying, Alcestis should wear a mask which is a somewhat stylized representation of her actual face. This mask, which is unreal, is her living face, and it is the only face that her husband has ever seen. At the moment of her death she removes this false face and holds it in both hands before her. Immediately, so far as Admetos is concerned, she has become a strange thing, a sufficiently remote subject for the romantic rhetoric in which his vanity indulges almost throughout the rest of the play. When, in the *Exodos*, she is brought back by Heracles, she is still carrying her mask before her. Looking upon her real face, Admetos is troubled by a certain resemblance; but he does not know her until, at the moment of her re-entrance, so to speak, into life, she replaces the

2 The little girl, Perimelê, is also indicated; but in this case we have been ruthless.

familiar false face that he has always known. Admetos, who is certainly the Greek Torvald Helmer, has never really known his wife at all. At the moment of his greatest need, and of her surest love, he finds her a complete stranger.

Dudley Fitts.
Robert Fitzgerald.

KING OEDIPUS

This version of Sophocles' play was written for the Dublin players, for Dublin liturgical singers, for a small auditorium, for a chorus that must stand stock still where the orchestra are accustomed to put their chairs, for an audience where nobody comes for self-improvement or for anything but emotion. In other words, I put readers and scholars out of my mind and wrote to be sung and spoken. The one thing that I kept in mind was that a word unfitted for living speech, out of its natural order, or unnecessary to our modern technique, would check emotion and tire attention.

Years ago I persuaded Florence Farr to so train the chorus for a Greek play that the sung words were almost as intelligible and dramatic as the spoken; and I have commended that art of hers in *Speaking to the Psaltery*. I asked my Dublin producer Lennox Robinson to disregard that essay, partly because liturgical singers were there to his hand, but mainly because if a chorus stands stock still in half shadow music and singing should, perhaps, possess a variety of rhythm and pitch incompatible with dramatic intelligible words. The main purpose of this chorus is to preserve the mood while it rests the mind by change of attention. A producer who has a space below the level of the stage, where a chorus can move about an altar, may do well to experiment with that old thought of mine and keep his singers as much in the range of the speaking voice as if they sang "The west's awake," or sang round a binnacle. However, he has his own singers to think of and must be content with what comes to hand.

W. B. Yeats.

OEDIPUS AT COLONUS

I

The familiar art of the theatre was once a discovery, and this discovery took place not long before Sophocles began to write. His older contemporary Aeschylus was credited by Aristotle with having been the first dramatic poet to use a second actor. The dramaturgy—though not the poetry—of Sophocles therefore emerged immediately from what we should call the archaic. We may justly admire the extent of its emergence. The Greek drama as Sophocles found it stood to previous Greek entertainment somewhat as the movies of our century stand to the art of the stage. His work might perhaps be compared with that of the director Eisenstein, for he mastered and intelligently extended a new medium.

The two main elements in cinema are the art of the stage and the arts of mechanical reproduction. The two main elements in Greek drama were the national religious ritual, composed of singing, dancing and spectacle, and the national entertainment of epic recital. How these elements came to be joined is conjectural. It is known that professional men called rhapsodes had for centuries recited the Homeric stories, and, considering the many lively speeches in Homer, it is probable that these rhapsodes were skillful mimics. It may well have occurred to someone six centuries B.C. to employ the arts of story-telling and mimicry to enhance the choral dithyrambs at the Dionysian festival. A certain dancer would imitate a leading character of the song; the rest of the chorus would exchange verses with him. So, possibly, it began. A century later Greek drama had developed into the "miming of an action" and had become, undoubtedly, very exciting.

This fact may be borne in mind. For if the story of the murder of Agamemnon or the doom of Oedipus should seem to anyone less dramatic than a modern action movie, it is fair to remember that a mere one-man narrative about Agamemnon or Oedipus was enthralling enough to the Athenians, let alone a representation in which the events themselves, the heroes themselves, were set in motion before their eyes.

II

Aristotle, who particularly admired Sophocles' work, bears witness to the power of Greek tragedy in his time. And Aristotle said, among other things more open to misinterpretation, that the quality of a tragedy could be discovered as well by reading it as by going to see it produced. This should be a comfort to us, and we may add that so far as Greek plays are concerned, reading is nowadays a somewhat safer approach. Attempts have been made to reproduce the Greek amphitheatre and what took place in it, but in English, for an audience reasonably robust, they have been in most cases perilous exhibitions. The nature of Greek dancing and choral singing is so obscure that they cannot be reconstructed with any certainty; nor, if they could, would there be much point in the reconstruction. These were arts that flourished in a religious atmosphere and for religious purposes that no longer exist.

For all the vigor of The Dance in our period, I should fear the effect of any choreography on the unity of a Greek play in performance. As for the singing, more is perhaps possible. In the Abbey Theatre production of Yeats' *King Oedipus*, the choruses were chanted by singers trained in Gregorian music, and the effect is said to have been impressive. Yet, since I have no trustworthy theatre or singing group in mind, I have left this version of *Oedipus at Colonus* almost bare of suggestions for its production; and I have called the choruses choral poems, thinking that if the play were staged it would be luck enough to have them well spoken.

It may be, indeed, that radio is the most nearly satisfactory means of presenting a Greek play to a modern audience. Euripides' *Alcestis* and Sophocles' *Antigoné*, in translations by Dudley Fitts and myself, were broadcast over a National Broadcasting Company network on successive Sundays in 1939. Despite certain faults hard to avoid in routine and hastily rehearsed radio productions, both plays were fairly effective. It is easy to see that such a manner of presentation, appealing wholly to the ear and imagination of the audience, avoids the difficulties of costuming and staging that must plague any stage performance.

III

Oedipus at Colonus is reckoned on ancient authority to have been the last of more than one hundred plays by its author. It was composed probably in 406 B.C., when Sophocles was eighty-nine years old. Some of the play's peculiar interest lies in this fact, and in various matters implied by this fact. At the time of its composition the Peloponnesian War between Athens and Sparta had been in progress for more than a quarter of a century. To Colonus, where he was born, and to the great and hard-pressed city of which he was a beloved citizen, Sophocles paid his tribute in this play. Though Athens was still undefeated, her lands had already been laid waste; and the verses about the olive trees may well have moved their first readers or auditors to tears. The play was not produced in the theatre until 401 B.C., four years after the death of Sophocles and three years after the starvation and capitulation of Athens. *Oedipus at Colonus* is therefore one of the last considerable works known to us from the period of Athenian genius.

Like the six other extant plays of Sophocles, it is the work of a mind in the highest degree orderly, penetrating and sensitive; an enlightened mind aware of the moral issues in human action, and a reverent mind aware of the powers that operate through time and fortune on human affairs. But it is first of all the work of an artist, a maker of plots and poetry, and it is only from the ever-ambiguous expression of art that we may divine his thought or his theme. Accordingly we have here no such lucid revelation of Athenian intellect as we find in the history of Thucydides or the dialogues of Plato. For its original audience the play shimmered with implications that are lost to us. Yet even we cannot fail to see in it the last, long reach toward truth of an artist who was formed by his great epoch and who perfectly represents it.

It would be hard to imagine any tribulation more severe than that endured by Oedipus, king of Thebes. At the summit of his power he discovered himself damned, by his own pertinacity discovered that he had horribly offended against the decencies by which men must live. In one day he fell from sovereignty and fame to self-blinded degradation, and later he was driven into exile. He comes on the stage a blind beggar led by a girl. The Athenians had no romantic notions about vagabondage or exile; in their eyes Oedipus had been reduced to the worst extremity, barring slavery, that a noble man could suffer.

But the atmosphere of the place to which the old man comes is an atmosphere of shadiness, blessedness and peace; and the contrast between Oedipus in his rags and the beauty of Colonus is an effect of which we are at once aware, an effect not unlike that of Odysseus's awakening in the pretty island of Phaeacia. Only here the poet's purposes are not so simple. For this is a grove sacred to the Furies, and the Furies are those spirits of retribution by whom sinners, murderers especially, and Oedipus in particular, have been pursued. It is furthermore well known to Sophocles' audience that in the *Eumenides* of Aeschylus, years before, these spirits were persuaded by Athena to reconcile themselves to the superior rule of Athenian law. Thus gentled, so to speak, in Attica, they have nevertheless great intrinsic power, and must be treated with tact. And they are indeed, as we see here symbolized, the divinities with whom Oedipus must make his peace.

To the Victorian mind there may have been something odd in the character and demeanor of this old man whom adversity might properly have purged into sweetness and resignation. His fund of both these qualities is limited. The dignity of Oedipus is never in doubt, but observe that this dignity is not of the sort associated with patriarchs. It is not incompatible with a scornful and artful wit, nor with a sort of fighting alertness: witness his persuasive remarks to the Attic elders who try to dismiss him from the grove. Nor is it incompatible with a definite savagery. The quick anger in which he killed his father and goaded Teiresias, long ago, into telling him the truth—it is, if anything, fiercer in his old age. A literal thirst for blood appears in his prophecy to Theseus of war between Thebes and Athens, and this primitivism in Oedipus is all the more evident by contrast with the calm Athenian hero. Against Creon and against his son he becomes a tower of passion and disgust.

In what, then, is his dignity? Why is he not merely an obsessed and vindictive old man? It should be remembered that one of Oedipus' distinguishing qualities was, in the first place, his intelligence. He saved Thebes once by solving the riddle of the Sphinx. He saved the city again by solving with furious persistence the riddle of his own birth. And in this play we see once more the working of that intellect, driving this time toward a transcendence of the purely human. During the years in which Oedipus has probed his own guilt he has come to terms with it. Though innocent of willful murder or incest, he has made expiation for what he recognized as his share of responsibility in those acts. Without reference to Freud we may perceive that in this whole fable of Oedipus the great poet is giving us to understand that the nature of man is darker than men believe it to be. Yet Oedipus is not penitent, for he has also recognized that the powers controlling life have, in a sense, chosen him as their example and instrument.

Thus it is not alone through passive suffering that the spirit of Oedipus attains power and blessedness. His rage and sternness in his last hours are the means of an affirmation, the most profound this poet could make. We recognize Oedipus' right to pass sentence on Creon and on his son, though by our first and easy standards neither would seem to deserve the curse pronounced on him. Creon is tricky and heartless, but he is "obeying the command of the State"; Polyneices has been thoughtless of his father and fiercely jealous of his brother, but he does not seem a bad young man. In the larger context of Oedipus' fate, however, we may discern that their sins of meanness, of avarice, of irreverence, are no less grave than the sins of passion for which Oedipus was punished: that in condemning them to the merciless justice soon to descend, Oedipus acts thoroughly in accord with a moral order which his own experience has enabled him to understand.

And this may clarify for us the beautiful ending of the play. Oedipus has indeed endured his suffering with courage, but it is not until he has acted, and acted as the agent of divine justice, that the passionate man is fit to embody and to symbolize human divinity. Only then the Furies stand at his side; only then the gods receive him. And only then is bitterness lifted from him. We should note that in his farewell to his daughters he assures them that "one word makes all those difficulties disappear." This is the final word of Oedipus and of the tragedian. For, as a great Polish writer has written, "suffering is the lot of man, but not inevitable failure or worthless despair which is without end—suffering, the mark of manhood, which bears within its pain a hope of felicity like a jewel set in iron. . . ."

IV

The quality of Sophocles cannot be rendered in the English of the King James Bible. Neither can it be rendered in the English of Bernard Shaw, of Maxwell Anderson, or of Philip Barry. Rendered well, it would seem equally acceptable English to Jonathan Swift and to Ernest Hemingway. It can be exactly rendered only in what might be called the English of Sophocles. This requisite furnishes the translator with the fascination of what is, strictly speaking, impossible. I am merely prepared to assure the reader that this version is not a paraphrase or an adaptation, and that it is intended above all as a just representation of the Greek. Except for one or two variant phrases, I have followed the Oxford text of Sophocles as edited in 1923 by A. C. Pearson, Regius Professor of Greek at the University of Cambridge.

V

The main dialogue in Greek dramatic poetry was cast in a regular meter (iambic trimeter) which may be imagined as a sort of unrhymed alexandrine. A formal meter, it was at the same time, by virtue of its quantitative and non-syllabic basis, more flexible and perhaps more expressive than the French alexandrine. A line of six stresses or accents is possible in English, and has even been carried off with some success, but for purposes of dramatic dialogue it is neither traditional nor appropriate, being slow and foreign to the natural rhythm of our speech. The iambic pentameter, or five stress line, has not these disadvantages, and it has furthermore been brought to great subtlety and expressive precision not only by the later Elizabethan poets but by writers in our own day. This therefore was the meter chosen for rendering the dialogue.

The diction of Sophocles was smooth. It has been likened by a modern critic to a molten flow of language, fitting and revealing every contour of the meaning, with no words wasted and no words poured on for effect. To approximate such purity I have sought a spare but felicitous manner of speech, not common and not "elevated" either, except by force of natural eloquence. The Greek writer did not disdain plainness when plainness was appropriate. As in every highly inflected language, the Greek order of words was controlled, by its masters, for special purposes of emphasis and even of meaning; and such of these as I have been acute enough to grasp I have tried to bring out by a comparable phrasing or rhythm in English. This I hold to be part of the business of "literal" rendering.

The difficulties involved in translating Greek dialogue are easily tripled when it comes to translating a chorus. Here the ellipses and compressions possible to the inflected idiom are particularly in evidence; and in the chorus, too, the poet concentrates his allusive power. For the modern reader, who has very little "literature" in the sense in which Samuel Johnson used the term, two out of three allusions in the Greek odes will be meaningless. This is neither surprising nor deplorable. The Roman writer, Ennius, translating Euripides for a Latin audience two centuries after the Periclean period, found it advisable to omit many place names and to omit or explain many mythological references; and his public certainly had greater reason to be familiar with such things than we have. My handling of this problem has been governed by the general wish to leave nothing in the English that would drive the literate reader to a library. Two examples should suffice.

On page 413, "the sea-surrounded west Where Agamemnon's race has sway" is a translation of words whose dictionary meaning is "the great Dorian island of Pelops," in other words the Peloponnesus. The Greek word for island which is Latinized as "nesus" was often applied to bodies of land that we should not properly define as islands. Hence "sea-surrounded" is a more exact rendering here. "Agamemnon" for "Pelops" is

582 · APPENDIX: COMMENTARIES

a greater liberty, to which purists may object on the ground that the legendary period of this play antedates that of the Trojan War and of Agamemnon, Pelops' most celebrated descendant. I chose Agamemnon because he is celebrated, and because he is quite as legendary to us as Pelops was to Sophocles.

On page 427, "that torchlit Eleusinian shore": this line and the following stanza refer to the holy shrine of Eleusis, sacred to Demeter and Persephone the goddess of the underworld, where a ritual of communion and revelation took place by torchlight every September. The initiates in these rites were sworn to secrecy by priests of an order called the Eumolpidae, or "sweet-voiced." The shrine, partly subterranean, was on the rocky shore of the bay of Eleusis behind the island of Salamis, about fourteen miles northwest of Athens. It is not clear precisely what the Eleusinian mysteries consisted of, but it is clear that they illuminated the life after death and afforded great spiritual solace to the devout. Sophocles' friend, Pericles, esteemed them of such importance to the Athenian state that he rebuilt the shrine. Finally, Eleusis was one of the places included in the "unification of Attica" carried out, according to Athenian tradition, by Theseus. . . . I have tried to give the essential meaning and quality of this passage for readers who cannot be expected to have the foregoing information.

Rhyme as we know it was unknown to Greek poetry. Rhymed verse structures are much more remote from the Greek choral forms than iambic pentameter is from the iambic trimeter of their dialogue. And since it is desirable so far as possible to retain the character of the Greek poetry in the English, rhyme constitutes one of the farthest formal departures that we can make. Moreover, the artifice of rhyming draws the translator irresistibly toward the addition of strokes of his own beyond the content or connotation of the text. Yet except by the use of rhymed stanzas and other formal devices of English verse, at least in certain instances, I do not see how the highly wrought regularity of the Sophoclean choruses, the lyricism deliberately distinct from dialogue, can be conveyed in untortured English. It has seemed to me necessary to convey these qualities, if possible; to convey them with the least possible increment of my own, but, when ingenuity should fail, to convey them even at the expense of absolute accuracy.

Thus, on page 414, the god of ocean is called "the son of Time," where the Greek refers to him as the son of Cronus, another name for Zeus.

Rhyming encouraged me to take this liberty, but it is also, I think, justified by the power of Time, the abstraction, which may well be an equivalent to us of the Almighty under one of his aspects. So far as I know, the greatest liberty I have taken is found on page 428 in the choral refrain. The only basis in the text for a refrain is the significantly emphatic way in which Sophocles twice repeated the verb in the line translated, "For God will see some noble thing," etc. But the refrain bears further repetition, and it strengthens a strophe and antistrophe which in English rendering must otherwise be somewhat weaker than the preceding ones.

ROBERT FITZGERALD.

ANTIGONE

> *Et quod propriè dicitur in idiomate Picardorum horrescit apud Burgundos, immò apud Gallicos viciniores; quanto igitur magis accidet hoc apud linguas diversas! Quapropter quod bene factum est in unâ linguâ non est possibile ut transferatur in aliam secundum ejus proprietatem quam habuerit in priori.*
>
> ROGER BACON

I

In the Commentary appended to our version of Euripides' *Alcestis* we wrote: "Our object was to make the *Alcestis* clear and credible in English. Since it is a poem, it had to be made clear as a poem; and since it is a play, it had to be made credible as a play. We set for ourselves no fixed rules of translation or of dramatic verse: often we found the best English equivalent in a literalness which extended to the texture and rhythm of the Greek phrasing; at other times we were forced to a more or less free paraphrase in order to achieve effects which the Greek conveyed in ways impossible to English. Consequently, this version of the *Alcestis* is not a 'translation' in the classroom sense of the word. The careful reader, comparing our text with the original, will discover alterations, suppressions, expansions—a word, perhaps, drawn out into a phrase, or a phrase condensed to a word: a way of saying things that is admittedly not Euripidean, if by Euripidean one means a translation *ad verbum expressa* of Euripides' poem. In defense we can say only that our purpose was to reach—and, if possible, to render precisely—the emotional and sensible meaning in every speech in the play; we could not follow the Greek word for word, where to do so would have been weak and therefore false." We

have been guided by the same principles in making this version of the
Antigonê.

II

We have made cuts only when it seemed absolutely necessary. The
most notable excision is that of a passage of sixteen lines beginning with
Antigonê's long speech near the end of Scene IV, which has been
bracketed as spurious, either in whole or in part, by the best critics.
Aristotle quotes two verses from it, which proves, as Professor Jebb
points out, that if it is an interpolation it must have been made soon
after Sophocles' death, possibly by his son Iophon. However that may
be, it is dismal stuff. Antigonê is made to interrupt her lamentation by
a series of inferior verses whose sense is as unsatisfactory as their sound.
We quote the Oxford Translation, the style of which is for once wholly
adequate to the occasion:

"And yet, in the opinion of those who have just sentiments, I honoured
you [Polyneicês] aright. For neither, though I had been the mother of
children, nor though my husband dying, had mouldered away, would I
have undertaken this toil against the will of the citizens. On account of
what law do I say this? There would have been another husband for me
if the first died, and if I lost my child there would have been another
from another man! But my father and my mother being laid in the grave,
it is impossible a brother should ever be born to me. On the principle of
such a law, having preferred you, my brother, to all other considerations,
I seemed to Creon to commit a sin, and to dare what was dreadful. And
now, seizing me by force, he thus leads me away, having never enjoyed
the nuptial bed, nor heard the nuptial lay, nor having gained the lot of
marriage, nor of rearing my children; but thus I, an unhappy woman,
deserted by my friends, go, while alive, to the cavern of the dead."

There are other excisions of less importance. Perhaps the discussion of
one of them will serve to explain them all. Near the end of the Exodos,
Creon is told of his wife's death. The Messenger has five very graphic
lines describing Eurydicê's suicide, to which Creon responds with an
outburst of dread and grief; yet two lines later, as if he had not heard
the first time, he is asking the Messenger how Eurydicê died. The Messenger replies that she stabbed herself to the heart. There is no evidence
that the question and reply are interpolations: on the contrary, they
serve the definite purpose of filling out the iambic interlude between two

lyric strophes; but in a modern version which does not attempt to reproduce the strophic structure of this passage they merely clog the dialogue.
Therefore we have skipped them; and the occasional suppression of short
passages throughout the play is based upon similar considerations.

III

In a like manner, we have not hesitated to use free paraphrase when a
literal rendering of the Greek would result in obscurity. Again, the discussion of a specific instance may illuminate the whole question.

After Antigonê has been led away to death, the Chorus, taking a hint
from her having compared her own fate to that of Niobê, proceeds to
elaborate the stories of mythological persons who have suffered similar
punishment. The Fourth Ode cites Danaê, Lycurgus, the son of Dryas,
and Kleopatra, the daughter of Boreas and wife of the Thracian king
Phineus. Only Danaê is mentioned by name; the others are allusively
identified. The difficulty arises from the allusive method: Sophocles'
audience would be certain to recognize the allusions, but that is not true
of ours. To what extent can we depend upon the audience's recognition
in a day when, to quote Mr. I. A. Richards, "we can no longer refer with
any confidence to any episode in the Bible, or to any nursery tale or any
piece of mythology"? We can assume that the story of Danaê is still
current; but Lycurgus is forgotten now, and the sordid Phineus-Kleo-
patra-Eidothea affair no longer stirs so much as an echo. Nevertheless,
Sophocles devotes two of his four strophes to this Kleopatra, and he
does it in so oblique a manner that "translation" is out of the question.
We have therefore rendered these strophes with such slight additions to
the Greek sense as might convey an equivalent suggestion of fable to a
modern audience.

IV

The Chorus is composed, says the Scholiast, of "certain old men of
Thebes": leading citizens ("O men many-charioted, in love with Fortune") to whom Creon addresses his fatal decree, and from whom he
later takes advice. Sophocles' Chorus probably numbered fifteen, includ-
ing the Choragos, or Leader; its function was to chant the Odes and, in
the person of the Choragos, to participate in the action. In a version
designed for the modern stage certain changes are inevitable. It cannot be
urged too strongly that the words of the Odes must be intelligible to the

audience; and they are almost certain not to be intelligible if they are chanted in unison by so large a group, with or without musical accompaniment. It is suggested, then, that in producing this play no attempt be made to follow the ancient choric method. There should be no dancing. The *párodos*, for example, should be a solemn but almost unnoticeable evolution of moving or still patterns accompanied by a drumbeat whose rhythm may be derived from the cadence of the Ode itself. The lines given to the Chorus in the Odes should probably be spoken by single voices. The only accompaniment should be percussion: we follow Allan Sly's score of the *Alcestis* in suggesting a large side drum from which the snares have been removed, to be struck with two felt-headed tympani sticks, one hard, one soft.

V

A careful production might make successful use of masks. They should be of the Benda type used in the production of O'Neill's *The Great God Brown*: lifelike, closely fitting the contours of the face, and valuable only as they give the effect of immobility to character. On no account should there be any attempt to reproduce the Greek mask, which was larger than life size and served a function non-existent on the modern stage—the amplification of voice and mood for projection to the distant seats of the outdoor theatre.

If masks are used at all, they might well be allotted only to those characters who are somewhat depersonalized by official position or discipline: Creon, Teiresias, the Chorus and Choragos, possibly the Messenger. By this rule, Antigonê has no mask; neither has Ismenê, Haimon, nor Eurydicê. If Creon is masked, we see no objection, in art or feeling, to the symbolic removal of his mask before he returns with the dead body of his son.

DUDLEY FITTS.
ROBERT FITZGERALD.

PROMETHEUS BOUND

The *Prometheus* is unlike any other ancient play. Only in the most modern theater is a parallel to be found. There is no action in it. Aristotle, first of critics, said that drama depends on action, not character.

There is only character in the *Prometheus*. The protagonist is motion-less, chained to a rock. None of the other personages do anything. The drama consists solely in the unfolding of Prometheus' character by means of conversation. It is the exemplar that tragedy is essentially the suf-fering of a great soul who suffers greatly.

The dialogue is sustained with an admirable art. Each of the minor personages, however brief his appearance, is an individual, clearly char-acterized. Nothing in the picture is blurred. Force is a rough careless villain; Hephestus, the Fire God, a feeble, kindly tool; the chorus, gentle conventional-minded girls, who can find courage enough in a crisis; Hermes, a crude youth, much set up by his high office, but beneath his grand assumption unsure of himself.

Ocean's character merits a fuller consideration for the reason that the traditional view is that Attic tragedy did not admit of comedy or humor. The textbooks all tell us that it was unrelieved by any lighter touch, and so gained an intensity of tragic effect impossible to Shakespeare's check-ered stage of light and shade. But most readers will agree that the comedy of Ocean's talk with Prometheus is beyond dispute. Ocean is a humorous creation, an amiable, self-important old busybody, really distressed at Prometheus' hard fate, but bent upon reading him a good lecture now that he has him where he cannot run away; delighted to find himself the person of importance who has pull with Zeus and can get that unprac-tical fool, Prometheus, out of his not entirely undeserved punishment; but underneath this superior attitude very uneasy because of Zeus, who "isn't so far off but he might hear," and completely happy when Prome-theus finally gives him a chance to save his face and run off safely home. When this dialogue is understood as humorous, the commentators and translators are relieved of what has always been a stumbling block to them, Ocean's four-footed bird. If it is accepted as axiomatic that a Greek tragic drama cannot have anything humorous in it, the bird with four feet undoubtedly presents difficulties. It is hard to see it as a tragic adjunct. But the Athenian spectators were at least as keen-witted as we are today, and when there appeared on the stage an enormous, grotesque bird with a pompous old man riding on its back, they had no more trouble than we should have in recognizing a comic interlude. Ocean is a figure of fun, and the steed he bestrides is there to give the audience the clue.

None of the points so far taken up will seem strange to the modern reader, but a real difficulty is presented by Io, a distracted, fleeing creature, quite mad, who seems now a girl and now a heifer, and by her talk with Prometheus, running into hundreds of lines, which consists largely of geography. These are matters that an ancient and a modern spectator would necessarily look at differently because so much of what was known to them is strange to us and vice versa. Io and her descendants were dear, familiar figures to Aeschylus' audience, always recognized with pleasure. On the other hand, Io's journey over the earth, which only the most devoted lover of Aeschylus today can help finding long, was delightful to the Greeks of long ago. The world outside of Greece was a place of wonder and mystery, and to lift the veil ever so little was to command the deepest interest. Geography was thrilling. It stayed so for a long time, as we know from one who won a lady's heart by stories of the Anthropophagi and men whose heads do grow beneath their shoulders. "These things to hear would Desdemona seriously incline." Shakespeare's audience and Aeschylus' were one on this point.

Milton's Satan is often called Prometheus injected with Christian theology, but the comparison falls to the ground. For all Satan's magnificence, he is, to use Prometheus' words, "young—young." Shame before the other spirits keeps him from submission quite as much as his own ambition. Beside him Prometheus seems experienced. He has learned what is important to him and what is not. He is calmly strong, loftily indifferent, never to be shaken, because he is sure, both of what he wants and what he means to do. He stands forever as the type of the great rebel.

A more interesting parallel is with Job, who when wronged to the utmost submits to irresistible power. He knows that all Jehovah has done to him is utter injustice, but in the end, confronted with the Almighty who can divide the waters and find the way of the thunder and set bounds to the sea, Job gives up: "I know that thou canst do all things. . . . Wherefore I abhor myself and repent in dust and ashes." Prometheus, too, is faced by irresistible force. His body is helplessly imprisoned, but his spirit is free. Just as with Job, the unconditional surrender is demanded of him. He refuses, and with his last words as the crumbling universe falls upon him, he asserts the injustice of the Almighty: "Behold me. I am wronged."

EDITH HAMILTON.

INDEX OF NAMES

The transliteration of Greek names is a thorny subject: some writers prefer the Latin system while others move, with all sorts of intermediary eccentricities, more closely to the Greek. In these plays the spelling of each translator has been retained and the variants—even at the risk of the obvious—are listed in the following index.

Abbreviations: AG., Agamemnon; ALC., Alcestis; ANT., Antigone; ELEC., Electra; EUM., Eumenides; HIP., Hippolytus; MED., Medea; OC, Oedipus at Colonus; OT, King Oedipus; PV, Prometheus Bound; TROAD., The Trojan Women.

ACHAEAN, ACHAIAN: Greek

ACHERON: a river of Hades

ACHILLES: son of King Peleus of Phthia; mightiest of the Greek chieftains in the Trojan War

ACHILLEUS: TROAD.] see ACHILLES

ADMETOS: son of Pheres; husband of Alcestis

ADRASTOS, ADRASTUS: a king of Argos; father-in-law of Polyneices, q.v., and leader of the expedition of the Seven against Thebes

AEA: a district of Colchis, q.v.; hence, AEAN: MED.] pertaining to this district

AEGEUS: a legendary king of Athens; son of Pandion and father of Theseus, qq.v.

AEGISTHOS, AEGISTHUS: son of Thyestes, hence first cousin of Agamemnon and Menelaos

AENIAN: ELEC.] of the Aenianes, a Thessalian tribe

AETNA, AITNA: a volcano in Sicily; burial place of Typhon, q.v.

AETOLIA: a district in middle Greece, south of Thessaly

AGAMEMNON: King of Argos; overlord of all the Greek princes

AIGAIAN: TROAD.] the Aegean Sea

AIGISTHOS: see AEGISTHOS

AIGYPLANKTOS: a mountain in the district of Megaris, southwest of Mt. Cithaeron

AIAS, AJAX: "the lesser Ajax" (as distinct from the Telamonian Ajax, or Ajax the Great); son of King Oïleus of Locris; violated Cassandra during the sack of Troy

AKASTOS, ACASTUS: son of King Pelias of Iolkos, q.v.

ALCESTIS: daughter of Pelias and wife of Admetos

ALCMENA, ALKMENA: wife of Amphitryon; seduced by Zeus in her husband's shape, she gave birth to Heracles.

ALEXANDER: AG., TROAD.] a name for Paris, q.v.

ALPHEUS: HIP.] a river in the Peloponnesus

AMAZONS: PV] a race of warrior women living on the bank of the River Thermodon, in Pontus

AMMON: the name given Zeus in his cult in Libya

AMPHIARAOS, AMPHIAREUS: one of the seven Captains supporting Polyneices in the Theban expedition

AMPHION: ANT.] a Theban prince, husband of Niobe

AMYKLAI: a town in Laconia

ANDROMACHE: wife of Hektor

ANTIGONE: daughter of Oedipus and Jocasta; ANT.] affianced to Haimon, son of Creon of Thebes

ANTIOPE: Queen of the Amazons; HIP.] mistress of Theseus and mother of Hippolytus; possibly confused here with her sister Hippolyta, q.v.

APHRODITE: goddess of Love

APOLLO: god of the Sun

ARACHNEUS, ARACHNOS: a hill in Argolis, near Mycenae

AEROPAGUS OC] the highest judicial assembly at Athens; EUM.] instituted by Athena

ARES: god of War

ARGIVE: poetic epithet for Greek or Grecian

ARGO: MED.] ship in which Jason and his companions sailed in quest of the Golden Fleece

ARGOLIS: a province in the Peloponnesus

ARGOS: capital city of Argolis

ARGUS: PV] the hundred-eyed guardian of Io, q.v., after she had been turned into a white cow by Zeus; slain by Hermes at the bidding of Zeus, his ghost pursued Io in the shape of a gad-fly

ARIMASPI: a legendary people, one-eyed, living in the unknown territory north of the Scythians

ARKADIA: a province in the middle of the Peloponnesus

ARTEMIS: sister of Apollo; goddess of the hunt; esp., HIP.] patroness of virgins

ASCLEPIUS, ASKLEPIOS: god of medical art; son of Apollo; ALC.] slain by Zeus, avenged by Apollo

ASCLEPIUS ROCK: HIP.] probably a reference to the shrine of Asclepius at Epidaurus, his birthplace

ASOPOS: a river in southern Boeotia, flowing into the strait of Euripus

ASTYANAX: infant son of Hektor and Andromache

ATALANTA: an Arkadian princess, mother of Parthenopaeus, q.v.

ATHENA, ATHENE: daughter of Zeus; goddess of Wisdom, of the Arts and Sciences; tutelary goddess of Athens

ATHOS: AG.] a mountain in Macedonia about forty miles west of Lemnos

ATLAS: PV] brother of Prometheus; sided with the other Titans against Zeus

ATREIDAI: members of the House of Atreus, q.v.

ATREUS: son of Pelops; father (but see PLEISTHENES) of Agamemnon and Menelaos; brother of Thyestes, whom he caused to eat the flesh of his own sons

ATTICA: a province of Greece situated in Hellas proper; capital, Athens

AULIS: a port in Boeotia; scene of the gathering of the Greek fleet against Troy, and of the ritual sacrifice of Iphigeneia, q.v.

BACCHANAL: HIP.] see MAENADES

BACCHANTES, BACCHANTS: see MAENADES

BARCAEAN: ELEC.] a native of the Libyan town of Barcê in the province of Pentapolis

BOEOTIA: a district of eastern Hellas

BOSPORUS: PV] a strait connecting the Black Sea and Maeotis, q.v.

BROMIUS: a surname of Dionysus, q.v., as βρόμιος, "the tumultuous one"

CADMOS, CADMUS: the legendary founder of Thebes; father of Semele, q.v.

CANOBUS: PV] a city in Egypt on the Nile Delta

CAPANEUS: one of the seven Captains supporting Polyneices in the Theban Expedition; ANT.] struck down from the ramparts of Thebes by a thunderbolt hurled by Zeus

CASSANDRA: daughter of Priam; beloved of Apollo, who gave her the gift of prophecy and later, repulsed, ordained that no one hearing her should believe her; priestess of Apollo, ravished by Ajax at the fall of Troy

CASTALIA: a spring, sacred to the Muses, on Mt. Parnassus

CAUCASUS: a mountain range extending from the Black Sea to the Caspian

CECROPS: the legendary founder of Athens; supposed to have migrated to Attica from Sais, in Egypt, thus introducing Egyptian arts and sciences

CENTAURS: a Thessalian race, half horse and half man, offspring of Ixion and a phantom of Hera

CEPHALUS: husband of Procris, the eldest daughter of Erechtheus

CEPHISUS: a river in Greece, rising at the foot of Mt. Parnassus

CHALKIS: chief city of Euboea, across the Strait of Euripus from Aulis

CHALYBIANS: PV] a people of Pontus, in Asia Minor, noted for their iron mines and forges

CHAOS: the mother of Night

CHARON: the ferryman of Hades

CHARYBDIS: a whirlpool in the Sicilian Strait, opposite Scylla, q.v.

CHRYSOTHEMIS: a daughter of Agamemnon and Clytemnestra

CILICIA: a region in southeastern Asia Minor; hence, PV] CILICIAN, pertaining to this region

CIMMERIA: PV] a Thracian isthmus in the present Crimea

CIRCE: a Ligurian sorceress who had

the power to transform men into swine

CISTHENE: PV] a legendary land of uncertain location; home of the Gorgons, q.v.

CITHAERON: a mountain range in southern Boeotia; scene of the exposure of the infant Oedipus

CLYTEMNESTRA: daughter of Leda; sister of Helen; wife of Agamemnon;. mistress of Aegisthos

COCYTUS: a river in Hades

COLCHIS: a country in Asia on the eastern shore of the Black Sea; the land of the Golden Fleece

COLONUS: a deme of Attica near Athens

CORYBANTES: the priests of Cybele

CORYCIA: a nymph beloved of Apollo; associated with a grotto on Mt. Parnassus, the Antrum Corycium, sacred to Pan; hence, EUM.] CORYCIAN, as adj.

CRANAUS: EUM.] a mythical king of Athens, successor to Cecrops, q.v.

CREON: (I) OT, OC, ANT.] brother of Jocasta, q.v.; King of Thebes after the death of Polyneices and Eteocles; father of Haimon and Megareus; (II) MED.] a king of Corinth, destroyed by Medea

CYBELE: an Asiatic goddess; adored as Magna Mater, the Mother of the Gods, in secret, cruel rites

CYCLOPES: the giant one-eyed armorers of Zeus, killed by Apollo in retaliation for the killing of his son Asclepius

CYPRIAN, CYPRIS: epithets of Aphrodite

DANAANS: Greeks

DANAE: daughter of Akrisios, King of Argos; confined by her father in a brazen chamber underground (or, some say, in a brazen tower), she was nevertheless seduced by Zeus in the form of a golden rain, and bore Perseus, q.v.

DANAOS: a legendary king of Argos, of Egyptian origin

DARDANOS: a son of Zeus; founder of Dardania, in the Troad; ancestor of the kings of Troy

DAULIS: a city in Phocis a few miles east of Delphi

DEIPHOBOS: TROAD.] a son of Priam and Hecuba

DELIAN: adj. from DELOS

DELOS: an island in the Aegean; birthplace of Apollo and Artemis

DELPHI: a city in Phocis; seat of the celebrated Oracle of Apollo

DELPHUS: EUM.] founder-king of Delphi, in whose reign the Oracle of Apollo was established there

DEMETER: daughter of Kronos; sister of Zeus; goddess of Agriculture

DICTYNNA: HIP.] a city in Crete; also, an epithet for Artemis, q.v.

DIKE: ELEC.] the personification of Divine Justice

DINDYMUS: a mountain in Mysia

DIOMED: ALC.] a king of the Bistones, in Thrace; son of Ares

DIONYSOS, DIONYSUS: son of Zeus and Semele; god of Wine

DIRCE: a spring near Thebes

DODONA: a city in Epirus, famous for an oak grove in which was an oracle of Zeus

DORIAN: adj. from DORIS

DORIS: a country of Greece, south of Thessaly; home of one of the most powerful of the Hellenic tribes

DRYAS: a king of Thrace; father of Lycurgus, who was driven mad by Dionysus

ELECTRA: daughter of Agamemnon and Clytemnestra

ELECTRYON: ALC.] a king of Mycenae; son of Perseus and Andromeda; father of Alcmena, hence grandfather of Heracles

ELEUSIS: a city in Attica sacred to Demeter and Persephone

EMPYREAN: OT] the highest heaven, sphere of pure fire

EPEIOS: TROAD.] the builder of the Wooden Horse of Troy

EPIDAURUS: a city in Argolis on the Saronic Gulf, famous for a shrine of Asclepius

ERECHTHEUS: a legendary hero, King of Athens; ancestor of Theseus

ERIDANUS: HIP.] the River Po

ERINNYES: the Furies, spirits of Divine Vengeance; EUM.] finally reconciled by Athena to Athenian law; see EUMENIDES

EROS: son of Aphrodite; god of Love

ETEOCLES: son of Oedipus and Jocasta; killed by his brother Polyneices in the assault upon Thebes

ETEOCLUS: oc] one of the seven Captains supporting Polyneices in the expedition against Thebes; killed under the walls of Thebes by Megareus, q.v.

EUBOEA: a large island lying along the coast of Locris, Boeotia, and Attica; hence, adj. EUBOEAN (EUBOIAN)

EUMELOS: son of Admetos

EUMENIDES: "the Gracious Ones": euphemistically for the Erinnyes, q.v.

EURIPOS, EURIPUS: a narrow strait between Boeotia and Euboea

EUROTAS: a river in Laconia

EURYDICE: ANT.] wife of Creon of Thebes

EURYSTHEUS: ALC.] a king of Argos and Mycenae; grandson of Pelops; by a decree of Zeus granted authority over Heracles, whom he forced to undertake the Twelve Labors

EURYTUS: HIP.] father of Iole

FATES: three goddesses — Clotho, Lachesis, and Atropos—who determined the course of human affairs

FORCE: PV] (Κράτος) a demon, slave of Zeus

FURIES: see ERINNYES

GAIA: "Earth"; wife of Uranos; mother of Oceanos and the Titans

GANYMEDE: son of Laomedon and brother of Priam, qq.v.; cup-bearer of Zeus

GERYON: a famous monster, three-headed, three-bodied, killed by Heracles

GORGON: PV] any one of three monstrous sisters with wings of gold, hair entwined with serpents, hands of brass, and impenetrably scaled bodies; ALC.] the Gorgon Medusa, whose eyes had the power to turn men to stone

GORGOPIS: a bay in the Corinthian Gulf

GRAIAI: "gray ones"; daughters of Phorcys and guardians of the Gorgons, qq.v.; they possessed only one eye and one tooth among them

HADES: the world of the dead

HAIMON: son of Creon of Thebes

HARMONIA: daughter of Ares and Aphrodite; wife of Cadmus, hence mother of Semele and Ino, qq.v.; MED.] symbolically, in this play, as the mother of the Muses

HECATE: a mysterious goddess of the race of the Titans; identified with several other divinities, as Selene in heaven, Artemis on earth, and Persephone in Hades, hence represented as *Triformis* (with three bodies) or *Triceps* (with three heads); generally, a goddess of sorcery and witchcraft

HECUBA: Queen of Troy

HEKTOR: TROAD.] a son of Priam and Hecuba; most beloved of the Trojan heroes

HELEN: sister of Clytemnestra; wife of Menelaos

HELICON: a mountain range in Boeotia, sacred to Apollo and the Muses

HELICONIDES: the Muses; see HELICON

HELIOS: an epithet of Apollo, as god of the Sun

HEPHAESTOS, HEPHAESTUS, HEPHESTUS: god of Fire; son of Zeus and Hera

HERA: wife of Zeus

HERACLES, HERAKLES: son of Zeus and Alcmena; most famous of the legendary heroes of Greece

HERMAIAN AG.] the Crag of Hermes, on the Island of Lemnos

HERMES: messenger of the gods; ALC.] guide of souls departing to Hades; PV] emissary of Zeus to Prometheus

HESIONE: PV] a daughter of Oceanos, given by him in marriage to Prometheus after the latter's theft of fire

HESPERIDES: daughters of Atlas, q.v.; guardians of a grove of golden apples on an island west of the Strait of Gibraltar

HIPPOLYTA: an Amazonian queen, daughter of Ares, slain by Heracles; sister of Antiope, q.v., with whom she is sometimes confused as the mother of Hippolytus

HIPPOLYTUS: bastard son of King Theseus of Athens

HIPPOMEDON: one of the seven Captains supporting Polyneices in the expedition against Thebes

HYMEN (also HYMENAIOS): god of Marriage

IACCHOS: ANT.] a name of Dionysus

IDA: a mountain near Troy; hence, adj. AG.] IDAIAN

ILION, ILIUM: Troy

INACHOS, INACHUS: founder of Argos; son of Oceanos and father of Io, qq.v.

INO: daughter of Cadmus and Harmonia, qq.v.; wife of King Athamas of Thebes, who, maddened by Hera, destroyed her and her two children

IO: daughter of Inachos; priestess of Hera at Argos; beloved of Zeus, who turned her into a white cow in order to conceal his adultery from Hera

IOCASTE: ANT.] see JOCASTA

IOLE: daughter of King Eurytus of Oechalia, beloved of Heracles

IOLCOS, IOLKOS: a port in Thessaly, ruled by Pelias; home of Alcestis

IPHIANASSA: ELEC.] see IPHIGENEIA

IPHIGENEIA: a daughter of Agamemnon and Clytemnestra; sacrificed at Aulis by her father in order to expedite the sailing of the Greek forces against Troy

ISMENE: a daughter of Oedipus

ISMENOS, ISMENUS: a river near Boeotian Thebes, sacred to Apollo

ISTER (also ISTROS): the lower reaches of the Danube

ITHACA, ITHAKA: an island in the Ionian Sea; home of Odysseus

ITYS: son of Tereus and Procne; murdered in his infancy and served up to his father at a feast

IXION: a Thessalian king; father, by a phantom of Hera, of the Centaurs

JASON: husband of Medea

JOCASTA: wife of King Laius of Thebes, q.v.; mother and, later, wife of Oedipus

KADMOS: see CADMUS

KALCHAS: a soothsayer; high priest and prophet of the Greeks in the Trojan War

KAPHERIAN: TROAD.] pertaining to Kaphereus, a promontory on the south shore of Euboea

KASSANDRA: see CASSANDRA

KASTOR: TROAD.] a brother of Helen

KERCHNEIA: PV] a lake in Argolis

KIRKE: TROAD.] see CIRCE

KITHAIRON: see CITHAERON

KLYTAIMESTRA: AG.] see CLYTEMNESTRA

KOKYTOS: see COCYTUS

KRATHIS: TROAD.] a river in Magna Graecia, in southern Italy, whose waters were fabled to redden hair

KREON: MED.] see CREON

KRISA: ELEC.] a town in Phocis

KRONION: an epithet of Zeus, as son of Kronos

KRONOS: son of Uranos and Gaia; father of Zeus

LABDACIDAE: descendants of Labdacus, q.v.

LABDACUS: an early king of Thebes

LACEDEMONIA: Sparta

LAERTES: TROAD.] a king of Ithaca; nominally, the father of Odysseus

LAIOS, LAIUS: a king of Thebes; father of Oedipus; killed by Oedipus in fulfilment of an oracle

LAKEDAIMONIA: see LACEDEMONIA

LAKONIA: see LACONIA

LAOMEDON: TROAD.] a king of Troy; father of Priam, Ganymede, and Tithonos, qq.v.

LARISSA: a city in Thessaly

LEDA: wife of King Tyndareus of Sparta; by him, or by Zeus (who seduced her in the shape of a Swan), the mother of Clytemnestra, Helen, Kastor, and Polydeuces, qq.v.

LEMNOS: an island in the Aegean

LERNA: a marshy district near Argos

LETO: mother by Zeus of Apollo and Artemis

LIBYA: a region in Africa

LIGURIAN: TROAD.] epithet of Circe, q.v., as living on the Ligurian island of Aiaia

LIMNAE: HIP.] a lake district in Laconia, sacred to Artemis

LOCRIS: a district in Greece, extending from Thessaly to Boeotia

LOXIAS: an epithet of Apollo in his function as interpreter of Zeus

LYCAON: ALC.] "wolf-man"; a son of Ares, overcome by Heracles

LYCIA: a country in southern Asia Minor

LYCIAN: OT] epithet of Apollo, of ambiguous meaning: as "born in Lycia" (Λυκία); as "god of Light" (*λύκη); as "wolfslayer" (λύκος)

MAENADES: the priestesses of Dionysus, especially in the frenzies of the god's rites

MAEOTIS: the Sea of Azov

MAKISTOS: a mountain in Euboea

MEDEA: daughter of King Aietes of Colchis; sorceress; wife of Jason, q.v.

MEGAREUS: a son of Creon of Thebes; killed in the assault of the Seven against the city

MENELAOS, MENELAUS: brother of Agamemnon; husband of Helen

MENOECEUS, MENOICEUS: father of Jocasta and Creon of Thebes

MEROPE: wife of King Polybus of Corinth; foster-mother of Oedipus

MESSAPION: a mountain on the coast of Boeotia, east of the Asopos

MOLOSSA: a plateau in Epirus; location of Dodona, q.v.

MUNYCHIA: a port of Athens

MUSES: nine goddesses presiding over the liberal arts and sciences; daughters of Zeus and the nymph Mnemosyne

MYCENAE: an ancient city of Argolis

MYKONOS: an island, one of the Cyclades group

MYRTILOS: ELEC.] a son of Hermes, murdered by Pelops, q.v.

NAIADES: nymphs of fresh water

NEOPTOLEMOS: son of Achilles; also called Pyrrhus

NEREIDES: nymphs of the sea

NIGHT (Νύξ): EUM.] daughter of Chaos; mother of the Erinnyes

NIOBE: daughter of Tantalus; wife of Amphion; mother of fourteen children killed, because of her arrogance, by Apollo and Artemis; transformed, in her grief, to a rock on Mt. Sipylus

OCEAN, OCEANOS: son of Uranos and Gaia; god of Streams and Rivers

OCEANIDES: PV] the three thousand sea-nymph daughters of Oceanos and Tethys

ODYSSEUS: King of Ithaca; wiliest of the Greek chieftains at the siege of Troy; TROAD.] advises the murder of Astyanax

OECHALIA: a city in Euboea

OEDIPUS: son of Laius and Jocasta; slayer of his father and husband of his mother

OINEUS: a king of Calydon in Aetolia; father of Tydeus, q.v.

OLYMPOS, OLYMPUS, a Thessalian mountain; the seat of the gods

ORESTES: son of Agamemnon and Clytemnestra

ORPHEUS: a philosopher, poet, and musician, widely celebrated in the early legends; ALC.] won permission by his music to bring his wife back to earth from Hades

PAIAN: ALC.] physician of the gods; name transferred to Apollo in his function of Healer

PAIDAGOGOS: a slave performing the modern function of tutor or governess; ELEC.] old friend and tutor of Orestes; MED.] attendant of Medea's sons

PALLANTIDAE: the fifty sons of Pallas (II), q.v.; failed in their attempt to murder Theseus, Aegeus' son and successor; slain by Theseus, who, to expiate the shedding of kindred blood, underwent a year's exile in Troezen

PALLANTIDS: HIP.] see PALLAN-TIDAE

PALLAS: (I) an epithet of Athena, q.v.; (II) HIP.] a son of Pandion and brother of Aegeus, qq.v.

PAN: an Arkadian rural god

PANDION: King of Athens; son of Erechtheus; hence, symbolic of Athens

PARIS (also called ALEXANDER): a son of Priam; lover of Helen, q.v.

PARNASOS, PARNASSOS, PARNASSUS: a mountain in Phocis, sacred to Apollo and the Muses; at its foot were Delphi and the Castalian Spring, qq.v.

PARTHENOPAEUS: OC] one of the seven Captains supporting Polyneices in the expedition against Thebes